RELIGION
& POWER

RELIGION & POWER

Pagans,
Jews,
and
Christians
in the
Greek East

DOUGLAS R. EDWARDS

New York   Oxford
Oxford University Press
1996

Oxford University Press

Oxford   New York
Athens   Auckland   Bangkok   Bogota   Bombay
Buenos Aires   Calcutta   Cape Town   Dar es Salaam
Delhi   Florence   Hong Kong   Istanbul   Karachi
Kuala Lumpur   Madras   Madrid   Melbourne
Mexico City   Nairobi   Paris   Singapore
Taipei   Tokyo   Toronto

and associated companies in
Berlin   Ibadan

Copyright © 1996 by Douglas R. Edwards

Published by Oxford University Press, Inc.
198 Madison Avenue, New York, New York 10016

Oxford is a registered trademark of Oxford University Press, Inc.

Library of Congress Cataloging-in-Publication Data
Edwards, Douglas R.
Religion and power : pagans, Jews, and Christians in the Greek
East / Douglas R. Edwards.
p.   cm.
Includes bibliographical references and indexes.
ISBN 0-19-508263-X
1. Church history—Primitive and early church, ca. 30–600.
2. Christianity and other religions—Greek.   3. Christianity and
other religions—Roman.   4. Christianity and other religions—
Judaism.   5. Judaism—Relations—Christianity.   6. Rome—Religion.
7. Middle East—Religion.   8. Power (Social sciences)—Rome.
I. Title.
BR185.E38   1996   95–35320
291'.093—dc20

1 3 5 7 9 8 6 4 2

Printed in the United States of America
on acid-free paper

Preface

This project was born of my intense interest in having conversations with colleagues in archaeology, classics, ancient history, Jewish studies, and New Testament studies. I was disturbed by the seeming disinclination of New Testament scholars and classicists to examine the bountiful information on epigraphic, sculptural, architectural, and other material remains available in numerous journals and archaeological reports when dealing with literary material from the same period. Such data has a tremendous potential for elaborating the contexts in which literary texts came to fruition. An important part of my intellectual journey occurred when I read Simon Price's *Rituals and Power.* Price's book, along with others that explored the interaction of religious symbols and power, stimulated my investigation into the nature of power and its association with the use of symbols.

But the ancient world is a large arena even when one concentrates on religious and mythic symbols used in the Greek East during the first two centuries of this era. One cannot be completely conversant with all literature associated with paganism, Judaism, and Christianity, much less the material culture associated with each or the methodological contributions of anthropologists, sociologists, deconstructionists, narratologists, and the innumerable "-ists" one could name. I have had to be selective, which undoubtedly will generate some dissatisfaction. For instance, I have not referred extensively to the Mishnah, and a number of pagan and Christian narrative voices are little heard. I can only hope that broad strokes, combined with specific examples, will be illuminating as well as challenge others to delve more deeply into such rich territory. My own interests now extend across strict disciplinary boundaries. I simply can no longer read the New Testament, Josephus, Plutarch, or an ancient romance or view an ancient sculpture, building, or coin without first trying to visualize the social, political, and cultural framework in which it was read or viewed. Indeed, attempts to ignore context rely on an "implied" contextual setting that may have little relation to the realia that exist. Recent studies that extend across old disciplinary boundaries and take seriously the contextual framework of narratives suggest that a number of my colleagues feel the same way.

Wolfson College, Oxford   D.R.E.
May 1995

Acknowledgments

This project could not have been undertaken without the contributions and insights of persons whose own expertise in ancient history, archaeology, epigraphy, New Testament studies, intertestamental studies, classics, or Jewish studies made them astute critics of my shortcomings in those areas. Certain elements in this study had their inception while I was in graduate school. They were challenged, honed, and sometimes altered to their present form through long hours of critical discussion with my advisers: Howard Clark Kee, Charles R. Beye, and J. Paul Sampley. Yet, as so often happens, it was only after my dissertation was completed that the significant questions became clear. Residual elements of the dissertation remain, but the present work bears little resemblance to its predecessor. Any sucess this book has in achieving its aims must be attributed largely to the many persons who have given generous amounts of their time to critique and discuss my ideas. John North, Luther Martin, Fergus Millar, Ewen Bowie, Consuelo Ruiz-Montero, Vernon Robbins, and David Lupher offered sage advice that clarified my direction at both early and later stages. Ronald Hock and Richard Pervo perused early drafts of my first two chapters and provided many useful comments. Joyce Reynolds read drafts of the sections on Aphrodisias and kept me from making some critical mistakes. Special thanks go to Martin Goodman, who commented extensively on the first four chapters and saved me from committing certain grievous errors. Simon Price and Richard Pervo read the complete manuscript and made astute observations throughout. Any shortcomings that remain must fall squarely on my shoulders.

The work could not have been finished without financial support from a number of sources, including a 1991–92 National Endowment for the Humanities Fellowship, which, in conjunction with a Martin Nelson Junior sabbatical grant from the University of Puget Sound, allowed me the luxury of studying at Oxford University in 1991 as a visiting scholar at the Oxford Centre for Postgraduate Hebrew Studies. An additional John Lantz sabbatical grant from the University of Puget Sound enabled me to complete the manuscript at Wolfson College, Oxford, in 1995. Lectures at numerous locations permitted me to test key ideas discussed in this book. These venues included the Institute of Classical Studies (lecture organized by Riet van Bremen and Guy Rogers); the Oxford Centre for Postgraduate Hebrew Studies; the International Association for the History of Religions international meeting in Rome; the Galilee Conference in Hanaton, Israel (organized by Lee Levine); the conference "Images of Empire" (organized by Loveday Alexander); a series of lectures at the University of South Dakota (organized by Judith Sebesta); seminars at the international and national meetings of the Society of Biblical Literature; the Ancient World Symposium at the University of Puget Sound; and the University of Vermont. I benefited enormously from the comments of those who attended.

Special thanks are also due Carol Avery, who has typed and edited more versions of this manuscript than she or I care to remember. Nicole Mulhausen provided editorial help at a crucial stage. Cynthia Read and her editorial staff have been the model of patience and helpfulness. But one person deserves the greatest credit. She has borne the brunt of all the travel, long hours of study, and fitful ruminations, and contributed in ways only she and I know. Mary, my love, I dedicate this book to you.

My thanks also go to those publishers who have allowed me to modify and incorporate portions of earlier articles and essays: "The Social, Religious, and Political Aspects of Costume in Josephus." In *The World of Roman Costume*, ed. Judith Lynn Sebesta and Larissa Bonfante, 153–59. Madison: University of Wisconsin Press, 1994 reprinted with permission of the University of Wisconsin Press. "Defining the Web of Power in Asia Minor: The Novelist Chariton and His City Aphrodisias." *Journal of the American Academy of Religion* 62.3 (Fall 1994) : 699–718. "The Socio-Economic and Cultural Ethos of the Lower Galilee in the First Century: Implications for the Nascent Jesus Movements." In *The Galilee in Late Antiquity*, ed. Lee Levine, 53–73. Cambridge: Harvard University Press, 1992. Reprinted with permission of the Jewish Theological Seminary of America. "Religion, Power, and Politics: Jewish Defeats by the Romans in Iconography and Josephus." In *Diaspora Jews and Judaism: Essays in Honor of, and in Dialogue with, A. Thomas Kraabel*, ed. J. Andrew Overman and R. S. MacLennan, 293–310. University of South Florida Series in Ancient Judaism. Atlanta: Scholars Press, 1992. "Surviving the Web of Roman Power: Religion and Politics in the Acts of the Apostles, Josephus, and Chariton's *Chaereas and Callirhoe*." In *Images of Empire*, ed. Loveday Alexander, 179–201. Sheffield: Sheffield Academic Press, 1991.

Contents

RELIGION
& POWER

Introduction

Power and its association with religious and mythic symbols permeate society. In 1991, as I worked on this book, the Iraqi conflict provided both sides an opportunity to invest traditional religious and mythic symbols with power. Iraq's leader, Saddam Hussein, associated his rule with such powerful military and religious figures as Saladin and Nebuchadnezzar, whose own battles drew on religious symbols. Visual symbols on currency, architecture, posters, and television spots combined religion and the historical and mythic past to bolster the power and prestige of his regime.[1] Similarly, our symbol-laden media portrayed former president George Bush, with head bowed, praying for the allies during church services. The Israeli–Palestinian accords of 1993 saw President Bill Clinton citing passages from the Hebrew Scriptures and the Koran to help reconcile old adversaries. Countless other examples could be cited. The use of these images is not solely crass political manipulation. Religious and mythic symbols have long been deployed to elicit powerful responses within communities.[2] Often the urgency and seriousness of impending or potential conflicts contribute to the resurfacing and rearticulation of potent symbols.

Symbols from religion permeate American society.[3] "In God We Trust" still graces the back of U.S. coins. Do religion and economics here intertwine? Or is the religious slogan simply a meaningless symbol? The answer no doubt depends on the audience, the occasion, and the time in which the question is asked. It requires no great feat of imagination to envision the response to any proposal seeking to remove the phrase. Symbols carry a latent power and when proffered at a particular time may tap into unnamed presuppositions. The power of a symbol becomes clearest when its "taken-for-granted" status is called into question. Reciting the Pledge of Allegiance and using money with "In God We Trust" are not mere rote exercises or valueless economic routines. Their symbolic value becomes clearest when challenged or interpreted in a manner different from the "normal." If religious and mythic symbols percolate with such force through our "secular" world, how much more so in antiquity, where secular/religious distinctions were rarely made?

This study examines how implied and overt use of religious and mythic symbols enabled pagans, Jews, and Christians in the Greek East to define as well as to negotiate their role amid many power networks during the first two centuries of Roman imperial rule and devotes special attention to the Flavian through Trajanic periods (70–117 C.E.)[4] The early centuries of the Roman Empire witnessed a number of changes that would profoundly affect its character (if not the course of Western civilization): the consolidation of imperial power; the political rise of powerful members from local elite classes in the Greek East; increased popularity of local and foreign cults; redefinitions of what Judaism meant; the rise of new groups, most notably the Christians. Religion played a significant role in the arenas of discourse (both real and imagined) that occurred within and among pagan, Jewish, and Christian communities.

A study of this sort has a number of hurdles to clear before it can begin, not least of which is clarification of key terms. That task is made especially difficult because of the lengthy debates surrounding each of the principal terms used in my title. I offer provisional definitions for each and note that the study itself best illustrates their use in the early imperial period of the Roman Empire.

By the time of Augustus and throughout the fourth century, the Greek term for religion, θρησκεια, came to refer to worship and practices associated with the cult of the dead,[5] Apollo at Delphi, Aphrodite at Aphrodisias,[6] Artemis at Ephesus, Zeus Panamaros at Stratonicea, Dionysus at Teos, Athena, the imperial cult, Jewish practice,[7] and even Christian practice (Acts 26:5; Col. 2:18; James 1:26, 27; 1 Clement 1:45).[8] Clearly, the modern-day distinction between cult and religion did not apply.

"Religion" here is used in its broadest sense to denote practices, beliefs, or patterns of behavior (albeit often unsystematic) associated with a sphere deemed sacred or divine. Here I follow what has become the classic functional description of religion by Clifford Geertz:

> A religion is: (1) a system of symbols which acts to (2) establish powerful, pervasive, and long-lasting moods and motivations in men by (3) formulating conceptions of a general order of existence and (4) clothing these conceptions with such an aura of factuality that (5) the moods and motivations seem uniquely realistic.[9]

"Pagans" are understood as those who performed cult acts or worshiped or recognized a deity or deities but were neither Christian nor Jew.[10] The Judaeo-Christian bias surrounding the term is obvious but nothing has replaced it. The danger, of course, is that, by lumping "pagans" together under one term, one can fail to recognize the complexity and diversity that existed. I have sought to avoid that where possible.

The term "Jew" (Greek *Ioudaios,* Latin *Iudaeus*) has raised many troublesome issues.[11] It has often implied someone whose identity rests within a monolithic system of practice and belief generally modeled on the rabbinic tradition developed in the second and subsequent centuries. Many works argue persuasively that Judaism was quite varied and that the term "Jew" had many connotations.[12] In this study, the term applies to those non-Christians[13] who acknowledge themselves as Jews for ethnic, religious, or cultural reasons or are acknowledged as such by others.

The term "Christian," at least for the period that I examine, is even more troublesome. Clearly, the word designated certain unique groups by the end of the first century, as indicated in Acts of the Apostles, which states that the followers of Jesus were first called Christians at Antioch (Acts 11:25). Some have challenged the notion that Christianity and Judaism were sharply separate enterprises and prefer to see a variety of Jesus-centered Judaisms, in other words, a messianic form of Judaism.[14] If one accepts that various Judaisms existed in the first century, then the model has merit. Nevertheless, by the late first and early second centuries, a break between a Gentile-dominated Christianity and certain Judaisms had begun to develop, so that one can consider Christianity a separate religious movement.[15] In this study "Christian" refers to any individual who understood Jesus as significant for his or her belief or practice.[16] This obviates the need to address whether individuals like Paul, who was a Jew, or the author of the Gospel of Matthew viewed themselves as Jews who interpret the tradition properly or as Christians, now separate from (and hostile toward) Judaism.

The Greek East had a distinctive character in the Roman Empire. It consisted of a vast territory ranging, as Peter Brown characterizes it, from "the Danube to the Euphrates, and from the Black Sea to as far south as the upper Nile and westward to Cyrenaica."[17] Much of this region was bound by a common Greek culture and a professed, if not always practiced, allegiance to Rome. Yet even those who promoted Greek culture were often conversant in the distinctive and often ancient culture(s) of their particular regions.[18] Regional studies, therefore, are of the utmost importance in understanding the Greek East as whole. Yet certain patterns do seem to unite the Greek East. These will be the focus of this work, always recognizing that actual events were more complex and nuanced. The study draws heavily on the substantive literary and material remains from the central region of the Greek East (especially Greece, Macedonia, the province of Asia, Pontus, Bithynia, and Lycia) as well as from more peripheral areas such as the northern Black Sea region and the Graeco-Roman Near East (Syria, Arabia, Judaea, and Egypt).[19]

Finally, I address what may be the most important word in my study, namely, "power." Discussion of power has a long history. At its most basic level, power addresses the question, "To what extent, and how, can we get what we want?"[20] Power also implies systemic relationships. Such relations can be negative and repressive or positive and liberating. In either case power, even imperial power, generally operated with tacit consent between ruler and ruled. As Foucault has argued:

> What makes power hold good, what makes it accepted, is simply the fact that it doesn't only weigh on us as a force that says no, but that it traverses and produces things, it induces pleasure, forms knowledge, produces discourse. It

needs to be considered as a productive network which runs through the whole social body, much more than as a negative instance whose function is repression.[21]

On one level, this study examines how religious symbols enable persons operating in systemic relations to "get what they want." On another level, while exploring how persons immersed "in nets of power relations" are constrained in their efforts, this study "simultaneously uncover[s] the means by which human beings have the ability to resist and challenge those relations."[22] Such activities may be explicit, assumed, or performed with little thought. This study elucidates how pagans, Jews, and Christians in the Greek East applied religious symbolic discourse to make sense of "nets of power relations" operating in imperial, regional, local, and cosmic arenas.[23]

I.

Religion and the
Symbolics of Power:
Message and Significance

Religious symbols permeated the Roman world. Visual displays and rhetorical flourishes on public and private monuments, coins and in literary texts provide ample testimony for the ways local elites in the Greek East acquired or consolidated power during imperial Roman rule. Local elites and their affiliates had at their disposal many religious symbols (the "symbolics of power") to mediate the intersection between religion, society, and politics. Studies that have examined that intersection—most notably on the imperial cult of Asia Minor, the power of images in the Age of Augustus, and the images associated with Roman arches in Rome—illustrate how invisible but real "webs of power" bound rulers and ruled in networks of visual and verbal discourse.[1] As this study will show, members of local elite classes and their affiliates in the Greek East drew on religious symbols to negotiate various power relationships in the Roman Empire. How did those associated with the elite classes in the Greek East incorporate the language of religion in their public and private lives? In what ways did religion help them stipulate their own identity and power within the networks of forces that coursed through local, regional, imperial, and cosmic networks of power?

The rule of the Flavians, Nerva, and Trajan ushered in an age that saw increased consolidation of power under imperial rule and a drawing of political and cultural boundaries that set the character of discourse in the Roman Empire for the next three centuries.[2] Between the reigns of Vespasian and Trajan, most of the New Testament and a number of noncanonical texts were written, reflecting a variety of responses to the figure of Jesus. Jews, who composed a few new texts in this period, had to define their relation to Rome and their neighbors with greater care.[3] Both groups had to express their symbolic discourse within the rubric of the structures established and run by local elites in cities and towns across the Greek East. Various Eastern religions (notably, those of Isis and Mithras), Greek cults (such as those of Zeus,[4] Artemis, and Aphrodite), and the increasingly important imperial cult provided significant vehicles for members of the local elite establishment to utilize religious and

7

mythic symbols to express their power and prestige locally, regionally, and often in association with imperial and cosmic power. The resultant discourses provided the framework, as we shall see, in which members from all levels of society participated and responded. Philosophers and writers like Dio of Prusa, Epictetus, and Plutarch have that much in common with such "outsiders" as Babatha, a Jewish woman who carried the Roman-approved title to her land with her while apparently participating in the Bar Kochba revolt.[5]

How significant, moreover, were religious symbols? Modern researchers have offered widely different interpretations. Some see such symbols as auxiliary, largely unimportant, or politically motivated;[6] others see them as significant and dominant, although somehow separate from place and audience. For many, symbols that display salvific overtones or Judaeo-Christian values become "significant"; those symbols that do not, remain marginal. Similar symbols may even receive different emphases depending on the interpreter's, rather than the early writer's, construct. Religious deities and heroines in ancient romances, for example, become literary topoi and "entertain"[7] their readership (and therefore have peripheral importance); similar symbols in Christian or Jewish literature such as the Apocryphal Acts or Joseph and Aseneth[8] edify, instruct, and serve a "religious" purpose. Anachronistic divisions like these, as we shall see, often ignore or downplay how religious symbols in even so-called entertaining material reflect and shape the webs of power in which the author and the audience participated.[9]

One still hears how traditional Greek deities such as Apollo or Aphrodite lost their religious vitality in the Roman period and were replaced by salvationistic deities (e.g., Mithras, Jesus, Isis) that appealed to the "religious" sensibilities of lost souls in a complex, unforgiving environment.[10] In the past, interpreters placed undue stress on religious symbols that proffered personal salvation and future reward amid a wide-open world full of insecurity and uncertainty.[11] Christocentric categories such as personal salvation and future rewards are not used here as the sole rubric to evaluate religious symbols, not even for "Christocentric" movements. Rather, I examine how religious symbols helped resolve strategic power relationships (both real and perceived) between various key parties in the Greek East. Put differently, I evaluate "power" relationships in the Greek East by exploring how persons utilized religious symbols to organize political, social, and cultural dimensions of their sacred cosmos.[12]

Much overlap occurred in the general responses to power made by pagans, Jews, and Christians. Many agreed or at least tolerated the attitudes of ruling elites in the Greek East, who largely discouraged subversive or alternative thinking. Such elites stressed "one particular way of ordering and organizing society as authoritative and God-given."[13] What made their "system" tolerable was that their power was largely "diffused," not explicit, even though their practices and behavior seemed to them natural, moral, and self-evident.[14] Yet each group had certain distinctive responses to the "webs of power" operating at that time. Epictetus, the former slave and eminent Stoic philosopher of the late first century, articulates how all groups agree on the importance of striving for the holy life:

When, then, does contradiction arise? . . . This is the conflict between Jews and Syrians and Egyptians and Romans, not over the questions whether holiness should be put before everything else and should be pursued in all circumstances, but whether the particular act of eating swine's flesh is holy or unholy.[15]

What separates these groups are their respective attitudes toward what constitutes a holy act. Even apparently explicit symbols could convey different meanings depending on one's particular circumstance or experience. Religious symbols are idiosyncratic: local situations or particular time periods bear heavily on their interpretation. At the same time, these very symbols could form part of an organic, semi-integrated system that participated in political, social, and cosmic networks of power.

THE DILEMMA OF SPECIFIC EXAMPLES VERSUS GENERAL PATTERNS

The historian's dilemma invariably revolves around deciding which specific examples or general patterns best depict the character of past events. How does one provide a high level of detail or statistical analysis (what Clifford Geertz calls "thick description") for an individual text or archaeological site and still avoid the black hole of tedious detail?[16] Without lapsing into easy or trite generalizations, to what degree must one examine the general social and cultural currents in which the specific material occurred?[17] And what reality do such currents have?

Texts, sites, sculptures, and coins represent slices of the ancient world from particular perspectives or worldviews. Well-chosen examples illuminate general patterns even though they offer at best marginal glimpses.[18] Due consideration, of course, must be given to how the same symbol functions in different locales or at different times. This will be done where possible. But the paucity of evidence (archaeological and literary) does not always permit such an analysis. The haphazard nature of some archaeological finds makes overgeneralization a constant hazard.[19] According to Stephen Jay Gould: "the beauty of nature lies in detail; the message, in generality. Optimal appreciation demands both, and I know no better tactic than the illustration of exciting principles by well-chosen particulars."[20] Anyone who deals with the past knows how well the term "history" could substitute for Gould's "nature." Still useful is Max Weber's notion of ideal types, that is, typical patterns that serve as heuristic models whose vitality becomes apparent through specific cases.[21] In this study I seek to balance Weber's "ideal types" and Geertz's "thick description."

Aphrodisias, a small city in Caria (Turkey), will frequently serve as a specific test case that elucidates general patterns in the Greek East during the Roman period. For example, local and imperial coin issues minted at Aphrodisias parallel others found throughout the Roman Empire. The messages conveyed by coins are often unique to their city of manufacture and result from the particular circumstances that led to each coin type's creation. Analysis of

Aphrodisias's "rhetoric" and "iconography of power" as displayed on its coins highlights specific concerns of the city and its local elite classes at the time of minting, most particularly, as we shall see, the promotion of the goddess Aphrodite. When one looks at other cities, especially in Asia Minor, one finds that their elites also used coins and particular deities to elaborate their local and regional power. By comparing the local and Greek imperial coins at Aphrodisias with coins from a number of cities in Asia Minor bearing religious symbols and with coins from the rest of the Greek East, one can discern the way members of the elite classes utilized generally available symbols to define their particular relation to imperial, regional, and cosmic power.[22] The "symbolics of power" found in texts and embedded in the iconography, epigraphy, coins, and architecture provide the data with which to discern the constructions of reality influencing both those who conceive and send the message and those who receive it at different periods.

LANGUAGE AND POWER:
THE LITERARY EVIDENCE

A text does not mirror reality but rather displays the author's conception of reality. As E. L. Carr notes, "No document can tell us more than what the author of the document thought—what he thought happened, what he thought ought to happen or would happen, or perhaps only what he wanted others to think he thought, or even only what he himself thought he thought."[23] In addition, however, modern interpreters must devise strategies for discerning large contextual patterns reflected in the text. Some have sought to resolve the relation of text and context(s) by analyzing how an ideal reader might respond to the text (reader-response).[24] This potentially fruitful approach, however, is frequently limited by very narrow (if any) analysis of the contexts of various readers, often ignoring altogether the assumptions, language, or the use of symbols from the writer's day. The best clue to an author's participation in various webs of power remains the author's own work. There one can often find historical data and social and cultural conventions of the day. Particular language, themes, and choices of images connect a text and its author with the world. Yet a narrative also operates as an integrated unit quite apart from its constituent parts. Writers create narrative worlds that operate by their own internal rules, with no explicit connection to the real world. Both features must be kept in mind.

Three near contemporaries provide lucid illustrations on the intersection of power and religious symbols in their respective traditions. Chariton of Aphrodisias (a pagan), Josephus (a Jew), and Luke (a Christian) each lived and wrote around the time of or during the Flavian through Trajanic periods. Significant similarities in style and content occur, although probably not because of direct literary relations between them; rather, they belong to an environment (the Greek East under Roman control) with which they interacted in remarkably similar ways.[25] Each author provides a snapshot of how those associated with the elite class in the Greek East incorporated the language of religion to define their own sense of identity and power within a world dominated by many forces, most particularly Roman presence and power, the power exhibited by local elites, and cosmic power. Chariton, Josephus, and Luke provide textual evidence of our "well-chosen particulars" that elucidate "exciting principles."

ICONOGRAPHY AND POWER:
THE MATERIAL EVIDENCE

This study deals not only with literary evidence but also with coins, sculpture, epigraphy, and buildings that convey perceptions and assumptions about the construction of power.[26] Images, as Paul Zanker notes, reflect "a society's inner life and give insights into people's values and imagination that often cannot be apprehended in literary sources."[27] To discern a society's "inner life" means taking a hard look at the "landscape" in which such features occur. "Landscape" here is used to mean "the entire surface over which people moved and within which they congregated. That surface was given meaning as people acted upon the world within the context of the various demands and obligations which acted upon them."[28] The difficulty, of course, is that a coin once made or a monument once built, like a piece of literature, takes on a life of its own.[29] Coins in the imperial period commissioned by local elites often had the image of the emperor on the obverse and some iconographic presentation on the reverse, which frequently included religious symbolism.[30] A connection (either real or perceived) existed between the imperial power network and the local elites, who often sponsored these coins.[31] Such coins conveyed to the viewer the power and prestige of the emperor; they also bolstered the power and prestige of the local or regional officials who sponsored the work. Values and authority were intimately tied to coin issues and had real persuasive power.[32] A. Wallace-Hadrill's observation regarding symbols on Augustan coinage rings no less true for provincial coinage in the Flavio-Trajanic period. The symbols are meant to persuade on several levels:

> [T]hey attempt to persuade the user that the coin is legitimate by presenting images that will command respect . . . they lay claim to the user's respect for the images they present, and so tend to legitimate the regime that issues them. . . . The coins persuade by offering images of authority.[33]

Religious images on coins were powerful symbols by which officials made sense of their relation with cities, regions, and Roman power. To a degree, those who issued the coins helped define the nature of the power relations by associating imperial power, their city, and themselves with significant religious symbols. Yet coins (or monuments or literature) could lose their original symbolic power and acquire a new meaning in a new context.[34] Thus Epictetus can disparage the use of Neronian coins in light of Nero's new status as persona non grata during the Flavio-Trajanic period.[35] And communities that honor the Senate's *damnatio memoriae* of Domitian by excising his name from honorific inscriptions redefine the monumental structures of which his name was a part. In short, monuments or, for that matter, any ancient vehicle of human expression can

> take on an ambiguity through time. They may be locales of ritual observance, where models of social order may be made explicitly, or, silent and almost unnoticed, encountered in the routines of daily life, but each time a new mark was made on the landscape, those who came after might accommodate that scar into their own understanding of the world.[36]

Such public expressions supply much of what we can know about life in the Greek East. Fergus Millar rightly cautions against looking for what people "really" felt when peering at a coin, gazing at a monument, or even participating in a ritual act. Communal assumptions, rather than individual reverence, loyalty, or gratitude, emerge through public actions, verbal displays, artifacts, and buildings.[37] At the very least, the material evidence displays the perception of power through the lenses of those who dedicated them. And they do convey to a degree the underlying assumptions about what constituted proper relations.

Several additional caveats must be made. Coins, architecture, epigraphy, sculpture, and literature from this period have one distinct bias: they primarily represent an elite perspective. One need not be overly apologetic in this regard, since the perspective of elites in the Roman world dominated most of the political, religious, and social landscape.[38] Even those who challenged certain aspects of the behavior often did so within the framework of prevailing elite attitudes. Jesus' didactic response, "Whose likeness appears on this coin?" to the question, "Is it lawful to pay taxes to Caesar?" indicates the power implicit in such images (Mark 12:14–17 = Matt. 22:15–22 = Luke 20:20–26), a point assumed in the narrative by the questioner and by Jesus.[39] The imperial Greek coin issues of many cities that display the head of the ruling caesar with a local or regional symbol indicate the vitality such association had for local elites, who endeavored to participate in the webs of power permeating the empire. The dialectic of local power with empirewide power (most notably the emperor's) was important for both sides. Each power base informs the other: Roman as symbolized by the emperor and local as symbolized by the demos, specific individuals, or religious figures. Members or affiliates of the local elite structure in the Greek East who issued coins, wrote and sponsored books, dedicated sculpture and buildings, or sponsored festivals often exhibit the interplay between local, regional, imperial, and cosmic power.[40] From all sides people in antiquity encountered the elite view of the world through texts, coins, iconography, building programs, sculpture, and epigraphy.[41]

A second problem is that ancient sources such as coins and epigraphy are often found isolated from their original context of buildings, sculptures, and related realia. Only recently have interpreters seemed to realize that the context of an inscription is almost as important as what is written.[42] The issue of context is further complicated by the lack of precision in dating epigraphic remains (normally through the letter forms, monument style, language, formulas, and so forth).[43] Nevertheless, the dating now done must serve as the best, if sometimes inadequate, heuristic device to help frame the discussion.

A third issue concerns the relative paucity of coins, urban architecture, art, and epigraphy, not to mention the accidental character of their discovery for the period under study. Indeed, for Christianity during this period such material is virtually nonexistent.[44] Ramsay MacMullen has estimated that the material evidence for the period 150–450 C.E. is fifty times greater than the from Hammurabi (1800 B.C.E.) to 150 C.E.[45] Thus any analysis of the Flavio-Trajanic period must paint broad strokes at best. But interpretation always involves selection. I endeavor to be clear as to what I select and what it shows. Despite MacMullen's cautionary observation, a significant body of literary and archaeological evidence does exist. Indeed, the material remains include an impressive number of coins from across the empire, and thanks to the "epigraphic habit" of the period,[46] we have a significant corpus of material that constitutes its own genre and provides us with some of our best sources for this period.[47]

In chapter 2, I address the wider social and historical context, with special attention to the Flavio-Trajanic period. I examine some of the prevalent issues that make this period so crucial for understanding the development of paganism, Judaism, and Christianity in the first centuries of this era. I also discuss further why Chariton, Josephus, Luke, and the city of Aphrodisias serve as our "well-chosen particulars" for this study.

Chapter 3 begins a series of thematic studies in which I elucidate some of the general ("ideal") principles of the period. I explore the significant role played by ancient religious symbols as groups and narrators reinvested them with meaning. The most dramatic examples come from "newer" movements associated with Isis, Mithras, or nascent Christianity. Yet, even so-called civic cults such as those of Artemis of Ephesus and Aphrodite of Aphrodisias had adherents throughout the Roman world. Some movements had made an impact earlier, but their widespread acceptance at many levels of society and on such a large scale in the late first and early second centuries was something new. The role of tradition in the political, social, and cultural affairs of the empire became increasingly important for proponents of these groups.

In chapter 4 I examine the role of cosmic power in social and political interactions, especially as local elites drew on it to define their role within other power networks. Fundamental is the way in which pagan, Jewish, and Christian groups and writers reinterpreted power networks, especially those governed by the Romans and local elites, and fit them within a cosmic framework that stressed the power of a particular deity (or deities).

In chapter 5 I describe how the real or perceived spread of particular movements across the *oikoumene* (known world) provided symbolic capital for the power and prestige of a deity (and the associated group). I describe how particular sacred places (e.g., the Temple in Jerusalem, the Artemesion in Ephesus) provided symbolic power for persons outside their immediate area.

In chapter 6 I look at the role of cosmic power brokers, that is, specially designated individuals who mediated the power of the deity within particular groups. I offer examples of the type of people who served as power brokers among pagans, Jews, and Christians, as well as the social, political, and cultural roles such individuals played. These human symbols were fundamental to the social coherence of a group, notably by their stress on ethics, education, and maintaining a proper relation to the current political order. I also look at the role that religious symbols play in social maintenance. This leads to a discussion of the importance of presenting religious or mythic symbols to the public to foster social cohesion.

In chapter 7 I discuss how symbolic images pertaining to the future influenced the way people interpreted their relations in the present. Such symbols were not simply responses to a "world grown large." They presented the future in ways that enabled individuals and groups to address the webs of power entangling them in the present.

To summarize, I examine how elites and those affiliated with them in the Greek East established much of the symbolic discourse within which most persons in the empire had to operate. People drew on the antiquity of the worship of their deity (or deities),[48] stressed the power and presence of the deity across the *oikoumene,* acknowledged individuals who mediated between the divine realm and human society, emphasized legitimate social customs and the current legal system promoted (but not always practiced) by powerful regional and international political figures, and made clear the deity's activity behind the scenes, influencing political and historical events. Members or associates of a local elite or aristocratic class often sought to use religious traditions to display for their audience (whether through literature or epigraphy or sculpture) the group's deity as the major arbiter of power within a newly defined all-pervasive web of power. They did so to make their place within the larger society as a whole and as a means to consolidate their power base, in their locale, their region, and their cosmos.

2.

The Power Game:
Setting the Stage

Between Augustus and Hadrian, something changed in the Greek East. A century and a half of imperial rule had altered both the nature of Roman rule and the manner in which those in the Greek East responded to it.[1] Imperial power still revolved around the emperor, a power based on decades of precedents. Senators and equestrians from Italy continued to play important roles in the maintenance of the empire. Yet, the faces and families who ruled had changed substantially. The senatorial and equestrian classes had huge turnovers each generation: up to 75 percent for senatorial families and even more for equestrian families.[2] Still visible in the Greek East were well-placed families associated with dynasts such as Herod the Great,[3] with the ruling class of Sparta,[4] or with powerful freedmen like Zoilos of Aphrodisias.[5] Such individuals and groups had ruled the Greek East on behalf of the Romans through much of the first century.[6] By Hadrian, however, most local dynasts in the Greek East had disappeared, and local authority often resided in powerful individuals and local councils, populated by local elites, some previously affiliated with former client kings or with ruling elites or freedmen, and others from new families who had risen to power.[7]

THE CIVIC WORLD OF THE PAGAN GREEK EAST

The Graeco-Roman city dominated the landscape of the Roman Empire in the East and it was in this context that the pagan, Jewish, and Christian movements formed in the first two centuries of this era.[8] Establishing and fostering the economic and social growth of the cities were part of the program of power and prestige that governed much of what the emperors (especially the Flavians, Nerva, and Trajan) and their regional and local affiliates in the Greek East did.[9] They built roads connecting much of the empire locally and regionally with Rome and sponsored or encouraged building programs by local elites throughout the Greek East.[10] To be sure, rural areas often developed their own local

identity.[11] Yet, no neat separation between city, town, and countryside generally existed; intricate webs of power often bound city and country along economic, social, political, and cultural lines.[12] Within those webs, the city remained a significant and distinctive center for the cultural apparatus and
identity of the empire and local elites.[13]

The Flavio-Trajanic period marked an important juncture in the Roman
Empire's relation with the Greek East.[14] The period saw a consolidation of
power over the century-old empire, with battles for new territory largely
relegated to areas east of the Euphrates and the north by the end of Trajan's
reign. The last major internal military threats to Roman rule from the Greek
East occurred during the Flavian period, with conflict coming mostly from a
few factions within Judaism and from sporadic outbreaks in several frontier
areas of the empire.[15] More significant, the Greek East flexed its cultural and
political muscle, perhaps because of changing imperial tastes by Latin-speaking
emperors. Literature written in Greek grew in quantity (if not quality) while
works in Latin saw a marked decline.[16] The incorporation of local elites from
the Greek East into the Roman political structure increased significantly under
the Flavians, with some local elites rising to great prominence in the Roman
system.[17]

Fresh from his triumphs over his rivals, Titus Flavius Vespasianus, the son
of a tax collector, became emperor in 69 C.E. One of the *novi homines* (new
men)[18] who began to wield great power in this period, he moved quickly to
establish his credentials as a military leader, an action that had strong Roman
precedent.[19] The Jewish revolt fulfilled this agenda nicely; the war significantly
affected the Flavian iconographic program through the reign of Vespasian's son
Titus.[20] The Jewish war enabled Vespasian to highlight the benefits of his
autocracy, especially stability and prosperity acquired through military victory.[21] Equally important, Vespasian reinvested with meaning traditions (or
perceived traditions) associated with the reign of Augustus, the golden age
when another civil war had ended and when some believed the Pax Romana
had shone its brightest.[22] The Augustan program itself had drawn strongly on
Greek models;[23] nevertheless, the monuments maintained a strong Roman
character that stressed "a revival of the *mores maiorum*: Augustus, the citizen in
his toga, stands as moral exemplar to his people."[24] Moral reform was renewed
with vigor under Vespasian and even more fervently under Domitian, which
later writers more sympathetic to the senatorial classes roundly criticized.[25]
The Flavian period saw increased conservatism among many elites, especially
compared to the perceived excesses of Neronian rule.

The desire for a traditional base in the religious and political past was
certainly not unique to the Augustan and Flavian periods. A number of local
elites in Rome and the Greek East drew on the past before the turbulent period
that followed Nero's death and would do so many times afterward. Vespasian's rule, however, like that of Augustus before him, marked an important
turning point within the Roman Empire and its association with the Greek
East. The Flavian consolidation of power was paralleled by a closer linkage of
the far-flung empire as the Flavian period witnessed an extensive expansion of

the road system that connected major urban areas in the Greek East.[26] This linkage coincided with a renaissance for cities and Greek culture in the Greek East that continued for another two centuries.[27] Power became more centralized in the emperors, and municipal embassies appear to come under increasing imperial control, especially during Vespasian's reign.[28] In some areas in the Greek East during the Flavio-Trajanic period, imperial authorities increasingly sought to identify distinctive ethnic groups and regions, a process that may have affected Jews and Christians as well.[29] As urban centers increased, more local elites became active in local, regional, and imperial policies.[30] The abrupt change in leadership, however, from the aristocratic Julio-Claudian line to the Flavians, members of the Italian "bourgeoisie,"[31] raised troubling questions for local elites in the Greek East. How were past relationships with Rome, with their region, and with their community to be treated? What power networks (political, social, cultural) were still operative? How were local elites to construe their place with the entrance of this new and unknown component in the power equation?

Religious symbols continued as powerful instruments for negotiating the new contours of power brought on by the Flavian ascendancy. Traditional deities in the Greek East continued to provide locales with powerful "collective images of concord and parity."[32] Local elites in towns across the Roman Empire did not simply use or ignore religious symbols as so much excess baggage.[33] Religious symbols supplied potent images that enabled their proponents to gain adherents, acquire or maintain power or prestige, bolster believers, respond to detractors, and associate with what many felt was the true force behind the world, divine power. Of course, rarely did this mean the creation of neat theological principles or systematic presentation.[34]

During the Flavian period, local elites in the Greek East established a firm presence in the new political environment.[35] Vespasian drew on such elites to fill in the recurring gap of available leaders and to have key areas of his imperial power network firmly controlled by trustworthy associates, persons who served with him in the army, like Tiberius Julius Celsus Polemaeanus, or in other ways proved their allegiance, like Tiberius Iulius Alexander, who was of Jewish origins and was the first to proclaim Vespasian emperor in Egypt and later in all probability was prefect of the guard.[36]

Building programs in the Greek East often paralleled those initiated by emperors such as Augustus and the Flavians. Herod the Great's well-known building exploits show the lengths to which some local elites in the Augustan period went. Theaters, marketplaces, and arches sprouted up during the Flavian period, a building spree by local elites that continued well into the third century.[37] The importance of local elites is evidenced in numerous ways, especially their extensive use of prestige items such as marble on public buildings. During the middle of the first century C.E., marble trade in the East escalated, especially because of regional building projects sponsored by local elites. Prior to this, most marble was directed toward Rome.[38] Equally revealing is the increased presence of theaters in the late first and early second centuries in places like southern Syria, Arabia, Galilee, and parts of Judaea.[39] Some, like the theater of Sepphoris in Galilee, may have been built by local dynasts or elites in the early part of the first century; for Sepphoris that would be Herod Antipas, who refounded the city as the capital of Galilee in 4 B.C.E. Like many buildings built during the early first century, it was apparently extensively renovated between 70 and 180 C.E.[40]

Such building activities parallel the rise in the late first century of local elites from the provinces playing active roles in the social and political affairs of Rome. Further, more senators than ever before came from the provinces during and after Flavian rule, grants of citizenship became more accessible, and urban areas increased significantly.[41] "This amounted to the development of a broadly homogeneous imperial aristocracy and the unification of local elites, together with some assimilation of wider strata of the population."[42] Crisis had brought opportunity and increased centralization of power, in the Senate and emperor on an imperial level, and in councils and certain key individuals on the local level.[43]

Many local elites in the Greek East learned well how to fit Roman power within their Hellenistic frame of reference. Even one of the more interventionist of Roman cultural and political strategies, the Roman colony (*colonia*)—characterized by Roman law, Latin language, and Roman culture—took on much of the character of the Greek city that preceded it.[44] Nevertheless, the locus of power, the imperial pyramid descending from emperor to senators downward, remained jealously guarded. In Rome at least, old prejudices against the Greek East died hard, as the late-first- and early-second-century Roman writers Juvenal (9.14) and Martial (10.761) indicate.[45] Some local elites in the Greek East recognized they had to operate in a world where Rome had the political and military upper hand. Plutarch, a prominent and influential participant in the local elite structure of Athens and a member of the equestrian class, admonished Greeks who sought to rule under Roman power not to overstep their offices or rely on their ancient roots and past glories to legitimate their power.

> You rule as a subject, over a city set under the jurisdiction of proconsuls, of the procurators of Caesar. . . . This is not ancient Sardis or that old power of the Lydians. You must keep your robes in check, and cast your eye from the generals' office to the tribunal . . . observing the Roman senators' shoes above your head.[46]

A number of local elites skillfully heeded that advice.[47] Some, as the quotation itself implies, did not.

Religious images provided elites in the Greek East with an array of symbols to negotiate their local and regional aspirations within the context of Roman power. To an extent, cosmic power redefined the obvious limits of participation by local elites in the Roman web of power, limits that were all too evident even among the *philoromanoi* (friends of Rome). No city better elucidates this negotiation than the Greek city of Aphrodisias in Caria of Asia Minor. Here local elites long understood the power of the emperors within the rubric of their deity, Aphrodite. As we shall see, they maintained Greek identity and pride by defining Roman power within their view of cosmic power, an action essential for their political and social identity. For towns in the Greek East like Aphrodisias, of course, it was important that the Roman leadership agreed for the better part of three centuries and allowed them to retain a number of special civic privileges. Like many from the elite classes in the Greek East, elites in Aphrodisias promoted a dialectic in which local or Roman power confirmed the power of their civic deity and its proponents; in turn, the power of the deity affirmed local or Roman power (at least from the local groups' perspective).

The city of Aphrodisias acquired increased stature in the latter part of the first century B.C.E., its prosperity and prestige paralleling the rise of Octavian and the Julio-Claudian line. Although Aphrodisias had certain unique features in its interaction with imperial authority, it typifies in many respects the desire of local elites to fit themselves within the new imperial regime. Excavations over the past thirty years have provided enormous amounts of epigraphic, architectural, and sculptural evidence that supplements earlier epigraphic forays in the area.[48] In many respects the city saw no major changes when the Julio-Claudian line was replaced by the Flavian line. The Sebasteion, or imperial cult complex, begun during the reign of Tiberius and continued through Nero, apparently functioned within the civic context at least through the early second century.[49] Such evidence reminds us that a good deal of continuity existed even when dramatic events occurred in the political leadership, such as the transition from Nero to Vespasian. Thus, though Vespasian denigrates the image and memory of Nero (as Trajan does for Domitian),[50] he nevertheless stresses how he continues what had come before. Dedications added to old complexes by local elites on behalf of the Flavians or the completion and expansion of public buildings such as the theater at Aphrodisias emphasize the continuity with what went before while at the same time reframing the relation of imperial power to the local civic context.[51]

Thus, although some of the best evidence comes from the Julio-Claudian period at Aphrodisias, clear evidence also exists that the city, like many others, sought to continue its power within the new period begun by the Flavians. Indicative is a dedication from Aphrodisias to honor Domitian (later changed to Vespasian) at the provincial temple of the emperors in Ephesus.[52] Another inscription records Trajan's donation of money to repair earthquake damage at Aphrodisias. The money had come from a bequest left to him from a wealthy member of the elite class at Aphrodisias.[53] Trajan also issued a ruling to Smyrna, reprinted on the wall of the theater in Aphrodisias, that affirmed Aphrodisias's rights as a free city, which permitted it to continue avoiding payment of common liturgies in Asia.[54] An architrave block in a large basilica west of the agora apparently contains the name of Titus.[55] A portrait statue of Domitian, a head of a Flavian priest, and a bust of Trajan have been found,[56] which indicate the ongoing connections made between some local elites in the city and imperial power. The fact that the goddess of the city was Aphrodite also enabled the city to adapt to the changed circumstances of Flavian rule, perhaps in part because some elite women in the Flavio-Trajanic period (including those in imperial households) closely identified themselves with Aphrodite/Venus.[57]

Aphrodisias provides excellent examples of the patterns appearing in the all-important civic arenas of the Greek East in the transition from Julio-Claudian to Flavio-Trajanic rule. In addition, it provides a useful context for the novelist Chariton's work, who claims to come from the city. Certainly, a social and cultural environment does not determine the entire meaning or significance of a literary work, but it can elucidate aspects of the elite structure and the worldview that the author and his audience took for granted.

Chariton of Aphrodisias, the Pagan

An anonymons editor of the first English translation of *Chaereas and Callirhoe* noted that the work had "much the appearance of a true story . . . containing a great variety of incidents, all well prepared; and very artfully interwoven; with scarce anything improbable and improper and the whole drawn up with a gravity of stile becoming an historian."[58]

Chariton, a little-known author from Aphrodisias in Caria, at first glance represents an odd choice for this project. The work is obscure and the author came from a small city in Asia Minor. Further, the narrative action occurs shortly after the Peloponnesian War (431–404 B.C.E.), which permits few opportunities for explicit mention of Rome or events contemporary with the author. Yet these are some of the very features that make his text attractive for this study. Chariton's text reverberates with the author's concern to address issues of identity and the intersections between imperial, local, and cosmic power. Chariton's "thoroughly provincial" approach provides innumerable examples of "people's attitudes, of their 'civilization' in the sense that they live in society and reflect the values accepted by that society."[59] Further, the text was read by an audience that was no doubt aware of interchanges between Roman provincial authorities, local elites, and others in the Greek East. Finally, archaeological and epigraphic remains from over thirty years of excavations at Aphrodisias, many of them roughly contemporary with Chariton, provide important visual clues to the use of religious images by local elites.[60] Such evidence helps us evaluate some of the religious images in the narrative of Chariton. In turn, Chariton's text highlights the effort of local elites across the Greek East to obtain or maintain a modicum of power within the Roman Empire.[61]

Chariton's *Chaereas and Callirhoe* is the earliest complete, extant Greek romance.[62] It was written between 50 and 150 C.E., with an early-second-century dating probable.[63] Five separate papyrus fragments of Chariton's text found at ancient Karanis and Oxyrhynchus in Egypt, locations far removed from the author's native home of Aphrodisias in Caria of Asia Minor, indicate that it, like other ancient romances, had a degree of popularity in the late second and third centuries.[64] One fragment, written on expensive parchment, suggests that some readers were well-to-do. Another was found in the brick tomb of a member of the local elite in a cemetery outside Kom Ushim (ancient

Karanis) in Fayum, Egypt.[65] The readership remains a debated issue but probably included members of or persons affiliated with the elite classes in the Greek East.[66]

Chariton's personal attachment to the local elite structure in Aphrodisias is evident in his opening remarks. In book 1.1.1, he identifies himself as a secretary (υπογραφευς)[67] to a rhetor, Athenagoras, in Aphrodisias. The names Chariton and Athenagoras are found in inscriptions at Aphrodisias, which, combined with the content of Chariton's text, has lead most interpreters to conclude that the Carian Aphrodisias is the Aphrodisias mentioned in Chariton's work.[68] As a secretary for a rhetorician Chariton would have intimate knowledge of the administrative operation of a city in the Greek East, as portions of his novel betray.[69]

Few interpreters disagree that religious themes are amply represented in Chariton's narrative,[70] though they have tended to interpret those themes along two extremely divergent tracks. Either the religious element was further proof "that the novel was seriously centered on religious ritual," or it showed the novel as only "sentimental and sensational."[71]

For many modern interpreters, *Chaereas and Callirhoe,* like the Greek romances and other Greek novels in general, becomes a form of light reading or entertainment.[72] Unfortunately, definitions of entertainment tend to fall into vague or anachronistic psychological categories that fit almost any narrative. One commentator, for example, argues that entertainment in the ancient romances stems from one or more of the following attributes: satisfaction of emotional needs, wish fulfillment, escape, and intellectual or aesthetic pleasure.[73] Another interpreter simply labels Chariton's piece a Hellenistic operetta.[74] Both definitions largely ignore or downplay the prominence of religion in the Greek novels and the promotion of social and cultural mores amenable to elites in the Greek East. In addition, they provide little in the way of a credible social or cultural context for reading such "entertaining" material.

On the other extreme is the view of Reinhold Merkelbach that religious motifs indicate that the Greek novels are *Mysterientexte,* texts that display now lost mystery rites for initiates or insiders, most especially for the goddess Isis. He argues that one of the earliest romances, Chariton's Greek novel, is a misconceived effort to write such a "mystery text."[75] Others temper the role of religion in the Greek novels by stating that the novels display the myth of the isolated person in Hellenistic society or operate as aretalogies.[76] Jack Winkler sees both tracks as "conjecturing in the dark" since the ancient world was largely silent on both mystery cults and popular sentiment. "The silence of serious reverence enshrined the one; the silence of critical disdain dismissed the other."[77] Yet even Winkler grants that an author can take standard motifs and invest them with religious meaning.[78]

Religion in Chariton's romance may be more profitably examined by drawing on my earlier definition that looked at religion as a significant feature in the construction of systemic power relationships. I will argue that Chariton of Aphrodisias did not write his Greek novel simply for pleasurable reading, "distraction for distraction's sake," or for salvific or ritualistic purposes. I intend to demonstrate how he drew on Greek heritage and the religious past to depict the goddess Aphrodite controlling the whims of Fate and the machinations of political figures. Like many local elites across the Greek East during this period, he celebrates Greek identity, reaffirms Greek religious and cultic associations, and promotes the Greek past.

JEWS IN THE GREEK EAST

By the time Augustus grasped the reins of imperial power, Jews had already established a legitimate legal presence in the empire. The first-century writer Valerius Maximus notes:

> The Romans gradually developed an official policy toward the Jews living within their empire. It was not until the middle of the [. . .], when Judaea came under direct Roman rule, that the unique nature of this ethnic and religious group was acknowledged and granted special protection. Despite its exclusive monotheism, Judaism was given the status of a *religio licita* [legal religion] and the Jews were accorded special privileges of maintaining their ancestral cult and lifestyle wherever they lived.[79]

Such rights appeared to be guaranteed at least through the Julio-Claudian period, even though tensions existed between Jews and non-Jews in areas of the empire, notably Egypt.[80] The Flavian period, however, marked a significant change in attitude on the part of the Roman leadership.[81]

No general remarks can do justice to the complexity of the Jewish situation throughout the Greek East, especially during the Flavio-Trajanic period. Significantly, the period begins with the ruthless crushing of the Jewish revolt in Judaea against Roman rule between 66 and 70 C.E. and ends with Trajan squelching another Jewish revolt in North Africa and Cyprus in 115–17 C.E.[82] The subsequent tax by Vespasian on all Jews in the Roman Empire (the *fiscus Iudaicus*) at the very least highlighted the difference between Jews and non-Jews in the Roman Empire.[83] That difference was seized upon by Latin and Greek authors alike.[84] Most of the Jews who did participate in local and imperial affairs were members of the Herodian family, a few elites such as Josephus, and those who dissociated themselves from their Jewish heritage such as Tiberius Alexander, Philo's nephew, who became prefect in Egypt.[85] This setting apart (though not total) of Diaspora Judaism's leadership contrasts sharply with the much heavier involvement of Jews in the Antonine and Severan periods, when certain traditions even associate Judah ha-Nasi, the compiler of the Mishnah, with the emperor Antoninus.[86]

To a degree, as we shall see, Jews during the Flavio-Trajanic period sought to define again their tradition (the Temple having been destroyed) and their relation to local and imperial power networks. In certain areas such as Egypt and Cyrene this proved completely unsuccessful. In other areas, notably in Asia Minor and Galilee, Jews came to participate at almost every level of civic life. This process of redefinition came at a time, as I have noted, when local elites in the Greek East were acquiring more power and were reclaiming and reasserting their own traditions. Josephus's attacks on Greek traditions while building up the Jewish faith represents one approach by Jewish elites to deal with a sporadically hostile non-Jewish environment.

Apparently for some Gentiles the arguments supporting Judaism and its God found a positive resonance. The degree to which overt proselytizing occurred remains a matter of debate, as does the character of the response.[87] Yet no doubt some non-Jews responded positively to Judaism during this period in ways ranging from admiration to outright conversion.[88]

Josephus, the Jew

The works of Josephus, a first-century aristocrat from Judaea, reflect a man whose world had undergone a radical, if not traumatic, change. Indeed, Josephus asks his readers' indulgence as they read his history of momentous events: "I cannot conceal my private sentiments, nor refuse to give my personal sympathies scope to bewail my country's misfortunes" (*BJ* 1.9). Josephus, more urgently than Chariton, must negotiate issues involving imperial and local Greek elites' approaches to cosmic power. The Jewish war of 66–73 C.E. was still fresh in Greek, Roman, and Jewish minds. Indeed, Josephus's own benefactors, the Flavians, continued to make political capital of the war, as is evident from the Judaea Capta coin series minted throughout the empire, statuary celebrating the victory, and the building of Titus's arches in Rome.[89] In part Josephus had to legitimate the status of the Jewish people within the Graeco-Roman world, especially because of scurrilous attacks and false histories written by Greek historians (*AJ* 1.5, *BJ* 1.7–8). Josephus was one of a large number of elites who sought to redefine their relation with the local, regional, imperial, and cosmic networks. Unlike most, however, he was a member of a people who had moved from being only one of the many subjugated peoples in the Roman Empire (as nicely illustrated in the *ethne* reliefs at Aphrodisias)[90] to become the centerpiece of the Flavian propaganda program.[91]

Josephus is an ideal choice for my study. He addresses the disastrous Jewish defeat, which included the destruction of the Jerusalem Temple, a central symbol for many Jews, and pays particular attention to the role Rome played in the scenario. He confronts explicitly how Jews should have responded to imperial power and, most important, how they now should interpret Roman power and presence. Josephus's several works written after his capture by Vespasian provide most of what we know about Jews in the first century. In *The Jewish War* (ca. 75–79 C.E.), *Antiquities of the Jews* (93–94), *Vita*, or *Life* (93–94 [less likely 100–101 or later]), and *Against Apion* (post 93–94?)[92] Josephus reflects, with varying consistency,[93] the Jewish relation to Roman power primarily by placing it within the context of Jewish tradition.[94] As we shall see, he stresses the antiquity (and thus the legitimacy) of the Jewish movement, its presence across the *oikoumene*, the fact that in many political and historical events affecting the Jewish nation (including the Roman victory) the Jewish god stands behind historical events as well as agents of Rome who govern appropriately (and therefore on behalf of the Jewish deity) or inappropriately (and therefore against the norms set forth by their own government). Josephus's work illustrates well how one member of the Jewish elite class reinterpreted the Jewish people's role amid intersecting webs of power by drawing on his tradition and religious symbol system.

CHRISTIANS IN THE GREEK EAST

Generally, Christians, like Jews, occupied the fringes of local and imperial networks of power. Unlike Jews, however, they had no series of legal precedents to establish their legitimate place in the Roman Empire or well-placed elites such as the Herodian family, the philosopher Philo, or the historian Josephus to serve as their advocates (with the possible exception of Luke and such sponsors as Theophilos). Initially, Roman and local officials in the Greek East appear not to have distinguished Christians from Jews.[95] Claudius's expulsion of Jews from Rome on account of a rabble-rouser named Chrestus (possibly a reference to Christus)[96] indicates that imperial power made no real distinction, viewing such confrontations as an internal Jewish debate.[97] In Nero's reign, however, greater distinctions were apparently made, although in this instance our sources (primarily Tacitus, Suetonius, and Josephus) may reflect their own period more than Nero's.[98] It was during the Flavio-Trajanic period that some imperial and local powers began to recognize Christianity as separate from Judaism. The most explicit examples, of course, are Pliny's letters to Trajan discussing his approach to those who professed Christianity and Trajan's approval of the severe response (death) to those who persisted in continuing their "obstinate" practice. Nevertheless, little evidence exists of systematic persecution of Christians during the reigns of Domitian and Trajan.[99] Only in the latter part of the second century and in the third century do more severe and widespread persecutions occur, as illustrated in the numerous stories of martyrdom in the church fathers and the spectacular presentations in the Apocryphal Acts (e.g., Thecla, a convert of Paul, rejects the advances of the leading member of the local elite, who also happens to be a priest of the imperial cult).[100] Christian symbols distinct from the surrounding culture make their appearance in some areas around 180 C.E., perhaps as part of the Christian response to increased persecution.[101]

The first and early second centuries, therefore, represent a crucial juncture in the development of the Christian movement as it sought to define itself within a pagan environment increasingly bent on reclaiming its own powerful traditions. In addition, Judaism, with which Christians had great affinity in light of their respective claims to similar roots, was as we have seen reevaluating itself. Most of the New Testament texts and those of the early church fathers written during this period reflect diverse Christian groups using religious symbols to help sort out their relation to their pagan surroundings, their attitude toward Jews, and their increasingly uncertain interactions with imperial power. Almost all our evidence is literary since Christians do not appear to have a distinctive material culture until the mid-second or third century.[102]

Like Judaism, Christianity appealed to a number of people, as evidenced by its fairly rapid expansion across much of the Roman Empire. This may reflect an initial use of established lines of communications among Jews throughout the Roman Empire, which is suggested in Acts (where Paul typically visits synagogues first), in Paul's letters (where he reiterates his Jewish roots), and in the fact that most of the early leadership was Jewish. The edict of Claudius and the persecution of Christians by Nero indicate that significant friction developed between certain Jews and Christians at an early stage.[103] By the Flavio-Trajanic period, connections with contemporary Judaism were stretched thin (except for a few Jewish Christians).[104] Hostility between Jews and Christians became more pronounced, as evidenced in the literature (especially from the Christian side). Yet the movement apparently attracted people from most sectors of the society except perhaps from the upper echelons of power, although some have suggested that members of Domitian's own family may have been involved.[105] The empire provided an environment in which the movement could flourish;[106] the increased importance of cities in the Greek East and the apparent ease of travel between cities and villages during the Flavio-Trajanic period offered additional opportunities for people to encounter this spreading movement. Acts suggests that a class of Gentiles became very attracted to the movement; called god-fearers, they either joined the movement or supported it out of their personal funds. That proselytes existed is assured. That a class of "god-fearers" who had first been attracted to Judaism existed as early as the first century is more problematic, but clearly such a group had formed by the third.[107] The Christian movement during this period sought to define itself within the elite framework that dominated the political and cultural landscape of the Greek East. It also appropriated some of the same religious symbols as certain Jewish groups, creating literary, if not real, confrontations. Christianity's espoused quest for converts apparently attracted a number of people to their ranks. For the Flavio-Trajanic period the best examples of these processes come from the writings of Luke.

Luke, the Christian

H. J. Cadbury has concluded: "it is far more important to know the personality of the author than his name, to know his purpose in writing than his profession, to know the technique of his age than the exact year, to know his position in the transmission of history than his habitat."[108]

Luke, an anonymous Christian author, wrote two books dedicated to a Theophilos, probably a wealthy patron and certainly portrayed as someone of status.[109] Luke wrote his texts, the Gospel of Luke and Acts of the Apostles, between 85 and 115 C.E., with a probable date of between 85 and 90.[110] The Gospel of Luke's elegant and stylistic prologue and Luke–Acts' dramatic episodes and use of speeches by the main characters indicate an author well versed in the literary conventions of his day.[111] His understanding of the imperial, regional, and local power networks operative in the Greek East is evident throughout his work, especially in Acts. The disciples of the new Jesus movement encounter Jewish religious leaders in Jerusalem, Roman magistrates, Asiarchs (wardens of the imperial cult in Asia Minor), and innumerable persons affiliated with political and religious networks of power.[112] His work is the most polished of the Gospels. Generically, Acts has affinities with historiography, biography, and the ancient novel.[113] No texts in the early Christian corpus serve as better starting points for addressing Christian responses by persons associated with elite power structures to local, regional, imperial, or cosmic power as it was manifested in social, economic, political, or cultural spheres in the Greek East.[114]

Luke writes at a key juncture for the nascent Christian movement. Not only have most of the initial leadership died, but various Christian groups are receiving greater attention from the elite power structure and those affiliated with it. Luke, more than any other New Testament writer, provides stark and often vivid examples that argue for the Christian movement and the Christian god as major forces within the elite and imperial power networks operating in the Greek East during the Flavian period.[115]

CONCLUSION

The Flavian period inaugurated a significant change in Rome's long-standing relation with the Greek East. Local elites rose in prominence in imperial circles and played increasingly important roles in negotiating benefits for their home cities. Sponsorship of civic cults allowed local elites to incorporate religious and mythic images associated with particular locales as part of the field of symbolic discourse being articulated throughout the empire. Naturally, local elites in the Greek East had been involved with imperial power prior to the Flavians, and many of the same symbols were used. Indeed, Chariton's text would thematically fit comfortably anywhere between Augustus and Hadrian. What distinguished the Flavio-Trajanic period was the increasing involvement of local elites in the Greek East in the power equation, the move to consolidate power on the part of the Flavians, and, as we shall see, the increasing effort by local elites to emphasize the power and prestige of their local traditions.

In this period of consolidation and resurgence of Greek pride, Jews in many parts of the Roman Empire faced increasing uncertainty and in some cases hostility. The period saw several significant Jewish communities and one of Judaism's central symbols, the Temple, destroyed by Roman authorities. The requirement that the Jewish population as a whole pay the *fiscus Iudaicus* linked all Jews in symbolic fashion to the destruction of the Temple. While local elites in the Greek East (with the exception of Jewish elites in Palestine) were acquiring greater prominence in the empire and stressing their own traditions, Jews found themselves in an awkward position, still recognized (and therefore legitimate) but suspect. It is no accident that Josephus writes tracts that stress the legitimate role of Jews in the past and present.

Christians during the Flavian period were in an even more precarious position. Increasingly, they recognized themselves and were recognized by others as separate from Jews (an association that would not have benefited them much in any case). Because initially the Christian movement expanded mostly in urban areas, Christians faced the very Greek elites who were consolidating their own power and who were not inclined to tolerate a movement composed of people who denied the existence of their gods. Luke depicts in narrative form what must have occurred to some extent as the Christian movement spread from city to village. The civic arena of the Greek East during the Flavio-Trajanic period provided the structure in which pagans, Jews, and Christians established patterns of relations that would form the basis of their interactions for at least the next three centuries.

3.

The Power
of the Past

A real tradition is not the relic of a past that is irretrievably gone; it is a living force that animates and informs the present. . . . Far from implying the repetition of what has been, tradition presupposes the reality of what endures.

—Stravinsky, *Poetics*

Symbols of the "past," mythically infused with timelessness . . . attain particular effectiveness during periods of intensive social change when communities have to drop their heaviest cultural anchors in order to resist the currents of transformation.

—Cohen, *The Symbolic Construction of Community*

How are we to interpret the role of tradition in the Greek East? Does a core of inherited cultural traits pass from generation to generation, or do persons symbolically construct the past to speak to the present?[1] Individuals who copied Homeric themes in literature or emulated the sculptural programs of fifth-century Greek sculptors did not receive a static and clearly articulated tradition. Certainly, the artists of antiquity believed they had appropriated faithfully and accurately fixed and immutable traditions. Innovation was viewed with suspicion, if not outright hostility.[2] Ancient protests to the contrary, the particular images selected from the past took on a new life, a new existence, when they reappeared in literature, sculpture, art, and architecture. These individuals reinvented tradition.[3]

Religious and mythic traditions in literature and iconography helped define and order arenas of power for those proffering or observing them, most notably within the political, social, and cosmic spheres. The antiquity of religious and mythic traditions heightened the power and prestige of leaders and secured or reaffirmed the relationship between rulers and ruled on a number of levels: between the emperor and the Greek cities, between local elites and their constituents, as well as between coequals, such as cities within a region.

PAGAN PERSPECTIVES ON THE PAST

Cities throughout the Greek East drew on myths and religions that had long associations either locally or within wide-ranging religious traditions.[4] In the late first century, Sparta reclaimed Lycurgus, the Spartan lawgiver, as well as its ancestral religious traditions.[5] Ephesus promoted the goddess Artemis and, in the process, acquired political and social advantages, as did the city of Aphrodisias in Caria with Aphrodite.[6] Tyre had the god Heracles, a favorite of Alexander the Great and subsequent victors.[7] Antioch of Pisidia promoted the Iranian moon god, Men, now thoroughly Hellenized.[8] The island of Samos had the goddess Hera. Jerusalem, prior to its destruction in 70 C.E., drew on long religious traditions within Judaism to acquire a powerful place in the symbolic vocabulary of Jewish groups across the Roman Empire and extending even to its neighbor, the Parthian Empire.[9] The Temple proved such a potent symbol that Jewish rebels in the revolts of 66 C.E. and 132 C.E., when minting their coins, drew on images that evoked worship in Jerusalem.[10]

The association of cities with venerable mythic and religious traditions, no doubt assisted by Augustus's earlier archaizing ventures, had long precedent. The desire for reclaiming the past, however, became particularly acute during or after periods of crisis, such as those preceding Augustan and Flavian rule.[11] Both reigns followed disruptive civil strife in Rome and the empire, and both Augustus and Vespasian sought to establish or maintain firm rule in a fragmented and politically insecure environment. Yet tradition was a mechanism not just for maintaining the status quo in the midst of change but also for interpreting profound new changes within prescribed parameters.

Local elites in the Greek East did not simply acquiesce to Roman power and presence. The past, and especially the religious past, had symbolic power to provide local elites' essential tools with which to construct or maintain a stable environment. Indeed, the use of religious traditions by local elites in the Greek East during the Flavio-Trajanic period played a key role in their quest for power and prestige within the framework of the Roman Empire and within their local and regional environments. Such archaism, as Paul Cartledge and Antony Spawforth note, was part of the

> larger cultural and political conditions of the Greek world under the Flavians and Trajan, a time which saw the early stirrings of the great renaissance of cultural activity in the Greek provinces under the principate, for which the peace and prosperity of the Roman Empire provided the necessary precondi-tions.[12]

Efforts to archaize do not, as some suggest, rest with "a flight from the present" where Greeks had little real political power.[13] Local elites sought and achieved a modicum of power within the imperial network. The latter was largely set by the Romans, but it was, to a degree, fluid, created in part by the very acts of the local elites. Thus, Sebaste in Phrygia, which had no strong Greek tradition, commissioned a founding legend that associated Apollo with the foundation of their city. This commission parallels a rise in oracular activity in the latter part of the first century and beginning of the second.[14] At Didyma, between 50 and 90 C.E., Claudius Damas, who held numerous honorific titles in the city, renewed and revised the ancient religious and oracular institution associated with Apollo.[15] Such activities bolstered local elites' (and their cities') power and prestige and tapped into a rich source of cosmic power.[16] Dio of Prusa reflects how increased competition for power and prestige occurred among cities in the Greek East. Nicaea in Bithynia, he says, claimed that it was "inferior to no one of the cities which were famous either for nobility of origin or for the number of inhabitants" (39.1). These examples aptly illustrate the active attempts by local elites to enter the network created by Roman imperial power through the incorporation of a prestigious past.

Of course, local elites depended on the goodwill and patronage of the Roman ruler.[17] A clear example is Nero's grant of independent status to Athens; the grant was revoked by Vespasian, a sign that at least for Athens the change in imperial administration had a real impact. Similar actions took place against Rhodes, Byzantium, and Samos under Vespasian.[18] Although Titus reinstated some civic privileges to those who had lost them under Vespasian, the message was clear. Vespasian also consolidated power by bringing the Greek East under more direct control of Roman officials.[19] Nevertheless, the endless train of embassies,[20] so evident from sources as disparate as the writings of the Alexandrian Jew Philo, to copies of letters found at Aphrodisias, Athens, Ephesus, and Delphi, indicates that local elites in the Greek East played key roles in setting the tone and character of the relations between imperial power and the provinces.[21]

Increased concern for local religious traditions coincided with the more active participation by the local elites of the Greek East in the Roman power structure, a process that reached its zenith during the Second Sophistic (late first through early third centuries).[22] Not atypical is a family from Roman Thespiae whose family tree can be traced from the third century B.C.E. to the third century C.E.[23] The family's pivotal period for acquiring power and prestige occurred during Flavian rule when two members received Roman citizenship. At that time, one of them, Philinus, a friend of Plutarch, donated heavily to the local temple of Eros (the most significant deity of the city) and served as agonothete of the festival of Eros.[24] During the Flavio-Trajanic period, local elites like Philinus sought to "reassure themselves that Greece had a claim comparable to that of Rome" and therefore "began to dwell more and more in their principal cultural activities, on the political greatness of the past."[25] This was not mere avoidance of confrontation with Rome or an antagonistic response to Roman power.[26] Rather, it reflects a redefinition of the networks of power. By setting the power relationships within their traditional rubrics, local elites created a symbolic arena in which the Romans tacitly, and sometimes reluctantly, participated. At this level local elites wielded a good deal of power, albeit still within the Roman sphere of influence.

A stark visual example of how various worlds and the religious and mythic past could intertwine within the life of one individual comes from the monument at Athens of Caius Julius Antiochus Ephiphanes Philopappos, yet another friend of Plutarch.[27] Philopappos's grandfather was Antiochus, king of Commagene, who, according to Josephus, was accused by the governor of Syria, Caesennius Paetus, of sedition during the first Jewish revolt (*BJ* 7.219–20). Vespasian, Josephus states, had Commagene occupied because of its strategic position between Syria and Cappadocia, and Antiochus was brought to Rome in chains. Vespasian, however, had him released, and the family was treated with every honor. A mere forty years later, his grandson Philopappos is a prestigious member of the elite class in the empire.

Like his name, Philopappos's monument, erected in Athens between 114 and 116 C.E., shows how he participated intimately in three arenas:[28] his dynastic ties to Commagene; his Roman ties as citizen, suffect consul, and Arval brother (one of only twelve, including the emperor, who interceded with the gods to support the imperial family);[29] and his citizenship and archonship at Athens.[30] Latin inscriptions and a depiction of his *processus consularis* commemorated Philopappos's inauguration as consul in 109 C.E.[31] The panel even includes accompanying lictors. Yet Philopappos integrates his Commagenian origins. In the procession, the god Heracles, a favorite of the Commagenian dynasty (as well as of Trajan), appears in the chariot in which Philopappos rides, suggesting a divine association.[32] Further, Philopappos wears not the laurel crown normally associated with Roman consul processions but the rayed crown, a feature common to his Commagenian ancestors at their coronation. Diana Kleiner concludes:

> In the frieze of his tomb Philopappos is represented at the apex of his Roman career and perhaps at the high point of his life. By donning a rayed crown, however, he indicates that he has not lost sight of his Commagenian origins, of the kingship he claims on his tomb, or of the divinization and worship that was the Commagenian king's due after his death.[33]

Dynastic ties are still important despite the fact that the kingdom of Commagene was absorbed into the Roman Empire by Vespasian in 72 C.E.[34]

Greek influence makes its appearance as well. One statue presents Philopappos in the heroic nudity of the Greek tradition, and a now lost inscription mentioned his archonship in Athens.[35] Yet even here his background as a dynast from Commagene surfaces. He

> appears divinized among his illustrious ancestors on the facade of his tomb situated on a high and prominent peak in Athens. Despite the purely Graeco-Roman form of the monument and its sculptural decoration the kinship between Philopappos' Athenian tomb and the hierothesia of his royal Commagenian predecessors is also clear.[36]

Philopappos's life and his monument, on the one hand, are unique.[37] Few dynasts or their descendants in this period achieved the power and prestige that Philopappos had within the Roman web of power. Nevertheless, as Fergus Millar notes, he was in many respects a "highly typical figure of the age."[38] The monument and the life of Philopappos reflect a widespread desire by local elites in the Greek East to retain and emphasize their ancient heritage while integrating it with the imperial power system. Philopappos's affiliation with the highest levels of Roman authority replaced neither his association with a proud dynastic past nor a civic affiliation with Athens. Various power networks in which he participated intertwine. When one so intimately connected to Roman power nevertheless highlights his ancient foreign roots in a Greek center of learning, it should not be surprising when those less closely affiliated with Roman authority structures place importance on a prestigious past as part of their effort to negotiate the webs of power in which they operated.[39]

In the flurry of first-century scrambles to acquire and maintain prestige, the antiquity of "the ancient mysteries" made them especially inviting. Epictetus provides ample evidence in his discussion of the mysteries at Eleusis. When one comes to participate in the mysteries, he comes with sacrifices, prayers, and

> with his mind predisposed to the idea that he will be approaching holy rites, and holy rites of great antiquity. Only thus do the Mysteries become helpful, only thus do we arrive at the impression that all these things were established by men of old time for the purpose of education and for the amendment of our life. (3.21.14–15)

In like fashion a first-century C.E. inscription from Thessalonica legitimates the cult of Isis and Sarapis by emphasizing its establishment two centuries earlier. The inscription depicts a certain Eurynomos. In a dream Sarapis instructs Eurynomos to worship Sarapis and Isis. The event, purported to have occurred in the third century B.C.E., legitimates the practice of the cult in first-century Thessalonica.[40] Likewise, on another inscription dedicated in Magnesia on the Maenander the dedicant claims to copy a stele in Memphis, Egypt, in an effort to appropriate authority associated with the antiquity of the cult.[41]

At Sardis, a first- or second-century C.E. inscription claims to rewrite in Greek an Aramaic edict written ca. 365 B.C.E.[42] It states that the temple wardens of Zeus are not to take part in the mysteries of Sabazios, Agdistis, and Ma. The rewriting of the text five hundred years later indicates the power of the ancient tradition for those still worshiping the gods. The creation of archaizing texts shows how people appropriate power associated with "ancient, venerable times" to meet current concerns.[43] The exclusive character also suggests how persons reemphasized allegiance to a particular cult.

Antiquity gave a degree of legitimacy not easily acquired elsewhere.[44] Long debates and careful genealogies established a religion's credentials; novelty was viewed with suspicion, especially when special privileges from Rome were sought. The antiquity of a religion concerned the Romans a good deal. One of Augustus's first acts was to rebuild and refound cult centers that had ancient roots.[45] The reformulated past provided powerful roots and stability on which to set the new order. Antiquity of a cult or religion carried with it the mark of power, permanence, and legitimacy so crucial in a world of previous disorder and religious, social, and political chaos.[46] The Flavians, who found themselves needing both to establish their legitimate rule and to provide order, sought ancient roots as well as continuity with the Age of Augustus, which acquired its own symbolic significance in the Flavian period.[47] The Flavians, therefore, were not unsympathetic to local elites who drew on the antiquity of their religion or cult to help define their relationship to Rome. This allowed local elites to acquire and maintain authority and prestige in a world with many competing powers. Adherents of certain religions required the necessary credentials.

The great weight given precedent in the Roman Empire also explains the flood of petitioners and embassies from the Greek East to the Romans, which left an indelible mark on the form and character of the emerging empire.[48] This process becomes clear in the letters from Roman emperors displayed in the theater at Aphrodisias, part of the public iconography of the city. In several instances the second- and third-century inscriptions reconfirm special privileges established as early as Julius Caesar.[49] At Delphi, also, a series of inscribed imperial letters shows the importance of the famous oracle of Apollo. In 90 C.E. Domitian responds to an embassy from Delphi that disputed claims by the amphictyonic league regarding new procedures to be observed at the Pythian Games. He writes the proconsul that the ancient procedures are to be observed, a nod toward tradition and reaffirmation of the past.[50] A regional power struggle over the proper role of the Delphi oracle and associated games is mediated by imperial power.

Religious traditions played an important role in various grants and privileges given to cities and towns, as did being on the proper side of any conflict (as Aphrodisias makes abundantly clear in its bid to become and remain a free and federated city). Plutarch remarks that false claims on divinity will become known because "their good fame flourished only a short time, and then, convicted of false glory and imposture, with impiety and unlawfulness, 'of a sudden, like smoke arising' (as Empedocles had said) they flew off" (*Moral* 360 C). As R. MacMullen argues, people believed that true divinity "will prove itself by its wide or long-lasting impact on the human scene."[51] It remained imperative, therefore, for cities and local elites to stress through visual and literary programs the antiquity of their deity if they hoped to bolster or sustain their power and prestige within the confines of the Roman Empire. Chariton and his city, Aphrodisias, played the game remarkably well.

Chariton of Aphrodisias and the Past

Chariton understands clearly the power that the glorious Greek past held for his audience. Traditional themes and symbols permeate his narrative. He situates his story in a historical period when Greek power still meant something, and he employs renowned historical persons who embody the ideals of the "true" Greek (at least as Chariton envisions him or her).[52] In style and structure the work appears as a history or biography of the daughter of Hermocrates,[53] the naval commander who, according to Chariton's revisionist description (1.1.1,3), became the leading political figure and war hero in Syracuse after the defeat of the Athenians[54] in the Peloponnesian War.[55]

Chariton describes the appearance of his hero, Chaereas, and of his heroine, Callirhoe, in heroic terms rich with popular mythic images. These images, which Grundy Steiner labels "graphic analogues,"[56] draw on the reader's awareness of the arts, including sculpture, for which Aphrodisias was famous.[57] Chaereas is compared to statues and pictures of Achilles, Nireus, Hippolytus, and Alcibiades (1.1.3),[58] individuals renowned for either their prowess in war or their physical appearance. Chariton often exploits literary as well as visual sensibilities, especially Homer, whom he skillfully reuses. Like many authors in the Hellenistic and Roman periods, he rewrites the cosmic power structures permeating Homer into a new "epic" form that fits the concerns of his own period.[59] Certain powerful elites in the Greek East were associated by artists with heroic figures of the past in literature and sculpture;[60] like those artists, Chariton "rewrites" Homer to portray Chaereas's superior and heroic appearance on his return from the gymnasium before his fateful meeting with Callirhoe: "radiant as a star" (*stilbon hosper aster*), with the flush of exercise blooming on his face "just as gold on silver" (1.1.5).[61]

Chariton often adapts traditional sayings. In a suicide speech to an absent Callirhoe, Chaereas admonishes her to shed a tear. "Even if in Hades people forget the dead, even there I shall remember you, my dear." Here, Chariton adapts Achilles' speech to his dead companion Patroclus (*Iliad* 22.389–90), transferring the power of the epic to the novel. Chariton draws again on Achilles' anguish over the loss of Patroclus (*Iliad* 24.10–11) when he describes the inability of the king of Persia to sleep after encountering Callirhoe: "Lying now on his side, now on his back, now face down" (6.1.8).[62] Chariton uses Homer to emphasize how even imperial power, here represented by the Persian king, is rendered immobile by the power of Aphrodite as manifested through her human representative Callirhoe.

The period following the Peloponnesian War provides the narrative backdrop for journeys by the protagonists across the greater part of the ancient Greek East and even into the heart of the Persian Empire, Babylon itself. The Persian Empire was a popular motif in portions of the Greek East, and Chariton skillfully draws on the tradition. Indeed, his city, Aphrodisias, had connections with Persia at least mythically; archaeological evidence indicates that some local elites associated the city's founding with Ninos, mythical founder of the Assyrian and Babylonian Empires. The connection appears to be part of Aphrodisian attempts to reinterpret a powerful ancient figure within the new reality of Roman imperial power. A relief panel found at Aphrodisias has Ninos dressed in Roman imperial garb sacrificing to an altar with an eagle on it while a companion in Roman military garb looks on.[63] Ninos is also shown with Semiramis, both presented in Roman dress as part of a series of relief panels perhaps originally from a third-century C.E. building complex for provincial affairs.[64]

Political connections between Syracuse and Ionia and Persia are confirmed in Chaereas's concluding speech to the assembly at Syracuse on their return: "I made the Great King your friend [*philos*] by restoring his queen as a gift to him, and by sending back their mothers, sisters, wives, and daughters to the highest Persian nobles. . . . Sometime another expedition of yours shall sail from Ionia and its leader shall be the grandson of Hermocrates" (8.8.10–11).

Chaereas, the heroic military victor, Callirhoe, the human vehicle of Aphrodite, and Aphrodite herself symbolize political alliances, social stability, and marital reunion. The pattern may well draw on "symbolic discourse" from Hellenistic and later Roman accounts that stress an eastern conquest (first by the Greeks, then the Romans), a dynastic marriage, and the restoration of peace by a son born to the dynastic union.[65]

The reference to a son draws on a related tradition with even more explicit connections to Rome: the myth of Aeneas. At Miletus crowds see Callirhoe with her newborn son as she prepares to pray before Aphrodite's cult statue: "[S]he took the child in her arms, and thus presented a most charming sight, the like of which no painter has ever portrayed, nor sculptor fashioned, nor poet described to the present day; for no one of them has created an Artemis or an Athena holding a child in her arms" (3.8.6). Aphrodite, whose political power is equal to that of Athena and Artemis, surpasses them in her ability to bear a child, most notably Aeneas, who becomes the founder of the Roman Empire. Callirhoe's child serves as a founder for Syracuse along the lines of an Aeneas.[66] Callirhoe operates as Aphrodite's representative and performs civic and religious roles throughout the narrative.[67] Descriptions of Callirhoe often allude to attributes that the readers would certainly have recognized as affiliated with Aphrodite.[68] He also alludes to famous areas associated with Aphrodite, notably her famous birthplace on Cyprus. Such allusions allow Chariton to show the power of Aphrodite by drawing on mythic elements familiar to his audience. Not surprisingly, his city also used popular mythic images of Aphrodite since it apparently had no ancient local traditions on which to base its association with Aphrodite.[69]

Chariton weaves explicit quotations and allusions from ancient writers and available visual images into the fabric of his narrative, enabling his audience to identify the heroic appearance of his principal characters and the power of Aphrodite within imperial, regional, and local authority networks. He plugs into his narrative taken-for-granted mythic and historical themes, which he apparently holds in common with his audience. Because these components are transformed to suit the program of Chariton, the readers understand the old heroic and mythic features within the new narrative framework that Chariton creates and within the social context of their own situation, that is, as local elites or their affiliates in the Greek East who operate under the aegis of Rome. This process need not have been fully understood by either writer or audience. As Nock has observed, the "dominant attitudes" in the Graeco-Roman world, especially in the period following the Flavian era,

> were those of classicist culture and practical action, with a strong emphasis on plain morality and the control of the passions (notably anger), a matter-of-fact belief in direct divine action by miracle and sign, and some predilection for the idea of survival without preoccupation or precision of thought about it.[70]

As so many others who cited or used tradition, Chariton cares more for what it contributes to his own time than for attempting a faithful reconstruction of his sources. Chariton's use of popular literary sources such as Homer, his setting of the story in a significant period in Greek history, and his use of myths and locations associated with the goddess Aphrodite would appeal to a pagan audience in the Greek East who drew on the Greek past to negotiate power relationships in the empire. The setting and the traditional elements, as I show later, form the structure that elucidates for Chariton's reading audience the power of the goddess Aphrodite, which extends throughout the entire *oikoumene,* if not the cosmos itself; it elucidates the significant role that power brokers (especially representatives of the local elites) play in the process of acquiring and maintaining power and the key role that ethical responsibility and proper paideia (education) of elites play for the maintenance of a stable society. Chariton, like so many of his contemporaries, understands the potent power of a vital past for a present age.

JEWS AND THE PAST

Judaism and nascent Christianity operated within, but were never fully a part of, the local elite structures established throughout the Greek East, especially following the Jewish defeat in the first revolt. Members of the Jewish Diaspora did increasingly participate in civic affairs in the late second and third centuries C.E., but this period falls outside the primary focus of my study.[71] There were loose affiliations earlier, as evidenced by a synagogue decree honoring Marcus Titius, Roman governor at Cyrenaica[72] and the possible affiliation of the synagogue at Acmonia with Julia Severa, a prominent woman who was priestess of a local pagan deity. With the exception of the Herodian family, one finds outside Judaea few Jewish or Christian equivalents to local leaders like the freedman Zoilos of Aphrodisias, who during the first century B.C.E. is acknowledged with pride in an inscription as having been chosen as a priest of Aphrodite ten times, a decree prominently displayed in the city.[73] Elites with explicit Jewish connections left few extant public, civic declarations, especially in the Flavio-Trajanic period. Nor did archons or major public officials openly declare themselves as Jews or Christians. Evidence does exist for Jews serving in the military, on city councils, and even as a city magistrate. Most of these occur either before the war of 66–70 C.E. or after the Trajanic period and even then represent a small fraction of the inscriptions that deal with such categories.[74] Perhaps public animosity toward such "atheistic" organizations, especially by Greek elites in the Greek East, played some role.

Within Jewish groups ancient roots and tradition provided identity, stability, and a way to construe the world. The antiquity of Judaism had obtained a degree of legitimacy within the Roman world.[75] Julius Caesar acknowledged and protected Jewish rights, possibly because of the critical aid provided by Antipater, the father of Herod the Great, in Caesar's war against Pompey. Augustus continued certain special privileges (notably the right to pay taxes to the Temple in Jerusalem and acknowledgment of Sabbath worship). Claudius used the precedent set by Augustus to allow Jews to practice their customs in Alexandria, although he did not give them rights as Alexandrian citizens.[76] The antiquity of Jewish practices as well as established precedent with the Romans prevented Jews in the Diaspora from being taken to court on the Sabbath and, prior to 66 C.E., from having their funds to the Temple confiscated by local elites. Nevertheless, civic participation by Jews in the Roman Empire should not be overstated, especially following the disastrous Jewish revolt.[77] The Temple tax, the most prominent symbol linking Diaspora Jews to their tradition, took on new symbolic value under Flavian rule as Jews across the empire were expected to continue payment but now to the Roman coffers.[78] The *fiscus Iudaicus* became an explicit sign of Roman power and prestige as well as Jewish subjugation for the Flavians and local elites, who sponsored some of the Judaea Capta coin issues.[79] Some relief came with Nerva, but primarily for Jews who no longer practiced their religion and who were now absolved from payment of the "Jewish tax." Notably, Nerva's reforms did formally recognize Judaism as a religion and not just as something ethnic, political, or hereditary.[80] The antiquity of the Jews, a feature respected by many Romans and Greeks, plus the early support from Julius Caesar and, later, Octavian no doubt had some bearing.[81]

For those who considered themselves Jews, the primary role of tradition centered on its treasure trove of symbols.[82] The perceived power of select symbols enabled each group to organize their lives and their sacred cosmos, especially in relation to their non-Jewish neighbors and the Romans. Responses could vary widely. Prior to 66 C.E., the Qumran community, near the Dead Sea, drew on the power of their tradition to place Roman power under the cosmic rule of their god.[83] Some Jews even combined Roman and Jewish traditions, as is evident in the third and fourth Sibylline Oracles. The results could be decidedly anti-Roman.

With the exception of Josephus, literary and material evidence from Jewish elites who operated during the Flavio-Trajanic period remains sparse. Coins, papyri, and tombs offer important information but are not plentiful. Those dating from our period provide some information about the role of tradition. An inscription probably from Egypt and dated to the first or early second century mentions a certain Papous who, with his wife and child, built a *proseuche* (Jewish house of worship).[84] The dedication and the obvious wealth needed to build an entire *proseuche* indicate someone with considerable resources. Nothing in the dedication draws on ancient symbols, but the inscription is useful in showing that local elites did exist in the Diaspora who continued to sponsor what came to be increasingly important centers of identity. The epitaph of a certain Abramos provides clear evidence of such a Jewish elite. As magistrate in the apparently largely Jewish city of Leontopolis, he participated in its civic affairs.[85] Another possible Jewish inscription from Egypt mourns the death of a woman about to be married. The inscription asks the passing stranger to mourn for her untimely death, when "suddenly Hades came and snatched me away, like a rose in a garden nurtured by fresh rain."[86] The apparent allusion to the myth of Persephone indicates that the dedicators of the stone, even if Jewish, had little difficulty in drawing on pagan sources to make sense of the loss of their loved one.[87]

Some literary sources exist. In 2 Baruch and 4 Ezra are reflected several common features of Jewish texts associated with this period. They both purport to derive from a famous figure of the past, a common feature of apocalyptic literature; they both draw extensively on biblical tradition; and they both deal with the disastrous aftermath of the first Jewish war by looking to the past (to discern Israel's sin) and to the future (to display Israel's salvation).[88] The Romans are never mentioned by name, but the comparisons drawn by the authors and the destruction of the Temple in Israel's past would be hard to miss for first- and second-century Jewish audiences. In 2 Baruch, for example, the destruction of the Temple does not occur because of the enemy's (i.e., Rome's) power. Rather, God's angels topple the walls so that the enemy forces cannot brag that it was their doing (7.1–2). God destroyed the Temple through his holy angels because of the sin of the people, the latter also a key theme of Josephus.[89]

Less antagonistic responses toward imperial power also appear, especially prior to 66–70 C.E. In Bernike in 25 C.E. the Jewish *politeuma* honored Marcus Titius, who was the Roman governor of Cyrenaica and Crete. The meeting in which the resolution was passed occurred on the Feast of Tabernacles, a point mentioned in the inscription. The resolution was put on Parian marble and placed in a prominent place in the amphitheater.[90] The mention of the Feast of Tabernacles, a significant Jewish festival, and its association with the Jewish assembly provides a Jewish temporal frame of reference in which the public, civic gesture is set. The inscription is displayed in a prominent pagan and public space[91] and honors a public figure within the temporal rubric of the Jewish festival. Tradition becomes part of the symbolic and visual discourse in which the Jewish community defined itself within and in relation to imperial and local power. Sometimes the honors could be reversed. Though early, a rededication possibly dating to the last half of the first century B.C.E. reads: "On the order of the queen and king, in place of the previous plaque about the dedication of the *proseuche* let what is written below be written up. King Ptolemy Euergetes (proclaimed) the *proseuche* inviolate. The queen and king gave the order."[92] The rededication draws on past precedent, a common fact of civic life in the Greek East. The allusion to prior precedent for the maintenance of the proper status of the *proseuche* has frequent parallels in Josephus, who alludes to the past precedent of Augustus to emphasize the legitimacy of Jewish religious practices.

The law, the biblical tradition, the celebration of the Sabbath, and even the figure of Moses also provided potent symbols from the past for the community and an attraction for some non-Jews.[93] Such traditions (and the flexibility of interpretation) provided significant resources for Jews, who grappled with a world not often sympathetic to their goals and aspirations. In some instances, the symbols were significant enough to influence non-Jews as well, as seen most dramatically in an epitaph set up by T. Flavius Amphikles, a pupil of the philosopher Herodes Attikos, for his son. The epithet clearly draws on Deuteronomy 28 when it warns against anyone interfering with the tomb.[94]

Adherents to other religions in the eastern end of the empire, especially

Syria–Palestine,[95] also stressed the antiquity of their religions. Philo of Byblos, writing in the late first or early second century C.E., argues in his *Phoenician History* that the antiquity of the Phoenicians displays the prestige of the Phoenician past, putting it on par with the best that Greek tradition has to offer.[96] Such promotion of ancient roots occurred in all Phoenician cities.[97] As Elias Bickerman notes, writers in Egyptian, Babylonian, Phoenician, and Jewish traditions (notably Manetho, Berossus, Philo of Byblos, and Josephus) looked back to their primeval roots. "Speaking *qua* 'Orientals' but in Greek, these intellectuals from the East all display the same apologetic accent and are univocal in the face of the Greek conqueror."[98] The Romans were a significant factor in this interaction, as were local elites, who, drawing on Greek traditions, were increasingly competitive.[99]

The power of tradition becomes starkly clear during the first Jewish revolt, providing symbolic ammunition for those leading the revolt. Rebels minted their own coins using a palaeo-Hebrew script instead of the normal Greek or Latin, and they used images associated with the Temple, both actions in clear defiance of the Roman authorities.[100] Sixty years later, the evidence is even more explicit in the second major revolt in Palestine against Rome. The leader, Bar Kochba, had stamped over the head of the Roman emperor an image of the Temple (destroyed in the first revolt) on a new large local silver coin.[101] Grape clusters on Bar Kochba's coins also associated his revolt with the divine bounty promised in the biblical tradition. The fluid character of such symbols can be seen when rabbis in the second century use the same grape-cluster motif but this time in clear opposition to its association with a revolt against Rome.[102] Likewise, the menorah, so prominent as part of the spoils in the triumph on Titus's arch,[103] became a key symbol for Jews in the mid–second century C.E., primarily in funerary and synagogue art. It was studiously avoided by Jews between the destruction of the Temple and the Bar Kochba revolt, probably because of its powerful association with the destruction of the Temple during that period.[104] Such ancient symbols and traditions held more than antiquarian interest for those proffering them. Current power and prestige, primarily within local and regional spheres, had greater credence when tied to long-established (and thus continually powerful) traditions.[105]

The stakes could be high. Josephus's repudiation of Manetho's claim that Jews were simply errant Egyptians associated with lepers carried significant social and even political ramifications (*CA* 1.229–50). Native Egyptians had distinctly fewer rights and thus less power in the Roman system than the Greeks, who were citizens of Alexandria and thus allotted a greater say in the affairs of the city, especially during the Flavian period. Jews in Egypt apparently still had a special status, although not citizenship.[106] Moses as Egyptian or Moses as founder and lawgiver had implications for Jews across the land, especially following the disastrous Jewish defeat in Palestine at the hands of the Flavians.[107]

Most elites in the Greek East, even Jewish elites,[108] were not anti-Roman. Greek elites, nevertheless, stressed their Greek past to lessen the "contrast between the immense prosperity and the distressing dependence of the contem-

porary Greek world."[109] The same might be said for Jews such as Josephus or
Justus of Tiberias in the period between the two revolts. In post–70 C.E.
Palestine, the reuse of tradition made a difficult period tolerable. After all, God,
as 2 Baruch,[110] 4 Ezra, and Josephus claimed, worked through history and
would reestablish his elect people. Such use of tradition dominated Greek,
Roman, and Jewish worlds through the Roman imperial period (and, of
course, afterward).[111]

Josephus and the Past

Through Agrippa's famous speech, Josephus makes clear that the Jewish
movement was ancient. Agrippa's point, of course, emphasizes the potential
destruction facing all Jews if a revolt against Rome takes place (BJ 2.399).[112] As
Josephus concludes upon witnessing the destruction of Jerusalem: "Neither its
antiquity, nor its ample wealth, nor its people spread over the whole habitable
world, nor yet the great glory of its religious rites, could aught avail to avert
ruin" (BJ 6.442). Such statements also indicate to the reader the extent (and, by
implication, the importance) of the Jewish people and their religion. This
becomes explicit in Josephus's Antiquities. Josephus emphasizes that God works
through history, rewarding those who follow the sacred laws and setting up
"irretrievable disasters" for those who transgress them (AJ 1.15). Josephus
goes to great lengths to stress the antiquity of the Jewish movement and its
recognition as a legitimate movement by Roman officials. All this means nothing however if the adherents stray from God's purposes. Josephus, who may
have seen himself as a latter-day Jeremiah,[113] depicts the venerable roots of
Jewish tradition, where the main lesson of Jewish history, he argues, is that
those

> who conform to the will of God, and do not venture to transgress laws that
> have been excellently laid down, prosper in all things beyond belief, and for
> their reward are offered by God felicity [eudaimonia]; whereas, in proportion as
> they depart from the strict observance of these laws, things (else) practicable
> become impracticable, and whatever imaginary good thing they strive to do
> ends in irretrievable disasters. (AJ 1.15; cf. 1.20)[114]

Josephus's portrayal of Solomon highlights the interplay between the
power and prestige of Jewish tradition and sin, which can bring down the most
powerful. Josephus presents an altered version of the biblical account of Solomon's court (cf. 1 Kings 10:14–29 = 2 Chron. 9:13–28), fashioning a portrait of
a fabulously wealthy potentate (AJ 8.182–86). Both the biblical and the Jos-
ephan accounts extol Solomon's wisdom. Josephus, however, embellishes the
biblical account, adding that Solomon's escort included two thousand tall
young men dressed in tunics of Tyrian purple, who "sprinkled their hair with
gold dust so that their heads sparkled as the gleam of the gold was reflected by
the sun." The account brings to mind Josephus's account of Vespasian's triumph in Rome, in which even the servants were clothed in garments of true
purple lined with gold (BJ 7.137). No doubt would remain in the reader's mind

as to the power, wealth, and immense (awesome?) prestige that existed in Israel's glorious past. Solomon was a rich and powerful king whose wealth and prestige rival, if not surpass, any in the known world, past or present. Yet, even Solomon's resplendent power does not prevent the turn of fortune in Solomon's kingdom when Solomon lusts for women and turns to foreign idols (*AJ* 8.187–98). Even the most powerful, Josephus indicates, are susceptible to God's wrath. Josephus's portrait of Solomon's court is one of many that high-light the power of Israel's heroic ancestors. Nevertheless, Josephus portrays such power as legitimate only when it operates within the boundaries set by the Jewish God. God humbles even mighty figures like Solomon for their sins. Josephus leaves little doubt where the ultimate power lies.[115]

Josephus lists several motives for his writing of *Antiquities*: the fact of his participation in events that merited exposition; to counter the prevailing igno-rance "of important affairs of general utility" (*AJ* 1.3); to discern whether his ancestors were willing to communicate information; and to discover whether Greeks in the past had sought to learn Jewish history (*AJ* 1.9). Josephus makes abundantly clear that the Jewish religion has great antiquity:[116] "The things narrated in the sacred Scriptures are, however, innumerable, seeing that they embrace the history of five thousand years and recount all sorts of surprising reverses, many fortunes of war, heroic exploits of generals, and political revo-lutions" (*AJ* 1.13). That this proved a major concern for Josephus becomes even clearer in his summary of the importance of *Antiquities* made to Epaphroditos in *Against Apion*. "In my history of our Antiquities, most excel-lent Epaphroditus, I have, I think, made sufficiently clear to any who may peruse that work the extreme antiquity of our Jewish race, the purity of the original stock, and the manner in which it established itself in the country which we occupy today" (*CA* 1.1).

Josephus, who tied ancient traditions to proper codes and conduct, typified the heightened and pervasive quest in the Greek East in the Flavio-Trajanic period for ancient precedents.

> [P]ersons who have espoused the cause of order and law—one law for all—and been the first to introduce them, may fairly be admitted to be more civilized and virtuously disposed than those who lead lawless and disorderly lives. In fact, each nation endeavours to trace its own institutions back to the remot-est date, in order to create the impression that far from imitating others, it has been the one to set its neighbours an example of orderly life under law. (*CA* 2.151–52)

Josephus enters the competitive fray, promoted by local elites who emphasize their own ancient traditions. Their claims, Josephus asserts, cannot compete with Jewish tradition: "I maintain that our legislator [Moses] is the most an-cient of all legislators in the records of the whole world. Compared with him, your Lycurguses and Solons, and Zaleucus, who gave the Locrians their laws, and all who are held in such high esteem by the Greeks appear to have been born but yesterday" (*CA* 2.154). Reflected here is the increased competition between groups, each drawing on its own tradition to substantiate current claims to power and prestige. For Josephus, the law is integrated with every aspect of the social and cultural life of Jews. "Religion governs all our actions and occupations and speech; none of these things did our lawgiver leave unexamined or indeterminate" (CA 2.171). Elias Bickerman is largely right that intellectuals affiliated with Eastern religions in the Greek East "had to choose between Athens and Jerusalem, or Memphis, or Babylon."[117] He neglects, however, the ability of such individuals to participate in a variety of power networks in some measure by interpreting them through the lens of their tradition. Josephus effectively presents a tradition whose antiquity is generally unquestioned and that allows him to place the Jewish people in the scramble for power and prestige in the Greek East.

CHRISTIANS AND THE PAST

Some in the new Christian movement took full advantage of the powerful role played by tradition (the biblical tradition) to seek a degree of accommodation with Roman and local authorities. Such overtures, of course, were not always welcomed by local elites in the Greek East. The apostle Paul acknowledged the power of the state (Rom. 13) but was persecuted by pagan as well as Jewish leaders (2 Cor. 11:23–27). The author of Acts portrays vividly the varied responses from local elites throughout the Greek East toward the new movement. The conflict with pagan local elites in the Greek East is graphically portrayed in the mid- to late-second-century work the Acts of Paul, in which Thecla spurns the advances of a member of the local elite who also happens to be the priest of the imperial cult (Acts of Paul 3.26).[118] Justin Martyr, writing between 153 and 155 C.E., drew extensively on biblical tradition as well as Greek philosophy in his defense of Christianity.[119] While arguing that Christians obeyed the state, he also made clear that it might be a good idea for the emperor to recognize the error of his ways in order to not burn in hell, an attitude not likely to sit well with the imperial authorities.[120] Q. Iunius Rusticus, Justin's judge and Emperor Marcus Aurelius's adviser and friend, counciled that Justin's admission that Christians followed the law yet refused to "obey gods and submit to the emperors" was, as Elaine Pagels notes, a direct challenge to "traditional patterns of piety," in which "family, city, and state are perceived as sacred, unconditional, and inviolate, wholly bound up with religious sanction."[121] Justin Martyr represents a later development of what was to become clear to many both within and outside the movement: the interpretation of scriptural tradition put Christians at odds with certain key tenets that were at the core of Graeco-Roman society, notably the nature of the family, the character of proper civic life, the relation to the state (especially the emperor), and the role of the gods. From the Christian perspective, scriptural tradition helped to define the power equation they understood as truly operative, that is, the power of God as interpreted through Christian sages.

Writers in the first through early second centuries C.E. who associated themselves with the Christian movement drew heavily on scriptural tradition.[122] What little information we have of Christians in the years between 30 and 117 C.E. comes primarily from literary sources.[123] The so-called early Jewish–Christian symbols in Palestine[124] have little validity.[125] Pilgrimages to sacred sites, however, may have played an important role, possibly at a very early stage.[126] Most writers of the New Testament use biblical tradition to bolster their position against competitors within the movement or against Jewish power structures. Less often do they use tradition to address other networks of power within society. Of greatest interest here are those texts that deal most explicitly with the type of power wielded by Greek elites and Rome.

Pliny's well-known letter to Trajan while governor of Bithynia indicates that the Christian movement had become illegal within the Roman Empire at least during the reign of Trajan (98–117 C.E.) and probably before.[127] Persecution of Christians at the hands of imperial and local authorities finds clear expression in several New Testament texts. Tradition, both recent and ancient, becomes a key part of Christian writers' attempts to make sense of their current suffering. The writer of 1 Peter uses the suffering of Christ at the hands of the authorities to serve as a model for the current suffering of those Christians in northwest Asia Minor who are servants or slaves.

> For one is approved if, mindful of God, he endures pain while suffering unjustly. For what credit is it, if when you do wrong and are beaten for it you take it patiently? But if when you do right and suffer for it you take it patiently, you have God's approval. For to this you have been called, because Christ also suffered for you, leaving you an example, that you should follow in his steps. (2:19–21)

The author, who probably wrote in the latter part of the Flavian period or at the beginning of the reign of Trajan[128] expects the present evil age to end shortly: "The end of all things is at hand" (1 Pet. 4:7). Jesus and Old Testament traditions provide powerful symbols with which to deal with the present: "God's patience waited in the days of Noah, during the building of the ark, in which a few, that is, eight persons, were saved through the water" (1 Pet. 3:20). Such an emphasis on patience may explain how the author can hold a similar attitude toward the world as the writer of Revelation but come to a distinctively different response toward the authorities that control it. Like Paul in Romans 13, the author of 1 Peter stresses proper moral conduct before Gentiles "so that in case they speak against you as wrongdoers, they may see your good deeds and glorify God on the day of visitation" (1 Pet. 2:12). The proper connection to the imperial web of power is also made explicit. "Be subject for the Lord's sake to every human institution, whether it be to the emperor as supreme, or to governors as sent by him to punish those who do wrong and to praise those who do right" (1 Pet. 2:13–14). The author reflects the effort by some early Christians to draw on their unique traditions about Jesus and on ancient biblical tradition to cope with an environment increasingly hostile, suspicious, and sporadically violent toward their movement.

The Letter to the Hebrews, replete with Platonic allusions, also depicts the suffering of Jesus as a model for Christians, who should strive for peace with all

(Heb. 12:3, 14). The Letter to Titus, written toward the latter part of the first century, argues that one should display model behavior so that opponents cannot refute the movement (Titus 2:7). With the exception of Acts, however, the New Testament writers are largely silent about the role tradition played in the encounter by Christians with local, regional, and international networks of power, though power remained a potent issue for the writers.[129] But the writings do show one thing clearly. Christian communities, in part through their great social mobility,[130] offered an opportunity for persons left out of or stymied in local, regional, or Roman arenas to participate in powers quite unattainable to those not part of the group, especially life after death.

Other than the New Testament texts, several Christian writings of the late first and early second century shed some light on the powerful role tradition played in coming to grips with the often confusing issues of power in the Greek East. Clement of Rome (93–96 C.E.),[131] the writer of the Didache, and Ignatius of Antioch, who died in Rome between 110 and 117 C.E. and wrote six letters to churches in Asia Minor and a seventh to Polycarp of Smyrna, were the precursors to later apologists of the church like Justin Martyr, who drew even more explicitly on Greek, biblical, and Christian traditions to counter extreme prejudice toward the Christian movement.[132] Generally these writers address internal community difficulties or theological issues and seldom mention the broader power networks in which they often involuntarily participated. Ignatius of Antioch, however, provides a glimpse of such networks: "For when you heard I had been sent a prisoner from Syria for the sake of our common name and hope, in the hope of obtaining by your prayers the privilege of fighting with beasts at Rome, that by so doing I might be enabled to be a true disciple, you hastened to see me."[133] Such allusions to suffering, rife in much of the Christian literature of this period, reflect at least the perception on the part of Christian leaders of overt hostility toward them by outside groups.

A possible early iconographic example of Christian (though more probably Jewish) art illustrates the general perception. In the Roman catacombs exists an early-second-century portrayal based on the Book of Daniel showing the burning of Shadrach, Meshach, and Abednego by Nebuchadnezzar.[134] The three symbolize martyrs who refuse to worship an imperial image; a fourth-century depiction of the scene replaces Nebuchadnezzar with the Roman emperor and the image to be worshiped with a bust of the emperor on a column.[135] From the Cain and Abel story in the Old Testament to the execution of early leaders such as Paul and Peter, Jewish and Christian figures became the paradigm of the true Christian, who endured persecution in an increasingly hostile environment.[136]

The period between 70 and 117 C.E. was a time of formative change and consolidation for the nascent Christian movement in the Roman Empire. By its end Roman authorities apparently understood that Christianity was not a branch of Judaism even though the writers of Matthew, John, 1 Peter, and Luke–Acts see the Christian movement as the proper expression of Judaism. Increased visibility brought with it suspicion, hostility, and sporadic punishment by local and imperial authorities. Tradition helped many groups make sense of the inequities inherent in the Roman system. The scriptural tradition placed the various expressions of early Christianity within a long and venerable past. The Christian traditions associated with Jesus, Peter, Paul, and other early leaders also provided part of the mythos by which persons structured their lives. For some, Greek philosophical systems (most notably the Platonic) offered a framework for writers, such as the author of Hebrews, to reinterpret both the sacrificial system of Judaism and the death of Jesus. The author's view that Christ represented the true high priest and served as the true sacrifice, in contrast to his human and earthly counterparts, had real implications for those who sought to live within power networks dominated by local elites and imperial representatives.

> But recall the former days when, after you were enlightened, you endured a hard struggle with sufferings, sometimes being publicly exposed to abuse and affliction, and sometimes being partners with those so treated. For you had compassion on the prisoners, and you joyfully accepted the plundering of your property, since you knew that you yourselves had a better possession and an abiding one. (Heb. 10:32–34)

For those who withstood the social and cultural pressures, the rewards were very real. "Therefore do not throw away your confidence, which has a great reward. For you have need of endurance, so that you may do the will of God and receive what is promised" (Heb. 10:35–36). The past served as the guide for those in the present to achieve true power in the future. This attitude, especially prevalent in Luke's work, was a leitmotiv in almost every Christian writing from this period. It becomes more explicitly stated in the apologists of the second century and the martyrologies of the third.[137]

Luke and the Past

Luke, more than any other Christian writer of his day, draws on the power of Jewish and Jesus traditions to address local, regional, and imperial arenas of power.[138] The reader could have little doubt about the antiquity of the movement. Mary, the mother of Jesus, associates Jesus' birth with promises made to Abraham (Luke 1:55). Zechariah, the father of John the Baptist, links the birth of Jesus to Abraham, David, and the "prophets of old" (Luke 1:69–73). Luke connects these predictions to a significant event of the Roman Empire, the decree by Augustus to enroll the world (Luke 2:1). Mentioning this decree, as well as noting that Quirinius was governor of Syria of the time, does not merely date Jesus' birth. Nor is it simply a device to show Luke's acumen in writing a historical tract. The narrative effectively subsumes Augustus's act within the Christian god's activity in history. The decree of Augustus served that god's plan, a plan revealed to the prophets as early as Abraham. Roman decisions simply further the activity of God.

Luke draws on other ancient and powerful elements. The antiquity of Jesus' lineage is made explicit in Luke 3, when in his genealogy, Luke links Jesus to Adam, the first human. Further, a series of speeches in Acts by various

Christian leaders make the connections with ancient predictions clear. Peter ties Jesus' activity to figures in Jewish tradition such as Moses and Samuel, who predicted that a prophet would come to save the people (Acts 3:23–24).[139] This interpretation, Luke argues, clashed with other Jewish views of the tradition. Stephen, one of the seven deacons selected by the Twelve Apostles, is accused of trying to change the "customs which Moses delivered to us." Stephen responds in a lengthy speech that details the connection of the Jesus movement to Jewish tradition extending back to Abraham (Acts 7). It is the Paul of Acts, however, who summarizes best the role of tradition. In his speech to the synagogue in Antioch of Pisidia, he states, "And we bring you the good news that what God promised to the fathers, this he has fulfilled to us their children by raising Jesus; as also it is written in the second psalm" (Acts 13:32–33). Even within the context of his trial, Paul tells a Roman ruler and a Jewish king that

> To this day I have had the help that comes from God, and so I stand here testifying both to small and great, saying nothing but what the prophets and Moses said would come to pass: that the Christ must suffer, and that, by being the first to rise from the dead, he would proclaim light both to the people and to the Gentiles. (Acts 26:22–23)

By connecting the Christian movement to the great figures in Israel's past, to its ancestral law (Acts 22:3), its ancestral god (28:14), and its ancestral customs, Luke reformulates the character of the power network in which Christians dealt with imperial, regional, and local power. Perhaps Luke seeks to benefit in some measure from the toleration provided Judaism by Roman authorities.[140] More to the point, he places the Christian movement within a venerable tradition that stated clearly the Christians' powerful and prestigious past to those inside and outside the movement. It was part of a competitive process in which a powerful and potent tradition was the minimal requirement for a movement to achieve a degree of legitimacy for adherents and to attract followers.

CONCLUSION

The venerable past provided vital symbols and themes that bolstered the acquisition and maintenance of power and prestige by local elites in the Roman Empire. The past helped pagan elites in the Greek East to order a world formerly plagued by civil war and internal strife. The reign of Rome under the newly established principate of Augustus motivated local elites in the Greek East as well as the Augustan Empire itself to restructure the past to fit the demands of the present. Augustus was presented in heroic form and associated with the gods in many parts of the Greek East. Local elites affiliated themselves with venerable deities that had ancient traditions and with the Roman principate.

The Flavians, seeking stability, peace, and continuation of power, followed the Augustan example. Patterns of relationship established in the Augustan period soon took on the force of law. Precedent formed a crucial part of the world of the Greek East and its relation to Rome. Groups such as those that followed Isis or Dionysus, initially viewed by members of the elite classes as outside the proper bounds, gradually became integrated into the power structures, most often on a local level but sometimes in circumstances that held much wider implications. The Flavians, for example, accepted and even promoted the Isis cult. Other groups, notably the Druids in Britain, some Jewish groups,[141] and Christians, had increasing difficulty in integrating and participating in local and empirewide networks of power. Indeed, they often became victims of those powers. Increased emphasis on the past could mean greater exclusion for those whose practice threatened (or was perceived to threaten) the status quo.

Diaspora Jews participated to an extent in local civic affairs, although most of the evidence is either late or predates the first revolt. The revolt of 66 C.E. and the subsequent revolts of 115–17 and 132–35 placed Jews throughout much of the empire in a precarious position. Flavian programs up to Domitian promoted the Jewish defeat of 70 C.E. in iconography, a practice repeated in many parts of the Greek East, especially on coins. To be sure, in the Antonine and Severan periods, Jewish participation in and cordial relations with local and empirewide power networks increased substantially. But the period between 70 and 117 was marked by uncertainty and tension. Like Greek elites, some Jewish writers of this period, notably Josephus and the authors of 2 Baruch and 4 Ezra, drew on tradition to show Jewish audiences, if no one else, that Jewish power and prestige had existed since time immemorial and would be restored in God's good order.

For the Christians the period between 70 and 117 was a time of growth, consolidation, and encounter with a political environment increasingly unsympathetic to their views. Sporadic outbreaks of violence occurred, especially in Asia Minor, and Roman authorities such as Pliny became more involved. In a period when Greek pride and power were on the rise for elites in the Greek East, the Christian movement brought its own, competing view of tradition. To a degree it may have had its effect, if Pliny's letter can serve as evidence. Some people, he notes, admitted to becoming Christians as long as twenty-five years earlier, and worse, the "contagious superstition" had spread through cities, villages, and rural districts. The temples had been deserted. A combination of punishment and a resurgent Greek pride no doubt influenced greater numbers to go back to pagan temples and sacrificing. "[I]t is easy to imagine what multitudes may be reclaimed from this error," Pliny conveys to Trajan, "if a door be left open to repentance."[142]

Tradition (whether pagan, Jewish, or Christian) became a bellwether for the maintenance of a proper and ordered society. Empty temples meant a disordered world for Pliny. It no doubt meant the opposite for the Christian movement, who in their own manner participated in the competition between local elites in the Greek East. Both stressed the power of their traditions. For pagans, Jews, and Christians the power and importance of their deities increased (at least internally) when they showed that their connection to those deities tapped into structures of cosmic power that had ancient and venerable roots. It allowed participation within an arena of symbolic discourse that valued the role of a venerable past.

4.

Cosmic Connections: Defining the Arena of Power

Images of the divine world permeated ancient society. Connecting with the divine world was serious business and occupied persons at almost every level. Members of elite classes in the Greek East and those associated with them actively sought the continuing benevolence of a god or gods. Many appropriated symbols associated with the divine world to bolster, maintain, or redefine their relation to political, social, and economic arenas of power. The stakes could be high. Tax breaks, acquisition of prestige, or the right to provide asylum could go to those cities whose elites argued effectively for legitimate and long-standing cosmic connections. Those who fell outside "proper" channels of divine power could suffer severe social, political, and economic sanctions. The gods had to be appeased. Jewish and Christian groups, who claimed to have access to a power greater than any other, also had their adherents in the larger society. Even though generally on the fringes of power, Jews and Christians often drew on their own cosmic power bases as they conversed (even if only internally) with the power networks controlled by local elites or imperial power. This chapter examines how pagans, Jews, and Christians in the Greek East used divine or cosmic symbols to negotiate power relationships within the Roman Empire.

PAGANS AND THE POWER OF THE DIVINE

The starting place for understanding how cosmic power served as a crucial vehicle for both local elites in the Greek East and those on the fringe of power such as Jews and Christians is again the city. Here, local elites interacted most directly with imperial power, providing a loose framework in which all groups operated. These elites often drew on cosmic connections to help negotiate their relation to local, regional, and empirewide power networks. Persons who wished to participate in the imperial network of power as well as local and regional networks often had to acknowledge the power and presence of the cosmic realm associated with those arenas. The Flavian establishment of municipalities in the West offers a probable, though not conclusive, parallel. The Flavian charter for the Spanish city of Salpensa states that those who receive the office of duovir, aedile, or quaestor must take an oath in public to Jupiter, to the deified emperors Augustus, Claudius, Vespasian, and Titus, and to the municipal gods. The penalty for not taking the oath was 10,000 sesterces.[1] At the very least, this indicates the close tie between economic and political power at the local level in the West and the emperors, the Roman gods, and the local deities. Again it must be stressed that Roman power and local elite power in the Greek East were not synonymous, nor was power unidirectional, emanating solely from the Roman side. Especially revealing are cities like Aphrodisias in Caria and local elites in the Greek East who had particularly close relations with the Romans but who make clear that their local deity (in Aphrodisias's case, Aphrodite) frames the character of the power relationship between themselves and imperial rule.

Nor was the confluence of power and religion simply a manipulative ploy on the part of local elites to keep the Romans and the general populace in line. This unduly downplays the powerful role religion played in the public and, though less discernible, private lives of individuals in the ancient world.[2] Skeptics of divine power in antiquity certainly existed. One undated grave stele asserts that "in Hades there exists no boat, no ferryman Charon, no custodian Aiakos, no dog Kerberos; all we who are dead below have become bones, ashes, and nothing else."[3] But the preponderance of evidence suggests such sentiments were minority voices and wielded little real power.[4]

Dio of Prusa, a citizen of Nicomedia in Asia Minor and a well-educated member of the elite class in the Greek East, saw a clear relation between the cosmic realm and political power. One needed, he argued, the correct balance of political and cosmic power in order to achieve ethically responsible and just rule. Kings, for instance, should derive their powers (*dynamis*) and their stewardship from Zeus; in doing so they will govern justly according to the laws and ordinances of Zeus and enjoy "a happy lot and a fortunate end" (*Discourses* 1.45). Not surprisingly, Dio reappropriates Greek myth and the Homeric tradition to illustrate the dire consequences of not following Zeus's will:

> [H]e who goes astray and dishonours him [Zeus] who entrusted him with his stewardship or gave him this gift, receives no other reward from his great authority and power than merely this: that he has shown himself to all men of his own time and to posterity to be a wicked and undisciplined man, illustrating the storied end of Phaethon, who mounted a mighty chariot of heaven in defiance of his lot but proved himself a feeble charioteer. (*Discourses* 1.45–46)

Dio reflects the widely held attitude of his day that the divine world informed proper governance and that it behooved any who ruled to pay close attention to divine expectations.

Cities in the Greek East knew well the connection between the divine world and political governance. Many cities had long associations with particular deities, who were an important factor in their diplomatic and political discourse. The city of Stratonicea in Asia Minor, for example, celebrated through much of the imperial period its victory over the renegade Labieuus Parthicus (40 B.C.E.) by the sudden and miraculous epiphany of Zeus Pan-amaros, interpreting the historical victory within a cosmic framework of power.[5] When Parthicus revolted against the rule of the Romans, several cities in Asia Minor, including Stratonicea and Aphrodisias, remained loyal to the Romans. As usual, local elites played a significant role in the resultant symbolic discourse centered on the event. Chaeremon, mentioned in an inscription that celebrates Zeus's epiphany in the war, was probably related to a distinguished family that had a long record of support for the Romans in the late Republic and early imperial period.[6] The inscription, like four hundred others found near the temple dedicated to Zeus at Panamara, testifies to the many epiphanies and miracles performed by the god. A typical inscription, dating to the late first century C.E., states that "the greatest and most wonderful Zeus of Panamara saves the city," a sign of Zeus's ongoing power and presence.[7] R. MacMullen vividly recreates the scene that must have greeted visitors to Panamara: "wherever the eye rested, there must have been the inscribed and painted letters of honorific decrees, testimony to miracles, or regulations specifying the music and victims appropriate to this or that act of supplication or thanksgiv-ing."[8] Activities associated with the deity exhibited the intersection of cosmic, regional, and local power networks. Local priests invited neighboring cities and cities as far away as Miletus and Rhodes to attend festivals in the god's honor.[9] The priest setting the image of the god on horseback and journeying to nearby Stratonicea symbolized the deity's role in unifying the local area. Strato-nicea's theater, which served as both civic and entertainment center, and as the hieron of Panamara[10] became a festive site filled with revelry; free oil was given in the public baths, and cash, wine, and meals were passed out to the poor.[11] For participants and observers, Zeus's beneficence was exhibited through the activity of his agents, who, being members of the elite class, displayed the power of the deity and their own power through association by sharing wealth and food with the local populace and visitors to the area. Asso-ciation with the divine realm had distinct social and political advantages.

Cities (and individuals) often saw particular deities as providing power and prestige, a type of divine euergetism (benefaction) that was often emulated by local elites. Some deities spilled outside their civic boundaries, notably Artemis of Ephesus, who supposedly had mystic letters inscribed on her statue that could serve as a charm or, according to Plutarch, even expel demons (*Moral* 706 e).[12] Belief in divinity (one or many) meant participation in a primary source of power. Attempts to draw on divine power ranged from individual requests for a deity to intervene in one's romantic ventures[13] to corporate ventures such as Stratonicea's seeking divine aid for its war effort. Entreaties for divine help (and their subsequent recording on stone or papyri) were taken seriously.[14]

No cult better illustrates the intersection of imperial, cosmic, regional, and local rule than the imperial cult in the Greek East.[15] The imperial cult exhibited a fluidity and continuity that generally transcended the divisions normally established between the Julio-Claudians, the Flavians, and the Antonines. Vespasian promoted it more aggressively in parts of the empire than had previous emperors. The imperial cult was, as Peter Garnsey and Richard Saller note, novel, ubiquitous, and "a conveyor of imperial ideology, a focus of loyalty for the many, and a mechanism for the social advancement of the few."[16] It was a vehicle in which elites in the Greek East could negotiate the rather lopsided military and political power relations that existed. Benefactions on the part of the emperor played a role in his depiction as a god, especially when powerful local elites benefited directly from Roman rule. When Nero restored the Greek city of Acraephiae to the status of a free city, Epameinondas, high priest of the emperors for life, placed steles in two very public arenas, the agora and the temple of Apollo. The following excerpt addresses in part the resultant intersection of cosmic, imperial, and local powers:

> Since Nero the lord of the whole universe, greatest emperor, holding the tribunician power for the thirteenth time elect, father of his country, dawned as a new Sun for the Greeks, especially chosen to benefit Greece, and revered our gods in return for the fact that they had always stood beside him for his care and protection; and being the one and only emperor for all time, mightiest philhellenic Nero Zeus Eleutherios [Zeus of Freedom] gave, granted and restored the indigenous and immemorial freedom previously removed from the Greeks to its ancient condition of autonomy and freedom . . . ; therefore it was decided by the magistrates, councillors and people to dedicate for the present an altar by [the statue of] Zeus the Saviour, inscribing it "to Zeus Eleutherios Nero forever" and to establish statues in the temple of Apollo Ptoios jointly with our ancestral gods of Nero Zeus Eleutherios and of Thea Sebaste Messalina.[17]

The local elites who sponsored this inscription incorporated Nero as "Zeus of Freedom" into their new political environment and their long-standing association with ancient, venerable deities. Nero (the "mightiest philhellene") is interpreted through the lens of Greek tradition, placing his power within the symbolic network so important for the local society. Power networks operate on a number of levels in this inscription. The emperor certainly has the ability to grant freedom for the city, but that grant, from the local elites' perspective, simply restored the city to "its ancient condition of autonomy and freedom." Further, only the city, primarily through its magistrates and council (*boule*), which wielded the bulk of local power,[18] had the right to give its full allegiance to the emperor, to name him Zeus Eleutherios, and to associate him with their ancestral gods. Benefactions elicit allegiance and recognition, entailing reciprocal relations, freely offered between persons of different statuses, key features of patronage in the Roman world.[19]

The placement of statues and an altar in the temple of Apollo Ptoios indicates that local elites incorporated the emperor's divinity within the framework of a prominent local deity.[20] Here, imperial power operates within (under?) the cosmic power network run by the local elites. The inscription exhibits the importance of the deity for regional interactions, especially since Zeus Eleutherios played a key role for the League of Greeks in nearby Plataea.[21]

Certainly the association of the emperor with the divine world and with the proper degree of *eusebeia* (piety) "emphasized that the subjects were dependent on the emperor as on the gods," who maintained a stable world when worshiped properly.[22] As S. Price notes, Aristides remarks that upon hearing the emperor's name, people praise and worship him, uttering "a two-fold prayer, one on the ruler's behalf to the gods and one to the ruler himself about his own matters."[23] The dual nature of the prayer is intriguing. While prayers are offered to the ruler as to a god, the community itself serves as an intermediary with the gods on the emperor's behalf, a significant juxtaposition of power. Cosmic power intertwines with the social and political power of local elites, who in turn mediate imperial power locally, regionally, and cosmically.[24] Association with the cosmic realm as exemplified in the inscription was not mere ceremony hiding political or social ambitions. It helped maintain the stability of local, regional, imperial, and cosmic power relations.[25]

But cosmic power often had more immediate implications. For individuals in a corporate setting the threat of an angry deity helped control inappropriate social behavior. Villagers in northeastern Lydia set up inscribed stones that invoked the judgment of local deities on a variety of issues. The all-seeing god was summoned to determine such things as whether an orphan was mistreated or who stole clothes from the bathhouse. In one case, dated to 98/99 C.E., Twelve Scepters, modeled on priest's scepters, are invoked to protect tombs; those who violate the tombs, and their families, risk the gods' divine wrath.[26] As Lane Fox argues, such examples do not prove that people believed that the divine world intruded on every aspect of their lives. Nevertheless, they indicate that the divine realm was a significant part of a system of relations maintaining and controlling even aspects of daily behavior. In addition, the use of inscriptions involved the purchase of expensive stone and the employment of specialists to carve it.[27]

The gods sometimes served as the vehicles of appeasement among members of society. An inscription from the village of Keryzeis in Lydia was dedicated by Galliko, a female slave of the village, as a ransom for Diogenes, possibly a sign of some "sinful relation."[28] Depicted above the text was the god Men, who was originally an Iranian moon god and had adherents in the Greek East for over five hundred years beginning in the third century B.C.E.[29] The public character of the inscription and the identification of the dedicant and the deity show the clear confluence of divine power and the proper order of local society. The god Men appears in a number of settings that indicate the god's importance for at least some in the Greek East. One inscription, dated to 143 C.E., records a certain Artemidoros, who dedicates on behalf of all his relatives ("both those who are aware and those who are not") and who because of an injunction must pay a ransom (*lutron*) "to Men Tyrannos and Zeus Ogmenos and the gods in his company."[30] One can assume that the well-being of society and of the extended family of Artemidoros is at issue. That pattern is seen in another late inscription from Sardis, dated to 160/61 C.E., to Men, blessing the god for providing a wife.[31]

A number of inscriptions indicate Men has punished someone for omitting proper ritual activities or committing a sin against the god or other persons. In Maionia, a late-second- or early-third-century inscription describes a woman who had failed to acknowledge in public the god Men Axiottenos's role in the recovery of a jewel.[32] Another inscription admonishes a person for allowing his pigs to wander (dated 114/15 C.E.); yet another rebukes an individual who did not serve Men when called and subsequently went insane (118/19 C.E.); still another late inscription condemns to death a banker who cheated and a woman who poisoned her son-in-law (156/57 C.E.); another admonishes the theft of a himation from the local baths.[33] Wrong acts against persons cause the god to expose and then punish their sin.[34] Several men donate their hair to the god Men, "as is the custom and holy ransom" apparently to appease the god for some grievous act committed.[35]

So-called Eastern religions played a significant role in defining the character of cosmic power in the Greek East. The influence of the goddess Isis, for example, continued into late antiquity.[36] At Athens, she is associated on a stele with Hermes, Aphrodite, and Pan in the first century B.C.E.[37] By the early part of the second century C.E. an entire sanctuary to Isis existed. One prominent woman sponsored monumental repairs at that time, including to the cult statue of Isis.[38] Greek culture appropriated Persian (or what was perceived as Persian) culture, whose symbolic field continued its influence, though in altered form.[39] The god Mithras, associated with the Persians in literary sources, had acquired a degree of popularity by the end of the first century.[40] At Mysia, a carving of Mithra wearing a Phrygian hat dates to 77/78 C.E., making it one of the earliest monuments to the god.[41] Mithraism had a considerable following among soldiers and merchants if current finds are any indication. The secrets of Mithras allowed individuals to obtain a modicum of power through association with a deity whose power extended throughout the cosmos. In the Nabataean Kingdom, the cosmic power of local deities strengthened a strong, local tradition that enabled local elites to deal with the encroachment of imperial power.[42] The interaction among Hellenistic, imperial, and local cultures was often subtle and complicated.[43] Many people simply took for granted that the divine world and the everyday world were intertwined. Social behavior had divine implications.

Aphrodisias

Aphrodisias serves as an excellent model to illustrate how local elites in the Greek East drew on cosmic power to interpret their relation to imperial, regional, and local networks of power. The symbolic discourse associated with the goddess Aphrodite dominates the civic landscape of Aphrodisias from the time of Octavian through the Severans. Certainly other deities were worshiped in the city and even promoted, but none approached the symbolic power embodied in the city's namesake. No structure shows this more clearly than the city's magnificent Sebasteion, or imperial cult complex.

The Sebasteion was built between the reigns of Tiberius and Nero and lasted into the Flavian period. It exemplifies the intimate connection between Aphrodite of Aphrodisias, the Julio-Claudian house, and Rome from the perspective of local elites in the city, a link stemming from the Julio-Claudian claim of descent from Aeneas, son of Aphrodite.[44] Epithets of various emperors in inscriptions on the walls of the theater, also dedicated to the goddess Aphrodite, make clear that the bond between Rome and Aphrodisias is Aphrodisias's Aphrodite, the *prometor,* or "ancestral mother."[45] Even more explicit, a dedication on the bath complex names her Aphrodite Epiphane, the *prometor* of the gens of the caesars.[46]

In the Sebasteion visitors encountered several inscriptions that dedicate the complex "to Aphrodite, the divine emperors, and the demos,"[47] a pattern common on civic buildings in Aphrodisias from Tiberius onward.[48] The complex reflects the integration of the rule of Aphrodite, the rule of Rome, and the rule of the demos, especially the local elites who sponsored the complex. The complex portrays the power relations operative as key local elites see them. The issue of who read such inscriptions need not concern us here. Certainly, local elites could read them. In any case, the inscriptions reflect the taken-for-granted attitudes of those who sponsored the complex (and probably of the rest of the city, which benefited from it). The fact that people took the trouble to eliminate troublesome names (e.g., "Nero" and "Aphrodite" by the Christians)[49] and placed so much importance on the public display of laws indicates the powerful symbolic importance attached to such public displays.

Aphrodite, named first in the building dedications,[50] plays a primary role in the web of power uniting the power of the local governing authority (the demos) and imperial authority (the Roman emperor). The fourth party, of course, though unmentioned in these dedications, are the local families who sponsored the complex. These families acquired local (and perhaps wider) prestige by their association with the powers that governed the political and religious realities of their day. Such associations were not just gratuitous acts or power-grabbing ventures. They were a way to conceptualize (and visualize) the intersections of local power (the demos and local elites), imperial power (the Romans and their affiliates), and cosmic power (Aphrodite). The association of different strands and levels of power was a pattern repeated in many diverse ways across the Greek East by local elites, especially those who linked the imperial cult with local deities.[51]

The niches of the monumental propylon (outer gateway) of the imperial cult complex at Aphrodisias offered additional displays of power for the viewer. There, the viewer saw busts or statues of Aphrodite Prometor, Aeneas, and various members of the Julio-Claudian family. The busts and statues stress the connection between the goddess Aphrodite and the founding (and power) of the Julio-Claudian line. For Aphrodisias, the power of Aphrodite defines and legitimates the power of Rome, a point made clearer when one entered the complex. There one saw at the far end of the complex a temple dedicated to Aphrodite and the emperors and a series of panels along the two porticoes that displayed mythic scenes (including Aphrodite and Aeneas) and scenes of imperial victory.[52] And it should come as no surprise that a first-century C.E. decorative marble plaque found within the foundations of the south portico of the Sebasteion portrays the cult statue of Aphrodite of Aphrodisias having homage paid to it by the personification of the city.[53] Key local elites viewed Aphrodite's favor as absolutely crucial to the continued existence of the city.

Letters recorded on the wall of the theater at Aphrodisias indicate that Roman authorities from the triumvirate to the Severan periods understood that the goddess was the titular head of the city. Descriptions of Aphrodite as "the goddess who is among them" (8.1.38), "ruler" (18.1.4), "founder" (25.1.4), and "source of the city's name" (49.1.2) indicate the Romans' recognition of Aphrodite's long and close relationship with the civic identity and the importance such associations had for the local elites who received and, in the second and third centuries, recorded the documents on the theater wall for all to see.[54] The audience for these documents was primarily a local and regional one. Aphrodite mediated a crucial relation among Rome, the region, and the city (including most importantly the local elites), a matter of pride and prestige and power. The city, region, and visitors were to take notice.

Aphrodite's importance continued in the Flavian period. Silius Italicus writes that Vespasian took to Cyprus the palm of the Idumaeans (= Judaea) for Aphrodite's triumph, where a hundred altars burned offerings to celebrate the conquest.[55] Titus offered sacrifices to Aphrodite, indicating his willingness to associate with the deity. Aphrodite at Corinth is even given a Flavian hairdo.[56] A bust of a priest of Aphrodite from the Flavian period found at Aphrodisias prominently displays on his crown the bust of Aphrodite flanked by a male and a female bust, probably of Helios (sun) and Selene (moon). Usually such crowns had portraits of the emperor and his family and were associated with the imperial cult.[57] A good example, though late, is a bust of Diogenes, a priest from the Severan period, that has Aphrodite of Aphrodisias as the center figure on his crown with eleven busts of the imperial family, four on the left and seven on the right.[58] The association of local goddess and imperial power could not be more explicit. From the iconographic (and as we saw, epigraphic) perspective, Aphrodite represents the cosmic force that unites imperial power with the power of local elites such as Diogenes and the demos of the city. The connection was long-lived, as indicated by busts associated with the cult of Aphrodite and local elites that appear well into the fifth century. A statue, possibly of a priest, was found in the "Atrium House" near the Sebasteion; the figure holds a cult statuette of the goddess Aphrodite of Aphrodisias.[59] In addition, the letters associated with the theater indicate that as late as the third century C.E., the Roman emperors Severus and Antonius declare Aphrodisias "more closely related than others to the empire of the Romans because of [the goddess] who presides over your city, your existing polity and its laws which have survived unchanged up to our reign."[60] Established precedent, as noted previously, carried great weight.

A deity's manifestation of power could include appearances, a leitmotiv from Homer through the Roman imperial period.[61] P. Agelaos dedicated an inscription that included the fact that he was an official of the "most distinguished, manifest, most visible [epiphanistates] Goddess Aphrodite."[62] There seems no reason to doubt the sincerity of the dedicator. As we have seen, miracles and divine manifestations percolated through the world as far as many were concerned. Recognition of the divine powers operative and associating with them through sacrifice and other prescribed activities meant that one could appropriate, to a degree, that power.

References to divine power sometimes appear to border on the mundane. When Adrastus Apollonios, a priest of Helios and chief priest of Vespasian's temple in a city on the Maeander River, built an aqueduct during the time of Domitian, he dedicated it to the goddess Aphrodite, the emperor Domitian and his house, and the demos, again associating cosmic, imperial, and local power networks.[63] A regional connection exists as well; Apollonios, as benefactor, links Helios and Aphrodite and their respective cities, reflecting a form of *homonoia,* or peace. In similar fashion, Xenophon's *Ephesiaca* depicts the hero and heroine acknowledging the power of several deities: their city goddess, Artemis of Ephesus; Helios, the god of the Rhodians, whom they visit; and Isis. This is not simple syncretization, that is, combining the attributes of many gods; nor are they worshiping all deities as if they were simply manifestations of a single deity. Rather, it follows a pattern fairly popular in the Greek East and typified by Apollonios's dedication: the association of a deity with a particular location.[64] Such associations also allow, as in Apollonios's dedication, someone to assert or profess the power of his or her own deity.

The regional stress on mutual cooperation between cities (*homonoia*) and the role played by the gods in this cooperation are made all the clearer in *homonoia* coin issues from a number of cities in Asia Minor.[65] C. J. Howgego draws attention to a number of cities in Asia Minor that used *homonoia* issues to establish or confirm social and economic interactions.[66] Aphrodisias, for example, features the cult statue of Aphrodite of Aphrodisias with those of other cities under the label *HOMONOIA* (e.g., Ephesus, Antiochia, and Neapolis).[67] A coin issued during the reign of Commodus commemorates an alliance between Phrygian Hierapolis and Carian Aphrodisias and depicts Aphrodite of Aphrodisias and Apollo of Hierapolis engaged in a *sacra conversazione* before a sacrificial altar.[68] Such coin issues generally included (1) the emperor on the obverse, (2) cult statues of the deities of the cities represented in some form on the reverse, and (3) *homonoia* written below the cities' names. S. Price argues that cities in Asia Minor had no real power to make treaties and that such implications are misleading, especially when real power began to lie with the Roman authorities.[69] Nevertheless, the stress on harmony and kinship remained, and such gestures were important to cities.[70] Deities mediated the power within the regional alliances, bolstered the prestige of the divine realm in human activity, and provided the basis for political and economic ties.[71] Dio of Prusa illustrates what this could entail. He sought to establish *homonoia* between Nicomedia and Nicaea, each of which claimed for itself the title "first city" on its coins (the basis of Nicaea's claim was its greater antiquity, larger territory, and central location).[72] He emphasizes their interchange of produce, ties of family and friendship, proxeny, worship of similar gods, and celebration of similar festivals. The emphasis on local deities may have taken on added significance in the imperial period. The use of Aphrodite of Aphrodisias, for example, in affirming regional bonds contrasts with an earlier association of *homonoia* with Zeus in a treaty Aphrodisias made with Plarasa, a neighboring village. Aphrodite, rather than the Roman Zeus, becomes the mediating force in treaty relations, a subtle move to a local frame of reference that dictates, even if symbolically, the power relations with regional, imperial, and cosmic arenas.[73]

Aphrodisians saw their deity as having more than just local significance. The universal power of Aphrodite is best symbolized by Aphrodisian cult statues, which are similar to the cult statues of Artemis at Ephesus.[74] The Aphrodisian statues display mythic images of Aphrodite's power over the underworld, sea, sky, and earth.[75] The statues are typically divided into four zones. A colossal Aphrodite found at Aphrodisias serves as a good representative.[76] On the lower zone are displayed three erotes sacrificing incense, a frequent motif found on funerary reliefs.[77] The scene above it shows Aphrodite riding over the waves on a sea goat (Capricorn) and accompanied by a dolphin. The third scene portrays Selene (moon) and Helios (sun), while the final scene has a picture of the Three Graces. These zones depict, respectively, Aphrodite's power over the underworld, sea, sky, and earth.[78] Statues of Aphrodite of Aphrodisias have been found as far away as Portugal, with a good number found at Rome itself.[79]

Greek cities like Aphrodisias used the myths, symbols, and general popularity of their deities to define themselves amid the Roman world of the first and second centuries C.E. A deity's appearance throughout the *oikoumene* on statues and coins displayed for the observer or the reader the power, significance, and prestige of the city, local Greek elites, and the deity. When an imperial provincial coin issue from Aphrodisias (54/55 C.E.) depicts the bust of Nero and Agrippina on one side and Aphrodite as Tyche holding a statue of the cult image of Aphrodite on the other,[80] the iconography of power associates the emperor and his power with Aphrodite, who for the city provided the very sustenance and prosperity it enjoyed within the context of that Roman power. The city benefited from the cosmic realm and from the empire.

As with most western Greek cities, Aphrodisias had to define itself in relation to the rising Roman star. For Aphrodisias, group identity and group success—at least among the ruling class[81]—centered on Aphrodite. The wealthy and powerful in Greek cities were not the only beneficiaries. A form of welfare was established in which the whole town participated in games, festivals, and religious observances generally paid for by the wealthy. Aphrodite symbolized the city's relations with Rome[82] and surrounding cities and preserved the social and political fabric of Aphrodisias via her control of the cosmos itself.

With few exceptions, the Flavio-Trajanic period saw a continuation of this attitude in Aphrodisias. Having been granted a measure of autonomy under Julian rule, the city was successful in its bid to become a free city, despite changed circumstances brought on by the Flavians. Building and renovation projects continued and may have actually increased.[83] An inscription found at Ephesus, dedicated during the reign of Domitian and recut to honor Vespasian after Domitian's death, asserts that the demos of Aphrodisias was "devoted to Caesar, being free and autonomous from time past by the grace of the emperors, dedicated (this) in the provincial temple of the emperors at Ephesus, of their own grace, on account of their loyalty to the emperors and their goodwill to the city of Ephesus which is the temple-warden." The dedication was supervised by Aristion, a member of the local elite class who, the inscription states, was a priest of Pluton and Core and "a curator of the fabric of the temple of the goddess Aphrodite."[84] The inscription draws on the recent past and on imperial power to reassert Aphrodisias's independence from regional obligations to contribute to the provincial cult at Ephesus. The addition of Aristion's religious connections to Pluton and Core (chthonic deities) and Aphrodite affirms both his personal power and prestige and, at the least, an indirect association of those deities (especially Aphrodite) in imperial, regional, and local power networks. The fact that he mentions that he is a curator, or holder, of the fabric of the temple of Aphrodite indicates the prominence (at least as perceived by Aphrodisians) obtained by association with the goddess.

The interplay between local power and imperial power during the Flavian period is also clear in an edict (unfortunately fragmentary) made by the Roman proconsul of Asia, Silius Italicus, a poet, who apparently reaffirms several local decrees that made it illegal to catch, keep, or scare doves in Aphrodisias.[85] Also mentioned is the cult of the goddess, presumably Aphrodite. Here imperial power takes a rare hand in controlling the social and sacred areas of Aphrodisias. The decree presumably functioned similarly to the emperors' letters to the city inscribed on the theater wall, that is, as a visible statement by imperial authorities affirming the power embodied in local elites and the divine power of Aphrodite. One of the letters on the theater wall, a copy of a letter sent by Trajan to Smyrna, reiterates Aphrodisias's right to avoid payment of common liturgies.[86] The documents inscribed on the theater walls, Aphrodite's appearance on coin issues, her cult statue, and the inscriptions on some graves that indicate that those who desecrate the site will have to pay a fine to the temple of Aphrodite display the visual and verbal "rhetoric of power" that local elites used with great success from Augustus through Trajan to highlight the power and prestige of Aphrodite, patroness of the city.[87] No sudden transformations occur during the Flavian period or afterward at Aphrodisias.[88] Local elites continued their vigorous participation in local, regional, and civic affairs. The premier personage at Aphrodisias when the city first made significant connections to the new imperial power at Rome in the first century B.C.E. was a freedman named Zoilos.[89] Two generations later, when imperial rule had acquired a degree of stability as an institution, a major benefactor at Aphrodisias like Tiberius Claudius Diogenes, who obtained Roman citizenship under Claudius, could seek and obtain the prestigious high priesthood of Asia.[90] Local elites at Aphrodisias built on the powerful connections with the new imperial order established by Zoilos and his generation. They sought and acquired greater prestige at regional and imperial levels by sponsoring monumental building projects, acquiring honorific titles, and obtaining Roman citizenship, activities that occurred in other parts of the Greek East. This period stands at the threshold of the Second Sophistic, when prominent Aphrodisians such as the lawyer L. Antonius Ti. Claudius Dometinus Diogenes become part of a large-scale participation of elites from the Greek East in the imperial network of power.[91]

The public posture of local elites at Aphrodisias toward the power of Aphrodite as the civic agent of the city did not prevent association or worship of other deities. Coins sponsored by the Boule itself show that Sarapis and Isis made inroads into the civic realm at Aphrodisias much as they had done throughout the Roman Empire, especially in the Flavian period.[92] In part this was due to the limits placed on who could occupy a prominent position within the cult of Aphrodite, a position reserved for the most prominent (and the wealthy). To obtain power or prestige, other cults offered an outlet, although this did not necessarily compete with the civic prominence of Aphrodite's cult, as coins, statuary, and epigraphic evidence amply illustrate. Henotheistic attitudes allowed persons to worship a particular deity without denying the existence and power of other gods.[93]

Chariton of Aphrodisias and the Goddess Aphrodite

Not surprisingly, deities show up prominently in the ancient romances. For Chariton, the principal deity in his narrative is the goddess Aphrodite. Aphrodite works behind the scenes through her divine agent, Eros, and through her reluctant human agent, Callirhoe, to display her power. The author states that Aphrodite arranges both marriages of Callirhoe (2.2.8, 2.3.5, 6.1), reunites Chaereas and Callirhoe (8.1.3,5), and overrules the whims of Tyche (8.1.3). Chariton also has significant figures acknowledge the power of Aphrodite throughout the narrative.[94] Aphrodite, however, is no Homeric goddess who dons human form and walks among mortals. She remains distant, though omnipresent, throughout the narrative. In narrative guise, we see an Aphrodite with much the same abilities as the one depicted iconographically and epigraphically at Aphrodisias.

Eros, as Aphrodite's agent, arranges the meeting of Chaereas and Callirhoe during a festival for Aphrodite (1.1.6); controls the political assembly that pressures Hermocrates, the father of Callirhoe, to agree to the marriage (1.1.12); and guides the separate expeditions of Chaereas and Callirhoe to a surprise meeting before the Persian king Artaxerxes (4.7.5). His attack on the psyches of major political figures renders the self-control and political acumen of these men useless, making clear that human reason stands little chance against the power of Aphrodite (1.1.10, 2.4.5, 4.2.4, 6.1.9, 6.3.2,9).

Aphrodite plans the marriages; Eros carries them out. In 1.1.3 the author portrays Eros as arranging the match between Chaereas and Callirhoe, whereas in 8.1.3 he shows Aphrodite behind the action. The author describes Aphrodite's thoughts regarding her previous anger at Chaereas for rejecting "her kindness after receiving from her a gift more superlatively beautiful even than Paris' prize."[95] Even when Eros seems to act independently, the results serve the ends and purposes of Aphrodite.[96]

Eros, fond of contention (*philoneikos*), is viewed as a cruel tyrant (4.2.3) and master of a person's psyche. According to traditions associated with poets and sculptors, who depict him with the bow and arrow, "things the most light and unstable" (4.7.6), he alters the will of those who seek to oppose him.[97] He controls assemblies, launches expeditions, and leads the bride in marriage (3.2.5). At one point in the narrative, when Egypt revolts from Persia, an action brought about by Tyche (6.8.1), Chariton implies that Eros's power can be usurped by Tyche. Even here, however, Eros lurks. The Persian king, in the midst of all the preparations for war, does not neglect to inform his servants to bring the heroine, Callirhoe, along with the rest of the harem (6.9.7).

Tyche, the third principal divine force, appears as both hostile and benign in Chariton as well as in other romances (especially Apuleius's *Metamorphoses*). Tyche compromises Callirhoe's honor when Callirhoe finds herself pregnant and must make the choice of saving her baby or her honor. Tyche is the one "against whom alone human reason has no power."[98] Then, in words reminiscent of Eros, Tyche is described as a divinity who loves strife (*philoneikos*) when she unexpectedly reveals Callirhoe's pregnancy to her (2.8.3). Tyche makes known where Callirhoe has been taken after the discovery of her empty tomb (3.3.8). Tyche causes the seizure of letters from Mithridates and Chaereas to Callirhoe explaining that Chaereas lives, thus setting the stage for the two to journey to the king of Persia (4.5.3). Tyche causes all discussion regarding Callirhoe's lawful husband to cease in Babylon when the Egyptian revolt occurs.

As powerful as Tyche is, however, the author makes clear that Aphrodite is more so.[99] When Tyche plans to keep Callirhoe hidden from Chaereas while both are on the same island, Aphrodite thinks the plan outrageous and, feeling pity for Chaereas, overrides Tyche's plan and brings Chaereas and Callirhoe together again (8.1.3). Chariton draws on a common feature associated with Tyche in the Graeco-Roman world: her ability to bring about unexpected turns of events and to create sudden changes in fortune. Yet Tyche's machinations only lead inexorably to the final chapter, the reunion of those who have been separated. Even Tyche serves the final aims of Aphrodite, that is, to test and train (*gymnadzein*, 8.1.3) Chaereas and Callirhoe until they are prepared to be reunited.[100] Little wonder then that Chariton concludes his narrative with Callirhoe in the temple of Aphrodite praying to Aphrodite that she never separate Callirhoe from Chaereas again (8.8.16). Callirhoe (and, by this time, the reader/hearer) knows where the power resides.[101]

For Chariton, as for his city, Aphrodisias, and most areas in the Greek East, the world is marked by many forces, both divine and human. His narrative shows clearly that local power networks (such as symbolized by the city of Syracuse or the local shrine of Aphrodite outside Miletus), imperial power networks (symbolized by the king of Persia), and cosmic power networks are interpreted, if not integrated, through the lens of Aphrodite's power.[102]

JEWS AND THE POWER OF GOD

Jews generally understood cosmic power as the power of the Jewish god within the parameters of human history. Of course, the view of that activity could vary, from the philosophical musings of Philo of Alexandria to the historical reconstructions of Josephus.[103] Some evidence exists for Jewish involvement in pagan cults, but especially in the literary sources, those who identify themselves or are identified by others as Jews and who draw on divine power stressed the power of the Jewish god.[104]

Prior to the first Jewish war, Judaism in the Greek East dealt directly and indirectly with a plethora of power networks proffered by local elites and imperial officials. Epigraphic evidence for Jews in the Flavio-Trajanic period is relatively sparse in the Greek East. Jews were viewed with antagonism in certain regions and by certain Roman writers. Hostile broadsides from Alexandria (a longtime site of animosity toward Jews) no doubt had their parallels in other areas of the Greek East.[105] The period saw at least two revolts identified with Jews, which were put down by the Romans (the Jewish revolt in Judaea, of course, in 66–73 and the revolt in 115–17 in Egypt, Cyprus, North Africa, and Mesopotamia) and which no doubt contributed to some antagonism.[106]

Nevertheless, a degree of accommodation between Jews and non-Jews took place. Legal contracts reflect one intriguing area. At Gorgippia, in the north Black Sea region, a dedication from 67/68 C.E. reads "To God the Most High, Almighty, Blessed, under the reign of King Rescuporis, loyal to the Emperor and friend of the Romans, pious, in the year 364, in the month of Daisuis, I Neocles son of Athenodoros set at liberty under Zeus, Ge, Helios (the slaves of . . . bred in my house?) . . . and undisturbed by all my heirs and may go where they want because of my valid order."[107] Probably Jewish, the dedicator, Neocles, mentions his god, pagan deities, and a king loyal to the Romans, integrating cosmic, local, and imperial power. The occasion? The freeing of slaves under Zeus, Ge (Earth), and Helios (Sun). Even if one agrees that this is an "indispensable juridical formula in acts of enfranchisement,"[108] it nevertheless indicates the intimate association of cosmic power with political and social actions such as freeing a slave. The social act of freeing a slave is placed within the rubric of the Bosporan king, whose rule frames the action between the two parties. In addition, the mention of the Romans indicates how the king himself (or at least his affiliates) situate their power within the rubric of Roman power.[109] The apostle Paul's letter to the slave owner Philemon takes a similar approach, though without the pagan overtones. The Christian god alters the relation between the slave and his master. Divine power redefines human relationships.

Another inscription from the same area, this time certainly Jewish, because it is placed in a synagogue (*proseuche*), also contains the pagan ending to Zeus, Sun, and Earth as witnesses to the manumission of a slave.[110] Nothing shown thus far would be particularly unusual for any person emancipating a slave or performing some other legal act, with the exception of the opening remarks mentioning the Most High God. Explicit and implicit rules governed this social discourse. Jews had slaves; therefore, they had to obey the rules established by the powers that allowed slavery. Short vignettes such as these epigraphic examples provide a brief glimpse into the way people constructed their lives, what powers they acknowledged, accepted or tolerated and what powers they did not. In our earlier example of enfranchisement, Neocles, acknowledges that the powers of the Bosporan king and his allies, the Romans, helped frame the social act of emancipation. The act of inscribing and publicly displaying it does as well. He need not have done this. Presumably he could have let the slaves go without such acknowledgment or not had slaves in the first place or revolted. These legal and quasi-legal documents may not tell us how individuals really felt about imperial and regional powers, but they do tell us what power(s) individuals acknowledged publicly, whatever their private feelings were. And the powers Neocles acknowledged were the same as his pagan neighbors acknowledged, with one important exception. Neocles dedicated his action before the Most High God, presumably for him the most powerful player in this group.

What makes such legal documents intriguing for our purposes is when one finds unlikely persons acknowledging such imperial, regional, and cosmic allegiances. The archive of Babatha, at one time a well-to-do Jewish landowner from the village of Mazoa, south of the Dead Sea, comes immediately to mind.[111] These documents (written as early as the 90s to as late as August 132 C.E.) provide powerful evidence for aspects of village life in the transition between Nabataean rule and the coming of Roman rule in 106 C.E. Babatha may have died in the Bar Kochba revolt against Rome (132–35 C.E.).[112] It is striking that she carried around legal documents that place her land acquisition within the framework of the very powers against whom Bar Kochba fought.[113] The ideological implications of framing a legal contract were apparently not lost on those participating in the revolt, as land lease contracts written under the authority of Bar Kochba indicate.[114] The political ramifications could not be more overt.

Babatha's own set of documents reflect the structural changes (if not the character of the "webs of power" themselves) brought on by Roman rule. The registration of her land begins by dating the document in the reign of Trajan (with a full list of his titles) and giving the dates of the two Roman consuls.[115] Babatha even swore to the truth of her census return by the *tyche* of the emperor.[116] Why did she continue to carry around documents whose only legitimacy rested in the authority granted them by the very power whose overthrow she apparently supported? Perhaps she was hedging her bets? Perhaps she and members of her village got caught up in events that rapidly spun out of control? Yet the deposit of her documents near a Bar Kochba stronghold seems at the least implicit acknowledgment of his authority. Whatever her professed reasons may have been, on one very important level she continued to acknowledge the power implicit in the legal documents. If she was swept rapidly into a revolutionary movement, she never fully broke the symbolic bonds that tied her to her former life.[117] The Babatha documents provide a glimpse of the rules and powers individuals implicitly and explicitly recognized and reveal that people sometimes harbored conflicting loyalties.

The pagan formula invoking Zeus, Ge, and Helios in the two inscriptions from the Black Sea area also merit comment. The phrase has a long and widespread tradition.[118] Menahem Stern finds in the formula a "dead letter" devoid of its "pagan character."[119] This seems too pat. Granted, persons like Neocles may have thought little about its implication. But its use presumes that the pagan formula was a necessary feature of the social act. The phrase indicates the web of power (including cosmic power) that people assumed and reacted to even if it conflicted with their own beliefs. Acceptance of the formula implies a degree of toleration. Symbols become "dead letters" only with difficulty. They may fall into a holding pattern only to be emphasized when events dictate. The underlying power network that one presupposes when performing such "taken-for-granted acts" becomes clearest when challenged. Sacrifices on behalf of the emperors' safety in the Temple in Jerusalem prior to the first Jewish revolt were apparently tolerated by most Jews. But when the sacrifices were discontinued, the power network generally implicit in such acts became clear. Both Romans and Jews recognized the seriousness of the Jewish revolt against Rome when the sacrifices were discontinued.[120] The dead letter sacrifice became very real indeed. When proper conditions reinvest symbols with significance, the latent power present in the symbols resurfaces.

An inscription found at 'Akrabah, twenty miles southeast of Caesarea Philippi in Palestine, shows the process from the pagan perspective. The inscription dates to 67 C.E., the second year of the Jewish revolt against Rome. "In the 18th year of the reign of our Lord, King Agrippa, Aoudeidos the son of Maleichathos made for Zeus the Lord the doors and their ornaments and the altar at his own expense from feelings of piety."[121] The dedication associates a pagan deity with the rule of the Jewish king Agrippa. The dedicator recognizes that the cosmic power of Zeus is manifested within the rule of his king. Again, the mention of King Agrippa's reign is no simple dating device. It suggests two spheres of power that the dedicator deems crucial. From the formal (if not personal) view of Aoudeidos, no apparent contradiction exists in participating in two spheres of power, one pagan and religious, the other Jewish and political.[122]

Josephus and the Jewish God

Josephus illustrates the complexity of Aoudeidos's intersecting spheres of power, albeit from the opposite perspective: the Jewish god and the Roman state. In *The Jewish War* Josephus rarely addresses the benefits of the Pax Romana.[123] When he does, he ascribes the benefits achieved by Roman peace largely to Roman virtue and not to tyche. Yet Josephus portrays Rome's world dominance as the outcome of divine will. The Jewish rebels failed to receive help not because God somehow supported the Roman Empire. Rather, Josephus perceives God moving from nation to nation, "giving the scepter of empire to each in turn; now He has bestowed it upon Italy."[124] Josephus's silence about the benefits of Roman rule in *The Jewish War* does not result from his fear that others might label him an assimilationist.[125] Josephus does not simply accept the yoke of Roman rule. Roman power is viewed through the lens of a powerful and prestigious Jewish god who works through history.

Josephus portrays even the Romans as subject to God's law. God often stands at the center of Roman victories in *The Jewish War,* primarily due to the wanton disregard of God's wishes by Jewish defenders. The Roman Cestius almost wins the city of Jerusalem early on in the campaign, but God "turned away even from His sanctuary and ordained that that day should not see the end of the war" (*BJ* 2.539). Titus, Roman emperor at the time Josephus writes this account, bolsters his men's courage by arguing that the Jewish god must be angry at the Jerusalem defenders and that "to betray a divine Ally would be beneath our dignity" (*BJ* 6.39–41). Josephus claims that "God it is then, God Himself, who with the Romans is bringing the fire to purge His temple and exterminating a city so laden with pollutions" (*BJ* 6.110). The brigands futilely try to hide from the Romans but are destined to escape neither God nor the Romans (*BJ* 6.371). When Titus surveys the massive walls of the Temple, he exclaims: "God indeed has been with us in the war. God it was who brought down the Jews from these strongholds; for what power have human hands or engines against these towers?" (*BJ* 6. 411).[126] Josephus had to make religious sense of the destruction of the Temple. His presentation concerned "God's purpose for the world and his arrangements for the destiny of nations, and centered on a scheme of sin and punishment."[127] Josephus stresses *stasis,* (civil strife) as a major sin against God and the cause of the nation's destruction.[128]

Josephus defines Roman power within a new rubric, the power of the Jewish god. As a writer in the Greek East he stresses for his reading audience the ancient roots and universal scope of the Jewish movement and the Jews' powerful deity as a major player in significant historical events.[129] As Josephus grapples with the import and trauma of the Jewish war, he effectively reformulates the context in which one answers why the Romans won or, better, why the Jews lost. In one sense, Josephus ironically turns the tables. The Romans did not so much win the war as the Jews, by disobeying God, lost it. Even Roman power operates, from Josephus's perspective, under the aegis of the Jewish god.

CHRISTIANS AND THE CHRISTIAN GOD

Christian attitudes toward imperial and local power centers do not play major roles in most Christian texts written in the Flavian and Trajanic periods. The Christian contacts with these power centers are interpreted through the lens of an all-powerful god. Paul's own letters indicate that encounters with regional and local leaders were not always friendly (2 Cor. 11:23–26). The author of Mark, writing in the late sixties, encourages his readers to stand fast as they are beaten in synagogues and brought before governors and kings (Mark 13:9). In the early second century, Ignatius's letter to the Romans depicts the trials facing an increasing (though still modest) number of Christians. "Fire and cross, packs of wild beasts, cuttings, rendings, crushing of bones, mangling of limbs, grinding of my whole body, wicked torture of the devil—let them come upon me if only I may attain to Jesus Christ."[130] The symbolic power of suffering and death played a crucial organizing role for Christian communities, who saw increasing suspicion, if not outright hostility, from those participating in the pagan structures in which they all lived.[131] Yet Paul's admonition to obey the imperial authorities and their representatives (Rom. 13) found frequent echoes in Christian writings during the Claudian through Trajanic periods. Most Christian writers advocated continued allegiance. In 1 Peter Christians, "as aliens and exiles," are admonished to maintain good conduct among the Gentiles and to obey the emperors and governors (2:11–17). For the author, cosmic power associated with God allows Christians to make sense of such imperial and local power structures.

For a number of early writers, the current sufferings only illustrate that the end of the present evil age is drawing nearer (1 Pet. 4:12–16). "For the time has come for judgment to begin with the household of God; and if it begins with us, what will be the end of those who do not obey the gospel of God?" (1 Pet. 4:17). Mark admonishes his hearers to "watch," for the end of the present age can come at any moment (Mark 13:33–37; cf. Didache 16:6–8). Suffering and death combine with an expectation of a new age, which will supplant the present age. The attitude toward cosmic power defines the character of that relationship. Thus, not surprisingly, most Christian texts take for granted that their God provides (and has provided) the framework of power within which their particular community understands its internal and external relations. This perspective, largely inherited from Jewish tradition, found ready acceptance by a movement that consisted of a clear minority.

Christians stressed the election of their group by God, and their activities displayed the power and presence of God. Both canonical and noncanonical texts from this period assume the special election of the group and a God who organizes and generally dominates the current world order. But explicit depictions of God's relation to imperial, regional, or local power structures are rare, especially compared with the writings of later authors such as Justin Martyr, Tertullian, or Origen, who discuss at length the Christian presence in a pagan world. The author of Luke–Acts remains the notable exception.

Luke and the Christian God

The reader of Luke has no doubt where the power resides in the interactions between the leading members of the movement and imperial and Herodian authorities, Jewish leaders, pagan crowds, and even philosophers. The Christian god controls events and employs human agents to accomplish his designs.[132] From the beginning Luke's narrative reveals the divine plan to the participants, a sharp contrast to Mark's stress on the messianic secret.[133] Several linguistic features show how God already knows the order of events. The use of *pro* prefixes on verbs indicates God's preordained work in the lives of those involved.[134] More pointedly, Luke uses *dei* to stress God's planned activities.[135] Luke here combines Old Testament prophetic tradition with the concept of necessity, which in the Greek worldview is often capable of controlling even the fate of the gods.[136] In Chariton's text, for example, Callirhoe's last act is a prayer to Aphrodite that states that all her toils were necessary (*heimarmenein*). Chariton, however, shows how Tyche's machinations simply play into the hand of Aphrodite. Likewise, God in Luke–Acts stands behind the machinations of present rulers, the action of the representatives of God, and the message contained in the Holy Scriptures.[137] What takes place "is necessary."

Peter's inaugural speech epitomizes the author's effort to show God standing behind the action of the narrative. Jesus' signs and wonders, Peter claims, were done at the behest of God (Acts 2:22), and even Jesus' death was according to the plan and foreknowledge of God (2:23), who intervened and raised Jesus from the dead (2:24). Indeed, Peter says, God had sworn to David that one of his descendants would be put on his throne (2:29). The Holy Spirit, given to Jesus by God, will also be given to those who ask for it (2:33–34). God has foretold all these events through the prophets (3:15 ff.), has raised Jesus from the dead (4:10), and created the universe ("Sovereign Lord, who made the heaven and the earth and the sea and everything in them"; 4:24). Even the imperial, regional, and local power structures embodied in Pontius Pilate, Herod, the Gentiles, and the people of Israel did whatever God had predestined to take place (4:28). Such a tactic proved a potent argument when dealing with competing pagan or Jewish claims. As evidenced through Scripture and revelation, the Christian god had decreed the events that were taking place. Justin Martyr, Tertullian, and others were to use this approach with great effectiveness.

A later speech by Paul before the people of Lystra echoes the theme that God has power over the cosmos itself:

> [Y]ou should turn from these vain things to a living God who made the heaven and the earth and the sea and all that is in them. In past generations he allowed all the nations to walk in their own ways; yet he did not leave himself without witness, for he did good and gave you from heaven rains and fruitful seasons, satisfying your hearts with food and gladness. (Acts 14:15–18)

God, who stands behind all the forces, actions, and creation of this world, falls within the same universal rubric posited for such deities as Isis, Artemis of Ephesus, and Aphrodite of Aphrodisias. The author's emphasis on the universal significance of the Christian deity reflects a growing desire to bolster individual and corporate security in a large and complex world, an attitude reflected at the highest levels of society.[138] Like Chariton, Luke shows his deity to have the kind of universal power capable of dealing with a diverse and sometimes hostile world, a world graphically portrayed in the wanderings of the disciples throughout the Mediterranean basin. The Christian deity stands behind the action in the narrative and maintains ultimate control over disruptive circumstances brought on by corrupt Jewish leaders, hostile crowds, scheming politicians, and even nature.

Luke traces the Christian movement from its inception through the journeys of Paul to Rome during the reign of Nero. Like Josephus in his *Antiquities,* Luke situates his movement within history and within the civic arena in which both writers reside. Luke's portrayal of the Christian movement's encounters with imperial authorities, local pagan elites, Jewish leaders, magicians, philosophers, barbarians, and crowds reflects the bewildering power networks within which the Christian movement had to define itself. Hints of actual contact with such groups already appear in Paul's writings. The Flavio-Trajanic period introduced a new set of issues that the nascent Christian movement had to address: increased promotion by local elites in the Greek East of their civic traditions and deities; increased suspicion of new groups, especially those that had Jewish trappings, because of the Jewish war; and participation in the Christian movement of persons with some status, as evidenced by Luke himself. The latter were no doubt especially concerned to understand how one participates in both the Kingdom of God and the kingdom of caesar. Luke's narrative portrait addresses all of those concerns. The encounters with political authorities by key figures in the movement from Jesus through Paul make abundantly clear that imperial representatives as well as the Herodians found absolutely nothing subversive or illegal about the movement. Suggestions that Luke's portrayal of these encounters was directed as an apologetic toward Roman officials make little sense, especially since the eschatological overtones of the text make clear that imperial rule has only a limited time to continue. Rather, Luke seems to be addressing the type of person to whom Josephus's works would appeal, people who participate in the Roman Empire and who would not find apocalyptic approaches appealing but who want to have a connection with a powerful cosmic benefactor. Luke's narrative provides a symbolic framework whereby people could participate in the movement while navigating a complicated set of power centers. Nevertheless, readers are intended to get a clear message as their narrative heroes encounter imperial power, local and regional power, Jewish power, and so on. The real power is the Christian god; political and religious leaders ignore that at their peril.[139]

CONCLUSION

Local elites in the Greek East drew on the power and prestige of pagan deities as they negotiated relations with other elites in their own community and in nearby cities and regions and with imperial authorities. Certain deities acquired special importance in the negotiations, sometimes because of careful planning and other times due to historical accident. Advocates of a deity stressed the universal significance and power of that deity even when the primary audience was local. Promotion of certain deities such as Artemis of Ephesus and Aphrodite of Aphrodisias proved extremely beneficial politically. More important, connections to the cosmic realm through powerful deities helped local elites define a power relationship, which pragmatically speaking was heavily weighted toward imperial authorities. This was often recognized. One way to reformulate that unequal relationship was to bring another powerful force into the equation, divine power. The close association of elites to that power gave them, at the least, a psychological edge. Rome ruled in cooperation with (and in some cases with the permission of) their deity. For certain cities whose deities the Romans explicitly acknowledged, this paid off handsomely both politically and economically. At the least, the cosmic world was a key part of the symbolic discourse that local elites and their cities used to negotiate their place within imperial power. Chariton and his city, Aphrodisias, fit right into this world. Both texts and monuments depict Aphrodite's power operating across the *oikoumene*.

Three significant historical events affected Jewish identity in the Flavio-Trajanic period and influenced the way Jews dealt with cosmic power. The first was the Jewish revolt in Palestine, which altered the status of Jews as a group in the empire.[140] The destruction of their most powerful symbolic center, the Temple, forced a reevaluation of what constituted proper relations with the divine. The second was the revolt by Jews in the Diaspora against Trajan, which resulted in the complete elimination of Jews in certain areas, notably Egypt. The last was more subtle, the decree of Nerva limiting the *fiscus Iudaicus* to those who openly practiced Judaism. The first two framed a turbulent period for many Jews (though not all). The latter set a precedent that was to identify Jews along more explicitly religious grounds, with far-reaching implications. That the Flavian war had an impact on Jews throughout the empire seems clear, though outside certain areas such as Egypt the archaeological evidence is less than forthcoming. Ostraca from Edfu in Egypt, apparently receipts from paying the *fiscus Iudaicus,* are dated by the year of the emperor and vividly depict what must have been greater imperial intrusion across the empire.[141] The tax may well have been degrading, because slaves, freedmen, and Roman citizens alike were expected to pay.[142] Even nonpracticing Jews had to pay. If M. Goodman is right, Nerva's reform, an apparent reaction to Domitian's vigorous enforcement of the code for practicing and nonpracticing Jews, had the unintended effect of moving Judaism from an ethnic identification to a religious identification.[143] If you said you were a Jew, you were legally a Jew. This also clarified the relation of proselytes, who now could openly declare their Jewish faith or simply associate with it.[144] This emphasis on religious affiliation coincides dramatically with the pagan elites' reclamation of ancient traditions to bolster their connections to ancestral cosmic authorities.

The Jewish response to imperial power and the resurgent activities of local pagan elites varied. The rabbinic schools, with some apparent exceptions, began to focus on the law and tradition as a means to understand the divine activity of God. So does Josephus. Others, however, such as the writers of 2 Baruch and 4 Ezra, understood events as harbingers of an apocalyptic future and the overthrow of the current authorities. Such writings expressed a sense of alienation that no doubt reflects the marginal role some Jews now played within the power structures governing their lives. Changes or the threat of changes often elicit the greatest feelings of alienation even when the changes are minor. Even Jews with a degree of wealth, like Babatha, who to all appearances had taken full advantage of the imperial system after it was established, were drawn, perhaps reluctantly, into the conflict.

Josephus, who generally seeks to emphasize that Jews maintained a united front (albeit a front with misguided representatives), depicts even Tiberius Julius Alexander, the nephew of Philo and prefect of Egypt, as a Jew who did not diligently follow the worship of God.[145] His little aside is part of a much bigger agenda: to define more precisely what constituted proper behavior for Jews, what precisely their relation was to the cosmic order, and how they were to deal with their altered status in the empire. Josephus's *Against Apion* reflects the increased competition that was part of the civic resurgence in the Greek East and that meant an ever present need (from his standpoint) to make clear the unique character of the Jewish god and the Jewish tradition. The implications were significant. Loss of the cosmic thread in the web meant, potentially, a significant loss in the other arenas.

Into this volatile environment of competing symbols of power came the Christians. Many of the Christian symbols surrounding cosmic power develop as part of a debate with some groups in Judaism. Yet Christians, for the most part, wrote for themselves or those attracted to the movement. The writer of Matthew stresses that the believer must adhere to the Jewish tradition, especially the law and purity, the same issues dominating later rabbinic writing. Paul, operating in the Julio-Claudian period, already reflects the beginning of this discussion for the Christian movement. But the boundaries between Jew, Gentile, and Christian were more fluid with Paul. By the writing of Luke–Acts at the end of the century that fluidity apparently became a caricature. In Luke's day Christian movements faced (perhaps only symbolically) Jewish and pagan groups increasingly bent on clarifying their identity in relation to other groups as they perceived them (especially those most closely linked to their own traditions). Christians do not seem to be in the forefront of these discussions until much later. But pagans and, especially, Jews occupied a good deal of space in Christian creations of power.

Jews and Christians negotiated their relations with local elites and imperial power by drawing on cosmic power. Unfortunately, we have scant evidence for Christians beyond their own literary sources to illustrate the complex interactions that must have existed. Our best literary evidence for Jews in this period comes from Josephus, who, like his near contemporary Luke, sought to come to grips with imperial and local elite power networks. Like certain elites in such cities as Aphrodisias and Ephesus, both understood their own deity as a powerful force (if not *the* powerful force) in the universe. Activities by the Romans, by local elites, and by themselves were interpreted through the lens of a deity who governed the universe and who set up structures within which all groups existed. What distinguished the Jewish and Christian groups, as represented by Josephus and Luke, from pagan elites in the Greek East was a symbol system that did not easily tolerate the view of the divine world promoted by those local elites, a view not fully shared by all Jews. In addition, the Jewish revolt of 66–73 and the subsequent use of their defeat in Flavian propaganda made Jewish and, by association, Christian perspectives suspect. It seems no accident, therefore, that both Luke and Josephus drew on language that percolated throughout the Greek East and that stressed the universal power of their respective deities to manage relations with imperial and local authorities alike.

Such rhetorical flourishes offered hope to their audiences of a degree of tolerance by imperial and local authorities, at least within the narrative world that they created. More important, they stressed the all encompassing power of their deities, which those outside (and inside) their believing groups ignore at their peril.

5.

Geography and the Sacred: Establishing Power Across the Roman Oikoumene

Defining space plays a significant role in human society.[1] How a people interpret their geographic surroundings illuminates how they perceive their world and their place in it. Territories (whether a site, a city, a region, or even an empire) were not neutral entities in the Graeco-Roman world. Often they were viewed as "having a relationship with the cosmos, religiously oriented and pervaded with sanctity."[2] In the empire Roman elites must have understood Rome to be the center of the *oikoumene*, aligned with heaven itself, as Vitruvius so aptly illustrates:

> Such being nature's arrangement of the universe, and all these nations being allotted temperaments which are lacking in due moderation, the truly perfect territory, situated under the middle of the heaven, and having on each side the entire extent of the world and its countries, is that which is occupied by the Roman people. . . . Thus the divine mind has allotted to the city of the Roman people an excellent and temperate region in order to rule the world.[3]

Certain areas take on a special character due to complex historical, social, or cultural factors, often with powerful results.[4] This chapter explores how groups in the Greek East created "mental maps" as a means to order their world and to negotiate their place within it.[5] What perception did adherents and detractors have of the distribution of a religion? What subsequent power did adherents perceive as a result? How did geography define the parameters of the sacred (e.g., Jerusalem as the holy city of the Jews or Ephesus as the holy city of Artemis)? What impact did that have on persons outside the sacred boundaries, especially as they negotiated their relationship to imperial, regional, local, and cosmic networks of power?

GEOGRAPHY AND THE SACRED
IN THE PAGAN GREEK EAST

The import of deities associated with sacred areas was not lost on those in the Greek East. Frequently, groups stressed the spread of their deity across the landscape of the Roman *oikoumene*. The actual or presumed distribution of a religious or mythic tradition across the *oikoumene* thereby played an important role in the perception of the power that a tradition wielded. Groups or individuals might also emphasize the inherent power of a particular space, a strategy of territoriality.[6] Deities or traditions linked to specific geographical areas could evoke powerful and sometimes conflicting responses in the Roman Empire. The name "Athens" might elicit the image of a venerable city of philosophers, the home of the goddess Athena, or an officious, meddlesome town dominated by magistrates on the Areopagus (*Chaereas and Callirhoe* 1.11.6). The import of Jerusalem's destruction could signify Roman power,[7] the sinfulness of a nation (Josephus, *BJ* 6.310–15), or the foreshadowing of the New Jerusalem (Rev. 21). The symbolic power of a place encouraged persons to allude to, appropriate, and even to transform the symbol to address the perceived needs of their audience (or themselves). Specific sites, especially religious ones, provided potent and powerful symbolic boundaries. When a symbol transcended its geographic location, it could interact with ancient society through the promotion of insiders or from the recognition of outsiders. Fundamental was the degree of power (local, regional, imperial, cosmic) that a religion or cult was perceived to wield by its promoters, its adherents, and outsiders.[8]

The world of the Greek East in the first centuries of this era was volatile and rife with possibilities for local elites. It was a world, as discussed earlier, in which Roman emperors progressively increased imperial power. The quest for power occurred locally and on an international stage. This process had its roots in the conquests of Alexander and their aftermath, and it took on new life during the Flavio-Trajanic period. Architectural changes illustrate this interaction between the Hellenistic world and imperial rule.

> In the whole body of architecture in Roman lands, the most striking and fundamental change in stylistic direction took place during the latter half of the first century and the early decades of the second. It was then that the sculptured, linear forms of the classical past were first firmly challenged by the canopied volume of the future.[9]

Challenged but not replaced, the classical building styles continued to dominate the landscape of the Greek East. Perhaps typical was the Sebasteion at Aphrodisias, which drew on the classical past rather than the canopied future. The Sebasteion at Aphrodisias was a formidable structure.[10] Anyone strolling through the completed complex in the Flavio-Trajanic period would encounter a powerful symbol of the Roman (and Aphrodisian) "mental map" of the *oikoumene*.[11] Reliefs and statuary that display mythological scenes and emperors in heroic guise dominate the landscape, conveying a sense of the power of Rome integrated with the power of gods.[12] Looking south one would see on reliefs depictions of emperors and gods above mythical scenes; looking north, allegories (e.g., Ocean, Day)[13] with emperors above them. Sacred geography here combines cosmic power (the activities of the gods) with political power in heroic guise.[14] But that was not all. Up to 190 reliefs may also have greeted the visitor. Spaced between the columns were *ethne* reliefs on bases that identified the origin of the group.[15] The *ethne,* as R. R. R. Smith notes, represent nations or groups that had been "simply defeated, or defeated and added to the empire, or brought back into the empire."[16]

The complex displays Roman power, which stretches to the furthest boundaries, including the cosmos itself, as evident in the mythological associations with deities and allegories. But the complex also changes the character of that sacred geography. The displays of the defeated or subjugated *ethne* may be based on models from Rome, but the framework for interpreting such groups is now Aphrodisias.[17] Several aspects of the complex make this evident. The emperors in heroic guise associated with Greek mythology illustrate the framework in which their victories are now understood. The dedication of the complex first to Aphrodite, then the emperors, then the demos, combined with explicit associations in some of the panels of Rome and Aphrodite (including Roma crowning the city), also set the complex within the power of Aphrodite.[18] Indeed, after traversing the long walkway that leads past depictions of emperors in heroic pose defeating enemies, mythic scenes of the gods, and *ethne* relief upon *ethne* relief, the visitor arrives at the temple dedicated to Aphrodite, which is filled with images depicting the power of Rome, the vastness of its empire, and its cosmic associations, all set within the domain of the goddess Aphrodite and her city.[19] One might say that the Aphrodisians have relocated Vitruvius's "truly perfect territory, situated under the middle of the heaven."

In the imperial cult geography and the sacred intersected. Like the cults of the Olympian deities or the cults of Isis and Mithras, the imperial cult initially focused on specific figures, not locations. The imperial cult probably developed from the cult of Roma and Augustus, which was roughly associated with a geographical center, Rome. By the end of the first century, however, the cult of the emperors had evolved to resemble the generic worship of the "gods" practiced in many locations. By the time of Trajan, the Capitoline triad of Jupiter, Juno, and Minerva had become significant in many parts of the Greek East.[20] These diverse representations of divine and political figures had two things in common. They were not site specific (as was, e.g., Artemis of Ephesus, at least in name), yet they had a sacred geography, generally associated with the particular locale in which they were located and, by implication, with Rome, the seat of Roman power. Certain imperial cult centers took on importance that extended beyond their local boundaries. The provincial imperial temple at Ephesus, for example, received dedications from cities and towns a long distance away.[21]

The association of the deity of a space with the Romans increased the power and prestige of the local elites. Moreover, it provided a mechanism by which to interpret Roman rule as operating within a matrix in which their deity played a major role. Geography worked in another way to highlight the prestige and power of a deity and those associated with it. The deity's presence across the *oikoumene* (whether in reality or simply professed locally) confirmed for those who professed allegiance its potent and universal power. Thus, the existence of cult statues of Aphrodite of Aphrodisias across the Roman Empire, as we shall see, suggests that the city's stress on the universal characteristics of their Aphrodite had some impact on its reception.

In the Flavio-Trajanic period, cults and religious movements moved through the Roman Empire, helping to reshape the nature of the empire itself.[22] Newer movements such as the worship of Mithras and Christ as well as established traditions such as the cult of Isis, the city cults of Artemis of Ephesus and Aphrodite of Aphrodisias, and monuments associated with the rural cult of Zeus from Doliche in Commagene and with Jupiter Optimus Maximus Heliopolitanus appeared in many parts of the empire.[23] People often maintained close ties with a particular deity that was linked to their actual or symbolic homeland.[24]

The Artemis cult at Ephesus is a good example. If the finds of her cult statue and cult complexes are any indication, many across the empire sought to associate with the Ephesian Artemis. Simon Price rightly notes that no unified religious system bound such sites together.[25] The degree of religious association in these various places is difficult to determine, as is how the worship of Artemis of Ephesus outside Ephesus factored into the power and prestige of Ephesian elites. Yet, it must have had some significance. Officials of Artemis of Ephesus were stationed at regional sanctuaries of the goddess.[26] Numerous writers, including Luke, indicate that the reputation of the Ephesian Artemis was considerable and widespread (Acts 19:27). And an inscription, though late (162/63 or 163/64 C.E.), indicates that Artemis's appearances throughout the *oikoumene* were very important for local elites at Ephesus.

> The deity over our city, Artemis, is honored not only in her own city which she has made more famous than all other cities through her own divinity, but also by Greeks and foreigners; everywhere shrines and sanctuaries have been dedicated, temples founded and altars erected to her because of her vivid manifestations.[27]

Power resides in the intimate relation local elites believe the goddess has established with Ephesus and in the fact that that association is acknowledged "everywhere" by the founding of associated religious sites. The perception that the cult extends across the *oikoumene* and the reality of the spread of the cult largely coincide in this instance. Shrines and cult statuettes of the goddess appear throughout much of the Roman Empire.[28]

Aphrodite of Aphrodisias offers another example. Bronze and ceramic statuettes of Aphrodite of Aphrodisias have been found in much of the Roman Empire (including Portugal, Rome, Ephesus, Athens, Leptis Magna, and even Baalbek), many apparently distributed during the second century.[29] These cult statues may have been purchased as religious souvenirs, paralleling the vigorous promotion by supporters of cults such as Artemis of Ephesus.[30] This contrasts with the view of R. Fleischer and M. Squarciapino that emigrating Aphrodisians carried the image of the goddess from their home city.[31] To be sure, some statues were dispersed in the first century B.C.E. when we have evidence for such emigrations, and Aphrodisians no doubt maintained their ties to the goddess of their home city when they joined the major influx of citizens from Asia Minor into Rome during this period. But most replicas of Aphrodite of Aphrodisias date to the second century C.E., which coincides with the full blossoming and expansion of cults across the Graeco-Roman world. Peter Noelke persuasively shows that the cult reached beyond the orbit of Aphrodisias and of Asia Minor.[32] Assured explanations of the religious function must await the discovery of dedicatory inscriptions in context with a cult statue, but the widespread dissemination of these statues indicates that those who had them acknowledged the goddess of this locale to some degree. Perhaps, as Noelke argues, the statues were spread by soldiers and civilians who had acquired a taste for eastern religions; evidence from Aphrodisias suggests that these groups were attracted to its cult of Aphrodite.[33] Clearly, the spread of Aphrodite of Aphrodisias parallels the vigorous activity of a variety of cults in the Flavio-Trajanic period and beyond, notably the cults of Artemis of Ephesus, Mithras, Isis, Men, and Dionysus.[34] The veneration of the goddess Aphrodite of Aphrodisias was part of a larger enterprise in which local elites promoted ancient civic organizations or archaic deities (whether oriental or Homeric/Hesiodic in perceived origin) associated with their civic centers, a pattern developed to a high degree in the Flavio-Trajanic period, as a means to achieve a modicum of power and prestige within the Roman web of power. Both Artemis of Ephesus and Aphrodite of Aphrodisias had important links to Roman rule, and the presence of the cult statues reflects their popularity in the Roman Empire.

The cult center dedicated to Aphrodite of Aphrodisias appropriated myths that had originated at other cult centers of the goddess; the cult's proponents tapped into mythic and religious symbols that lay beyond the boundaries of the city. Such symbols and myths proliferated. For example, Dionysius of Halicarnassus relates that during Aeneas's journey from Troy to the future site of Rome, he built a temple to Aphrodite at each major stop, including Thrace (*Roman Antiquities* 1.49.4), the island of Cythera (1.50.1), Leucus (1.50.4), and Actium, where, Dionysius notes, a temple to Aphrodite and Aeneas still exists (1.50.4). Such a tale helped explain the multiplicity of cults for a single deity, and of course, it gave the cults an added legitimacy to be linked with Aeneas, a figure of great importance for Augustus at the time Dionysius was writing. Interpretation of such myths, however, occurred within the unique presentation of a city or a writer. For Aphrodisias, circumstantial evidence for its deployment of myths and symbols comes from letters written by emperors that acknowledge Aphrodite of Aphrodisias as the key source of the city's fame. Aphrodite was also promoted regionally as the *homonoia* coin series and the distribution of the coins and the cult statues make clear.[35]

The spreading of deities across the Roman Empire is of course not limited to the Flavio-Trajanic period. The cult of Apollo, for example, had a widespread following in the Greek East from an early period, but only certain sites achieved the necessary notoriety to serve as oracular centers. The Greek sanctuary at Delphi remains the most famous example, serving as the center of the *oikoumene* in the ancient Ionian conception of the world.[36] Sanctuaries at Didyma and Claros in Asia Minor also had significant followings across the empire. Didyma, in fact, which had long been within the territory of Miletus, received questions for its oracle from Rhodes even though Rhodes had its own magnificent temple to Apollo.[37]

Why did cities display devotion to particular deities, often with great gusto and at times with such effectiveness that a deity's importance spread beyond the city, even attracting the attention of detractors? R. MacMullen argues that little evidence exists for "organized or conscious evangelizing in paganism"; in other words, no attempt was made to proselytize, present a system of beliefs, change people's lives, or convince people that the deity existed. Announcements of the deity, he argues, focused on the advantages of coming to the shrine to experience "healing, foreknowledge, or a feast."[38] Yet the distinction MacMullen makes seems a bit pat. MacMullen implies that pagan behavior contrasts with that of Christians, who do proselytize or evangelize. Yet most Christian material from the first and second centuries was relevant only to persons who already believed. Even the author of Luke–Acts, arguably the most cosmopolitan of the Christian authors, probably addresses his material to the converted. To be sure, he describes the conversions of Gentiles and Jews to the Christian god, but that is little different from the dedications made by countless individuals to innumerable deities across the Greek East. The criteria MacMullen uses to make his distinction seem Judaeo-Christian centered, which causes him to downplay a crucial element for many of these groups, the display of their deity's power. The reasons for presentations of the deity may have varied, as MacMullen rightly recognizes. Local elites in Ephesus may have emphasized the antiquity and mysteries of Artemis to heighten their own power and prestige, to gain prominence for their city, or to garner economic and political benefits from the imperial center or power. Their promotion of the perceived beneficence of their deity does not necessarily represent crass manipulation on their part. No doubt many, if not most, who promoted a deity like Artemis of Ephesus actually believed in her power to affect events. It seems futile to dismiss such activities as failing to meet standards adapted from later Christian activity. Indeed, New Testament writers often stress the healing power of the divine, the foreknowledge of God, and communal participation, the very things MacMullen argues are promoted by pagan cults.

Finally, some qualifications must be made concerning MacMullen's statement that no set system of beliefs or uniformity existed in the presentation and worship of a particular pagan deity (e.g., nothing like Aphroditism, Dionysiacism, Isaicism occurred).[39] Again, this appears to presuppose a Christianity that had an identifiable set of beliefs and that was largely uniform across the Roman Empire. Perusal of recent literature analyzing the New Testament and the spread of Christianity shows how diverse Christianity was in its beliefs and that it was anything but uniform. Indeed, most ancients appeared initially to consider it a form of Judaism, at least until the end of the first century.[40] Nevertheless, no one would confuse any form of Judaism or any form of Christianity that we know (with the exception of Gnosticism perhaps) with one of the pagan cults, even though they have many similarities (e.g., the power of the deity to affect crowds, the epiphany of the god). That is, there is something clearly definable about Judaism and Christianity. Yet the same could be said for many pagan cults. Few in antiquity would mistake Artemis of Ephesus with Aphrodite of Aphrodisias even though their iconographic presentations are similar. Certainly some groups claimed that other deities were simply their own deity by other names (e.g., the Isis aretalogy that states she is also Aphrodite, etc.). But generally speaking, the symbolism and iconography associated with the presentation of a deity would be apparent to the viewer and would draw on traditions that were common parlance in the empire, in the region, or in the locale. Aphrodite may acquire certain attributes based on a particular locale, but these did not disguise the more widely accepted attributes associated with her. Persons in antiquity had mental maps that covered the nature and location of deities, too.

Of course, the problem becomes less acute if one simply associates the deity with a particular town rather than with mythic traditions in literature. Thus, Artemis of Ephesus, Aphrodite of Aphrodisias, and the Jewish god of Jerusalem each have their specific symbols and iconographic program recognizable throughout the empire or at least to those in or near their locale. MacMullen recognizes this when he notes that duplication of physical features derives from "worshipers' sense of a sort of unitary character in cult."[41] Yet, it proves little to assert that because regional differences existed in a cult "no one enjoyed authority more than anyone else over questions of correct liturgy, iconography or temple construction."[42] The same could be said of Christian and Jewish groups in the first two centuries. Posing the issues in this way implies dependence on a model from the third and fourth centuries, when a particular religion, Christianity, came to dominate the political as well as religious scene. Even the imperial cult had no uniformity throughout the Greek East.[43] More useful is the fact that such cults display the power of their deities, which seems to demarcate their activities. In that sense they do "evangelize" or offer a "good message" of the power and beneficence of their deities. A type of collective presentation did occur from many groups. Conversion to a new way of being? No. Explicit proselytizing of one's deity? Probably not on any systematic basis.[44] Presentation or profession of the power of one's deity (often throughout the *oikoumene*) and those associated with it? A resounding yes.

Thus geography became part of the symbolic vocabulary of groups who wished to highlight the power and prestige of a particular deity and by association their own power and prestige. Some cities had deities with long-standing associations recognized throughout the empire (Jerusalem and the Jewish god, Delphi and Apollo, Doliche and Zeus, Artemis and Ephesus, Demeter and Eleusis). The symbolic and sacred focal point of power was the local site. Local elites promoted that power; others responded by offering sacrifices and prayers, making pilgrimages, or even establishing a similar or related cult in their own town. Local elites stressed these connections in part because it showed the widespread power of their deity. By the second century a number of these local deities had spread to many parts of the Greek East, satisfying at least their local adherents' criterion of universal power across a world grown large. Not surprisingly, the increased prestige of these deities (at least from the local elites' perspective) coincides with greater participation in local, regional, and imperial politics by local elites throughout the Greek East.

Some cities in the Greek East had no venerable tradition upon which to draw. Several, like Aphrodisias, devised other strategies. Aphrodisias stressed its deity's connection to emperors from the Julio-Claudian family, who had a longtime association with Aphrodite as the *promotor,* or first mother of the family. In effect, Aphrodisian elites capitalized on ancient and accepted traditions associated with Aphrodite. Thus, Aphrodite's famous birth at Cyprus and relationship to Aeneas could be legitimately appropriated in the iconography of the city. Use of ancient and venerable myths from other locations need not devalue the importance of a local deity. Indeed, the myths simply confirmed for her adherents what the special statue of Aphrodite of Aphrodisias embodied; the goddess had power throughout the *oikoumene,* a power that she uniquely bestowed on Aphrodisias, its local elites, and those who wisely chose to associate with them, notably the Romans and surrounding cities and territories.

The Sebasteion at Aphrodisias again provides an exemplar. Its scenes of emperors defeating their foes and its mythological scenes of the gods portray iconographically the vast expanse of the empire and its people under divinely sanctioned imperial rule. This fits the Roman perception of a world divided into nations and *ethne,* subservient to Roman power.[45] But that is not all. The complex, dedicated first to Aphrodite, then to the emperors, and then to the demos of the city shows how sacred geography can be nuanced to fit the needs of local elites. The complex depicts the power of Rome, but within a physical and symbolic space defined by Aphrodite and by her special city, Aphrodisias. The local elites who dedicated the complex and the demos, to whom it is also dedicated, participate in the divinely sanctioned power of Rome. Sacred geography, in this instance an imperial cult complex, becomes one vehicle by which local elites (as represented by the dedicants and the demos) negotiate their own power within the cosmic and imperial webs of power as symbolized in the complex. The location of this geographic symbol of imperial and divine power in Aphrodisias allows the local elites to associate with, if not define, that power.

Sacred space in the Sebasteion also defines the boundary between the civilized world and the area outside, in particular, barbarian regions. In several panels, the emperors in Greek guise are shown subduing the barbarians, a presentation that displays the superiority of imperial power and, of course, the superiority of those associated with it, in this case the Greek-educated Aphrodisians.[46]

As noted earlier, cults such as those associated with Isis,[47] Mithras, Dionysus, and the emperors had no central location; nevertheless, it is clear in their iconography and epigraphic records that their adherents often stressed their deities' universal power across the *oikoumene,* if not the cosmos. Certain sites could carry more importance than others (e.g., imperial worship at Ephesus), but the power operative here was not associated with a geographic center as much as with a divine personality (although even Isis was generally seen as coming from Egypt, Dionysus from Greece, the emperors from Rome, Mithras from the East [Persia?]). A cult at a particular location that had the proper combination of local promotion, empirewide connections, powerful local elites, and a long-established presence could even approach the kind of prestige achieved by Artemis of Ephesus. Indeed, Isis and Serapis made inroads into many cities and towns in Asia Minor, as is clear through local coin issues and such popular fare as the second-century romance by Xenophon of Ephesus. Did persons who worshiped such deities at a particular site understand themselves as part of a larger movement, albeit one with local peculiarities? Every indication suggests that they did. Although the emperor cult (and the other cults) had no apparent systematic theology, the emperors nevertheless were viewed as conveying power and prestige upon those who supported them. In other words, local manifestations of the deity had universal implications for local adherents. Such manifestations were linked to the political and social power networks of the locale. The prestige of a local cult was dependent on those who belonged to it and who promoted it. Thus the Isis cult in Rome and Pompeii could flourish because of the active support of the Flavians (notably Vespasian and Titus); the Mithras cult, through the close connections with the army.[48] The appearance of a cult, whether from the East or one of the Olympian deities, was seen by some writers as a sign of the universal power (and, of course, the prestige) of the deity and those associated with it, features that become clear in Chariton's *Chaereas and Callirhoe.*

Chariton of Aphrodisias and Geography: The Distribution of Power

Geographical change is often suggested as a key structural feature of the ancient romance.[49] Travel affords an opportunity for diverse and exciting action that creates tension and anticipation for readers.[50] In Chariton's text, travel across the breadth of the Mediterranean by the hero and heroine highlights the universal presence and antiquity of the cult of Aphrodite. Apparently drawing on an elongated version of the Greek world, the old Ionian view, Chariton treats the reader to a nonstop barrage of sites associated with Aphrodite.[51] As Callirhoe journeys from west to east, she encounters numerous temples of Aphrodite and their worshipers. Chariton opens his account with Callirhoe in a procession to the temple of Aphrodite in Syracuse during the public festival of the goddess.[52] When Callirhoe is carried by pirates to Miletus, she soon discovers a shrine to Aphrodite on the estate of her future husband, Dionysius, who holds the goddess in special honor (2.2.5). Much of the activity in the area centers on the shrine. Even Callirhoe's trip to Babylon provides an occasion for the author to stress Aphrodite's presence when even barbarian leaders acknowledge the power of Aphrodite. Stateira, the queen of Babylon, venerates the goddess (5.9.1), and Artaxerxes, the Persian king, offers sacrifices so that Aphrodite might intervene on his behalf with Eros (6.2.4).[53]

Chariton has both hero and heroine visit famous ancient cult centers of Aphrodite, notably, one on the island of Aradus (7.5.1) and the other at Paphos in Cyprus, which Chariton remarks was renowned in antiquity as the birthplace of Aphrodite (8.2.8). As noted earlier, ample evidence suggests that a belief in the antiquity of a cult was one of the prerequisites to the acceptance and maintenance of its power during the imperial period.[54] Chariton reflects that attitude as he sketches the journey of Chaereas and Callirhoe throughout much of the known world. During their travels the universal significance and presence of Aphrodite become clear to crowds, political leaders, and, most important, to the reader; even barbarians at Babylon recognize the power of this goddess through her representative Callirhoe. The continual appearance of cult centers and shrines of Aphrodite at every major juncture of the narrative establishes for the reader a symbolic landscape dominated by the goddess.

Key turning points in the narrative occur at sacred sites associated with Aphrodite. Callirhoe meets Chaereas on the way to the temple of Aphrodite, the same place where Callirhoe later asks Aphrodite to reunite them. At the shrine of Aphrodite on the estate of Dionysius, Callirhoe first meets her second husband, Dionysius, and dedicates her child; here also Chaereas learns the whereabouts of Callirhoe. At Aradus, Callirhoe weeps before the statue of Aphrodite and asks for knowledge of Chaereas (7.5.1–2). Chaereas sacrifices to the temple of Aphrodite on Cyprus and receives good omens from the priests, who, Chariton says, were also prophets (8.2.8 ff.). Chariton ends his narrative with Callirhoe at the foot of the statue of Aphrodite in Syracuse asking never to be separated from Chaereas again.

Geography and the sacred are integral to the fabric of Chariton's narrative. Temples of Aphrodite serve as places where prayers are offered and answered, where the antiquity of the Aphrodite cult is affirmed, and where the universal nature of the cult is verified. Callirhoe's journeys display Aphrodite's presence and power across the *oikoumene* and the ancient significance of Aphrodite and her cult. The presentation would not be lost on a readership thoroughly embedded in a culture replete with similar iconographic and literary presentations. Chariton's stress on a classical landscape that depicts the Greek worldview in its glory coincided with a perspective that had increasing popularity in the Flavio-Trajanic period throughout the Greek East.

THE JEWS OF THE DIASPORA:
THE POWER OF GEOGRAPHY

Jews across the Graeco-Roman world operated within a landscape dominated by pagan symbols. Yet they often drew on the symbolic power of a geographic center far removed from them. Many Jews prior to the first Jewish war had strong connections to Judaea and the religious base in Jerusalem.[55] Certainly, the Temple tax indicates this connection both from the Jewish perspective and in the minds of the Romans, who, after the first revolt, declared that all Jews were to pay in its stead a special tax administered by a Roman procurator, the *fiscus Iudaicus*.[56] As a key center, the Temple often drew on an adapted Ionian model of the world. The Ionian model understood the world to be circular, with three great continents: Europe, Asia, and Africa. At the center of the world was Delphi. As Philip Alexander argues, Jews replaced Delphi with a new center, Jerusalem.[57] Josephus notes that some people called Jerusalem the navel (*omphalos*) of the country (*BJ* 3.52).[58] In the Book of Jubilees the author draws on the table of nations listed in Genesis 10 and reinterprets it along the Ionian model. Thus, the three sons of Noah are equated with the three major continents: Japheth = Europe, Shem = Asia, and Ham = Libya (Africa).

Another model also circulated, apparently influenced by the Babylonian maps of the world. This suggests for Alexander that at least two schools of early Jewish geography existed, one that looked toward the east and one that looked toward the west.[59] A remarkable example of the eastern version may be found in a Tibetan map that has as its center the capital of Cyrus the Great, Pasargadae. Cyrus retained an important symbolic presence throughout antiquity, especially for classical authors. The map that celebrates the center of the world as Pasargadae is inscribed in Tibetan and appears in the Tibetan Shang-Shung dictionary, which consists of Buddhist teachings translated from the Shang-Shung dialect of northwest Tibet into Tibetan. The map is a rectangle, surrounded by a sea and oriented toward the east, filled with small rectangles in which the geographic names are written in the Tibetan script. David Stronach has noted that the date of the map seems to go back to the third or second centuries B.C.E.; because the southwest corner of the map locates Alexandria, the map cannot be much earlier than 300 B.C.E. In addition, the map fails to mention "the Queen Rome," which Stronach notes is cited in a later Tibetan map. The map includes a number of significant sites, notably in the west the city of Lanlin, which appears to correspond with Jerusalem.[60]

The map, which was probably adapted from a world map composed in Iran, shows starkly how the same area (in this case, Jerusalem) can be perceived in different ways. From the Ionian perspective, Jerusalem is part of the eastern hinterlands. In the Jewish adaptation of the Ionian system, it is the omphalos, or center of the world; in the eastern map that centered on Iran, it swings to the western reaches of the Parthian Empire.

Jerusalem, even after its destruction in 70 C.E., remained a powerful symbol for many Jews. As Philo of Alexandria observes in the early part of the first century, Jerusalem was

> the mother city not of one country Judaea but of most of the others in virtue of the colonies sent out at diverse times to the neighboring lands Egypt, Phoenicia, the part of Syria called the Hollow and the rest as well and the lands lying far apart, Pamphylia, Cilicia, most of Asia up to Bithynia and the corners of

Pontus, similarly also Europe, Thessaly, Boeotia, Macedonia, Aetolia, Attica, Argos, Corinth, and most of the best parts of Peloponnese. (*Legatio* 281–82)

The list is reminiscent of the one in Acts 2, which depicts Jews from across the empire gathering in Jerusalem on Pentecost. Jerusalem carried powerful, even cosmic, overtones.[61] It connected groups that may have had little in common except for a similar reverence for the city. Such lists emphasize the breadth of the movement.

Allegiance to the sacred center, Jerusalem, could strain relations with local elites or Roman authorities. The concession given Diaspora Jews to send tribute to Jerusalem proved too much for the Roman Flaccus, who in the first century B.C.E. confiscated money sent there by Jewish communities in Asia Minor. Cicero, in defending this confiscation, argues that Jewish privileges in this area were an egregious breach of Roman sovereignty and arrogant as well.[62] The sacred center in Jerusalem pulling Jews toward allegiance conflicted with the Roman center (at least in the arguments of Cicero), creating a tension never fully resolved. In 4 Maccabees, probably written in the first century C.E., the Temple serves as sort of a bank for private citizens to place their money (4:3). When the governor of the Seleucid king attempts to take the funds, economics and sacred space coalesce:

> Then the priests and the women and children made supplication to God in the temple to defend his holy place, which was being desecrated; and when Apollonius, with his armed soldiery, marched up to seize the moneys, angels on horseback appeared from heaven with flashing armor and filled them with fear and trembling. (4 Macc. 4:9–10)[63]

The Temple even provided divine protection for the savings of private citizens. Temple imagery also kept cropping up in Christian and rabbinic literature in the first and second centuries even after its destruction, which confirms the continual and potent symbolic power of the Temple.

Prior to its destruction, the Temple had powerful political associations. Josephus describes the tension between Roman and Jewish authorities to control this territory, epitomized in the struggle to have complete control over the high priest's garments. Clothing played a significant role in depicting various power relationships within society, and the concern over who controlled the high priest's garments, garments that had their own connection to cosmic geography, was no minor disagreement.[64]

Prior to the destruction of the Temple, Jerusalem served as a magnet in another way. Some Jews of the Diaspora felt a strong desire to be buried in Jerusalem. Most famous are the tombs of Helene of Adiabene and her family, recent converts to Judaism. Certainly a combination of factors are at work in such burials including the wealth of the individuals, depth of commitment, and opportunity. Underlying their desire was the symbolic captital associated with the city itself.[65] After the Roman destruction of the city in 70 C.E., the process became more difficult. The Romans' refusal to allow entrance into the city illustrated their awareness of the powerful pull this "place" had for Jews. Iconographic and verbal displays of symbolic discourse continue to center on the Temple and Mount Zion both before and after the destruction in 70 C.E.[66]

In the search for equally powerful sacred centers, many Jewish groups focused on the law and the synagogue. The Torah came to play an increasingly important role in synagogues; more elaborate Torah shrines and sacred portals were built beginning toward the end of the first century C.E.[67] The sacred portal served on tombs and in synagogues, as J. Lightstone observes, to mark "these locations as gateways to heaven, propitious (sacred) places for mediation between the divine and earthly realms. Indeed, the framing of these portals by cultic objects such as incense shovels, candelabra, shofar, and palm branches (lulav) lends further weight to such an interpretation of the portal motif."[68]

As early as the first century B.C.E. with the Tomb of the Patriarchs and extending through the third and subsequent centuries with the tombs of revered personages such as Rabbi Judah ha-Nasi at Beth She-arim, Jews created powerful "sacred spaces" that mediated the divine and mundane world.[69] The tomb of Judah ha-Nasi, who compiled the Mishnah during the Severan period, functioned in much the same way as saints' graves in the fifth and subsequent centuries, which exerted a strong pull on Christians who wished to associate with the power represented in a particular saint.[70] But the symbolic power of the Temple never completely faded.[71] A significant part of the Mishnah concerns Temple practice and sacrifices; because the Temple was destroyed, a symbolic reimaging occurred that emphasized the unifying role of the law.[72] During the Bar Kochba revolt, in 132–35 C.E., Temple symbolism played a key role in the coinage minted and contributed to the war effort. Recent archaeological and archival work at the northern Black Sea port of Chersonesus has revealed the significance of the Temple even in that frontier region of the Roman Empire. An inscription, written in Hebrew, was carved on a plaster wall probably associated with a public building (possibly a synagogue). The inscription dates somewhere between the second and fifth century C.E. and apparently mentions Jerusalem in the first line. If so, it represents a rare, if not unique, occurrence in the archaeological record.[73]

Jews in the Flavio-Trajanic period had no physical symbolic center. The Temple and Jerusalem were destroyed. Further, the symbol that had linked the sacred and geography lay in ashes and now served as part of the Flavians' own ideological geography, the conquest and triumph over a wayward Judaea and the reestablishment of peace and power over the Roman *oikoumene*. But Jerusalem never really faded as a powerful geographic symbol for Jews. It became an ideal, a vision, a possibility that dominated the thought of certain groups. Future restoration, a future sacred geography, shaped, if not dominated, the thought world of some groups. When Bar Kochba revolted against Rome, his coins bore the hope of a restored Temple, something that had plenty of precedents in the biblical tradition. Thus even without a physical temple, for some Jewish groups the sacred geography associated with it structured their understanding of the world in which they lived and the future they hoped would come.

No one offers a better look at the symbolic power of the Temple and of "sacred geography" within first-century Judaism than Josephus. The issues were central to Josephus, who had to make sense of the loss of two key symbolic geographic centers of Judaism, the Temple and Jerusalem.

Josephus and Geography

Josephus's works are replete with images that show the continuing power of the Temple for him in the latter part of the first century. His works also emphasize the spread of Jews across not only the Roman Empire but areas outside its borders. Both concerns lent credence to Josephus's connection of geography and the sacred. Further, the Temple and its destruction had universal import by emphasizing the allegiance that Jews pay to the Temple from all parts of the ancient world. This makes clear that the power of the Jewish god moves beyond the specific locale of Jerusalem and pervades the entire *oikoumene*. These points are best summarized in Josephus's rhetorical broadsides against those belittling the Jewish movement. In *Against Apion* he argues that

> unity and identity of religious belief, perfect uniformity in habits and customs, produce a very beautiful concord in human character. Among us alone will be heard no contradictory statements about God, such as are common among other nations, not only on the lips of ordinary individuals under the impulse of some passing moods, but even boldly propounded by philosophers; some putting forward crushing arguments against the very existence of God, others depriving him of his providential care for humankind. Among us alone will be seen no difference in the conduct of our lives. With us all act alike, all profess the same doctrine about God, one which is in harmony with our law and affirms that all things are under his eye. (*CA* 2.179–81)

To be sure, Josephus overstates Jewish unity on attitudes toward God and the law. Nevertheless, the perception of unity was crucial for a group that had served as the villains in the Flavian propaganda campaign for over a decade.

The Temple plays an important role in Josephus's interpretation of the war against Rome and, more broadly, of the Jewish attitude toward the Roman Empire. In his *Jewish War,* he addresses why something so central to Jewish identity has been destroyed. His reasoning has a long history in Jewish thought; the destruction resulted from the sin and arrogance of the people and in particular of those who had led the revolt. "God it is then, God Himself, who with the Romans is bringing the fire to purge His temple and exterminating a city so laden with poisons" (*BJ* 6.110). Josephus makes clear the cosmic geography of the temple. The colors of the tapestry covering the entrance to the sanctuary symbolized the universe itself (*BJ* 5.212–13). The interior contained "universally renowned" works of art: a lampstand, table, and an incense altar. Each symbolized the universal presence and power of God throughout the cosmos. The seven-branched lamp represented the planets, the twelve loaves on the altar represented the Zodiac and the year, the thirteen spices on the altar of incense came from sea and land (both desert and inhabited), signifying "all things are of God and for God" (*BJ* 5.216–18). Plated with gold, the exterior shown brilliantly in the sunshine like a snow–clad mountain (*BJ* 5.222–23). The dress of God's attendants, especially the high priest's, displayed the universal power of God embodied in this place (*BJ* 5.231–37). Josephus saw its destruction as the end of the "most marvellous edifice which we have ever seen or heard of, whether we consider its structure, its magnitude, the richness of its every detail, or the reputation of its Holy Places" (*BJ* 6.267).

The destruction of the Temple and of the sacred city Jerusalem had an inevitable character for Josephus. His explanation nevertheless epitomizes the power of its geographical significance and the universal spread of the movement even in this high moment of despair: "[N]either its antiquity, nor its ample wealth, nor its people spread over the whole habitable world, nor yet the great glory of its religious rites, could aught avail to avert its ruin. Thus ended the siege of Jerusalem" (*BJ* 6.442). Those who invented lies about what went on in the Temple, Josephus argues, disgrace one's intelligence, especially in belittling "a temple of world-wide fame and commanding sanctity" (*CA* 2.79).

The Temple served as a sacred locus for God's activity; it displayed the universal power and prestige that made key holy sites so prestigious in the ancient world. Titus himself, Josephus argues, recognized the grandeur of the site and did everything he could to save it. But for the sin of those Jewish revolutionaries, God would have not withdrawn his support and allowed its destruction. Josephus's narrative allows the symbolic power of the Temple to continue through his narrative. His narrative symbols illustrate a renegotiation of Jewish participation within the Roman Empire. In addition, Josephus's allusions to the widespread character of the Jewish movement ensure that his audience recognizes the power and prestige of the Jews, not only through history (as his *Antiquities* amply argues) but throughout the *oikoumene* as well.

CHRISTIANS AND GEOGRAPHY

The Christian movement had no actual geographic center from its inception through the Hadrianic period. Jerusalem and images associated with it, however, provided a plethora of significant symbols. Christians transferred the power of such symbols to the ideal realm, made easier by the Temple's destruction.[74] The Letter to the Hebrews devotes considerable space to contrasting the new high priest, Jesus, with the earthly high priest in the Temple (9:11–14). Drawing on Platonic imagery, it depicts the Temple as a "copy and shadow of the heavenly sanctuary" (Heb. 8:50). Sacred geography moves from a particular location where people mediate their relation with God to Christ, who "has entered, not into a sanctuary made with hands, a copy of the true one, but into heaven itself, now to appear in the presence of God on our behalf" (Heb. 9:24).[75]

The Book of Revelation talks about a new Jerusalem as a way to make sense of current conditions, in particular the persecution or perceived persecution of the Christians (Rev. 21:2–3). The new city has no temple because the temple will be God and Jesus (Rev. 21:22). Sacred space moves from a specific geographic location to spiritual centers: heaven and Jesus. In the early Christian movement, the Christian communities were the geographic sacred centers. Christians met in small groups, generally at "house-churches," made available by wealthy members of the groups. In the second and subsequent centuries, some of these churches expanded to become sacred gathering places in their own right.[76] By the latter part of the second century, this began to change as the movement located certain "pilgrimage" sites associated with Jesus, a practice that gained great impetus during the reign of Constantine in the fourth century.[77] But in the first two centuries, sacred geography consisted largely of the future Kingdom of God and the faithful remnants who existed throughout the Roman world. Jerusalem held symbolic capital but largely as a vehicle for promoting the central tenet of their faith, that Jesus was the Messiah already come.[78] The lack of a central symbolic geographic center allowed the movement to spread without encumbrances (or associations with locally based cults). This had the consequence, however, of putting it in competition or at least tension with local cults, which was recognized by Pliny in his letters to Trajan and portrayed in Acts in the encounter at Ephesus between Christians and followers of the Ephesian Artemis.

Some Christian communities and writers emphasized the spread of the movement through the *oikoumene,* a concern, we shall see, of special import to the author of Luke–Acts. Even texts apparently addressed to relatively specific groups such as the Gospels of Matthew and John indicate a concern (or at least an awareness of a concern) for the movement's spread among the Gentiles.[79] The movement, of course, held this attitude fairly early, as indicated by Peter's encounter with Paul and other Christians at Antioch (Gal. 2) and, of course, Paul's own mission across much of the eastern portion of the Roman Empire. Luke shows clearly how the movement has spread across the breadth of the *oikoumene,* a point that adds credibility to the author's claim that the movement has universal and worldwide significance.

Luke and Geography

Luke structures his two volumes using images of geography and the sacred.[80] The travel of his main characters across the Roman *oikoumene* show the reach of the movement "to the ends of the earth." He also locates the movement at key geographical spots sacred to others, such as Jerusalem, Athens, and Ephesus. In each case Luke demonstrates for his readers how the Christian movement is clearly superior to the movements encountered. In a sense the sacred spaces (assuming the philosophical tradition at Athens is a kind of sacralization) are shown as wanting.[81] Luke redefines the significance of the Temple by moving it out of the control of the Jewish leadership and, in effect, placing its symbolic power and that of the city of Jerusalem under the control of the Christians. Thus, Peter preaches at the Temple, and confrontations take place between the disciples and the Temple authorities (paralleling Jesus' earlier confrontation and cleansing of the Temple). Stephen's citation of Isaiah that God does not reside in "houses made with human hands" (Acts 7:48) condemns the wrong-headed practices associated with the Temple, though not the Temple itself, an assessment with which Josephus would have agreed.[82]

Jerusalem becomes the locus of the Pentecost and outpouring of the Holy Spirit (Acts 2), the beginning of the outreach to the Roman Empire, the convening of the Jerusalem Council, which set forth the criteria by which the mission to outsiders was to be handled, and, most important, the symbolic center from which the movement sprang. Luke reappropriates the powerful symbols of Jerusalem and the Temple for this nascent movement, an approach followed, albeit along different lines, in the Letter to the Hebrews and the Book of Revelation. As Loveday Alexander has argued, the mention of the names of the persons who are affected by the Holy Spirit in Acts 2 shows the influence of Jerusalem as the sacred center of the geographic world, much as was seen in the Jewish tradition, especially the Book of Jubilees. The names in this table of nations reflect the cardinal directions emanating from Jerusalem: "the East (Parthians, Medes, Elamites, and residents of Mesopotamia), the Center (Judaea), the North (Cappadocia, Pontus, Asia, Phrygia, and Pamphylia), the Southwest (Egypt and Libya), the West (Rome and Crete), and the South (Arabia)."[83] Indeed, the list of nations attending Pentecost may even have had astrological significance.[84] Luke portrays through words what the Temple at Jerusalem and the Sebasteion at Aphrodisias sought to display visually: a sacred center with universal, even cosmic, significance. The long-noted significance of Jerusalem in the Luke–Acts narrative as part of a geographic structure of the narrative is the author's attempt to show that the movement emanated from Judaism's sacred center. He reflects the continuing symbolic power of the city.

Like his pagan and Jewish counterparts, Luke emphasizes the antiquity and power of the Christian movement, which has spread throughout the *oikoumene*. He does not accomplish this by mentioning a plethora of Christian temples or shrines (as Chariton does) or through the appropriation of ancient Greek myths. Rather, Luke emphasizes, like Josephus, the movement's incorporation of established Jewish patterns: the writings of Scripture and the Jewish character of the movement. The speeches of Peter, James, Stephen, and Paul in Acts make direct links between Christ and the Covenant begun with Abraham and continued through Moses. The promise and fulfillment motif noted by many scholars[85] and the constant retelling of the Jesus story in light of Old Testament prophets and scriptures highlight the antiquity of the Christian movement. Luke also has Jesus, the apostles, and disciples go to synagogues and people's houses throughout the known world, often making converts at each stop.[86] In Acts, Paul's last speech occurs before a Jewish crowd in a synagogue. Not only does Luke associate the Christian movement with an acknowledged ancient religion, but he shows his readership a movement that, like the Jews (or like the cults of Aphrodite), dots the landscape of the ancient world.[87]

The structure of Acts, which begins at Jerusalem and ends at Rome, further emphasizes the universal scope of the mission; indeed, God creates and rules over all aspects of society. The travel of the apostles and disciples helps expand the movement.[88] Like the journeys of Callirhoe in Chariton's text, which reveal the power of Aphrodite extending from Callirhoe's native Syracuse to the "ends of the earth" (barbarian Babylon) during the fifth and fourth centuries B.C.E., travel in Luke–Acts provides the occasion for the power of the Christian deity to manifest itself throughout the *oikoumene*.

Luke ends his narrative with a sea voyage that allows one of his major characters, Paul, to complete the final stage of a journey that has consistently shown the power of the Christian deity. Luke underlines that power at journey's end. At Malta, the island on which the survivors of the wreck gather, Paul displays the power of God before barbarians (ironically appearing in the West as opposed to Chariton's East). When a poisonous viper wraps around Paul's hand, the barbarians think Paul a murderer who though rescued from the sea was receiving his just reward (as happens to the pirate Theron in Chariton's text).[89] Their attitude sharply changes when he does not die; they call him a god instead (Acts 28:6). Paul confirms his divine agency when he heals the father of Publius, the leader of Malta, and numerous others (28:7–8). This final climactic episode in Paul's voyage to Rome, another symbolic site, although here at the far reaches of Luke's geographic world, confirms for the reader the power and presence of Paul's god. In effect, even though under arrest, Paul proceeds to conquer Rome.

Paul remains preaching and teaching in Rome, symbolizing the ever widening movement. Luke's ending foreshadows future developments, keeps the narrative open-ended, and leaves the reader in anticipation. The travel of a deity's representative becomes the occasion for the manifestation of the power of that deity. The cause of the travel in Luke, whether due to persecution or the guidance of the Holy Spirit, serves the purpose of the Christian god. Outside forces that cause travel (census, persecution by Jews or local elites) are part of God's plan. Each stage of the journey across the *oikoumene* becomes another opportunity for the manifestation of the Christian god's power and, by implication, of the power of those associated with him.

CONCLUSION

Pagans, Jews, and Christians in the Flavio-Trajanic period could interpret the landscape in which they operated according to some common patterns. A group might emphasize the spread of their particular movement, no matter how wide. This could take several forms. Cities like Aphrodisias tapped into a rich mythic symbolic universe and long-standing traditions associated with locations throughout the Graeco-Roman world to highlight the power and importance of their own deity. Chariton was adept at drawing on such images. Likewise, Jews such as Josephus showed that their movement was widespread and had its own venerable myths. Further, their movement had implications for the entire *oikoumene*. Many ancient authors noted the spread of Jews across the entire Graeco-Roman world, which indicates the significance attached to its spread. Christians as well, especially the author of Luke–Acts, repeatedly claimed that the Christian movement had an auspicious past and also attracted adherents across the *oikoumene*. Whether such claims were actualized or were simply symbolic is another question. The point is that such claims tell us something about the authors' views of geography.

Sacred centers enabled people affiliated with them to stress the characteristics of their particular deity and promote the giving of offerings to the deity. This was a form of proselytizing or, better, an effort to promote the power and prestige of their deity. Jews stressed their own particular site: Jerusalem and its Temple. Christians, following Jewish tradition, made full use of Temple imagery and the power associated with it to adapt and in some cases reinvent the significance of the symbols for their own movement.

Key, of course, to any presentation of the geography of an area are the representatives who were seen by their respective communities as agents of the divine. These persons generally developed and presented the verbal and visual iconography of the sacred landscapes in which they and their deity operated. We examine next these "cosmic power brokers."

6.

Cosmic Power Brokers:
Human Agents and
Divine Emissaries

The divine world played an important role in the plethora of symbolic discourses between groups and individuals throughout the Roman Empire. Such activity needed interpreters and some system within which such agents could properly broker the power of the divine for the less informed. These agents were seen by groups as possessing special connections to the divine and sometimes were viewed as divine themselves. "That is why we even worship those persons as gods; for we consider that what has power to confer the greatest advantage is divine" (Epictetus 4.1.61). The particular power and special attributes of such emissaries depended on the history of the group, the circumstances in which an emissary worked, and the particular potent symbols operative for that group or that age.

Agents of the divine crossed the spectra of class, wealth, and status. The broker of miracles could be a fisherman from Galilee (Peter) or an emperor (Vespasian).[1] A priest or priestess could come from a hereditary line (Eleusis,[2] Sadducees and Levites) or be a member of the local elite (Zoilos of Aphrodisias). The common denominator generally was a perception by affiliated groups that these individuals had a special relationship with the divine.

This chapter examines the nature and role of cosmic power brokers in the Greek East. Who served as a power broker? What social, political, and cultural role did such an individual play when presenting or articulating divine power? How did such practices as miracles and oracles[3] or social graces as beauty, honor, and courage help cosmic power brokers depict or display divine power?[4]

PAGANS AND COSMIC
POWER BROKERS

Groups and societies drew upon religious symbols to organize themselves into cogent, functioning systems. Such symbols were not created solely by those with economic power, through religious or bureaucratic manipulation. Rather, significant symbols were a profusion of images and visions that percolated through an empire loosely bound by the administration at Rome. Certain themes dominated the discussion of those who participated or were affiliated with the elite classes in the Greek East: notably, a strong ethic (as defined by the group), paideia (a Greek way of life and education),[5] and a legitimate connection to the proper ordering of the world (most often understood as Rome's rule). The connection with Rome of local elites need not refer to their direct political involvement but implies at the least their acceptance, if not promotion, of the system of rules established by the Romans and affiliated elites.

Religious symbols were generally associated with local elite structures, often drawing from the literature most familiar to the educated. From the evidence available to us, cosmic power brokers frequently came from the elite classes or from people who were affiliated with them. It should come as no surprise, therefore, that religious and mythic symbols often fostered the social coherence of that group and stressed ethics, education, and the maintenance of a proper relation within the current political order. The stress on ethics and paideia was often contrasted with its opposites: bestial attitudes, crude behavior, and irrationality, features long associated with the "barbarian." Elite classes had long had a strong fear of mob rule and behavior. Ethics and education, promoted in literature and iconographic programs, helped stabilize, at least from the elite perspective, a potentially volatile situation.[6]

A system of benefactions (*beneficia*) created strong ties between persons of differing backgrounds and status that enabled the society to function effectively.[7] Benefactions, of course, preceded the Flavio-Trajanic period. A long inscription from the city of Kyme dated to 130 B.C.E. details at length the benefactions to the city provided by Archippe, a wealthy woman.[8] In 2 B.C.E. another woman, Lollia Antiochis, built a bath to honor Aphrodite Julia (the daughter of Augustus) and the demos. In turn she is referred to as the "first of women," an honorific title that set her apart in Assos.[9] Women played an important role in providing benefactions and serving as mediators between elites and nonelites and between the divine and local or regional bases of power. Some have thought such titles simply honorific and insubstantial, but that has been demonstrated to be too narrow a view.[10] Indeed, women became more prominent in the system of benefactions as people increasingly depicted the social system as part of a larger family system. Female members of the local elite classes participated in a benefactory system designed, not to threaten, but rather to support the existing social system (something done by males as well).[11] The lack of power of women priestesses compared with male priests may be overstated.[12] The oracle at Delphi, for example, wielded enormous symbolic import within power structures in antiquity. Clearly, women who served as functionaries of the divine supported, if not bolstered, the power of the elites and affirmed the current social system.[13]

A key component of the focus on the familial nature of society is the widely recognized pattern of patron–client relations, a pattern often integrated with divine power. A first- or second-century C.E. document from Egypt shows clearly the intimate connection perceived by some between patron, divine powers, and client. Here the client wishes his patron good health and then states: "For as you also make mention of us on each occasion by letter so I here make an act of worship for you in the presence of the lords Dioskouroi and in the presence of the lord Sarapis, and I pray for your safe-keeping during your entire life and for the health of your children and all your household."[14] Social stability revolved around the allegiance of clients to patrons; in turn, the relationship was solidified by the inclusion of the divine world. In this case, the client brokers for his patron's good health with the Dioskouroi and Sarapis.

Associations provided another forum for the intersection of religion and social behavior. One popular forum for persons involved in particular religions was the dining club or group celebration of a meal. A second- or third-century c.e. inscription from Egypt records an invitation to dine at a banquet in the dining room of the Sarapeion in honor of Sarapis.[15] Such gatherings provided an opportunity to mediate social interactions within a divine rubric. Meals in both Judaism and Christianity played similar roles in the structure of the communities, as Paul's letter to the Corinthians makes clear (1 Cor. 11:17–34).[16] Associations also played important roles as burial societies, extending in a smaller forum some of the same powers accorded to persons by the city.[17] This is aptly illustrated by an intriguing inscription placed in the Sarapeion at Opous in Thessalonica in the first century c.e. that describes a dream two centuries earlier. The dream tells a certain Xenainetos to persuade Eurynomos, his enemy, to receive Sarapis and Isis. The dream was confirmed, according to the inscription, by a letter found under his pillow. In turn, Eurynomos instituted the worship of these two deities in the household of Sosinike, who, the inscription states, "received them among her household gods and performed the sacrifices for some time." The cult continued through Eunosta, who "transmitted the (cult) and administered the mysteries of the gods among those who also were nonparticipants in the rites."[18] The power brokers range from Xenainetos, a figure in the past who receives the message via a dream, to the granddaughter of a woman who had begun to worship Sarapis and Isis many years after Xenainetos.[19] Clearly, the "epigraphic habit" so prevalent in the Greek East was an important means by which local elites could display how they served as the vehicles through which the gods benefited society.[20]

The promotion of Aphrodite across the Roman Empire amply illustrates the variety of ways elites served as cosmic power brokers. In the Greek East, magistrates often made communal votive offerings to Aphrodite as their guardian. F. Sokolowski cites a number of votive inscriptions from magistrates in Greek cities that stress Aphrodite as a "patroness of friendship and of harmony."[21] Police officials, supervisors, naval commanders, and those involved with penal facilities "paid most frequently their tribute to Aphrodite because of friendly relations existing among themselves or between them and the people." Epithets that proclaim Aphrodite as protectress of officials such as the *epistatai, timouchoi, synarchia,* and *nomophylakes* "describe really the harmony of the group doing their business."[22] Sokolowski also mentions that magistrates often made offerings to Aphrodite at the end of their military or civic service.[23]

An example of this occurs in *Chaereas and Callirhoe* when Chaereas offers sacrifices to Aphrodite at the end of his military ventures and before his return to Syracuse (8.2.8). Such instances indicate how those in power use iconography and texts to broker the power of the deity in the context of their jobs in society.

Aphrodisias again provides an excellent model. Local elites at Aphrodisias mediated or displayed or associated themselves with the power of Aphrodite through the dedication of buildings, the offering of sacrifices, and service as priests or priestesses of the cult. When such elites dedicate a building (e.g., the Sebasteion) at Aphrodisias to Aphrodite and specifically mention themselves as the dedicants, they show how they associate, if not negotiate, their own power with the power centers named in the dedication: Aphrodite (divine), the emperors (imperial), and the demos (local, civic). Such religious and political arenas reflect the "spectator culture"[24] and rhetorical displays, so prolific throughout the Greek East, that shaped or at least interpreted the interaction between ruler and ruled. As Cameron notes, "Showing, performance, and affirmation became as important as argument."[25]

In the imperial cult, local elites across the Greek East played key roles in serving as the representatives who brokered power relations between the divine, Roman, regional, and local power. Ti. Claudius Aristio, a prominent figure at Ephesus, served as archiereus of Asia in 88–89 C.E. and as high priest of the provincial temple of the imperial cult a short time later.[26] Aristio served in numerous other capacities that had religious and political overtones.[27] In a letter written to the Roman proconsul Lucius Mestrius in 88–89 C.E., Lucius Pompeius Apollonius from Ephesus negotiated with imperial power to continue the performance of the annual mysteries of Demeter. Apollonius draws on tradition and precedent to make his case. "Mysteries and sacrifices are performed every year at Ephesus, . . . , with much propriety and lawful customs."[28] He attaches letters showing the approval of such practices over the years by kings, emperors, and annual proconsuls (a strategy practiced in Aphrodisias in its letters written on the theater wall).[29] Apollonius serves on behalf of "those who ought to perform the mysteries," who "petition you through my agency."[30] Whether Apollonius is directly involved with the mysteries or whether he serves primarily as a benefactor or an advocate is unclear. What is clear is the key role played by this member of the local elite class in the negotiation between cosmic power (Demeter and her celebrants), imperial power (the proconsul), and local power (Apollonius). The petitioner, Apollonius, displayed the petition, in all probability, in public on a marble statue base, as a rhetorical assertion of his power and prestige as a power broker.[31]

Another clear example is the first-century C.E. Greek inscription dedicated by the demos and the Romans that honors Apollonis, a young woman from Cyzikos in Mysia, because of her parents' and husband's virtue (*arete*) and her moderation (*sophrosyne*).[32] Because she served as the priestess of Artemis, the temple overseers are to crown a statue (*agalma*) of Apollonis during the Artemis festival each year. Her statues were set up in association with the goddesses Aphrodite and Artemis. The lines of her (and her family's) power and prestige extend across many religious and civic boundaries throughout the city. Her statue is placed in a variety of civic contexts, including where persons are registered for marriage.

> Additionally, in order that the remembrance of her moderation [*sophrosyne*] may be visible to all the city, a statue of her is to be erected in one of the rooms on the Square Agora on its eastern portico, which lies between the office of the *timetai* and the *Agoranomion*. The *Kosmophylax* and his successors in this magistracy are to have the use of this office in perpetuity once it has been decorated. Those who register with the *Kosmophylax* the formalisation of their marriage are required to garland the statue of Apollonis which is dedicated in the office.[33]

Divine, imperial, and local power networks intertwine through the person of Apollonis, even after her death. The view in the Roman Empire that marriage was a stabilizing force helps us understand the significance and seriousness of the inscription, which concludes with the admonition, "May the decree be for the safeguarding of the city."[34] Local elites, who provided the priests and priestesses for cults across the Greek East, represented the divine world to the current society through a host of activities, even in death. Apollonis has a narrative parallel in the fictional heroine Callirhoe, who also, as a member of a local elite class, mediates intersecting power networks that wend their way through local, regional, imperial, and divine arenas.

Chariton of Aphrodisias:
Callirhoe and the Goddess Aphrodite

Chariton structures his work to underscore the relationship of his heroine, Callirhoe, with Aphrodite.[35] The narrative begins with a description that compares Callirhoe to the goddess and ends with Callirhoe praying at the base of Aphrodite's cult statue in Syracuse.[36] Throughout the narrative, Callirhoe acts out on the human plane various mythic and social roles of Aphrodite, roles that include Aphrodite's power to unite cities and nations, her appearance as goddess of love,[37] her civic association,[38] her close affiliation with the sea,[39] and her persuasive powers.

Chariton leaves little doubt that Callirhoe fits the paradigm of a woman from the local elite class. The daughter of Hermocrates, the Syracusan general, is cultured (7.6.5), even-tempered (1.2.6), virtuous, and well-bred.[40] Chariton describes Callirhoe as an absolutely amazing young woman,[41] the *agalma*[42] of all Sicily (1.1.1), whose beauty compares to that of Aphrodite Parthenos.[43] As Louis Robert notes, *agalma* generally refers to the statue for a god or a hero.[44] Callirhoe functions in the narrative as Aphrodite's human counterpart, apparently much like a certain Marcia (possibly a Jew) who, in an undated funerary inscription from Rome, is described as the "typos of golden Aphrodite."[45] "Typos" probably refers to Marcia's having received the imprint of Aphrodite in her manner and appearance.[46]

Callirhoe's human appearance embodies the *kallos* of the goddess Aphrodite (1.1.2).[47] In the ancient romances, comparisons of the human protagonist (both hero and heroine) with a deity are legion.[48] In certain instances, portrayals recall the practice in Graeco-Roman society (especially in Asia Minor) of associating members of the Roman imperial family with a god or goddess.[49] Women are often associated with Aphrodite. Agrippina and Caligula's sister, Drusilla, were each called the New Aphrodite.[50] At Assos in Turkey a bath was dedicated to Julia Aphrodite (Livia).[51] In addition, men and women of local elites at Aphrodisias during the Trajanic period and later served as priests and priestesss of Aphrodite.[52]

Such identifications may depict a ruling personage as another form of the deity or serve as honorific titles.[53] More to the point, however, association with a deity supported the maintenance of the political and social status quo. The practice began early. After the wife of Antiochus III, Laodice, established dowries for poor citizens' daughters, citizens established in her honor a new cult of Aphrodite Laodice. The "queen collocated with the goddess of love" and there occurred "a procession on the queen's birthday and sacrifices by all the brides and bridegrooms to the queen." Simon Price concludes that these "cults established the king and queen at the center of civic life, both political and social."[54] I would also add religious.

Callirhoe often appears at public events that join the civic and religious arenas (e.g., 1.1.11–12, 1.1.16–17, 2.3.5). Callirhoe's divine *kallos* overwhelms crowds and undoes the fortitude of political leaders. In Syracuse her divine appearance amazes (*thaumadzein*) the Greek crowd, and many (*polloi*) prostrate themselves before her (*proskunein*) (1.1.16). After the pirate Theron rescues Callirhoe from her tomb following her apparent death, he brings her to the country estate of Dionysius, the leading citizen of Miletus, in an attempt to sell her. Before presenting her, Theron uncovers her head and loosens her hair, actions that display her divine beauty.[55] Callirhoe's sudden entrance astounds (*kataplessein*) all who see her, and they think they have seen a goddess since rumor was that Aphrodite had appeared (*epiphainein*) in the countryside (1.14.1; cf. 4.7.5). Epigraphic evidence indicates that appearances by the goddess were seen as possible by Aphrodisians and non-Aphrodisians alike;[56] the reaction to Callirhoe would not seem far-fetched to Chariton's reading audience no matter their location in the Greek East.

Callirhoe's greatest impact on crowds comes on her journey to Babylon. At each point along the way, crowds turn out to see this "masterpiece of Nature, 'like unto Artemis or golden Aphrodite'" (4.7.5).[57] They were not disappointed. Callirhoe surpassed the reports. The journey concludes with her entrance into the city of Babylon. Despite Dionysius's attempt to hide Callirhoe under a *skene,* or awning,[58] word of her beauty had gone before their entourage, and "all of Babylon" poured out to see the sight. When Dionysius realizes that he cannot avoid the inevitable, he asks Callirhoe to come out. All in the crowd strain their eyes and their very souls (*psyche*). The result could easily fit a description of the Eleusinian mysteries. "Callirhoe's face gleamed with a radiance which held the eyes of all, just as when a great light is suddenly seen on a dark night."[59] Overcome with astonishment, the Persians prostrate themselves before her (*proskunein*) (5.3.9).[60] Callirhoe qua Aphrodite had conquered Babylon.[61]

The power of Aphrodite successively affects the significant political personages that Callirhoe meets. The first to encounter her power is Chaereas, who could serve as the paradigm for any aspiring member of the elite class in the Greek East. He has high political connections, a heroic appearance, and paideia. The son of Ariston, the second leading figure in Syracuse and political rival to Hermocrates, Chaereas is described by his friend and companion Polycharmus as "once at the very top in Sicily, in reputation, wealth, and handsome appearance" (4.3.1). Chaereas combines heroic features with popular Stoic virtues such as self-control, proper observance of the law, an aristocratic education, and an emphasis on reason—fine virtues to stress by Chariton, who was connected to a city that produced Alexander, an outstanding Aristotelian scholar.[62] Chaereas well represents the free and educated Greek who, especially in the latter part of the first century, sought to stress his proud heritage in the continual symbolic and quite real negotiations with Roman power. His training and bearing stand in marked contrast to the barbarian.[63] Chaereas's victory over the barbarian Persians (a feat his barbarian ally, the Egyptian king, cannot manage) compares favorably to the extensive set of barbarian defeats by imperial Rome depicted at the Aphrodisian Sebasteion. As R. Smith notes, the scenes in the Sebasteion show that Greeks in the Greek East now operate with Rome as "partners not subjugated recalcitrants," unlike the defeated barbarians.[64] In his battles, Chaereas displays the heroic features with which Greeks in the Greek East could identify. He becomes in the narrative the political and military power broker, the perfect companion to Aphrodite's representative, Callirhoe. The superiority of the educated Greek over the barbarian is repeatedly stressed throughout the narrative. Chariton shows clearly (from his perspective) where true grace (Callirhoe) and true honor (Chaereas) lie.

Aphrodite through her divine agent Eros causes Chaereas and Callirhoe to meet during the festival of Aphrodite.[65] Divine beauty (*kallos*) meets nobility (*eugeneia*). They fall in love (*pathos erotikon*) (1.1.16) and display characteristics closely linked with death. Chaereas is described as mortally wounded just as a hero in battle (1.1.7), sick (*nosos*), withered in appearance, and close to death because of the suffering of his noble soul (*dia pathos psyches euphuous*) (1.1.10).[66] Aphrodite, through Callirhoe, her human representative, overcomes the reason and control of a heroic and politically powerful figure, an action repeated throughout the narrative as she debilitates the *psyche* of Dionysius, the most powerful man in Miletus; Mithridates, the governor of Caria; and even Artaxerxes, king of Persia (probably alluding to Artaxerxes II Mnemon, 404–358).[67] Politically powerful figures must function within a new rubric: the power of Aphrodite.

Callirhoe has civic and religious import for Sicily and Syracuse.[68] Chariton places her beauty (*kallos*) on par with that of Aphrodite Parthenos herself (1.1.2), a possible allusion to Athena Parthenos, the premier deity of the political and religious life of Athens.[69] Chariton also implies that lawful marriage and family mean stability and continuity in society. Even in her second marriage, Callirhoe remains faithful to the memory of Chaereas. The marriage of Chaereas and Callirhoe symbolizes the very fabric of society itself. Disruption of the marriage disrupts society.

This is pointedly illustrated after her apparent death at the hands (or rather the foot) of her jealous and misinformed husband, Chaereas. Rumor quickly spread the word of her demise throughout all the city. The reaction? "From every side lamentations resounded, and the affair was very like the capture of a city" (1.5.1). At Chaereas's trial for the dastardly deed, he surprises everyone by refusing to defend himself. "Stone me to death in public. I have robbed our people of their crown [*apostephanoun*]" (1.5.5). When, after journeying across the Mediterranean landscape, Callirhoe returns to Syracuse,[70] she appears before the citizens (*demos*) in the theater at Syracuse: "[T]he people lifted their eyes to heaven, and praised the gods, feeling an even greater sense of gratitude for this day than for that of their victory" (8.7.2). Her return was more significant than the legendary victory over the Athenians in which the continued existence of Syracuse was secured. The author's selection of metaphors places Callirhoe, Aphrodite's representative, and a member of the local elite within the very fabric of Syracusan society.[71]

The first-century C.E. inscription from Cyzikos in Asia Minor honoring Apollonis again offers an important framework for understanding the relationship Chariton depicts.[72] The inscription, sponsored by the demos and the Romans who did business in the city, honored the deceased daughter (Apollonis) of a local elite because of the virtue of her parents and husband and because of her *sophrosyne*. The description of her funeral sounds very close to Chariton's portrayal of Callirhoe's, even to the point that Callirhoe, like Apollonis, is placed in an ancestral vault near the city's great harbor. Both have close association with a goddess, and both have significant civic connections. The real Apollonis and the fictional Callirhoe broker divine power as members of powerful local elite families through their association with a divinity and their exhibition of the proper social graces. These arenas indicate at least symbolically their participation in helping to maintain society's very existence.[73] The portrayals fit the Flavio-Trajanic period well. Women were increasingly active in the social and political affairs of local and regional areas, due in part to Greek and Roman law, which relaxed restrictions on them.[74] The prosperity and continued power of the state rested in women who conducted themselves properly.[75]

Callirhoe also brokers (albeit often reluctantly) the religious, political, and social dimensions of Aphrodite's power beyond the borders of Sicily.[76] In Miletus and, especially, at the country estate of Dionysius, its leading citizen, Callirhoe prepares for her second marriage, this time to her former owner, Dionysius. Returning from the temple of Aphrodite, Callirhoe approaches sailors, who prostrate themselves (*proskunein*) before her as if Aphrodite herself had appeared.[77] In preparation for the marriage, the city of Miletus is decked out for the sacred festival, and each person sacrifices at home and in the temple (not specified). The crowd (*plethos*) gathers at the temple of Homonoia, which

Chariton states is the traditional site for bridegrooms to receive their brides.[78] This also allows Chariton to present the overt political as well as marital implications of this union.[79] Certain empresses were associated with *homonoia*. Caligula's sister, Drusilla, is called Thea Homonoia,[80] and the Flavian Domitia in Asia is called Sebaste Homonoia.[81] Knowing that her beauty reflected "the nobility of fatherland [*patridos*] and race [*genos*]," Callirhoe put on the Milesian dress and bridal wreath. Only then does she turn and look (*apoblepein*) at the crowd. As one, they shout "*he Aphrodite gamei*" ("Aphrodite marries!") and give her all the attention of a deity or royalty, spreading purple cloth, roses, and violets before her and sprinkling her with perfume (3.2.15–17). The marriage between Callirhoe and Dionysius represents the union of two leading members from elite classes and depicts East (Asia Minor/Miletus) meeting West (Syracuse); the common bond is Aphrodite, as represented by Callirhoe, whose authority extends beyond political and social boundaries.

Aphrodite's political, social, and religious activities reach Babylon in yet another way. Chaereas, Callirhoe's first husband, joins an Egyptian rebellion against Artaxerxes, the Persian king, when he thinks the king has decided to give Callirhoe to his rival Dionysius (6.5.12). Chaereas is victorious in all his battles, and during the course of his campaigns he captures Callirhoe and Stateira, the queen of Persia, at Aradus. When Chaereas intends to keep the queen as a slave for Callirhoe, Callirhoe protests: "May the gods never inflict me with such insanity as to keep the queen of Asia as my slave, especially when she has been my friend" (8.3.2). "Friend," of course, is a key term used in treaties. Stateira's return to Artaxerxes affirms Aphrodite's authority through her emissary Callirhoe, as the interchange between Artaxerxes and Stateira makes clear:

> "What divine power has restored you to me, my darling wife! It is simply beyond belief either that my queen should have been lost, or that once lost, she should have been found again. How is it that when I left you on the land, I should get you back from the sea?" "You have me as a gift from Callirhoe," replied Stateira. (8.5.5–6)

Chariton's clever use of sea imagery probably alludes to Aphrodite's close connection with the sea, a connection made explicit elsewhere when Callirhoe prays to Aphrodite for a safe return voyage to Syracuse (8.4.10). Chariton elicits images of well-known sacred geography for the reader when Chaereas offers sacrifices to Aphrodite on Paphos, the legendary birthplace of Aphrodite, before their return to Syracuse. On her return to Syracuse, Callirhoe appears even more lovely, as if, Chariton tells the reader, Aphrodite herself rose (*anaduomenein*) up out of the sea, a direct association of Callirhoe with Aphrodite's famous birth from the sea (8.6.11) (see also the reaction of the boatmen at the estate of Dionysius; 3.2.14). Of course, numerous allusions to Callirhoe's role as cosmic power broker for Aphrodite have already prepared the reader. The fate of Theron, the pirate who took Callirhoe from the tomb, is particularly revealing. Returning with his band from Miletus to Crete, he is forced by a violent wind into the Ionian Sea, where they drift. "Thunder and lightning and prolonged darkness fell upon these villains, and Pronoia showed them plainly that until now they had had fair sailing only because of Callirhoe" (3.3.10). All the pirates die of thirst except Theron, who is rescued only to be crucified.

Through the agency (or benefaction) of Callirhoe, Aphrodite's representative, the king and queen of Persia are reunited, and thereby, an important bond is established with the most powerful imperial figures in the East. Chaereas and Callirhoe, born of noble Greek families and part of society's ruling elite[82] retain their superior presence and regain their power despite unfortunate circumstances *and* change of social standing. Even when Callirhoe is a slave, her *kallos* (beauty) is enhanced by slave's garments (2.2.4). Chaereas moves from prisoner/slave to the lowly underling of the Egyptian king, who is rebelling against the Persian king, to become the naval commander of the entire fleet. His regal bearing and paideia could not be hidden despite unfortunate changes in status (7.2.5). Even though traditional religious figures appear in the narrative (e.g., a priestess of Aphrodite at Dionysius's estate and prophets associated with Aphrodite at Paphos), Callirhoe and, to a lesser extent, Chaereas function as the real power brokers. After Chaereas's last battle, Chaereas and Callirhoe appear before the victorious troops after the capture of Aradus, and, "the sweetest fruits of war and peace, the triumph and the wedding were there combined" (8.1.12). Both attributes fit well the expected role of elites in maintaining the stability of society.

Chaeraes and Callirhoe display the expected virtues of the local elite class throughout the Greek East. Their narrative roles epitomize those members of the elite class who left numerous inscriptions, sculpture, and buildings dotting the landscape of the Greek East in the imperial period. In the view of ancient readers in the Greek East, Chaereas and Callirhoe appeared as vehicles through which relations between local, regional, imperial, and cosmic power centers were mediated, just like those local elites who served as priests and priestesses, on councils, on embassies, in the military, as equestrians or senators, or as part of a family, all necessary components of a stable society. For Chariton, of course, and for his city, the cosmic framework in which those operations took place was the power of Aphrodite, as mediated through her special emissaries.

JEWS AND COSMIC POWER BROKERS

Jews had a long history of intermediaries who negotiated within the various webs of power: Moses, kings of the Davidic line, prophets, seers, and a future messiah.[83] The voices of such venerable figures continued to mediate between various power centers through works such as 2 Baruch, 4 Ezra, and Pseudo-Philo that sought to portray the relevance of such figures for their own day.[84] The law, kingship, and the Temple played especially crucial roles for the establishment of proper boundaries for many who saw themselves as Jews. But who negotiated such power arenas in the first two centuries of this era? The issue is complicated by the unique circumstances that existed before and after the Jewish wars with Rome. Furthermore, the Diaspora itself was diverse and often varied from the situation in Galilee and Judaea. Thus, any description of the role played by Jewish cosmic power brokers must necessarily be limited. Particular attention will be placed on those who negotiated within the elite power structures. In addition, the principal focus will be on the Flavio-Trajanic period, in large measure because of the significant political and religious changes that it brought. Of course, earlier and later material will help illustrate the continuity or transformation of key themes or ideas.

One of the genres that played a key role in Christian literature after 70 C.E. and in Judaism prior to 70 C.E. was apocalyptic literature (e.g., 1 En., Dan.). Later Judaism tended to play down the apocalyptic perspective, especially following the disastrous Bar Kochba revolt. Yet, searching for the divine (and the future) through the symbolic discourse of apocalypticism did continue in several late-first- and early-second-century texts, notably 2 Baruch, 4 Ezra, and portions of the Fourth Sibylline Oracle. Each of the texts has a famous biblical personage (Baruch or Ezra) or a renowned semihistorical figure in antiquity (the Sibyl) serve as the cosmic power broker.[85] The reader is allowed to listen to the divine (generally either God or an angel) revealing itself to the special emissary. For those who felt that a gulf existed between the world as they once knew it and their current condition, apocalyptic discourse as mediated through great figures of the past held out a modicum of hope for the future. In most of the apocalyptic works from Daniel onward, the reward of faithful service by the remnant occurs in the future at some period of judgment. As the Sibyl says, "God himself will again fashion the bones and ashes often and he will raise up mortals again as they were before . . . and then there will be a judgment over which God himself will preside, judging the world again" (Sibyl. 4:180). The use of ancient and venerable figures was not limited to apocalyptically oriented texts. Philo and Josephus use Moses and other great figures of Israel's past to display the power of God.[86]

But who serves as cosmic power broker when we leave the narrative worlds of apocalypticism and philosophical discourse? Prior to 70 C.E., Temple functionaries served as key symbolic figures who integrated divine power with imperial power, regional power (especially local Greek and Samaritan cities), and Jewish groups both in Palestine and in the Diaspora. Significant priestly influence ended with the destruction of the Temple. Nevertheless, the continuation of priestly families in the aftermath of the first Jewish war is evident from evidence discovered at archaeological sites and the emphasis on priestly concerns in the Mishnah and Talmud.[87] This suggests that the priest as an intermediary with the divine may have retained some importance. Some writers in the post-70 period, however, saw the priests as part of the reason the Temple was destroyed in the first place, notably the author of 2 Baruch (10:18).[88] The attitude may explain in part the formation of rabbinic Judaism.[89]

Jewish elites often played a role similar to that of pagan elites. Nevertheless, as Martin Goodman has shown, Jewish elites in Palestine were largely ineffectual during the prerevolt period and were generally ignored in Palestine afterward, with the exception of the Herodian family, which stayed in power until Agrippa II's death in the mid-90s. The situation was different in the Diaspora; certain elites both prior to and following the first Jewish war participated in local councils and other civic assemblies. Jewish elites in Palestine could not prevent a second revolt under Bar Kochba, and it was only in the third century under the leadership of Judah ha-Nasi (Judah the Prince) that local Jewish elites, especially rabbis, exerted a modicum of power and influence.[90] The rabbis in the late second and third centuries display charisma and wonder-working in their dealings with local power centers.[91] First- and second-century rabbis (the Tannaim) are portrayed as holy men, although less frequently they are portrayed as charismatic figures or magicians.[92] S. Cohen argues that the second-century rabbis played only a small role in negotiating the power relations between the divine and the masses. Some examples do exist of such negotiations; such as an edict where rabbis condemned a Jew in Caesarea for sacrificing an animal to a pagan god.[93] But such instances appear limited, and the edict itself may have been ignored if received at all.

To define oneself as a Jew in the latter part of the first century had distinct social and political consequences. During Flavian rule, Jews still had distinctive rights in many communities across the Greek East, rights that exempted them from payment of certain taxes and participation in expensive sacrifices and festivals and that permitted them to worship their deity. Yet, as noted earlier, identifying oneself as a Jew also meant one had to pay the Jewish tax instituted by Vespasian on all Jews as a result of the Jewish revolt of 66–73.[94] When Nerva succeeded Domitian, he limited those who had to pay the tax ,which had the effect of defining more sharply who was or was not a Jew.[95] To deal with the power networks operative in the Roman Empire, Jewish groups sometimes drew on the benefactor and patron–client relationship. In Cyrene, a list naming high-ranking magistrates between 60 and 61 C.E., includes a certain Elazaros, son of Jason. Both Elazaros and Jason appear to be Jews who participated in the gymnasium at Ptolemais around the end of the first century B.C.E. and later became citizens.[96] Individuals like Elazaros in the Jewish Diaspora seem to have functioned as benefactors to some extent within the Graeco-Roman system as a whole. But, more important, they functioned in that way within their respective communities. This seems clearly the case for a certain Ptolemy, a Jew who built a cemetery for the local congregation at Tlos in Lycia during the first century C.E. His inscription commemorates the building of the cemetery in gratitude for his son's appointment as a local archon, presumably within the Jewish community itself.[97]

Evidence also exists for non-Jews participating in or serving as benefactors for local congregations. An inscription from Phokaia (or Kyme), probably third century C.E., illustrates this well: "Tation daughter of Straton, son of Empedon, having built (or furnished) the meeting room (*oikos*) and the precinct of the *hypaithros* at her own expense, bestowed a favour on the Jews. The synagogue of the Jews honoured Tation daughter of Straton, son of Empedon, with a gold crown and seat of honour."[98] Tation, probably a non-Jew, associates with the Jewish community by building, like a good benefactor, their meeting place. She probably belongs to the local elite class, as indicated by the naming of her father and grandfather. In turn, the Jewish community displays its power by its gift of a gold crown and, more important, by public acknowledgment in the display of the inscription itself and in her "seat of honour." That such a position would be desirable indicates how both parties contribute to the power networks that bind them both. To be sure, Tation may not have worshiped the Jewish god. Nevertheless, her contribution implies a recognition of the legitimate social significance of the group and her desire for recognition by them.[99]

Equally intriguing and more suitable for our period is the well-known late-first-century C.E. inscription from Acmonia in Phyrgia:

> This building constructed by Julia Severa was restored by Gaius Tyrronius Clades, head of the synagogue for life, and Lucius, son of Lucius, head of the synagogue, and Popilius Rufus, archon, from their own funds and from money contributed—the walls and roof, and they made safe the little door and all the remaining decorations. These men the synagogue honored with a golden shield on account of their virtuous life and their goodwill and zeal for the synagogue.[100]

Julia Severa, a Gentile from the city of Acmonia in Asia Minor, may have donated the synagogue to the Jews during the reign of Nero. She appears on coins issued under Nero[101] and served as eponymous magistrate and a priestess of local pagan cults.[102] The inscription records the repairs made on a building (*oikos*) built by her. Some have assumed that she was a benefactor and a god-fearer who built the building for the Jewish community. But perhaps she built it for some other purpose and later it may have been converted to a synagogue. The inscription remains unclear in that regard. At the least, however, the community associates itself with a famous local elite in an inscription meant for public display. They make clear that they function within the local elite systems operative in the first century.[103]

Jewish women played a significant role in public life, more significant than commonly supposed. B. Brooten has argued persuasively that women held some of the same offices as men (or at least the titles). Perhaps such titles were "honorary," but that makes them no less symbolically powerful.[104]

The boundaries established in Judaism with other religions or groups were not always sharply defined even within the more structured rabbinic traditions. When Rabbi Gamaliel travels to Acco, a Gentile city, and bathes at a bathhouse associated with Aphrodite, he is asked how he could break the law by associating with a pagan deity. Gamaliel redefines the character of the space he was in. "I never came into her domain. She came into mine. They don't say, 'Let's make a bathhouse as an ornament for Aphrodite.' But they say, 'Let's make Aphrodite as an ornament for the bathhouse.'" The function of the space, Gamaliel argues, was for taking baths and not as sacred ground for Aphrodite. Besides, no one treats her as a deity. Her statue, he says, stands "at the head of the gutter and everybody pisses right in front of her."[105] If the Gentiles do not take her seriously in that space, why should he? Other testings of the boundaries could be more dramatic, though again, examples are late. T. Flavius

Amphikles, a member of the Second Sophistic and a pupil of Herodes Attikos, drew on biblical tradition rather than Greek philosophy for the epitaph on his tomb.[106] In later periods the Greek magical papyri show where such agglutination could lead.[107] On some magical amulets, for example, one finds the tetragrammaton associated with other Jewish symbols (e.g., the menorah), and sometimes figures from Israel's past such as Abraham, Isaac, Jacob, or Moses appear with pagan deities.[108] Such efforts to negotiate with, if not manipulate, divine power had a ready attraction for all levels of society. Those who mediated such spells, the *magoi,* were often viewed as dangerous. John Gager sums up why they were often seen to be in conflict with other cosmic and political power brokers.

> The idea that *magoi* could dispense power on matters of central importance to human life; the idea that any private person, for nothing but a small fee, could put that power to use in a wide variety of circumstances; and the idea that all of these transactions were available to individuals who stood outside and sometimes against the "legitimate" corporate structures of society—all of these ideas presented a serious threat to those who saw themselves as jealous guardians of power emanating from the center of that society, whether Greek, Roman, Antiochene, or Rabbinic. Here was power beyond their control, power in the hands of freely negotiating individuals.[109]

The author of Acts recognizes the power inherent in magical practices, as we shall see, and substitutes, in effect, miracles by Christian cosmic power brokers. Josephus, in his *Jewish War,* reflects more mainstream concerns, especially the role of Temple functionaries and prophetic figures as cosmic power brokers who fail in their attempt to mediate the disastrous events facing Jerusalem and its Temple in the first century.

Josephus and Cosmic Power Brokers

Josephus, in writing his *Jewish War,* no doubt understood himself as a cosmic power broker, a prophetic messenger for the divine who explains the disastrous events that have overtaken the Jewish nation.[110] His writings seek to mediate through an interpretation of the events, an understanding of how divine power related to historical events, both the Jewish revolt and the subsequent Roman victory. His *Jewish War* is replete with specific historical explanations of the event, but always within the implied framework of someone who understands those events through the lens of the Jewish god, who works through history and punishes those who circumvent his authority. Josephus also highlights others who serve or function as cosmic power brokers, albeit sometimes altering facts to fit his presentation.[111] In *Antiquities,* many key ancient figures mediate cosmic power and display the proper noble virtues of self-control, wisdom, and justice, notably Moses, Abraham, Joseph, David, Solomon, and prophets.[112] I will focus here, however, on the *Jewish War,* with particular attention to individuals and groups that Josephus presents as mediating the power of the divine.

Josephus indicates that priests play a significant role in negotiating cosmic power. He mentions that he himself is a Hebrew, a native of Jerusalem, and a priest (*BJ* 1.3). He portrays high priests and members of the priestly order as the appropriate representatives for negotiating or discerning the will of God.[113] Indeed, Josephus apparently understood there to be three principal and sometimes overlapping vehicles of privilege associated with the divine: to command the nation, to serve as high priest, and to receive the gift of prophecy. For Josephus, John Hyrcanus embodied all three. He was

> the only man to unite in his person three of the highest privileges: the supreme command of the nation, the high priesthood, and the gift of prophecy. For so closely was he in touch with the deity that he was never ignorant of the future. Thus he foresaw and predicted that his two older sons would not remain at the head of the affairs. (*BJ* 1.68–69)

Priests functioned as God's representatives when Pompey attacked the Temple and his army begin to kill them. "The priests," Josephus notes, "seeing the enemy advancing sword in hand, calmly continued their sacred ministrations and were butchered in the act of pouring libations and burning incense; putting the worship of the deity above their own preservation" (*BJ* 1.150).

The Essenes also receive special consideration. Josephus, in a later discussion of Archelaus's reign, talks about Archelaus's dream in which he saw nine tall and full-grown ears of corn among which oxen were browsing. Archelaus sent for soothsayers and Chaldaeans to ask their opinions on its meaning (an apparent allusion to Joseph's interpretation of pharaoh's dream in Genesis). The soothsayers could not interpret the message, whereas a certain Simon of the Essenes interpreted the dream accurately; the ears of corn represented the years of rule that Archelaus had left, and the oxen indicated a revolution would soon take place. Josephus says that this was confirmed shortly thereafter (*BJ* 2.111–13). Essenes are described at some length by Josephus (*BJ* 2.119–61).[114] For Josephus the Essenes have a particular aptitude to serve as cosmic power brokers between the divine and this world: "there are some among them who profess to foretell the future, being versed from the early years in holy books, various forms of purification, and apophthegms of prophets; and seldom if ever do they err in their predictions" (*BJ* 2.159).[115]

Josephus understands that there was another kind of prophet, a false prophet, who seemed to have become quite popular in Palestine.[116] One was an Egyptian, a charlatan, who gained for himself the reputation of a prophet by collecting over 30,000 people and leading them into the desert. There he proposed a forced entrance into Jerusalem, attempting to set himself up as a tyrant of the people. Unfortunately for his followers, Felix, the Roman procurator, anticipated his activity, and although the Egyptian escaped, most of his followers were either killed or taken prisoner (*BJ* 2:261–63).[117]

But it is the revolutionaries against whom Josephus directs his harshest diatribes. One of the great sins of the revolutionaries was to set up a pretender as a high priest. The consequences were grave, in this case the cause of the destruction of the Temple itself. This particularly distressed Josephus since the high priest symbolized by his garment the cosmos itself and by implication served as the vehicle through which the divine worked.[118] In contrast, Josephus portrays positively certain local elites and priests who, when tensions start to mount with the Romans, attempt to mediate between the passions of the crowd and the provocations of the Romans led by Florus (*BJ* 2.315–16). Indeed, after the troops continued their provocations, Josephus says that

> every priest and every minister of God, bearing in procession holy vessels and wearing the robes in which they were wont to perform their priestly offices, the harpers also and the choristers with their instruments, fell on their knees and earnestly implored the people to preserve for them these sacred ornaments, and not to provoke the Romans to pillage the treasures of the house of God. Even the chief priests might then have been seen heaping dust upon their heads, their breasts bared, their vestments rent. They appealed by name to each of the notables individually and to the people as a whole not, by offending in so trifling a matter, to deliver up their country to those who were eager to sack it. (*BJ* 2.321–22)

The chief priests and the leading citizens in the council continued to try to mediate between local concerns and imperial power by meeting Herod Agrippa II to tell him of the atrocities committed by the Romans. After his response, Josephus says, "They indeed being men of position and as owners of property desirous of peace understood the benevolent intentions of the king's reprimand" (*BJ* 2.338).

That local elites serve as the emissaries of the divine becomes especially clear in a long speech of Herod Agrippa II to the nation before its uprising against Rome. After a long recitation that details how Rome has conquered every major power in the known world, he says:

> [T]he only refuge then left to you is divine assistance. But even this is ranged on the side of the Romans, for without God's aid so vast an empire could never have been built up. Consider too the difficulty of preserving your religious rules from contamination even were you engaging a less formidable foe; and how, if compelled to transgress the very principles on which you chiefly build your hope of God's assistance, you will alienate him from you. If you observe your Sabbath customs and refuse to take any action on that day, you will undoubtedly be easily defeated, as were your forefathers by Pompey, who pressed the siege most vigorously on the days when the besieged remained inactive. If on the contrary you transgress the law of your ancestors, I fail to see what further object you will have for hostilities since your one aim is to preserve inviolate all the institutions of your fathers. How could you invoke the aid of the Deity after deliberately omitting to pay him service which you owe him? (*BJ* 2.390–94)

Herod, like so many elites in the pagan world, sought to mediate between the local people, the divine, and the political and social conditions in which the populace found itself. A similar situation occurs when the principal citizens assemble with the chief priests and highest-ranking Pharisees to present an alternative to the revolutionaries, who had taken over the inner Temple. The emissaries expressed indignation at the audacity of the revolt, saying that their forefathers had adorned the sanctuary, largely at the expense of aliens, and had accepted gifts from foreign nations. No one had ever taken the step the revolutionaries had and forbidden non-Jews to make sacrifices.

> But now here were these men, who were provoking the arms of the Romans courting a war with them, introducing a strange innovation into their religion, and, besides endangering the city, laying it open to the charge of impiety, if Jews henceforth were to be the only people to allow no alien the right of sacrifice or worship. . . . In the course of these remonstrances, they produced priestly experts on the traditions who declared that all their ancestors had accepted the sacrifices of aliens. (*BJ* 2.414–15, 417)

Jewish local elites in Palestine functioned in much the same way as elites did across the Roman Empire. That is, they sought to mediate between imperial power, local power, and the proper conveyers of divine power. Unfortunately for them, they did not have the traditional backing of the populace or the full support of the Romans, unlike other areas of the empire. As Martin Goodman has pointed out, the lack of a strong base from which to operate made it almost impossible for them to control the elements instigating the Jewish revolt.[119]

The masses in Josephus function much like the chorus in a Greek drama. They recognize the power of the divine, although that recognition is little help against the leaders of the revolt, who are portrayed as treacherous and barbaric. Thus when a Roman garrison was massacred by the revolutionaries, the people recognize the cosmic implications of the atrocity.

> Seeing the grounds for war to be now beyond remedy and the city polluted by such a stain of guilt as could not but arouse a dread of some visitation from heaven, if not of the vengeance of Rome, they gave themselves up to public mourning; the whole city was a scene of dejection, and among the moderates there was not one who was not racked with the thought that he would personally have to suffer for the rebels' crime. For, to add to this heinousness, the massacre took place on the Sabbath, a day on which from religious scruples Jews abstain even from the most innocent acts. (*BJ* 2.455–56)

Josephus's own part as cosmic power broker who mediates between sacred and imperial and regional power deserves additional comment. After the destruction of the town Jotapata by Vespasian, Josephus, holed up in a cave, has dreams in which

> God had foretold to him [Josephus] the impending fate of the Jews and the destinies of the Roman sovereigns. He was an interpreter of dreams and skilled at divining the meaning of ambiguous utterances of the Deity; a priest himself and of priestly descent, he was not ignorant of the prophecies in the sacred books. At that hour he was inspired to read their meaning, and, recalling the dreadful images of his recent dreams, he offered up a silent prayer to God. (*BJ* 3.351–53).

Josephus makes his ability to discern the divine even more clear in his speech to Vespasian after his capture. "You imagine, Vespasian, that in the person of Josephus you have taken a mere captive; but I come to you as a messenger of greater destinies. Had I not been sent on this errand by God, I know the law of the Jews and how it becomes a general to die" (*BJ* 3.399–400). Josephus then proceeds to tell Vespasian that Vespasian will become caesar, ruler of land, sea, and the whole human race, which Vespasian, according to Josephus, gradually came to believe himself (*BJ* 3.402–4).

In some respects, Josephus even viewed Titus as an emissary of the divine. Titus, in leading the charge against Tarichaeae, says, "For lead I will, be sure of it, and will charge the enemy at your head. Do you then not fail me, have confidence that God is on my side and supports my ardour, and be assured that, beyond mere victory in this battle outside the walls, we shall achieve some further success" (*BJ* 3.484; cf. *BJ* 3.492–95). The subsequent victories by the Romans simply confirmed, for Josephus, that God was working through them.

CHRISTIANS AND COSMIC POWER BROKERS

Christians did not have the benefit of a social system that allowed systemic expression of cosmic power brokers, at least in public display. Nevertheless, literary sources depict Christians brokering the divine amid the imperial, regional, and local systems in ways similar to those of the elite classes throughout the empire. The first, and again perhaps obvious, power brokers were the writers themselves, that is, those who wrote the New Testament texts, the Didache, the Shepherd of Hermas, and other Christian works; each author sought to mediate and/or portray the role of the divine within society. The narrative itself becomes the vehicle through which the reader was to see the divine.

The early apostles and disciples soon were perceived as cosmic power brokers. Initially these apostles, who emulate Jesus, the ultimate power broker from the Christian viewpoint, were loosely understood to be persons especially endowed to interpret the biblical tradition. Originally, apostleship may have required having known the earthly Jesus. Paul's apologetic approach regarding his own apostleship suggests the importance of that connection (1 Cor. 15:1–3). As the apostles and earlier followers of Jesus died off, a gradual move toward a more hierarchic and institutional structure began to develop, although less structured models still operated. In the pastorals, the offices of bishop and deacon become more defined (1 Tim. 3:1–12), and the characteristics expected of persons holding such offices frequently paralleled or were similar to the attributes expected of members of the elite classes in the pagan world (temperance, dignity, gentleness, a manager of the household).

As the Didache indicates, some problems developed with prophetic figures who, drawing on earlier traditions within the Christian movement, wandered from community to community. The admonition that prophets should not overstay their welcome indicates that not all communities were equally clear on the roles such persons were to play. Defining the proper role of emissaries of the divine became a crucial matter for churches. How does one discern the authentic messenger from the "Christ peddler" (Didache 11:3–12:5)?

The letters of Ignatius indicate that certain individuals were understood to carry on the traditions initiated by Paul's movements across the Mediterranean world fifty years earlier. Ignatius and later key church figures such as Justin Martyr and Origen now represented the community before God and helped to negotiate the relationships with non-Christian and other Christian communities (see 1 Tim. 3:7). *Homonoia* became an important theme for Ignatius in much the same way as it had been for pagan writers.[120]

For the early Christian church, the paradigms for leadership and the membership of the church also centered on prophetic figures of the past. The letter to the Hebrews, for example, has a litany of Old Testament figures who serve as the models of faith (Heb. 11:2–40). These paradigms, in turn, were taken over by the later church, particularly in the second century.[121]

But writers continually returned to the apostles and, of course, Jesus as the ultimate exemplars for suffering and persecution. The Gospel tradition, notably the Gospel of Mark, stresses this role (e.g., Mark 13). By the end of the first and the beginning of the second century, leaders in the church themselves became the models. Paul's own letters now offered the proper paradigm. Ignatius, in the early second century, talks about being taken before the lions, noting that it is necessary for people to be willing to suffer and die for their belief. The Book of 1 Peter typifies the attitude: "Beloved, do not be surprised at the fiery ordeal which comes upon you to prove you, as though something strange were happening to you. But rejoice in so far as you share Christ's sufferings, that you may also rejoice and be glad when his glory is revealed" (4:12–13). In short, at first the leaders of the church were believed to be the emissaries or agents between the divine and the powers that exist in this world, and later this role devolved upon all believers.

An inscription, though late, shows the increase in power of those figures who served as cosmic power brokers in the church. A certain Kallistos, a slave, was set up in the banking trade by his Christian master, who subsequently became the bishop of Rome.[122] Such evidence illustrates how the Christian movement began to filter into local elite structures and operations and how the leadership in particular functioned much like local elites. This process can be seen already in the Acts of the Apostles.

Power brokers presented their case, as Averil Cameron rightly notes, through metaphor, image, and symbols to engage the empire. Thus, Jesus spoke in parables, scriptural allusions, and typologies. The New Testament canon itself in its various manifestations toward the end of the second century became the medium through which signs, symbols, and typology were developed by later writers.[123] A tension developed in the presentation among Christians because of the emphasis on understanding truth not through proof but rather through faith in such signs as the cross. Almost all writers argued for faith rather than logic. Yet, as Cameron observes, the presentation of that argument is usually through a rhetorical process that uses or draws on logic to make the case.[124] Thus, Ignatius of Antioch in the early second century drew on metaphor and on logic to present his position.

Beg only that I have inward and outward strength not only in word but in will that I may be a Christian not merely in name but in fact, for if I am one in fact then I may be called one and be faithful long after I have vanished from the world. Nothing merely visible is good, for our God Jesus Christ is manifest the more now that he is hidden in God.

This vision or mystical experience indicates the power of the divine as mediated through the vision of the key figure, in this case Ignatius.[125]

The Shepherd of Hermas also draws on visions that allow the reader to discern the divine. A young man says:

"Why do you ask for instant revelations in your prayer? Be careful lest you injure your flesh by heavy requests. The present revelations are all you need. Can you see greater revelations than those you have seen?" In answer I said to him, "Sir, I am only asking for a revelation complete in every detail about the three forms of the elderly lady." For answer, he said to me, "How long are you going to be without perception? It is your doubts that make you so and the failure to have your heart directed to the Lord."[126]

The rhetorical devices used in the presentation of the material serve for the reader the same role as any agent of cosmic power. As texts such as those written by Ignatius and the authors of the Didache and the Shepherd of Hermas become more significant for the later church, they served as the vehicles through which believers perceived and experienced the divine.

Tradition and telling the key aspects of Christian faith became central to those agents who served as intermediaries between God and world. Christian preaching and teaching, as Cameron notes, were often embodied in homilies. Like episcopal letters that used the argument of apologetic, these homilies

confirmed the structure of the Christian groups and continually reminded the faithful of the essentials of the system to which they now belonged. Preaching therefore became for most Christians the medium through which they were heard and regularly reminded of the interpretation of the scriptures, the relation of the Old Testament to the life of Jesus, and of both to the overall divine providence. While many preachers themselves saw their role as that of teacher, that function was carried out as much by the regular repetition and affirmation of familiar themes as by actual argument.[127]

No better early representative shows the movement toward the kind of rhetorical displays that become commonplace in later Christianity and presents a vision of the interrelationship between the scriptural heroes of old and the heroes of the early church than the writer of the Gospel of Luke and Acts of the Apostles.

Luke and Cosmic Power Brokers

Like Josephus and Chariton, Luke patterns his major characters in Acts, the disciples, on historical figures who had obtained mythic proportions by the first century C.E.[128] For Luke, this included the prophets as set forth in the Septuagint and Jesus, the founder of the movement.[129] Jesus' role as a paradigm for the disciples is perhaps most clear in the programmatic sermon in Luke 4:16–30. Jesus' ministry, in line with the ancient tradition of Elijah and Elisha, heralds the mission of the church for the outsider (Luke 4:25–27). His miracles and power of speech[130] affect crowds and political figures and set the pattern for the apostles and disciples, whose authority also includes teaching, preaching, and healing (Luke 9:1–2, 10:17–20; cf. Acts 2–5).[131]

Luke portrays Peter's denial prior to Jesus' trial in a heightened, more dramatic fashion than the Gospels of Mark and Matthew, adding to his Markan source "and the Lord turned and looked at Peter" (22:61), which captures the isolation and persecution of Jesus. The author places the denial scene right before Jesus' trial by the Jewish authorities, further sharpening his isolation; indeed, the burden for Jesus' trial falls on the Jewish authorities.[132] In Acts, the pattern of persecution continues against the disciples and apostles, who become, like Jesus, mediators of divine power expressing through their prophetlike speech and miraculous acts the power and presence of God (before crowds and political figures).[133]

Jesus brokers the power of God for his followers in Luke 24:48–49 and presents in programmatic fashion their responsibility; "you will receive power [*dynamis*] when the Holy Spirit comes upon you; and you will bear witness for me in Jerusalem, and all over Judea and Samaria, and away to the ends of the earth" (Acts 1:8).[134] Following the Pentecost, at which Jews from all over the Mediterranean world were gathered, Peter presents the purpose and the scriptural foundation of the Christian movement with a mixture of scriptural quotes and rhetorical proficiency (Acts 2:14–36). The audience (in this case Jewish) is overwhelmed ("pierced in the heart," *katenugesan ten kardian*) and responds, "what are we to do?" (Acts 2:37). The answer—to repent, be baptized, and receive the Holy Spirit (Acts 2:38–42)—remains fairly consistent throughout Acts.[135] Teaching and performing signs and wonders continue, so that the "sense of awe was everywhere" (Acts 2:43); indeed, "the Lord added to their number those whom he was saving" (Acts 2:47). The miracles at the hands of apostles cause amazement and wonderment (*thaumbos, ekstasis*) (Acts 3:10); and the apostles' words influence many to join the movement (Acts 4:4).

The power of speech and wonder-working continues with Stephen, one of seven chosen by the apostles to wait on tables (Acts 6:8–9). Further, Stephen's speech sets the events in the context of Jewish tradition, and Luke thereby stresses the continuity of Jesus and his followers with the ancient and respected religion of Judaism. Stephen calls Moses a powerful speaker and man of action (Acts 7:22), one rejected even though he was commissioned as a ruler and liberator (Acts 7:35), and one who led the people out of Egypt after working "miracles and signs" (Acts 7:36). Stephen cites Deuteronomy 18:15 to indicate that Moses foretold the coming of Jesus: "God will raise up a prophet for you from among yourselves as he raised me" (Acts 7:37).[136]

The combination *teras kai semeia* (signs and wonders), used at several important junctures in Acts,[137] draws on imagery from the Septuagint. God intervenes and gathers the faithful remnant (Joel 2:32; cf. Acts 2:19);[138] Moses guides the people out of Egypt. Signs and wonders highlight God's intervention in the affairs of the people Israel.[139] The Christian movement stands squarely in the prophetic tradition; the apostles and disciples are agents of God.[140] Thus, Philip, also one of the seven, drew crowds, who "listened eagerly" to him "when they heard him and saw the miracles that he performed" (Acts 8:6). Philip, like the prophets, possesses prophetic speech and the ability to perform miraculous acts.

Stephen receives an unfavorable response when he condemns those who refuse to follow Jesus. His stoning continues a pattern of persecution and opposition that forms a consistent structural component in Luke's portrait of the spread of the Christian movement.[141] The Acts account of the disciples and apostles is distinguished from the Septuagint account of the prophets by the use of deliberate geographical movement, the constant and purposeful meeting before political officials and crowds, and the rising dramatic scale of the narrative based on the conflict and intrigue that stands behind most of the movement.[142]

The presence of the apostles impresses, amazes, and makes clear the power of the deity just as the *kallos* of Callirhoe overwhelms crowds and political authorities. As with Callirhoe, the human representatives of the Christian god meet the officials of the political establishment. The results are as impressive as those portrayed by Chariton. In Acts 13:1, Paul, the primary figure for much of the remaining narrative, displays the obligatory ability to perform signs and wonders as well as to possess powerful speech. Before Sergius Paulus, the senatorial proconsul of Cyprus, Paul and Barnabas are called to tell the word of God (13:8). Paul displays the power of God by causing Elymas (a Jewish magician and another power broker) to go blind (13:7–8); as a result, Paul brings a prestigious convert, Sergius Paulus, into the fold. When the proconsul *sees* these events, he believes, being overwhelmed at the teaching of the Lord (13:12).

Seeing emphasizes the active role of the participant, who "sees," that is, "understands," the manifestation of the deity's power through these special representatives. The author lived in a world filled with visual images, so the emphasis on sight is not surprising. In Acts, Sergius Paulus's commitment is followed by Paul's lengthy speech in which he displays the prophetic features of the disciples as understood by Luke (13:17–42). For Paul, this begins a series of encounters that increase in intensity and that replay the twin features of the power of speech and the performance of signs and wonders. Following the Paphos event, Paul gives a long discourse that reiterates the covenants of Abraham, Moses, and David, concluding with Jesus' death and resurrection. In effect, the retelling of these stories serves to place the Jesus myth in the context of the other vital myths of Israel's past.[143]

Other figures associated with powerful centers of authority in the ancient world are affected by the speech and performance of God's agents. Philip encounters a eunuch, the official of the queen of Ethiopia (Acts 8:27) in charge of her treasury, who was puzzled about the writings of Isaiah. When Philip explains that the passage refers to Jesus, the eunuch seeks baptism and then continues on his way "rejoicing" (8:36–39). Likewise, Dionysius, a member of the powerful court on the Areopagus, becomes a follower after Paul's speech at Athens (Acts 17:34). In a final, dramatic trial before Festus, Paul relates his experience as an agent of God; Festus can only retort that Paul's great learning has driven Paul mad (Acts 26:24–25).

Luke's heroes also exhibit a form of paideia. Peter and John, even though viewed as unlettered by the authorities, amaze (*thaumadzein*) the high priest and the high-priestly family because their actions belie their training and social status (Acts 4:13; see also Luke 3). Paul gives speeches with a rhetorical flourish and polish that indicate an exceptional personality to his listening audience (e.g., Acts 17). From the standpoint of the narrator, the learned Paul (Acts 21:37–22:3) is so persuasive that he almost convinces Herod Agrippa II of his position (Acts 26:28). Ironically, some of Paul's listeners, such as the educated Athenians, are superstitious, a term often reserved in other literature for barbarians. Luke explicitly places barbarians only on Malta, in the West, a reversal of what would normally be viewed as the geographic location of barbarians (also contrasting the view in Chariton's and Xenophon's romances).[144] Paul's manner and appearance also suggest one who is learned and well educated. Despite his status as a prisoner, he amazes a Roman officer with his ability to speak Greek and Hebrew (Acts 22:37 ff.) He impresses a Roman procurator with his great learning (Acts 26:24). When the author mentions Paul's Roman citizenship, in effect, he places him higher on the social scale than many of those with whom he comes into contact, a factor Paul uses to great effectiveness with certain city leaders (Acts 16:35–38). Yet the message of God's emissaries does supersede the expectations of normal discourse among the elite classes in the Greek East. Festus, the Roman governor, struggles to maintain popular Stoic virtues such as self-control and reason but fails when faced with Paul's rhetoric concerning the Resurrection.

Luke also has key figures in the narrative compared to gods. At Lystra, when Paul heals a crippled man, crowds exclaim in their native language that Barnabas and Paul are the gods Zeus and Hermes respectively; the priest of the temple of Zeus himself wishes to offer sacrifices to them (Acts 14:8–13). The reaction by the apostles is sharp and quick: "But when the apostles Barnabus and Paul heard of it, they tore their garments and rushed out among the multitude, crying, 'Men, why are you doing this? We also are men, of like nature with you'" (Acts 14:14–15).[145] People are not to mistake the brokers of cosmic power as the source of that power, a motif seen in Chariton when Callirhoe also denies any divine status. Ironically, the protestations of Paul and Barnabas (as with Callirhoe) only heighten the audience's confirmation of their divine power. At Lystra the crowd is scarcely restrained from offering sacrifices to Paul and Barnabas after Paul finishes speaking (Acts 14:18). This scene contrasts sharply with the acclamation of godlike status to Herod Agrippa I offered by the people (*demos*) from Tyre and Sidon (Acts 12:20–23). According to Luke, Herod's subsequent death occurs because he appropriates a title reserved for God. Indeed, Luke contrasts his death with the continual expansion of the Christian movement: "But the word of God grew and multiplied" (Acts 12:24). A reader in the Greek East could not fail to note the *hybris* of Herod and its negative consequences.

Luke's cosmic power brokers confront other power brokers who represent Jewish and Graeco-Roman traditions. The miracles of the disciples and apostles follow a prophetic tradition (e.g., Elijah and Elisha) where such events serve a vital role. These become particularly important in confrontations with other purported cosmic power brokers. Philip overwhelms the magician Simon (Acts 8:4–13), and Peter condemns his request to buy the power apparent in the disciples: "May your silver perish with you, because you thought you could obtain God's gift with money! You have no part or share in this, for your heart is not right before God. . . . For I see that you are in the gall of bitterness and the chains of wickedness" (Acts 8:20–23). Paul's encounter with the Jewish magician ("a false prophet") Bar-Jesus, or Elymas, an advisor to the proconsul of Cyprus, Sergius Paulus, demonstrates for the reader that Paul presents the "true" picture of the divine to imperial rule (Acts 13:4–12). The mistaken belief by the priest of Zeus of Lystra that Paul and Barnabas's healings mean they are Hermes and Zeus provides the reader with another clear example where and through whom divine power truly does (and does not) operate (Acts 14:8–18).[146]

The confrontation with those who felt that the Artemis cult was threatened at Ephesus has often been cited as an example of the competition between the Christian movement and other religious movements (Acts 19:23–41). To be sure, Luke does not explicitly condemn the cult, only the fear of the statue makers that they will lose revenue. Yet the implications are clear. Only one god rules this world, the Christian god. Another incident may also serve as evidence for competition between religions. When Paul goes to Antioch in Pisidia, he encounters opposition from well-to-do women and the leading citizens of the town (Acts 13:44–50), possibly Roman magistrates of this Roman colony. As G. Horsley notes, epigraphic evidence shows that leading Roman men at Antioch were associated with the Men cult, which like that of Artemis of Ephesus was the cult associated with the city. Just as in Ephesus, the city's leadership may have feared that Paul and Barnabas would draw followers away from the city's god.[147] The narrative concerns of the pagans may have reflected a degree of reality. Pliny the Younger reports to Trajan that the temples have been emptied of worshipers, although the situation seems to be changing.[148]

Miracles are not the only vehicle used by the Christian god's power brokers. Rhetorical displays function in much the same fashion. As noted earlier, Averil Cameron observes that Christian discourse operated in an environment where rhetorical displays and public presentations were significant aspects of society.[149] That certainly seems the case in Acts. Luke has unlettered apostles (Acts 4:13) amaze crowds and opponents with their verbal virtuosity. Paul's rhetorical display at Athens leaves the philosophers speechless and, in a few instances, even convinced (Acts 17:16–33). His defense of the movement before Herod Agrippa II and Festus is so convincing that Herod Agrippa II responds (perhaps ironically) to Paul's arguments "Are you so quickly persuading me to become a Christian?" (Acts 26:28). Whether ironic or not, the passage presents for the reader the rhetorical flourish of a cosmic power broker who presents to imperial, regional, and local authorities the power of the divine. The disciples and apostles function here as paradigms for the church as envisioned by Luke. Embedded within the Jewish tradition, they operate freely (at least within Luke's narrative world) throughout the Roman Empire, displaying and mediating the power of the divine before imperial, regional, and local authorities. For the ancient reader (who is also a believer) the result is an affirmation of the inexorable spread of the power of the Christian god to "the ends of the earth" (Acts 1:8).

CONCLUSION

Divine power occupied a vital place in the social, political, and religious discourse among pagans, Jews, and Christians in the Greek East. The appropriate means with which to discern it came to dominate conversations in the Flavio-Trajanic period. The civic framework in which much of the discourse occurred was dominated by local elites, who held the priesthoods (some hereditary), built and maintained temples, facilitated alliances with political and religious centers, promoted their deities, and drew on ancient traditions (Greek in the case of most civic cults, "oriental" in the case of deities like Isis). Local elites like the freedman Zoilos at Aphrodisias in the first century B.C.E., who served as priest for life of Aphrodite, was a major benefactor to the city, and facilitated the very profitable connections to the Romans, helped to establish a pattern followed through the Severan period.[150] Under Claudius, local elites officiating at religious ceremonies or dedicating magnificent structures at Aphrodisias[151] or Eleusis[152] could be Roman citizens instead of freedmen. By the Flavio-Trajanic period, they might even be senators.

Chariton's portrayal of Callirhoe and Chaereas fits this period well. Both protagonists begin with the prerequisites desired of elites in the Greek East: paideia, high standing, good family. Through her appearance and *sophrosyne,* Callirhoe becomes the vehicle through which the divine (in this case, Aphrodite) displays its power. As discussed in preceding chapters, other power centers (imperial, regional, and local) are interpreted through the lens of Aphrodite's power. Chaereas emerges from his adolescent self-pity and jealousy to become the ideal man in the Greek East: pious, heroic, judicious, ethical. Ti. Claudius Diogenes and the other sponsors of the Sebasteion might have used the same script, as they too mine the Greek mythic past, merging it with heroic presentations of the victorious exploits of the emperors, all framed within the universal power of the goddess Aphrodite. Their activities had countless parallels throughout the Greek East, which provided societal, visual, and narrative frameworks within which other groups often had to define themselves and their power brokers.

For Jews, power brokers probably included local Jewish elites such as

Gaius Tyrronius Clades, Lucius, and Popilius Rufus in Acmonia, who in the latter part of the first century served as benefactors to their local Jewish communities through the restoration of the sacred space (the synagogue) and their "virtuous life, goodwill and zeal." Gaius was head of the synagogue for life, an office whose function is unclear. But it must have had similar significance as Zoilos's priesthood for life in the cult of Aphrodite. It implies that Gaius brokered to some extent the power of the divine, though the exact nature of that activity remains unclear. No doubt, however, it was Jews like Gaius who helped negotiate relations with the local, regional, and imperial powers. Philo as mediator and as interpreter of the divine is an excellent example. Examples for the Flavio-Trajanic period, however, are few and far between. Late traditions portray Rabbi Yohanan ben Zakkai mediating between the divine, imperial, and local authorities, though it is difficult to separate historical fact from legendary embellishment.[153]

Our best evidence, especially for this period, comes from literary sources. The texts themselves serve as the brokers of power, albeit usually directed toward a believing community and usually through association with a famous personage. Like the Sebasteion, which brokers the power of Aphrodite through the employment of mythic and heroic images presented within the physical structure of a monumental building, the texts broker the power of the Jewish god through the narrative structure of a book (or scroll). The voices are those of famous figures of the past: Baruch or Ezra or the Sibyl or even Philo (as represented in Pseudo-Philo). The authors draw on these figures (as well as Moses, David, the law, the Temple, and so on) to demonstrate for their readers the nature of God's activity. Often the presentation is decidedly apocalyptic, one natural response to the alienation felt by some Jews operating in an increasingly difficult environment. That approach had its following at least until the disastrous Bar Kochba revolt. The priests, of course, had long served to mediate divine power, and in some sense that tradition persevered (though considerably altered) through the writings and activities of the rabbis. Indeed, it is through the rabbinic schools that emphasis on the law, moral codes, and maintaining the vitality of the ancient traditions continued as significant vehicles through which interpreters sought to discern the role of the sacred.

Josephus, priest, prophet, interpreter of dreams, conversant with the law and the venerable traditions, represents the Jewish cosmic power broker par excellence. His entire corpus depicts the role of the Jewish god in the course of history, from the beginning through the Jewish wars and beyond. The rationales for his different books vary, of course, but underlying them all is a deep-felt quest for the role of the divine in events confronting the Jewish community in the aftermath of the Jewish war. Josephus offers us a unique look through the eyes of a late-first-century Jew at this significant period. The competition between pagan views of reality and Josephus's Jewish one becomes patently obvious in *Against Apion*. The real power behind the cosmic scene is demonstrably clear from Josephus's perspective. The degree to which he felt compelled to address the charges against Judaism as well as the false claims (from his perspective) of Greek religious superiority indicates the competitive atmosphere that Josephus encountered (at least as he perceived it). The later harangues against Judaism by Latin writers such as Tacitus (*Hist.* 5.5.2) and Juvenal (*Sat.* 14.96–104) and the revolt of 115–17 C.E. indicate that prejudice and hostility were real. Other power brokers such as astrologers are shown to be ineffective compared to their Jewish counterparts (as, e.g., Simon the Essene). Josephus, like his apocalyptic counterparts, paints a portrait of an ancient, venerable tradition filled with powerful figures like Moses, Abraham, Solomon, David, Simon the Essene, and Josephus the priest and interpreter of dreams who mediated God's activity in political and social events and come alive again as the reader views Josephus's brokered narrative.

The Christian texts from the Flavio-Trajanic period are a diverse lot, ranging from the set of community teachings (Didache) to a narrative depicting the movement from its inception to the death of Paul (Luke–Acts). We have even less information about possible Christians who sought to mediate for the Christian communities with outside groups. The bishops and deacons mentioned in Timothy may have had that role. But generally our sources are literary. For that reason they also function as narrative presentations of divine activity and power. Again we see the venerable Jewish tradition and figures associated with it play a major role (law, Temple, Moses, Abraham). But new mediators now dominate the narrative world, notably Jesus and the disciples. In virtually every text, Jesus mediates the power of God, whether in the guise of high priest (Hebrews), cosmic war lord (Revelation),[154] or prophet, miracle worker, Messiah (Luke–Acts). That new dimension, the nature of Jesus as mediator of the divine, becomes the vehicle by which groups carry on conversations with other arenas of power, notably imperial, pagan, and Jewish. Christian responses to that contact range from tolerance to outright rejection and expectations of imminent destruction, but all the texts have one thing in common: the current order will end. That belief paints even the apparent tolerance of Luke or 1 Peter with a different brush. The current imperial system may be powerful and need to be obeyed, but it will be replaced.

Luke presents a rare glimpse into the mind of a person living in the Flavio-Trajanic period who, like Josephus, understands the elite culture of the Greek East in which he must operate. Jesus and the apostles demonstrate the ethics, education, and piety so important in the Greek East. Their encounters with powerful groups such as Roman, Greek, and Jewish authorities, as well as with pagan cults, illustrate well the competitive world of the Flavio-Trajanic period. Luke depicts cosmic power brokers such as magicians, Jewish leaders and prophets, miracle workers, pagan adherents to the great civic cult of Artemis, Athenian philosophers, Roman leaders, and civic leaders to make one major point: the Christian god and his special agent, Jesus, represent the real power in the cosmos. Those who ignore that ultimately do so at their peril.

Cosmic power brokers in the Greek East took many forms, but their goals often overlapped: to discern and depict the divine for members of their own group and to use their power to negotiate relationships with other power centers. For Christians and some Jews, such negotiations could serve as a way to make sense of present suffering. Jesus and the disciples become the paradigm for Christians. In the pagan world (and, to a lesser extent, in the Jewish), local elites generally served as the power brokers, as displayed in the monuments and epigraphic remains spread all over the ancient world. Some groups remained outside "legitimate" structures, such as magicians, who nevertheless enjoyed remarkable popularity. Each group drew on its own tradition, its own deity or deities, its own sacred geography, and its own special set of materials to engage in a symbolically powerful discourse (if to no one else but members of its own group) mediated through cosmic power brokers. A significant number of these groups addressed the symbolic power of the future, a concern that often structured and informed conversations carried on in the present.

7.

The Power
of the Future

[A] mythic future . . . —like a mythic past—enters discourse in the present always and only for reasons of the present. What is more, such myths may well be (and have often been) contested territory as competing segments of society seek to appropriate them and turn them to their own interests, be those interests the preservation of the status quo or the reconstruction of society in some radically new form.

— Lincoln, *Discourse and the Construction of Society*

Symbols associated with the future occurred through media with long-standing traditions. Oracles, prophecies, votive offerings, cultic practices of the mystery cults, architecture, tombs, games, festivals, and treaties often framed images and symbols of the future that informed or expressed concerns that persons had in the present. Symbols of the future in antiquity often centered on "personal religion" or personal piety that sought salvation "through closeness to the divine"[1] as persons selected from a plethora of options to cope with the future. Yet "personal religion" meant more than an individual concern for one's future salvation after death. The benefactor who provided funds for a festival dedicated to a local deity may well have obtained "personal" as well as political satisfaction. Personal religion was also invariably associated with assorted webs of power. Rarely did one make a decision that did not include participation in a whole network of social, political, and cultural forces. The intensity of religious feeling by persons should not be downplayed because a practice may have resulted in political benefits or personal prestige. Neither should one ignore the significant role images of the future played in the intersections of imperial, regional, local, and cosmic power.

PAGANS AND THE POWER
OF THE FUTURE

Symbols from the past and the present often interweave with those of the future. For the provinces, stimulus frequently came from Rome. Official sponsorship of building programs in Italy and the provinces ensured the future of the state and provided concrete frames of reference that symbolized past glories, Rome's current achievements, and the empire's future stability. The famous arch of Titus built in the Roman forum celebrated the Flavian triumph over the Jews and alluded to the past, a connection made by Titus's brother Domitian, who completed the arch. The future glory of Rome and the Flavian house is duly symbolized in the apotheosis of Titus displayed at the top of the arch (continuing a Roman imperial tradition) and in the arch itself.[2] Domitian creates his own new links to the past, as his change in the iconography of coins indicates.[3] The continuance of the power of Rome and the Flavian family forms the constant thematic thread in these iconographic visions of the future. The appearance of arches throughout the empire celebrate not only the triumphs of Rome but also its enduring presence throughout its empire.[4]

The continued existence of the empire itself created a significant "symbolic horizon" for the conducting of everyday affairs. The "myth" of ongoing imperial rule guaranteed even mundane affairs such as contracts, laws, and economic interactions. Augustus's and, later, the Flavians' propensity to stress peace and continued prosperity under Roman rule further bolstered a myth of the unending power of Rome. Actions and transactions occurring today, the myth implies, will be honored tomorrow. Some in the Greek East even incorporated this into the fabric of their civic structure. A decree regarding a bequest to the city of Acmonia in Phrygia is guaranteed "by the eternity of the empire of the Romans."[5] A vision of the future, symbolically depicted, works to govern activities in the present. Thus it seems no accident that one of the acts of those revolting against Rome in the Jewish war of 66–73 C.E., after seizing Jerusalem, was to destroy the records of debts and contracts.[6] Without the vision of a Roman government ruling in perpetuity, the contracts and debts meant nothing, at least to those who did not share the vision. Yet this was not necessarily the case for all who revolted from Rome. Babatha, the Jewish woman who died during the Bar Kochba war, had a number of legal documents with her that discussed her landholdings and other legal contracts.[7] Many of the documents make clear that the interaction depicted occurs within the framework of imperial power, as the opening lines of Babatha's land registration indicates:

> In the reign of Imperator Caesar divi Traiani Parthici filius divi Nervae nepos Traianus Hadrianus Augustus pontifex maximus tribuniciae potestatis XII consul III, in the consulship of Marcus Gavius Gallicanus and Titus Atilius Rufus Titianus four days before the nones of December, and according to the compute of the new province of Arabia year twenty-second month Apellaios the sixteenth, in the city of Rabbath-Moab. As a census of Arabia is being conducted by Titus Aninius Sextius Florentinus, legatus Augusti pro praetore,

I, Babtha daughter of Simon, of Maoza in the Zoarene [district] of the Petra administrative region, domiciled in my own private property in the said Maoza, register what I possess . . .[8]

Imperial power (from an empire to a regional and to a local setting) frames the nature of the transaction in this document, publicly displayed after its completion. The relevance of the document for future transactions works only as long as the power of the empire continues to hold sway in some fashion. Presumably, even though Babatha was part of or associated with a revolt against Roman power, she kept documents obtained under Roman rule that were invested with Rome's authority to support any future legal claim to her land.[9]

Gifts or bequests were used by the emperors to bolster their power and the power of members of the elite classes whose support they needed. Local deities also played an important role. Between 102 and 116, Trajan used a bequest left to him by a member of the local elite class at Aphrodisias to help repair damage caused by an earthquake.[10] Trajan integrates his imperial prerogative with the power of the Aphrodisian Aphrodite, now firmly associated with the civic character of the city, by beginning the dedication "To the first mother [*prometor*] Aphrodite." The reference recalling Aphrodite's connection to the Julian clan stresses the continuity of Trajan's reign with the founding of imperial rule. Trajan also dedicates his gift to the demos, showing the intersection of divine, imperial, and local rule. The mention of specific local elites, one who originally left the bequest to Trajan, the other a priest (one presumes of Aphrodite or of the imperial cult), bolsters their local power and prestige. The public display of the inscription (location unknown) provided a continual reminder of the power of Aphrodite, the beneficence of the emperor, and the prestige of a local family whose money stimulated the connection in the first place and who now control the distribution for the benefit of the polity.

Public gifts such as the one at Aphrodisias, building programs, and festivals provided ways for local elites to become immortal. The extensive building activity by local elites throughout the Greek East has been noted already. The portrayal of local prestige and power, as well as leaving a legacy for the future, no doubt played an important role in people's decisions. The precedent was clearly established by Augustus, who could boast that he "left in marble that which he had found in brick." Clearly Suetonius's portrait of Augustus indicates how potent this image was for his own generation. Buildings implied a permanence and a continuation of one's presence. They also highlighted the power and prestige of the benefactor in the present. Simon Price rightly notes that imperial cult complexes indicated that "the rule of any given emperor would last for ever," and that "the successive erection of statues of new emperors implied the durability of imperial rule."[11]

One person made the connection between benefaction and personal immortality explicit in the city of Gytheion in southern Greece. His generosity is inscribed on stone pillars set up in the marketplace, on the imperial temple near the city gate, and on the gymnasium, "so that my philanthropic generosity should be conspicuous and acknowledged both by citizens and by visitors to the city." His rationale? "My idea is that I shall be immortal by virtue of this just and kindly gift."[12] This inscription dates somewhere between 161 and 169 C.E. and displays explicitly what must have been implicit for most benefactors. Donors, perhaps most donors, saw the establishment of memorials, festivals, and other honors in their name as a form of immortality. Memorials and festivals that began after one died also had significant implications for the present. The symbol of the future expressed in the memorial or festival commemorating the person's life and death displayed and sometimes altered power relations in the present. A legal change finalized in the Flavian period made the process even more attractive for local civic institutions. The change allowed local cities and towns to enforce contractual agreements made between them and donors who subsequently died. Prior to the Flavians, if someone in their will left money to a town for a festival or some other benefaction, the ruling officials of the town were obliged to wait on the good wishes and "honor" of those in charge of the person's estate to fulfill the will's stipulations. Continuing a process begun under Claudius, the Flavians allowed many local cities to become legal entities with the power to receive legacies and to sue for (and win) funds withheld by recalcitrant trustees of the estates.[13] Symbols of the future (the benefactions and their association with the deceased) took a more civic turn as imperial power strengthened the hand of local officials at the expense of the immediate family.[14] This change may have helped the renaissance in local cults through the late first and early second centuries in the Greek East as local elites saw their immortality tied to the religio-political structure of their local community.

Oracles,[15] prayers, divination, and vows played more recognized roles for persons who sought to make sense of present concerns through discernment of the future. These mechanisms provided groups and individuals a release from anxiety and distress, obtained requested success or profit, or placed persons in a situation that promised more control over an uncertain future.[16] They also provided divine legitimation for new practices through reference to ancient and revered media.[17]

The oracular role of deities such as Apollo of Delphi, Claros, or Didyma is well documented and need not be rehearsed here.[18] In the Flavio-Trajanic period they witnessed a revival as elites like Plutarch show a greater interest.[19] Sometimes the significance such oracular activity held for the social and religious well-being of the community comes from the most mundane examples. In the early part of the second century C.E., a group of workmen at Miletus placed their question to the oracle at Didyma and the subsequent response on the back wall of the theater, which they helped to build. They had asked the oracle whether they should break their contract to build a certain portion of the theater. In an obscure response, the oracle advised them to complete their task and then display their question and the oracle's response on the building itself.[20] Such practical consequences of oracular activity exhibit how the social and even economic arenas could be influenced by the divine realm. The oracle maintained and shaped (literally in this case) the civic landscape. Moreover, the dedication of the response offered public acknowledgment in a prominent civic structure of the oracular power of the deity for those who read the inscription in the future. Civic space, the theater, provided the framework for affirming and reiterating the power of the oracle for further generations.

When certain Jews and Christians wrote the Sibylline Oracles, they appropriated for their own use this powerful and popular way to determine the god's will.[21] The popularity of divination, especially through oracles, for all levels of society is evident in the number of fragments of questions to and answers from oracles.[22] A third-century document, the Astrampsychus, which records a series of proper questions one asks an oracle as well as a list of responses, make clear that slaves, soldiers, and women were clients of the oracles "as often as wealthy men and businessmen.[23]

Prayer as well as petition, often part of the oracular process, also closed the gap between the divine and the everyday world. Prayer helped people deal with a future often full of uncertainty, potential distress, and multiple possibilities.[24] A statue in the Valley of the Kings in Egypt was dislodged by an earthquake in the first century C.E. and began to give off a distinctive sound. Greek and Roman visitors to the site, especially in the late first century, believed that they heard the god Memnon in the statue's whisper. Large numbers of inscriptions remain, many inscribed with great detail and care.[25] Some visitors came from long distances to Egypt. One graffito describes a certain Hermogenes from Amasia, near the Black Sea, who writes: "I, Hermogenes, of Amasia have seen other chambers and was amazed, but when I visited this one of Memnon I, was completely astounded."[26] As H. S. Versnel rightly remarks, when persons in antiquity thanked or honored a "human or divine benefactor in word or deed," they rarely did so "without also ensuring [their] future."[27] An inscription became a personal witness, which, added to the other, countless inscriptions, authenticated one's association with a powerful and enduring deity.

Dreams, visions, and epiphanies determined the future or discerned the will of the god or gods. This, of course, has a long tradition in pagan and Jewish circles. The visitation of the gods, people believed, was not simply a phenomenon of the distant past. Dreaming addressed human concerns, ranging from whether one was loved to whether one would win in an athletic event or become successful in business ventures.[28] Dreams, as Peter Brown argues, became "the paradigm of the open frontier: when a man was asleep and his bodily senses were stilled the frontier lay wide open between himself and the god."[29] Dreams provided a vehicle for individuals and groups to visit the realm of the divine, to visit the gods. Through dreams the gods in turn could visit humans. In a world seemingly controlled by the whims of fate or human inconsistency, dreams and visions offered a modicum of security. They drew on publicly available symbolic discourse that enabled an individual to tap into the divine. This socially sanctioned discourse provided a brief glimpse into an uncertain and insecure future.[30] Dreams and visions were powerful mechanisms for discerning the future or for being captured by the divine; but discernment of the future came with its own set of fears. Maximus, a Roman decurion, wrote on a temple wall at Mandulis (Talmis, in Egypt) that "a sleeping nook induced me to descend even though I was a bit afraid to abandon myself to visions or dreams."[31]

One of the more telling exhibits of the hold the future had on the mentality of the Greek East is the massive body of evidence for votive offerings.[32] W. Burkert notes that such offerings bear witness to personal stories of "anxiety, hope, prayer, and fulfillment," to acts of "personal religion." Vows display "a major human strategy for coping with the future" and often denote intense religious experiences, "the search for some escape or help," often sought (and obtained), according to a number of inscriptions, through supernatural intervention in "dreams, visions, or divine command."[33] Votive offerings are often public events as well. Vows permitted wealthy individuals to express their concern for the future by erecting magnificent sanctuaries. Persons of more modest means used vows to obtain healings, safety in childbirth or sea voyages, and successful business dealings. Burkert stresses that votive offerings socialized

> anxieties and sufferings. The petitioner encounters the interest and reinforcement offered by priests and fellow worshipers. The vow is made in public, and the fulfillment is demonstratively public, with many others profiting from the investment, craftsmen, shopkeepers, and all those sharing in the sacrificial banquets.[34]

Personal desires to be healed, to remain safe on trips at sea,[35] or to have love reciprocated had corporate implications. Concern for the future was not simply an individual quest for meaning.

No aspect of human existence illustrates the corporate character associated with the appropriation of symbols connected with the future better than death. Symbols abound in the Greek East that deal with the death of loved ones, a person's own death, or the death of powerful figures in a community or society. One finds constant interplay between the life of a local elite and the various power networks in which the person played. As Elias Canetti argues: "No one who studies the original documents of any religion can fail to be amazed at the power of the dead."[36] Archaeological evidence exhibits a host of social roles played by the dead, including "legitimation of the social order, embodiments of land rights, martyrs to a holy cause, guardians of ancestral traditions or even an archaeological management resource. The living may conceal, embellish or justify their actual social relations through a relationship to the dead."[37] An inscription at Iulia Gordos in Lydia illustrates certain of these connections. Dated around 75/76 C.E., the inscription is on a white marble stele that served as the lid for the grave. The stele records honors given to a certain Theophilos, whose noble ancestry indicates his elite status. His list of offices includes serving as a general, an *agoranomos* (market overseer), and a frequent ambassador to Rome on behalf of the city. The inscription records that the council (*boule*), the people (*demos*), and the Romans "who are engaged in business among us" honored him with a painted portrait, gold bust, and marble statue.[38] The inscription commemorating his death exhibits how one's death serves as a vehicle to display the relation between Roman power (the

Roman businessmen) and local elites. Further, Theophilos, like many others from elite classes across the Roman Empire, participates in the Roman network of power through embassies to Rome on behalf of the city.[39] Even in death Theophilos's monument depicts for future generations the network of power operating during his life and after his death.

Some believed that after death a person could continue to communicate with the living and in some cases negotiate between the divine world and those who sought redress, comfort, or guidance. Of course, the belief that the dead communicated with the living (especially heroic figures) has a long history. Evidence suggests that such an attitude extended to members of local elite classes in the Greek East. At Thyatira in Lydia, a local cult association and the family of the deceased dedicated a funerary altar (dated to the second or third century C.E.) to Ammias, a former priestess of the association.

> To Ammias, her children and the initiates of the gods set up the altar with the sarcophagus for the priestess of the gods as a memorial. And if anyone wants to learn the truth from me, let him pray at (?) the altar for whatever he wants and he will get it, via a vision, during the nighttime and day.[40]

The power of the priestess while alive continues in the future, although we have no evidence in what fashion or how seriously the community viewed this after honoring her. Certainly the perception of her ability to communicate in the future played a role in the iconography of power at the time the inscription was commissioned and executed. Her power (or perceived power) displays the prestige of the association and her kin. Future communications promised through dreams or visions ensure her continued influence (and, by association, that of those who sponsored the inscription).[41]

Burials could also stress familial obligations to the deceased parent within a public context. A late Hellenistic inscription from Arsada in Lykia dedicated to Artemes by his wife charges their sons to sacrifice annually, one presumes in memory of their father. If they do not, they will be "sinners against god and the dead."[42] The public character of the inscription places familial obligation within a civic, as well as cosmic, context.[43] The civic connection is also patently obvious in the use of epithets against grave robbers, who if caught are expected to pay a fine to the local deity, the town, a local guild,[44] or, in certain Jewish inscriptions, to the local synagogue.[45]

A well-known inscription from Nazareth illustrates pointedly the intersection of death with imperial and cosmic power.

> Ordinance of Caesar. It is my pleasure that graves and tombs remain undisturbed in perpetuity for those who have made them for the cult[46] of their ancestors or children or members of their house. If, however, any man lay information that another has either demolished them, or has in any other way extracted the buried, or has maliciously transferred them to other places in order to wrong them, or has displaced the sealing or other stones, against such a one I order that a trial be instituted, as in respect of the gods, so in regard to the cult of mortals. For it shall be much more obligatory to honor the buried. Let it be absolutely forbidden for anyone to disturb them. In case of contraven-

tion I desire that the offender be sentenced to capital punishment or charge of violation of sepulture.[47]

The plundering or inappropriate re-use of an individual's grave had social and in some cases cosmic implications.[48]

Through death, individuals sought to maintain a connection with the group or groups that provided a sense of order and purpose. A certain Peplos in Ephesus established an association to continue his memory with appropriate rites to maintain his tomb.[49] Death and burial also provided friends and relatives the opportunity to make statements about the deceased's significance to the social fabric of a community. Customs associated with the burial and later activities at the tomb (routinized visits, anniversary memorials, a specific mourning period) provided "social support for mourners' psychic needs."[50] The memorial addressed future generations and often conveyed a message that exhibited the networks of power in which the deceased (and his or her associates) participated.[51] The social networks are most clear on tombs that include inscriptions warning all persons that the tomb was to remain inviolate in perpetuity. Honor and respect, key features of local elites' actions in the present, continued through the threat of economic and sometimes divine penalties. Tomb inscriptions for some freedmen in the first century B.C.E. and first century C.E. proclaimed the change of status of the deceased, a fact of particular importance to their families, who wished to continue and promote the prestige of such a change in status.[52] Funerary dedications, as B. D. Shaw observes, connote the value that the deceased had

> in overall networks of power of the whole society in which the family had an integral function. The act of placing a tombstone, of having it inscribed, was integrally connected with the webs of duties and feelings concerning the dead and, by extension, a mirroring of their status while still among the living.[53]

Nothing better illustrates the symbolic power of the future for members of the elite classes in the Greek East than the well-known inscription of C. Vibius Salutaris of Ephesus, who made a bequest to the Boule and demos of Ephesus in 104 C.E.[54] The public character of the inscription displays the intricate connection between the individual and imperial, local, and cosmic power networks.[55] Salutaris set up a series of bequests honoring the emperor, the goddess Artemis, and the city of Ephesus. As the following quotation illustrates, his bequest establishes a series of rituals in perpetuity.

> The care of the aforementioned sacred images, and the conveyance before everyone, from the temple into the theatre, and from the theatre into the temple of Artemis, will be done according to the bequest every year by two of the neopoioi and a beadle, and the guards [7 lines missing] . . . [his bequest] to be valid, unable to be changed, indissoluble, precisely similar for all time.[56]

The inscription was displayed prominently in the city and established future rituals intimately connected with the goddess Artemis, the city leadership, the emperor, and the local governors. The future rituals had current implications, as the accompanying letter by the Roman proconsul Aquillius Proculus indicates: "May I congratulate him that his piety toward the goddess and the Augusti, and his goodwill toward the city in the theatre now become clear to all."[57] There can be little doubt that they did, at least among members of the local elite class. When enacted, the rituals displayed the power present in the person of Salutaris. Key webs of power intertwine: imperial power as manifested in the dedication of the emperor and the confirmation of the proconsul and *legatus pro praetore* that those who break or attempt to change the rituals as set forth will incur a penalty paid to Artemis and to the emperor; local power as invested in the demos and Gerousia as well as in those assorted personages who participated in the processions; and divine power as invested in the goddess Artemis. The inscription itself, displayed in the theater, a prominent public place, becomes part of the future myth. This myriad of activities concerning the future underscored Salutaris's power and prestige in the city as recognized not only by the local demos but also by the Roman rulers and the divine world.

As argued earlier, euergetism and a willingness to participate in the Roman imperial system dominated much of the activity of local elites and their affiliates in the Greek East. Even so, local elites redefined that system within the rubric of their traditions and cosmic connections. Josephus acknowledges and even bolsters Roman power. God confirms it. Yet even Roman rule, his account makes clear, will run its course only to be replaced by a new order established by the Jewish god. The Christian writer Luke makes the point that God will replace the current powers even more explicit while still maintaining Roman rule as an instrument of the Christian god. Both remain, nevertheless, largely sympathetic or at least tolerant of the status quo.

Not all who drew on powerful symbols of the future viewed their relation to the imperial power structure with such sympathy or tolerance. Some pagan, Jewish, and Christian groups saw the current political, social, or cultural order as inherently bad, evil, or, at best, a nuisance.[58] Often such groups used the same symbolic field of discourse as more sympathetic counterparts. As Bruce Lincoln has observed:

> When previously persuasive discourses no longer persuade and previously prevalent sentiments no longer prevail, society enters a situation of fluidity and crisis. In such moments competing groups continue to deploy strategic discourses and may also make use of coercive force as they struggle, not just to seize or retain power, but to reshape the borders and hierarchic order of society itself.[59]

Works like the Acts of the Pagan Martyrs, written in Alexandria, the Jewish Fourth Sibylline Oracle, and the Christian Book of Revelation bluntly and with hostility place power within the strict domain of their respective deity or deities. The present for these groups shows that Roman rule and those associated with it have failed miserably. The symbolic discourse regarding the future portrays clearly the result: a new order is coming and the present powers will be demolished. This material reflects an attitude that some call "cognitive dissonance," whereby a group or writer has a strong sense of alienation with the powers that be. Resistance may well involve the "purposeful reproduction of ambiguous meanings, rather than the dualistic or monolithic meanings of state-sponsored ideologies or religions."[60] Such ambiguous use of symbols appears in the frontier regions of Britain, the Rhine, and the Danube. There, in the first and second centuries C. E., locals began to cremate their dead and then place the remains under tumuli. To Roman officials and soldiers, such burials may have seemed to imitate the round tombs in Rome, perhaps modeled on Augustus's mausoleum. But the burials also imitate practices from the Late Bronze Age and may indicate instead a "native reaction" against the Romans[61] or at least the "purposeful reproduction of ambiguous meanings." Some first-century funerary altars also suggest that those who commissioned them subtly used them to resist imperial power.[62] Even in Archaia, as early as the Augustan period, anti-Roman feelings surfaced through ritual expression and through the neglect of sacred landscapes associated with imperial rule (e.g., imperial cult complexes).[63] The latter represents a direct attack on the stable presence of the Roman Empire encouraged through the sponsorship of buildings and their maintenance.

Other vehicles for discerning the future, though not necessarily hostile toward imperial or political power, nevertheless encountered sporadic hostility from the ruling authorities. The concern for the future that permeated the ancient world finds clear expression in the fascination with astrology and magic.[64] Each in its own way allowed individuals to shape their present activities, often in association with an equally powerful tendency toward a deterministic view that saw the world dominated by the whims of fate. Astrology had obtained great status through the influence of the astrological schools in Babylon.[65] By the first century B.C.E., astrological signs and symbols permeated literature and to a lesser extent the iconography of the Graeco-Roman Empire.[66] Thus, the cult statue of Aphrodite of Aphrodisias displayed solar and lunar imagery depicting her intimate connection to (and control of?) the structure of the cosmos. The Egyptian goddess Isis, now thoroughly Hellenized, was portrayed with cosmic images.[67] Apuleius makes the astrological connection explicit in a way that had numerous parallels in our period. "[Isis] informed me how much I must spend on the ceremonies, and decreed that Mithras himself, her high priest, who, as she explained, was joined to me by a divine conjunction of stars, would administer the rites" (*Meta.* 11.22). Chapter 11 of the *Metamorphoses* marks the end of ten chapters of misery, uncertainty, and buffeting of the hero, Lucius. Isis, the high priest remarks, rescues people like Lucius from the vicissitudes of Fortune, whereas high birth, fine education, or powerful position could not (*Meta.* 11.15). Lucius's famous prayer to Isis celebrates her powerful impact on the future:

> Neither a day nor a night nor even a tiny moment passes empty of your blessings: you protect men on sea and land, and you drive away the storm-winds of life and stretch forth your rescuing hand, with which you unwind the threads of the Fates even when they are inextricably twisted, you calm the storms of fortune, and you repress harmful motions of the stars. (*Met.* 11.25)

This vision of a powerful deity controlling even the whimsical forces of fate in the present provided a modicum of security, especially for those who, like Lucius, had something to lose.

That concern for security may well have played a role in the popularity of the Mithras cult as well, especially among the military. The cult, which spread throughout the Roman Empire in the first through fourth centuries C.E., displays a clear association with the astrological interest prevalent in the ancient world. The signs of the zodiac and the symbols of the planets, the sun, and the moon appear on numerous paintings and reliefs in Mithraic shrines throughout the Roman world.[68] By the end of the first century, astrological images played an increasingly important role for those who sought to draw on cosmic power to make sense of their circumstances.[69] An ability to read or control the future gave individuals and groups a modicum of security (and power) to live within the present.

Magic also shaped the way people dealt with an uncertain future. Magic and astrology, though often outlawed, proved resistant.[70] Much modern debate has centered on the nature of magic in antiquity.[71] Ancient protests against magical activities often have the character of a reaction against the "Other," that is, those outside the accusing group.[72] Through the manipulation of particular formulaic devices, people sought to control events.[73] Practitioners attempted to manipulate to some extent the will of the gods, though they probably viewed their rituals as religious and not as magic.[74] Thus, a certain Thessalus, a student doctor, attached a section of magical rites to a work on medical astrobotany and dedicated the work to the Roman emperor.[75] This mid-first-century C.E. text indicates that Thessalus sought out a priest to help him understand and meet the god associated with the doctor's art, Asclepius.[76]

Defixiones (curse tablets), popular from the fifth century B.C.E. through the sixth century C.E., show the powerful attraction of trying to influence the gods. Generally inscribed on pieces of lead, they "intended to influence, by supernatural means, the actions or welfare of persons or animals against their will."[77] Generally, *defixiones* are found in tombs, chthonic sanctuaries, or underground bodies of water. D. R. Jordan notes that depositing a curse tablet into the grave of one who had died an untimely death (often a child) meant the petitioner could draw on the spirit of the unsettled dead to effect his desires.[78] Typical is a first- or second-century charm to make a woman love a man; next to the text is the drawing of a mummy.[79] Dating the *defixiones* is often difficult, but several have apparently been found in archaeologically verifiable first-century C.E. contexts. One intriguing example comes from the agora in Athens. Hecate in a variety of forms, Pluton (the god of the underworld), the Fates, Persephone, and Hermes are invoked to punish thieves who had taken some coverlets and a fleecy white new cloak.[80] A sample of the much longer inscription conveys the point: "I inscribe and consign to Pluto and Fates and Persephone and to Furies and every evil one, I consign also to Hecate eater of animals (or eater of what has been demanded by the god),[81] I consign to underworld goddesses and gods and to Hermes messenger, I consign the thieves who take their name from the little house of a certain slum quarter . . ."[82] A bat sketched with outstretched wings and numerous drawings of Hecate completed the stark appeal to the gods to resolve a breaking of the social covenant.[83] An early-second-century curse tablet from Amorgos in Greece asks Demeter to punish the persons or persons who encouraged slaves to escape.[84]

The quest to draw on the power associated with symbols of the future stemmed in part from the capricious nature of the present. Tyche, or Fate, symbolized better than anything else the potential sudden change in fortune that could occur to any individual, group, or even empire.[85] Whether viewed anthropomorphically as a fickle deity or as an abstract concept epitomizing the chance circumstances one encounters, Fate's role in the individual and corporate lives of people in the Graeco-Roman Empire had a significant influence on conceptions of the future.[86] The concern over an uncertain future and the role played by forces beyond individual control influenced the symbols popular among ancient writers, not least among the authors of the novels.

Chariton of Aphrodisias and the Future

Images that conjure up the potent power resting in the future greet the reader throughout Chariton's novel. The protagonists dream dreams that portend the future, utter prayers for deliverance that the goddess accepts or rejects, and build magnificent tombs that glorify the power and prestige of the dedicants and the dead for future generations. Chariton is quite aware of what plays well with his reading audience. The foreshadowing so popular with Chariton (and many of the novels)[87] parallels the intense desire on the part of many to acquire knowledge of the future. Chaereas and Callirhoe never quite know the future, but the reader does through foreshadowing and authorial (or at least narratorial) asides.

Toward the end of their journey, Chaereas and Callirhoe encounter individuals capable of reading the future. Not surprisingly, these people are associated with the cult of Aphrodite. The author explicitly states that the priests of Aphrodite at Paphos were prophets of the future (8.2.9). The appearance of such diviners assures the reader that the narrative is inhabited by persons who understand and come to grips with their future. But Chariton is not above playing with the reader's emotional concern for the future. When Callirhoe awakes in her tomb and hears tomb robbers trying to enter, she initially believes some divinity has come to take her (1.9.3). Her fear of an angry deity has a parallel in a first-century B.C.E. tomb inscription from Kyzikos in which the deceased, Apollodoros, describes Hades as an "Indiscriminate arbiter of life for all mortals, bitter Hades, who casts his envious eyes upon honourable things."[88]

The very quest of Chaereas and Callirhoe in their journey across the ancient landscape of the Mediterranean world indicates a desire to understand the character of the future, both one's personal future and the future of society itself. Chariton has his hero and heroine reunited by Aphrodite after endless sufferings and wandering. Why? Because Aphrodite considers outrageous Tyche's plan to continue to keep them apart (8.1.1–3). Aphrodite, like Apuleius's Isis and other deities who exhibit universal powers, has control even over the disruptive power of Tyche. Chariton presents the reader with the goddess Aphrodite, who, by her very nature, is able to control the whimsical forces of human and divine behavior. The final episode of the book highlights how the power of Aphrodite provides some certainty for the future. Here Callirhoe prays to Aphrodite that she never be separated from Chaereas again (8.8.15–16). By this time Callirhoe, and certainly the reader, know that Aphrodite is the source of future prosperity and stability.

A specific allusion to a future outside the narrative time of the text deserves mention. The child of Chaereas and Callirhoe, who is left with Dionysius, will return as a great king. This promise may imply that the child is an Aeneas figure who returns to the West as a conquering hero.[89] The allusion illustrates Chariton's wish to show important ties between the West and the East, especially the area around western Asia Minor. It displays the importance of the Greek world and its historical implications. Chariton, like so many others across the Greek East, understands a Greek-influenced future shaping and informing the present.

JEWS AND THE POWER OF THE FUTURE

Jews drew on many of the same models available to all groups to address an uncertain future. Judaism was no monolithic entity but remained richly textured, composed of very diverse groups of people spread across the Roman Empire. Jews sponsored buildings, offered dedications, employed magical techniques,[90] utilized astrological signs,[91] created oracles, interpreted dreams,[92] and sought information through culturally appropriate divine channels (notably, prayer and sacrifice) as defined by their particular group. No common principle determined who selected what approach. Yet, Jews had their own heritage (whatever aspect they wished to stress), and by the end of the first century were, as noted earlier, a clearly identifiable religious entity. How the symbolic power of the future helped them negotiate their relations with imperial and regional powers depended on a number of factors.

Not surprisingly, those Jews who built buildings and inscribed dedications as a means of leaving a legacy were members of Jewish elites, who had the most to gain by emulating (albeit through the use of their own symbolic discourse) ruling elites across the empire.[93] The Herodian family is the most visible of this group, and Herod's refurbishing of the Temple in Jerusalem is the most ostentatious example.[94] The Herodians, however, were exceptional among most Jews in one respect. Josephus and inscriptional evidence indicate that their beneficence extended to non-Jews as well as Jews. In contrast, most other evidence that identifies the dedicant(s) as Jewish is connected with the Jewish community.[95] Several unique symbols helped Jews express their connection to the future and to the cosmos, most notably the menorah and the Torah. The menorah, especially after the destruction of the Temple, took on particular significance and was depicted on walls of houses and tombs and on lamps, amulets, and rings.[96] Menorahs themselves have been found in synagogues and tombs.[97] The menorah as a visible symbol appears on a coin of Antigonus (40–37 B.C.E.); the most famous example is the one associated with the Temple cult (depicted on Titus's arch).[98] Ironically, the menorah, which is displayed on Titus's arch as part of the spoils of war, emphasizing imperial power and prestige, became a fundamental symbol for the identity and continuity of the Jewish people.

Ancient traditions, as argued earlier, also play a significant role in a community's construction of its power in relation to those around them. In Judaism the prophetic traditions were a vibrant part of Jewish identity, including the Diaspora. The Torah played a critical role in this identity.[99] After the destruction of the Temple, the Torah shrine became an integral part of synagogue structures, both within and outside Israel.[100] As A. T. Kraabel notes, Diaspora Jews' "reverence for the Scripture is manifested architecturally in the Torah shrines" in several important Diaspora synagogues.[101] Epigraphic examples also point to the power of biblical passages.[102]

As did the pagans, some Diaspora Jews depicted on funerary monuments symbols associated with the future that often expressed the power networks in which the deceased and his or her associates operated. A well-known inscription regarding a certain Rufina, dating to the second or third century, provides an excellent example:

> Rufina, a Jewish woman, head of the synagogue, prepared this tomb for her freedmen and slaves; and no one else has the authority to bury here anyone else. If someone dares to do so, he will have to give 1500 denaria to the most sacred treasury and 1000 denaria to the Jewish community. A copy of this inscription has been deposited in the public archives.[103]

Rufina, a member and leader of the Jewish community, immortalized her benefaction to her slaves and freedman and highlighted the authority and prestige of arenas with which she was associated (civic power and the Jewish community), which receive the fine if someone uses the tomb improperly. The public character of the inscription, a copy of which was also placed in the archives, illustrates how much this particular Jewish community operated within the web of power assumed by the general community. Other inscriptions associated with Jewish tombs also bring divine power into the equation.[104] Sometimes this was presented in dramatic fashion, as exemplified in a second- or first-century B.C.E. tomb memorial from Rheneia, a small island near Delos:

> I call upon and pray to God the Most High, the Lord of the spirits and of all flesh, against those who have treacherously murdered or poisoned the poor Heraclea, who died untimely, and who have unjustly shed her innocent blood; may the same happen to them who have murdered or poisoned her and their children; Lord, you who see everything, and you, angels of God, for whom

every soul humiliates itself on this day with supplications, (hoping) that you revenge her innocent blood and settle your account with them as soon as possible. [105]

As P. W. van der Horst notes, the epitaph "is a prayer of vengeance on Yom Kippur, which was evidently celebrated by the Jewish community on pre-Christian Delos."[106] Another inscription, written in the early part of the second century C.E. in the city of Thyatira, illustrates again how the inscription itself becomes a symbol of the future for all those who encounter it. This inscription integrates imperial power, Jewish power, and the power of local elites.

Fabius Zosimus, who had this sarcophagus made, put it on a holy place located before the city, near the sabbateion in the Chaldaean quarter, alongside the public road, for himself, in order to be deposited there, and for his very sweet wife Aurelia Pontiane, but no one else has the right to deposit someone into this sarcophagus. But if someone dares to do so or acts contrary to these (rules), he will have to pay 1500 silver denaria to the city of the Thyatirans and to the most holy treasury 2500 silver denaria, and, moreover, he falls under the law of tomb violation. Two copies of this inscription have been written, one of which has been deposited in the archive. This has been done in the most illustrious city of the Thyatirans when Catillius Severus was consul, on the 13th of the month Audnaios, by Menophilus the public notary, the son of Julianus. [107]

The last sentence shows how even the members of the Jewish community structured their future within the future of the imperial system and the affiliated local elite power network. The tomb violation prohibition only makes sense if the civic framework remains a vital force. Without the system, prohibitions against the inviolability of the tomb are largely meaningless.

Inscriptions indicate that some Jews had the same gloomy outlook toward existence after death as their pagan counterparts. Two inscriptions from Leontopolis in Egypt are particularly revealing. The first, written in the first century C.E., describes a certain Jesus, who explains to those who pass his tomb:

I went to Hades when I was sixty years old. Weep all together for the one who has suddenly gone to the secret place of eternity to dwell in darkness. And you, Dositheus, weep for me, for it is your duty to pour libations of bitterest tears on my tomb. You are my child, for I have gone away childless. All weep together for Jesus, the lifeless. [108]

The other inscription displays the important role that Abramos played in the life of his community.

When he had already achieved the span of 53 years, he who tames all himself snatched him off to Hades. O sandy earth, what a body you hide of the soul of the most blessed Abramos. For he was not without honour in the city, but wore the wreath of magistracy for the whole people in his wisdom. For you were honoured with the leadership of two places, generously performing the double duty. And everything which was fitting to you, soul, before you hid yourself, we, your family of good children, are increasing. But you, passerby, seeing the grave of a good man, say these fair words to him and depart: "May the earth be light on you for ever."[109]

The familial connection is also apparent in these two inscriptions. The continuity of the family (or of a friend, in the case of Jesus) symbolizes the future existence of the individual, a concept with a long history.

The prophets still held significance for some Jewish communities who saw the prophetic period as a time of past greatness. "There was once among men a shining light of the sun when the harmonious ray of the prophets was being spread abroad, a tongue dripping a beautiful drink for all mortals with honeyed sweetness."[110] Some Jews believed that certain of their contemporaries had the ability to predict future events, often events with dire consequences.[111] Until the Mishnah, much of this theology understands that God worked through history and exhibited his power through special emissaries and groups. Those individuals and groups were able to interpret, and thus elucidate for those in the present, the dangers involved in continuing along certain paths.[112]

The most obvious literary effort of this sort comes from groups who held an eschatological or apocalyptic view of reality. The prevalent attitude among such groups held that the present age or rule was not run properly. The symbolic discourse of the Essenes and the writers of the Sibylline Oracles typically asserted that those in charge (Rome or their representatives) would be removed in the very near future and replaced by proper representatives of God.[113] The writer of the Fourth Sibylline Oracle (first to early second century C.E.) typifies the attitude toward imperial power. Set in the past, the oracle narrates a litany of historical events that range from the attack of the Persians on the Greeks in the fifth century B.C.E. to the predicted return of Nero, believed by many to reside in Parthia (4:115–20).[114] For the writer, the most traumatic future event would be the destruction of the Temple. "A leader of Rome will come to Syria who will burn the Temple of Jerusalem with fire, and at the same time slaughter many men and destroy the great land of the Jews with its broad roads" (4:125–27). Prediction of destruction (in this case an already accomplished fact) had tremendous symbolic power and cosmic implications for communities oriented toward an age in its last stage of existence (Sibyl. 3:80–92). Participation in the evil of this age will result in judgment at the end, when "there will be fire throughout the whole world, and a very great sign with sword and trumpet at the rising of the sun." God will "burn the whole earth, and will destroy the whole race of men and all cities and rivers at once, and the sea" (Sibyl. 4:173–77). Readers of the Book of Daniel or texts from the Qumran community would have felt quite at home with this attitude toward the governing powers.[115] As George Brooke states regarding the depiction of Rome in the texts at Qumran, it is "militarily mighty, economically threatening, but ultimately cultically no match for the God of Israel."[116] This vision of the future structured the current behavior of those who believed in it. From the evidence in Josephus, some of the leaders of the Jewish revolt understood their work as part of the final battle against evil in the Last Days. Through the mid–second century C.E. a number of Jewish texts portray messianic expectations as the vehicle for dealing with present concerns.[117] As Benedict Anderson has noted, the idea of messianic time enabled the past and the future to merge in the "instantaneous present."[118]

But others, notably elites in the Jewish system, continued, and sometimes increased, their building activities. In particular, synagogues emphasized the role of Jewish elites within Graeco-Roman society as a stable force for the future.[119] This attitude contrasted with that of those who elected to follow a movement or an ideology that argued that the present age was an evil age and was about to end. In either case, perceptions of the future significantly influenced the responses to the present.

Astrological images also played a role in Jewish thought during this time. A tomb inscription from Corycos in Cilicia shows how powerful these symbols were for some. "Don't be despondent, for nobody is immortal except One, He who ordered this to happen (and) who has placed us in the sphere of the planets."[120] The connection of the individual to the structure of the universe was popular among a number of writers. In the Fifth Sibylline Oracle the zodiac portends the coming of catastrophic cosmic activity:

[W]hen the wheel of arched Axis, Capricorn and Taurus amid Gemini, revolves in mid-heaven, Virgo, coming forth, and the sun, fixing a belt all about its brow, shall lead. There will be a great heavenly conflagration on earth and from the battling stars a new nature will emerge.[121]

Astrological imagery permeates Jewish texts, ranging from the Wisdom of Solomon, Artapanus, and the Testament of Shem to the writings of the Dead Sea sect.[122] Astrological associations in Judaism, as in the pagan world, proved attractive because of the desire by many to discern more precisely their personal and corporate futures.

The use of objects to control or predict behavior or events appears often in Josephus.[123] Josephus ties such activities to venerable figures of the past. At one point an exorcist and countryman of Josephus named Eleazar "put to the nose of the possessed man a ring which had under its seal one of the roots prescribed by Solomon, and then, as the man smelled it, drew out the demon through his nostrils, and, when the man at once fell down, adjured the demon never to come back into him, speaking Solomon's name and reciting the incantations which he had composed" (*AJ* 8.47). The purpose of this action, Josephus claims, was to display clearly the "understanding and wisdom of Solomon . . . in order that all men may know the greatness of his nature and how God favoured him, and that no one under the sun may be ignorant of the king's surpassing virtue of every kind" (*AJ* 8.49). Jewish tradition had a strong influence on magic, and venerable figures like Moses or Solomon came to play an especially important role.[124]

The importance of a ring to control future events (especially demons' activities) has a close parallel in the Testament of Solomon. There Solomon tells a child to use a ring given to Solomon by the archangel Michael and fling it at the chest of the demon bothering the boy, which the boy does. Solomon then meets numerous demons, twelve of whom reside in the zodiac, others in stars and constellations, one in the moon, and thirty-six who rule over each 10 degrees of the 360-degree zodiac. The demons represent the evil or dark forces governing the world[125] and haunt tombs (17:2) and isolated areas (4:4). Each demon is brought under control by the commanding word of Solomon, who calls upon the opposite good force to counteract it. The account draws upon ancient tradition to interpret the forces affecting people as they dealt with an uncertain future: death, disease, wicked behavior, immorality, and, of course, fate itself. The Testament of Solomon presents a powerful figure of the past who, through the power of God, controls astrology and magic to assuage the concerns of a readership obviously familiar with the cosmological images presented. Like Isis for Apuleius, the Jewish god (and the Christian god for the later Christian redactor of the text)[126] holds sway over all the forces of the universe, even evil ones operating within the zodiac.[127]

The phylactery illustrates on a more intimate level this effort to control the future. At Qumran, phylacteries worn on the head or arm contained Scripture passages (some written in unbelievably small script).[128] The wearing of phylacteries reminded believers of their relation to God and the expectation that they would live godly lives. The term "phylactery" (*tefillin* in Hebrew) used in its broadest sense means a type of amulet used to ward off disasters for an individual or community. Phylacteries had a long history in the Greek world and the Near East.[129] Phylacteries of a different sort are mentioned in the Testament of Job (first century B.C.E. to first century C.E.). As an inheritance, Job gives his daughters phylacteries (multicolored cords in this instance) that are to be worn and which had curative properties when worn by Job. After he had put them on, "the worms disappeared from my body and the plagues, too. And then my body got strength through the Lord as if I actually had not suffered a thing. I also forgot the pains in my heart. And the Lord spoke to me in Power, showing me things present and things to come" (Testament of Job 47:6–9). When the daughters put on the cords, they began to utter the dramatic and ecstatic speech of angels, archons, and cherubim (48–50). The phylacteries served as a symbol of the desire to understand the future, a future understood by the writer to be governed by God.

Josephus and the Future

Symbols that express the power of the future permeate Josephus's texts in both his personal quest for meaning and in his description of others who attempt to define their relation to power networks operative in the human and divine realms. Even his texts become symbols meant to present Josephus and the Jewish people in a way that helps make sense of their current situation in the Roman Empire (*BJ* 1.11). As a member of the local elite class and, by his own account, affiliated with several significant religious groups (the priests and the Pharisees; *Vita* 7–11), Josephus was well acquainted with the way in which Jews in Palestine drew on images of the future in their dealings with the Romans, Greeks, other Jews, and God. One vehicle for predicting the future that had a long tradition in both pagan and Jewish circles was dreams. Josephus has dreams that portend good fortune either for himself (*Vita* 208–9; *BJ* 3.352–54) or for another, as when he predicts that Vespasian will become the future emperor (*BJ* 3.400–403).[130]

Many of Josephus's symbols of the future are intimately tied to the past. The concern among Jews for maintaining proper genealogies, for instance, guarantees that the priests, whose lineages must be demonstrated as pure, ensure the continuity of the movement into the future (*CA* 1.31–36). Because the prophets were inspired by God, they wrote clear accounts of events in their own day, which explains why Jews "do not possess myriads of inconsistent books, conflicting with each other" (*CA* 1.38). Not surprisingly, Josephus, like so many of his compatriots, asserts the power of the law for people in his own day: "[I]t is an instinct with every Jew, from the day of his birth, to regard them as the decrees of God, to abide by them, and, if need be cheerfully to die for them" (*CA* 1.42). Josephus believes that Moses viewed God as all-powerful and eternally unchanging (*CA* 2.166–67). The necessity to maintain the law for future generations and to believe in an unchanging God governs all actions of Jews, both present and future (*CA* 2.170). The law dictates ethical behavior, and behavior determines what happens to the individual and the group. The strength of the Jewish faith for Josephus is the integration of practical ethics and principled foundation. The law was to serve as "the standard and rule, that we might live under it as under a father and master, and be guilty of no sin through willfulness or ignorance" (*CA* 2.174). Josephus asks, "Could God be more worthily honoured than by such a scheme, under which religion is the end and aim of the training of the entire community, the priests are entrusted with the special charge of it, and the whole administration of the state resembles some sacred ceremony?" (*CA* 2.188). The entire *oikoumene* stands under the guidance of God. "The universe is in God's hands; perfect and blessed, self-sufficing and sufficing for all, He is the beginning, the middle, and the end of all things" (*CA* 2.190).

The priestly system, like the imperial system, provided a vehicle to guarantee future activities. Established by God, the priests "safeguard the laws, adjudicate in cases of dispute, punish those convicted of crime" (*CA* 2.194). The result of the law is a continuing legacy for all generations.

> What more beneficial than to be in harmony with one another, to be a prey neither to disunion in adversity, nor to arrogance and faction in prosperity; in war to despise death, in peace to devote oneself to crafts or agriculture; and to be convinced that everything in the whole universe is under the eye and direction of God? (*CA* 2.294)

Death and memorials appear in diverse guises in Josephus's understanding of the future. When Aristobulus was poisoned before he could reclaim his Jewish throne, his body was preserved in honey so that he could receive a proper burial in the royal tombs (*BJ* 1.184). Certain Essenes, likewise, integrated their belief in a future existence with proper ethical behavior:

> [T]heir aim was first to establish the doctrine of the immortality of the soul, and secondly to promote virtue and to deter from vice; for the good are made

better in their lifetime by the hope of a reward after death, and the passions of
the wicked are restrained by the fear that, even though they escape detection
while alive, they will undergo never-ending punishment after their decease.
(*BJ* 2.157)

Josephus notes that after caesar ruled in favor of Antipater's and Hyrcanus's claims to power in Judaea, he sent orders to Rome that the honors given
were "to be graven in the Capitol, as a memorial of his own justice and of
Antipater's valour" (*BJ* 1.200). Such inscriptions were common, the most
obvious being Augustus's will and testament, which was displayed in a number of cities (an extant version is found at Ankara). The memorial not only
highlighted past glories but served as a symbol of the ongoing power and
prestige of the empire. The building of cities, of course, also highlighted the
ongoing power and prestige of the benefactor. Josephus points out that Herod
founded Herodion as a memorial to commemorate his victory over the Parthians and their Jewish allies (*BJ* 1.265), built the second Temple, and presented
benefactions to numerous cities (*BJ* 1.401–28). Like so many members of the
elite class in the Greek East, Herod "perpetuated the memory of his family and
his friends" as well as himself in his building programs (*BJ* 1.419). His endowment of the Olympic Games in Greece should, Josephus states, "preserve an
unfading memory of his term as president" (*BJ* 1.428).[131]

Josephus addresses the sticky issue of how Jews are to honor imperial
power when offering sacrifices to images is prohibited by Moses. The accommodation, offering sacrifices on behalf of the emperor (*BJ* 2.197), represents an
honor given to no other person (*CA* 2.76–77; cf. *BJ* 2.197). The discontinuance
of the sacrifices by the rebels against Rome attacked the type of future taken for
granted or at least promoted by those Jews who had held power, that is, a
future in which Roman power continued to hold sway (*BJ* 2.409–10). The new
administration sought to make new laws establishing a different vision of the
future. The revolutionaries introduced a "strange innovation into their religion, and, besides endangering the city, laying it open to the charge of impiety,
if Jews henceforth were to be the only people to allow no alien the right of
sacrifice or worship" (*BJ* 2.414). This put their city "outside the pale of the
empire" (*BJ* 2.416) and, as he later asserts, outside the will of God (*BJ* 4.150–
57). Indeed, from Josephus's perspective, the rebels overthrew the very institutions that ensured the stability of the nation and the people. They murdered
Jewish elites and high priests, replacing them with their own base followers. In
doing so, Josephus asserts, they guaranteed a future of strife, turmoil, and utter
defeat, all because of their "insolence to the Deity" (*BJ* 4.150).

In Josephus's view, no event better epitomized the complete destruction of
the future fortunes of the people than the brutal murder of High Priest Ananus,
which, combined with the many other sacrileges of the rebels, caused God to
condemn the city and purge "the sanctuary by fire." The high priests, who had
worn the "sacred vestments, led those ceremonies of world-wide [literally
cosmic] significance and been reverenced by visitors to the city from every
quarter of the earth, were now seen cast out naked, to be devoured by dogs and

beasts of prey" (*BJ* 4.324). The murder of the very people who made a hopeful future possible, the priests, now guaranteed a future of misery and destruction. Often in the remainder of Josephus's account of the Jewish war, the dire warnings are repeated as the vestiges of true and proper Judaism (according to Josephus) are eliminated or attacked by the rebels. The result was complete anarchy. "Every human ordinance was trampled under foot, every dictate of religion ridiculed by these men, who scoffed at the oracles of the prophets as impostors' fables" (*BJ* 4.385).

Josephus firmly believed in the power of portents to depict the future. His work is certainly influenced by his concern for the proper ways of dealing with the power of Tyche, or *heimarmene,* a term that Josephus uses with some consistency.[132] Josephus recognizes the power of cosmological imagery in his description of the Temple complex. The temple curtain is depicted as various aspects of the cosmos and symbolizes that the Temple and, in particular, the Holy of Holies embody the very fabric of their existence. It is no accident that when Mark portrays Jesus' death, he has the curtain hiding the Holy of Holies ripping from top to bottom, a symbol of the rending of the cosmos itself at the death.[133] The power of such astrological symbols continues for a long time in Jewish tradition, symbolized best in the zodiacs that formed part of the fourth-through sixth-century C.E. mosaic floors of synagogues in Israel.[134]

Other instances indicate Josephus's concern to grapple with issues of the future as they impinged on the present. He notes a variety of portents that preceded the destruction of Jerusalem by the Romans. These included a star resembling a sword appearing over the city, the yearlong appearance of a comet, a cow giving birth to a lamb, and the massive gate to the inner Temple opening of its own accord (*BJ* 6.289–97). Such portents illustrate God's overriding care and provide, he argues, cues for persons to turn from sin and folly (*BJ* 6.310). Understanding properly these portents sent by God was crucial for Josephus. He tells the story of Herod the Great, whose land had just experienced an earthquake and an invasion by the Arabs (*BJ* 1.365–72). Herod's speech shows how critically important interpretation of such portents was for maintenance of the society. Herod says, fate (Tyche) is never permanently against or for one but goes from "one mood to the next" (*BJ* 1.374).[135] Disasters, whether they come from human beings or from God, "will never reduce the valour of the Jews" (*BJ* 1.376). What is more, natural disasters need not portend future calamities. Once they occur, their power to destroy is spent. In contrast, the breaking of universal laws (especially divine laws), such as the murder of Herod's ambassadors by the Arabs, will be avenged by God (*BJ* 1.379). After offering a sacrifice to God, Herod defeated the enemy. Determinism and astrological notions of fate do not determine the future; God does.

Natural portents, however, sometimes do carry clear signs of imminent doom. A great windstorm suggested that "the very fabric of the universe clearly foretokened destruction of mankind, and the conjecture was natural that these were portents of no trifling calamity" (*BJ* 4.287). Of course, reading the portents properly was the real difficulty. Josephus notes that opponents seeing the sign each determined that it was favorable to their position. The moderate party, led by the priest Ananus, believed that God "was directing the battle on their behalf." As Josephus points out, "they proved mistaken in their divination of the future, and the fate which they predicted for their foes was destined to befall their friends" (*BJ* 4.290).

CHRISTIANS AND THE POWER
OF THE FUTURE

Early Christians had at least three arenas within which their symbolic discourse on the future developed: the pagan world under the control of imperial power, the multifaceted Jewish environment, and other Christian groups. With some exceptions, most groups developed a powerful vocabulary that offered a future often in tension with, if not outright opposition to, prevailing pagan and Jewish visions of the day. This section examines more closely literary portraits of power that circulated among some Christian groups.[136]

The trappings associated with an elite worldview (buildings, proper dress, benefactions, hierarchy, correct social behavior) were integral parts of society's vision of a stable future, a perspective shared by many pagan and Jewish groups. Early on the Christian movement reacted to the power implicit in such signs and activities. Admonitions in early Christian texts against displaying the trappings of society in the community occur frequently. For example, wives should avoid outward signs such as "braiding of hair, decoration of gold, and wearing of fine clothing," all representative of elite lifestyles promoted throughout the ancient world (1 Pet. 3:3).[137] Instead, the writer promotes the "imperishable jewel of a gentle and quiet spirit" (1 Pet. 3:4). Of course, 1 Peter, like Romans 13, stresses that Christians are to work within the existing political system. "Maintain good conduct among the Gentiles, so that in case they speak against you as wrongdoers, they many see your good deeds and glorify God on the day of visitation. Be subject for the Lord's sake to every human institution whether it be to the emperor as supreme or to governors as sent by him to punish those who do wrong and to praise those who do right" (1 Pet. 2:12–14). However, the view of the future in 1 Peter makes clear that such worldly institutions have no real power. "The end of all things is at hand" (1 Pet. 4:7). Proper behavior of the community is crucial when the time of judgment comes in the near future, a time of great severity, especially for those who did not obey "the Gospel of God" (1 Pet. 4:17). The author of James has blunter opinions toward those who desire the trappings of the elite structure. "Come now, you rich, weep and howl for the miseries that are coming upon you. Your riches have rotted and your garments are moth-eaten. Your gold and silver have rusted, and their rust will be evidence against you and will eat your flesh like fire" (James 5:1–3).[138]

Christian traditions in the latter part of the first century circulated Jesus' response to the power implicit in the Herodian building program. "And as he came out of the temple, one of his disciples said to him, 'Look, Teacher, what wonderful stones and what wonderful buildings!'" (Mark 13:1 = Matt. 24:1–3

= Luke 21:5–7). The statement illustrates the impact buildings were intended to have on future (as well as current) generations. The prophetic response of Jesus, however, indicates how certain early Christian communities dealt with such displays of power. "And Jesus said to him, 'Do you see these great buildings? There will not be left here one stone upon another, that will not be thrown down'" (Mark 13:2). To be sure, this pronouncement initially came after or during the destruction of Jerusalem and the Temple in 70 C.E. Nevertheless, it shows how many in the movement redefined apparent arenas of power such as the Temple.[139] Moreover, the statement sets the stage for a long discourse in Mark 13 on future events, some no doubt occurring during the lifetime of the community and others anticipated (notably suffering and persecution). These symbols provided a means to cope with an ambiguous, if not dangerous, present. They also enabled a redefinition of the arenas of power, a theme I have discussed in other contexts. One image of the future, the stability and power of the Herodian rulers and elite classes as represented in the buildings, has been replaced by another, the future rule of the Christian god. Such rule, at least according to the Gospel of Mark and echoed in Revelation, the Didache, and even the more circumspect work of the author of Luke–Acts, can come at any moment. "And what I say to you I say to all: Watch!" (Mark 13:37). No symbol of the future more powerfully impinges on the actions of those in the present.

The image of the church itself served for some as the harbinger of stability and the guarantor of the continuation of the movement. Like the Roman government for the empire, the church became the vehicle in the present that ensures continuity of the movement into the future. That perspective is symbolized by the late-first-century author of the Shepherd of Hermas, whose text revolves around the question, "How shall I be saved?"[140] "'Who do you think that old woman is from whom you received the book?' and I said, 'The Sybil.' 'You are mistaken' says he; 'It is not the Sybil.' 'Who is it then?' say I. And he said, 'It is the Church.'"[141]

Like the Sibyl, the church is the prophetic voice of society, the predictor of the future, the one that defines a Christian's role in society. This allusion to the Sibyl tradition elucidates how the church symbolized the continuance of the movement much like a monument or a building or a venerated cult displayed for local elites a search for a future in an uncertain world. The Shepherd of Hermas, as Miller points out, provides an interesting model for how persons conceived of the role of dreams in the divine incursion.

> The beginning of his [Hermas] oneiric adventures, as he tells them, was not set in motion by petition nor by incubation at a shrine, nor by writing in myrrh on linen. Instead, Hermas was invaded by his dreams. For him the open frontier was more sinister than it was for others. He was easy prey for divine incursions across the boundary.[142]

The Christian movement always had a hard edge where the Roman Empire and local elites were concerned. Even reasonably sympathetic voices such as those found in Luke–Acts or Paul's letters contain elements that indicate tension with the status quo. Paul recalls how he was beaten by civic leaders. Acts of the Apostles shows ever increasing persecution of the movement, often at the hands of or at the least with the tacit permission of local elites in the Greek East. Yet neither comes close to overt hostility toward the Roman Empire, the Greek East, or the status quo. Not so the author of Revelation:

> Fallen, fallen is Babylon the great! It has become a dwelling place of demons, a haunt of every foul spirit, a haunt of every foul and hateful bird; for all nations have drunk the wine of her impure passion, and the kings of the earth have committed fornication with her, and the merchants of the earth have grown rich with the wealth of her wantonness. (18:2–3)

Little effort is needed to see that Babylon represents the Roman Empire.[143] Hostility is couched in terms intended for the insider. Merchants come in for particular criticism.

> The merchants of these wares, who gained wealth from her, will stand far off, in fear of her torment, weeping and mourning aloud, "Alas, alas for the great city that was clothed in fine linen, in purple and scarlet, bedecked with gold, with jewels, and with pearls! In one hour all this wealth has been laid wasted." (Rev. 18:15–16)

The mechanisms by which the empire maintains itself, notably trade and military prowess, come to nothing when the cataclysmic encounter with God's power occurs. The elites, who have occupied so many of our previous pages as the primary power brokers on at least a local and regional level, now will rue their involvement with the power of Rome.

Luke and the Future

Luke views the future as a significant part of the Christian message. Like most of the New Testament writers, he understands the Old Testament as a cacophony of prophetic voices speaking to the present and the future. Judas's death through bursting bowels took place because the prophetic tradition predicted that particular event long years in the past (Acts 1:17–20). For Luke, the activities of Jesus and his followers have the same prophetic overtones. Predictions and events display Jesus' second coming as the Messiah and the redemption of Israel and intensive mission to the Gentiles. Scripture and prophecy speak to a future that structures the very character of the movement portrayed in the narrative and, of course, serves as a model for readers in coming to grips with their own personal or group continuance. Like Josephus and Chariton, Luke understands the future as a crucial component in the interpretation and understanding of the past. Both impinge on the time in which each author is writing.

Luke illustrates his vision of the future against competing claims of a number of groups. He uses some of the religious practices so important for local elites in the Roman Empire to make clear that the true arbiter of the future is the Christian god. No example better illustrates this than Paul's confrontation with adherents of Artemis of Ephesus. When depicting the encounter, Luke cleverly never condemns worship of Artemis; that is simply the assumption made by overzealous and fearful craftsmen. Their fear causes them to be accused by the local authorities of running the risk of disturbing the peace. To all appearances the Christian movement comes off as nonsubversive. But subversive it is, as Luke shows through the speech of Demetrius, one of the silversmiths. "Men, you know that from this business we have our wealth. And you see and hear that not only at Ephesus but almost throughout all Asia this Paul has persuaded and turned away a considerable company of people, saying that gods made with hands are not gods" (Acts 19:26). This speech follows a series of miraculous events, including use of Paul's handkerchief to heal people. Such events, the authorial voice says, "became known to all residents of Ephesus, both Jews and Greeks; and fear fell upon them all" (Acts 19:17). From Luke's perspective, there is no doubt that the gods so important for the maintenance of the dominant elite structure did not have control over the future (or the present). That power resided in the Christian god.[144] The craftsmen in Ephesus had good reason to be concerned. Luke shows that many Gentiles (many belonging to the elite classes) are attracted to the movement, a feature of Luke that has long been noted. Typical for Luke is the response of Gentiles at Antioch of Pisidia, who upon hearing of their potential salvation "were glad and glorified the word of God; and as many as were ordained to eternal life believed" (Acts 13:48).[145] Readers of Luke, however, were by this time well conditioned to what followed such initial enthusiasm. In this case, Luke brushes in broad strokes the elite structure with which the Christian movement had to contend, one Jewish, the other pagan. "But the Jews incited the devout women of high standing and the leading men of the city and stirred up persecution against Paul and Barnabas, and drove them out of their district" (Acts 13:50).[146] The elite structure in Luke's narrative world no doubt reflected to some degree its counterpart in the real world, although the resistance to Christianity was perhaps not as virulent as the literary portrait suggests.

Like so many of his pagan and Jewish counterparts, Luke has individuals and communities pray, prophesy, and make vows. Prayer in Acts is an almost exclusively communal act. The apostles and important figures in Jerusalem pray before they determine the person who replaces Judas as the twelfth apostle (determined by the drawing of lots) (Acts 1:14, 26). The action is repeated when the seven Hellenists are selected (6:6) and when elders are appointed in churches (14:23). Prayer symbolizes the stability of the community and its intimate (and appropriate) tie to the divine. Although prayer does not necessarily portend future events (as we see in Chariton's text) it ensures the reader of a stable and secure future, at least within the parameters of Luke's view of the Christian community.

Prophecy on the other hand has explicit bearing on the future. The prophecy of Joel sets the stage for Luke's perspective in Acts. Sons and daughters, male and female servants, will prophesy, and people will dream dreams, all before "the day of the Lord comes, the great and manifest day" (Acts 2:20). Most of Acts illustrates that such events are occurring. Paul baptizes twelve disciples in Corinth, who then prophesy and speak in tongues (19:6). A prophet and prophetess recognize that the baby Jesus is the Messiah long predicted in the Scripture (Luke 2:25–38). King David foresaw the resurrection of Jesus (Acts 2:31), and other prophets foretold that Jesus would suffer and rise from the dead (Acts 3:18). The litany of prophecies presents a vital and certain future by which those in the community could structure their everyday behavior. Such behavior had profound implications for those participating in the community, something characterized throughout Luke in parables and stories designed to elicit proper ethical behavior. Often forgotten in the parable of the Good Samaritan is the initial question that led to its telling: "What must I do to inherit eternal life?" (Luke 10:25). Ethical performance had future consequences. No better example exists than Luke showing what happens to those who use their vows improperly. When the Christians Ananias and Sapphira renege on their agreement to sell property and give it to the community, they are struck dead immediately (Acts 5:1–10). Divine retribution against those who break their vows follows a pattern that permeated ancient society. Luke provides a clear vision of the seriousness of making such vows within the context of the Christian community.

Visions and epiphanies also portend future events, often as an explicit expression of God's power. Stephen sees Jesus at the right hand of God and the glory of the Christian god (Acts 7:55). Peter's vision of a sheet descending from heaven with assorted forbidden foods portends his future involvement (in the narrative) with the Gentile mission (10:9–16). This mission, of course, is one of the key themes throughout Luke–Acts. Other visions function the same way. Paul has a vision of a man from Macedonia bidding him to come to preach, which occurs shortly afterward in the narrative (16:9–10). God tells Paul in a vision that he must preach in Corinth (18:9). And an angel appears to Paul to tell him that he will be saved from a shipwreck so that he can appear before caesar (27:23). The visions in Acts function in the narrative much like visions in Chariton's ancient romance, that is, as portents of future activity in the narrative itself. The visions display in a readily available cultural script what the protagonists (and the reader) can expect in the narrative. Moreover, they emphasize the important connection between the divine world and the principal characters (and, by implication, the reader). Epiphanies also make clear the divine connection with the major protagonists. Significantly, the resurrected Jesus appears before the assembled apostles (1:3–10) and Paul (9:1–22; cf. 22:4–16; 26:9–18), the primary leaders of the early movement. Again, the narrative affirms for the reader the genuineness of the message reiterated in various forms throughout Luke–Acts. The resurrected Jesus, who suffered and died, this "Jesus, who was taken up from you into heaven, will come in the same way as you saw him go into heaven" (1:11).

Luke shows the movement in constant dialogue, if not confrontation, with competing systems of the future, including the imperial system, local Greek magistrates, Jewish political leaders affiliated with the Herodian family, and various Jewish groups. As we have seen, the magicians were another group that held an attraction for people, an attraction illustrated in a number of

Christian and Jewish texts.[147] Luke depicts magicians as unable to compete with God's true messengers or as recognizing that the true interpreters of the future are members of the Christian movement. Philip encounters Simon, who had practiced magic in the city of Samaria (Acts 8:9). Simon was considered to have the power of God, and people gave heed to him "because for a long time he had amazed them with his magic." The signs and miracles performed by Philip countered the power of magic, a point emphasized in Acts. When Peter and John arrive and lay hands on people, they receive the Holy Spirit. Simon sees this and offers money just as he would for buying magical books. Through Peter's narrative voice, Luke makes clear that such activities are not the proper vehicles for understanding the power of the future and the role of God. "Repent therefore of this wickedness of yours and pray to the Lord that if possible the intent of your heart may be forgiven you. For I see that you are in gall of bitterness and in the bond of iniquity" (Acts 8:22). In another encounter Bar-Jesus, or Elymas, whom the author calls the magician, "for that is the meaning of his name," confronts Paul. Elymas apparently has the ear of Sergius Paulus, the proconsul of Cyprus. Paul, who like Peter and James is filled with the Holy Spirit, looks at Elymas and says, "You son of the devil, you enemy of all righteousness, full of all deceit and villainy, will you not stop making crooked the straight paths of the Lord? And now behold the hand of the Lord is upon you and you shall be blind and unable to see the sun for a time" (Acts 13:9–10). The power of the signs and miracles of the appropriate messengers of the divine confront and defeat those who seek to control or recognize the future through inappropriate means, in this case magic.[148] Again, that confrontation is most clearly seen at Ephesus. Through Paul, according to Luke, God did extraordinary miracles so that "handkerchiefs or aprons were carried away from his body to the sick and diseases left them and the evil spirits came out of them." People became fearful and many became believers. Indeed, "a number of those who practiced magic arts brought their books together and burned them in sight of all; and they counted the value of them and found it came to fifty thousand pieces of silver." The key point the author wishes to make is that as a result of Paul's activity "the word of the Lord grew and prevailed mightily" (Acts 19:11–20).

In encounters with Jewish, Greek, and Roman power structures, Luke illustrates that the Christian movement has the true vision of the future, a future established and controlled by the Christian god. The birth of their leader, Jesus, fulfills Scripture (and God's plan) because of a tax decreed by a Roman leader. But it is Jesus the Messiah not Augustus the emperor who provides the historical framework for Luke's narrative, what Hans Conzelman so long ago recognized as salvation history.[149] The imperial system and its related elite structures throughout the Greek East become bit players in a drama with cosmic implications. Pilate, the representative of imperial power, finds no guilt in Jesus' activities, a pattern echoed throughout Acts. Herod Antipas, the titular head of the Jews, judges Jesus to be innocent. Luke contrasts these reasoned positions with the leadership of certain Jewish groups who demand Jesus' death and subsequently persecute the movement. Page after page shows powerful Roman and Jewish leaders such as Pilate, Herod Antipas, Festus, Felix, and Herod Agrippa II decree that Jesus and his followers are innocent according to the law of imperial Rome. Yet Pilate still rules that Jesus should die, and Festus can only call Paul crazy (Acts 26:24).[150] The future remains clouded for all these narrative characters. But Luke's readers understand. Luke shows explicitly that Christ's death, resurrection, and subsequent return follow a pattern set forth in the Scriptures. To be sure, the imperial and regional power structures are taken for granted by Luke. He even shows a degree of tolerance for such systems. It is important that he show the movement as not subverting such powers. But the reason is not because he agrees with the powerful vision of the future that most Romans, Greeks, or Jews took for granted and that so structured much of the discourse of this period (including Luke's). Rather, Luke recognizes that many in the Christian movement work within this structure and need to have some way in which to perform their everyday tasks.[151] The framework for their activity must be the vision of the future in which the resurrected Jesus returns to regain control of the world (Acts 1:11). Jesus became the foundation of the future. Luke has Peter state it bluntly: "And there is salvation in no one else, for there is no other name under heaven given among men by which we must be saved" (Acts 4:12).

CONCLUSION

Concern for the future permeated the Flavio-Trajanic period but probably no more than in the earlier periods of the empire. However, one of the changes during this period was the increasing political participation of local elites in the Greek East, who now wielded or had the potential to wield significant power within a more established empire. The donors of buildings and bequests and the priests and priestesses of local civic cults still came from local elites, but they were now often Roman citizens with the potential to become members of the equestrian or senatorial orders. Times had changed from the days when a freedman of Octavian (or Julius Caesar) like Zoilos of Aphrodisias was the principal power broker in his city. The period also brought increased competition between cities, which Pliny's letters to Trajan indicate led to ill-advised uses of public expenditures. Nonetheless, the building programs, the participation of local elites in most levels of imperial, regional, and local rule, and the increasing ease with which persons mingled across the empire provided the setting for competing claims for the future.

The Flavio-Trajanic period also saw a resurgence of cults across the empire. To be sure the cults of Isis and Dionysus had entered Rome itself long before. The difference was a tacit, if not overt, acceptance of certain cults by imperial authorities. The Flavians honored Isis. The Persian god Mithras (at least by tradition) became a favorite of imperial troops. The period saw a plethora of religious options, including the possibility of new cults (e.g., the one started by Alexander of Abonuteichos in the mid–second century). Adherents of particular religions often became more vigorous in their promotion of the power of their particular deity in a world populated by many possibilities.

Some of the so-called salvationistic movements that operated in the Roman Empire during the latter half of the first century have been touted as the primary harbingers of future power and promise. To be sure, such movements offered salvation and future reward to those who joined or at least partook of the mysteries. Yet, symbols associated with the future did not belong solely to the mystery cults, Jewish tradition, or the nascent Christian movement. Nor did such symbols only depict continuing existence for the individual. Symbols associated with the future often mediated power relations in the present for individuals and groups. Just as the past provided symbols for the reappropriation and consolidation of power, so symbols of the future promised association with or continuance of power, prestige, and meaning for those who proffered them. Mythic stories, religious rituals, building programs, bequests for festivals, all presented a vision of the future that helped define and confirm intricate webs of power operating in the present.

The future informed actions taken in the present. All manner of persons in antiquity sought out oracles, heeded prophetic pronouncements, or desired knowledge of the afterlife. To establish continuity and to provide a lasting legacy, many elites built architecture, sponsored festivals, and made treaties (at least symbolically). Their visions of the future created an environment that helped structure decisions made by those in the present. Chariton's text is replete with images of the future with which local elites in the Greek East could relate. Chaereas and Callirhoe are elites par excellence who, though buffeted by the whims of Tyche, pirates, politicians, and crowds, return to their homeland, Chaereas the heroic victor carrying the spoils of war, and Callirhoe, the light of Syracusan society embodying the power of Aphrodite. Greek paideia, Greek superiority, and Greek religion emerge victorious, themes displayed in countless ways by elites across the Greek East. Chariton embodies the civic mythos of elites in the Greek East, who understand their civic religious participation as guaranteeing a stable future.

With the destruction of the Temple and the forced payment of the *fiscus Iudaicus,* symbols associated with the future took on a particular significance for Jews. Jewish groups took various routes to stress a secure future, ranging from building buildings to appropriating images from the pagan world (such as the Sibyl) for their own use. Certain powerful and distinctive symbols kept cropping up, however, especially the Torah (law) and the Temple. Both shaped and guaranteed the future even after the latter was destroyed.

The symbol of the reestablishment of a Jewish kingdom also was powerful for some groups, a vision of the future that probably impacted events leading to the disastrous Bar Kochba revolt in Hadrian's reign. For certain Jewish groups, especially in Egypt, it became increasingly difficult to maintain their vision of the future in the midst of increasingly vigorous pagan promotions. The lack of tolerance by pagans in those areas and the aftermath of the Jewish war of 70 C.E. no doubt played a role in the Jewish revolt of 115–17 C.E. Pagans in other areas of the empire, such as Acmonia in Asia Minor, had quite amicable relations with Jews, to the extent that they even appropriated some of their symbols. These extremes depict the range of responses to the increasingly diverse religious environment in which people lived.

Josephus reflects well this transition period for Jews in the Roman Empire. He recognizes the stability and power of the Roman government (e.g., *CA* 2.72–73). He also answers attacks by local elites, such as the Egyptian Apion, who sought to build up his religion by denigrating the Jewish religion. Josephus responds that within the current competitive rush of all groups to link their institutions to a remote beginning, the Jewish religion has set the standard through the excellence of its law and its antiquity (*CA* 2.151–53). Honoring the law, practicing piety, promoting harmony, and certainty in the knowledge that God governs all activity structure the future for Jews, which all nations would do well to emulate.

The Christian communities, though also a diverse lot, generally had one common bond between them, the belief that a resurrected figure (however one understood his nature) had a key role in the present and future situation of a community of faith. Most Christian groups apparently saw themselves at odds with the assorted approaches to the future proposed in pagan and Jewish circles. Such Christian groups could draw on and even assume the cultural horizon in which they lived, but they adapted and oftentimes contradicted it, whether with benign tolerance, like Luke, or with virulent hostility, like the author of Revelation. Luke's two-volume work reflects the increasing competition for the true vision of the future. Luke depicts the various Jewish groups, magicians, pagan worshipers of civic cults, Athenian philosophers, imperial authorities, and the Herodian leadership and their alternative approaches to the future as subject to the power of the Christian god. This approach was taken even further in the writings of Justin Martyr and the early church fathers, who in the mid–second century and later persistently challenged proposed alternatives to the future (including those offered by "other" Christians), sometimes to the point of martyrdom. The die had been cast. For Christians, pagans, and Jews symbolic discourse associated with the future shaped the fabric of life for their respective communities and their response to those outside.

Conclusion

Religion in the ancient world provided multifaceted symbols with which to interpret competing, intersecting, and sometimes congenial forces. Such forces helped shaped who an individual or group was or could be. They clarified the relationships in which persons operated. They could even challenge the character and structure of the status quo. The past played an especially powerful role. Not only did appropriation of ancient symbols provide a foundation on which individuals or groups could build their own place within the networks of power but they drew on generally accepted vehicles of expression. Although disagreement might occur as to the significance or interpretation of a particular tradition, few denied the fundamental importance the past played in the creation of the symbolics of power. Indeed, some of the bitterest conflicts occurred between groups who sought to appropriate some of the same traditions. Whether the medium was literary or iconographic, the results were often the same.

The divine world permeated the ancient world, much more than many contemporary interpreters grant. Power associated with the gods and goddesses of the ancient world interacted with almost all spheres of ancient activity. From the choice of what images to depict on coins, to the freeing of slaves, to seeking advice or healing, the divine world was one arena of power that could not easily be ignored. To be sure, there were people who conducted business, paid taxes, and so on with little regard to the divine realm and even scoffed at the gods. But the civic structures that dominated the political, social, and economic landscape of the Greek East often vigorously promoted the deity or deities associated with their particular locale or group. Although groups did not necessarily proselytize, they certainly tried to demonstrate the power of their deities (and by association their own power). Thus, members of the elite class across the Greek East promoted through buildings and dedications their affiliation with a deity or deities of demonstrated power. Many of the displays may have had local audiences in mind. That certainly seems the case for Christians, even Luke. But the point is clear whatever the group. The gods and goddesses provided stability and powerful resources in a world sometimes ruled by the whims of Fate, unethical leaders, and other forces outside individual or group control.

Geography and the power of place proved important in presenting rhetorical and iconographic displays of power. A deity that had a presence across the known world, whether in the pages of Luke or Josephus or Chariton or in statuettes or temples, had power that extended over that territory. Widespread recognition increased the legitimacy of one's deity and provided reassurance, if not a measure of power, for those who associated with it. The claim by some groups, notably Jewish and Christian, that their people were spread across the known world also confirmed their association with a powerful deity. Of course, the only people who saw the iconographic displays of divine power may have been local citizens, and the only ones who read the claims of an author, like Luke, who contends his movement has spread to the ends of the earth may already have been believers. But that is just the point. Groups attempted to come to grips with the imperial, regional, local, and cosmic power networks all around them. One way to make sense of such networks was participation in a group that defined how one operates amid the competing voices for one's allegiance. For Josephus, imperial power and the loss of Jewish power make sense under a rubric he feels has long tradition. The Jewish god used the Romans as an instrument to punish a sinful nation. The Romans are powerful because God has allowed them to be powerful. Josephus may believe this; the authors of 2 Baruch and the Fourth Sibylline Oracle did not. But the point holds in any case. Josephus was one member of the Jewish elite class who drew on his tradition, the power of sacred geography, and his vision of the divine to reformulate the Roman victory and to significantly alter the character of the power relation. This method was practiced by a number of Jewish groups.

Luke does the same. The Christian god provides the framework in which the political activity in Luke's narrative takes place. Christians were to fine-tune this perspective in increasing confrontations with imperial and local power centers to the point where the cosmic power center, for some, completely replaced any need for negotiation. Luke does not go that far. But it should come as no surprise that this most amenable of writers to the elite system as it operated in the Greek East should continue much of the Markan eschatological language. The end may be delayed, but it is coming. Sacred geography for Christians and for Luke moves away from the association with a particular place on earth to the celestial realm. Heaven and the beings associated with it become the true sacred center. Jesus at the right hand of God, as Stephen sees him, or as the High Priest or True Temple or King makes perfect sense in approaches that now give ultimate weight to the cosmic or divine part of the webs of power.

But how groups perceive the future now begins to demonstrate clear differences, although even here significant overlap exists. Local elites for the most part understood the civic structure as the vehicle in which visions of the future played themselves out. The buildings and visual displays offered a continuity, as the empire itself did, in which people continued, gods continued, and the power equations so important to the maintenance of society—honor, status, benefactions—played themselves out. Some groups rejected this. Others tolerated or participated in several spheres in which other kinds of future needs, such as their personal salvation or future good health, could be met. Jewish groups sought and found a variety of ways to deal with the future: reliance on the synagogue structure, the Temple until its destruction, the coming of the Messiah. But one thing seemed to be part of most Jewish groups whose theology we know: the power of the Torah. The law became a symbol that gave credence and direction to the future. For Christians the power of the future overturned the present age and replaced it with the Kingdom of God. Some, like the Gnostics, defined that event allegorically and spiritually. Others expected a real and material change. Most expected it soon. The attitude toward other power centers ranged from acceptance and toleration to outright rejection and hostility. Yet sometimes the most virulent attacks were directed inward against groups who attached importance to some of the same symbols as those who railed against them. Josephus reserved some of his harshest invectives for those rebels who sought to enforce their version of the Jewish faith. Christian literature is replete with similar tirades.

This work has tried to offer some observations about the general patterns that percolated through the society, though the breadth and wealth of experience finally defies neat categorization. Religion helped individuals and groups to construe the world of which they were a part. Religious and mythic symbols permeated the world in which pagans, Jews, and Christians worked, played, fought, and did all the mundane things that people through the generations have done. Religion helped structure the networks of power that shaped or informed the relationships between pagans, Jews, and Christians in the Greek East.

Notes

CPJ	*Corpus Papyrorum Judaicarum*. 3 vols. Cambridge: Harvard University Press, 1957–64
CR	*Classical Review*
EPRO	Etudes Préliminaires aux Réligions Orientales dans l'Empire Romain
GRBS	*Greek, Roman, and Byzantine Studies*
HBD	P. Achtemeir, ed. *Harper's Bible Dictionary*. San Francisco: Harper & Row, 1985
HSCP	*Harvard Studies in Classical Philology*
HTR	*Harvard Theological Review*
IEJ	*Israel Exploration Journal*
IG	*Inscriptiones Graecae*. Berlin: G. Reimer, 1873–
IGRR	*Inscriptiones Graecae ad Res Romanas Pertinentes*. Paris: E. Leroux, 1906–27. Chicago, 1975
IGUR	*Inscriptiones Graecae Urbis Romae*. Vol. 3, ed. L. Moretti. Rome, 1979
ILS	*Inscriptiones Latinae Selectae*. Vols. 1–3, ed. H. Dessau, 1892–1916
JAAR	*Journal of the American Academy of Religion*
JbAC	*Jahrbuch für Antike und Christentum*
JBL	*Journal of Biblical Literature*
JDAI	*Jahrbuch des Deutschen Archäologischen Instituts*
JHS	*Journal of Hellenic Studies*
JJS	*Journal of Jewish Studies*
JMA	*Journal of Mediterranean Archaeology*
JMS	*Journal of Mithraic Studies*
JRA	*Journal of Roman Archaeology*
JRS	*Journal of Roman Studies*
JS	*Journal des Savants*
JSNT	*Journal for the Study of the New Testament*
JSOT	*Journal for the Study of the Old Testament*
JTS	*Journal of Theological Studies*
LIMC	*Lexicon Iconographicum Mythologiae Classicae*. 7 vols. to date. Zurich: Artemis Verlag, 1981–
MAMA	*Monumenta Asiae Minoris Antiqua*. 10 vols. to date. Manchester: Manchester University Press, 1928–
MDAI	*Mitteilungen des Deutschen Archäologischen Instituts*
New Docs.	Greg H. R. Horsley. *New Documents Illustrating Early Christianity*. 6 vols. North Ryde, New South Wales: Ancient History Documentary Research Centre, Macquarie Univ., 1981–
NTS	*New Testament Studies*
OGIS	*Orientis Graecae Inscriptiones Selectae*. Vols. 1–2, ed. W. Dittenberger, 1903–5
OTP	J. H. Charlesworth. *The Old Testament Pseudepigrapha*. 2 vols. Garden City, NY: Doubleday, 1983–85
PBSR	*Papers of the British School at Rome*
PCPS	*Proceedings of the Cambridge Philological Society*
P. Oxy.	*The Oxyrhynchus Papyri*. 1898–
RAC	*Reallexikon für Antike und Christentum*
RB	*Revue Biblique*

RE   *Paulys Realencyclopädie der classischen Altertumswissenschaft.* Munich: A. Druckenmuller, 1980

REG   *Revue des Études Grecques*

RPh   *Revue de Philologie de Littérature et d'Histoire Anciennes*

SBLDS   Society of Biblical Literature Dissertation Series

SBLMS   Society of Biblical Literature Monograph Series

SBLSP   *Society of Biblical Literature Seminar Papers*

SEG   *Supplementum Epigraphicum Graecum.* Leiden: A. W. Sijthoff, 1923–

SEOR   *Sylloge epigraphica orbis Roman*

SNTSMS   Societas Novum Testamentum Studia Monograph Series

STClas   *Studii Clasice*

Syll.   *Sylloge Inscriptionum Graecarum.* Vols. 1–4, ed. W. Dittenberger et. al., 1915–24

TAM   *Tituli Asiae Minoris*

YCS   *Yale Classical Studies*

ZPE   *Zeitschrift für Papyrologie und Epigraphie*

Introduction

1. See Huot 1991, 12–39.

2. Freedberg 1991; Castriota 1986; Arvidsson and Blomquist 1987.

3. Wills 1990.

4. This time period was important for pagans because a new regime, the Flavians, allowed increasing political participation by local elites in the Greek East. Hadrian heightened that power, beginning what many acknowledge as a new era in Roman relations with the East. For Jews, two wars bracket this critical period in their relation to Rome and other groups. The war with Rome under Hadrian (132–35) put the final touches on this relation. For Christians, 70 C.E. marks an important turning point because the significance of Jerusalem-based Christianity ceased. Some of the clearest references to Christianity from outside its own movement occur during the Trajanic period, demonstrating its increasing visibility in the empire.

5. *SEG* 8.13.1.2.

6. *IGRR* 4.1381.1.4.

7. See, e.g., 4 Macc. 5:7 and Josephus.

8. See Robert 1938, 227–35, for a full list of citations.

9. Geertz 1966, 4. See also Asad 1983.

10. For their discussions of the term "pagan," see Lane Fox 1986, 30–31; Chuvin 1990, 7–13; and Goodman 1994, 38.

11. Some have found the term "Diaspora Judaism" problematic, arguing that the term seems to imply a coherent cultural identity for all Jews outside Palestine. Rather, they suggest that each manifestation of Judaism be looked at within its own region (see, e.g., Price 1994). This is surely important criticism. Each Jewish member and community must be examined within the regional network of which they are a part. Nevertheless, the distinction between Diaspora Judaism and Palestine still seems important. Identification of Jews outside Judaea (or within for that matter) occurs largely because of particular symbols (e.g., the menorah), specifically Jewish names, the use of particular Jewish phrases, and the use of Hebrew associated with a building or funerary stone or whatever (see Horbury and Noy 1992, x–xi). In those cases an implicit or perhaps even

explicit connection with Judaea or Jerusalem or the Temple is intended. Of course, even here problems exist, as illustrated by Kraemer 1991.

12. See, e.g., Kraemer 1992b; Chilton 1992; Goodman 1990, 1994, 13, 41–46; Rajak 1992.

13. I add "non-Christians" to the definition because in some periods Christians used the term "Jew" to denigrate their Christian opponents. See Kraabel 1992a, 18–20.

14. See the discussion and bibliography in Overman and Green 1992.

15. Katz 1984. The specific use of the term "Christian" outside literary sources does not come until the third century (Kraemer 1991, 144), although one example may date to the mid–second century (*MAMA* 10.xxxvi). For further discussion see chapter 2.

16. See also Goodman 1994, 91.

17. Brown 1992, 5.

18. Ibid., 5–6.

19. See Millar 1993a, 243.

20. Boulding 1990, 9, 10.

21. Foucault 1980, 119.

22. Wartenberg 1992, xix.

23. See McCarthy 1992, 130.

Chapter 1

1. For religious symbols in Anatolia, see Mitchell 1993b, 11–31. For an excellent overview, see Lane Fox 1986. On the "symbolics of power," see Geertz 1977. On the imperial cult of Asia Minor, see Price 1984b. On the Age of Augustus, see Zanker 1988. On the imagery of Roman arches, see Wallace-Hadrill 1990, 147.

2. On this subject, see Syme 1936, 135–37; Magie 1950, 566–610.

3. See Goodman 1994.

4. On the cult of Zeus, see Schubert 1984.

5. It is probable that she also fell victim to the revolt. See Lewis 1989, 4–5, 65–70; Bowersock 1991.

6. See North's (1986) devastating critique of this perspective. See also Price 1984b; Brown 1992.

7. This becomes a leitmotiv in most analyses of the ancient romances. See the useful discussions by Pervo (1987, 102–4), Edwards (1994a).

8. On the Apocryphal Acts, see Pervo 1987, 122–31; Pervo 1994; Perkins 1985. On Joseph and Aseneth, see Chesnutt 1988; Kee 1983b; Burchard 1987, 109–17.

9. See Edwards 1994a.

10. This view has been convincingly discredited by Lane Fox (1986, 11–264).

11. This position has been rightly challenged by Price (1984b, 247; 1986, 29).

12. See also Price 1984b, 241–42. Berger 1967, 25–28; Boon 1982.

13. Cannadine and Price 1987, 2. See also Lukés 1977; Eisenstadt 1979, 21–33.

14. Mann 1986, 8.

15. Epictetus, *Discourses* 1.22.3–4.

16. Geertz 1975, 3–30.

17. This problem is addressed in Veeser 1989.

18. See Veyne 1990.

19. See the discussion, with bibliography, of the problems in *New Docs.* 3:22.

20. Gould 1989, 13.

21. See Weber 1949. The phrase "ideal types" is used loosely in this study to refer

to general patterns that seem to operate in pagan, Jewish, and Christian contexts, albeit with unique manifestations dependent on group, location, and time period.

22. For provincial coinage in the period 44 B.C.E. to 69 C.E., see the excellent and comprehensive collection in Burnett, Amandry, and Ripollès 1992.

23. Carr 1962, 16.

24. A fine discussion of this approach can be found in Winkler 1985, 1–24.

25. For the high incidence of "idiom and ideas" between Chariton and Luke–Acts and bibliography, see Edwards 1987. For the many similarities between Josephus and Luke, see Cadbury 1968, 169–83; Sterling 1992. See also Hemer 1989a, 94–95.

26. Cf. Marcus 1974.

27. Zanker 1988, 3.

28. Barrett, Bradley, and Green 1991, 8.

29. The focus here unless explicitly stated otherwise is on the power networks implied in the initial creation of the iconography.

30. See Howgego 1985.

31. Cf. Sullivan 1984. Sullivan downplays too much the important connection of local issues to the Roman Empire.

32. Crawford (1980) deemphasizes this point unduly.

33. Wallace-Hadrill 1986, 84.

34. Gregory 1994.

35. Epictetus, *Discourses* 4.5.17.

36. Barrett, Bradley, and Green 1991, 8.

37. See Millar 1984, 39–40, 56.

38. The dominance of the elite perspective is rightly stressed by Bruce Lincoln: "[T]he dominant discourse—including mythic discourse—in any age is the discourse of the dominant class. This does not mean that other groups are without their discourses and without their myths, nor that they are incapable of appropriating the myths and discourse of the dominant class, which they may also refashion and employ to telling advantage" (1989, 49–50).

39. See also Epictetus, *Discourses* 4.5.15–18.

40. Work in archaeology and geography has made much the same point. See Cherry 1987, 155.

41. See Alcock 1993, 1989a.

42. See, e.g., Beard 1985; Millar 1983a.

43. See Millar 1983a, 98.

44. Snyder 1985, 1–2; Finney 1994.

45. MacMullen 1990, 8.

46. MacMullen 1982, 233–46.

47. Millar 1993a, 247; Cotton, Cockle, and Millar 1995.

48. On the importance of tradition, see Bowie 1974. Cf. Brown 1978, 28.

Chapter 2

1. Millar 1993c, 80–81.

2. Morris 1992, 7–8 (with bibliography); see also Hopkins 1983, 123–27, 194–96; Jones 1992, 169–70.

3. E.g., the Herodians ruled until 96 C.E.

4. See Cartledge and Spawforth 1989, 143–59.

5. See Smith 1993; Robert 1966, 408–9; Reynolds 1982, 156–64.

6. See Braund 1984.

7. See the discussion by Hartmut Galsterer (1988) on the expectations of such persons during the Flavian period as displayed in the fascinating set of Flavian laws found on bronze tablets at ancient Arni (5 km. southwest of El Saujeco, Spain). For the Latin text with English translation by Michael Crawford, see Gonzalez 1986.

8. Millar 1993a.

9. On this topic, see Woolf 1992; Fulford 1987.

10. See Syme 1936, 141; MacDonald 1982, 182.

11. See Mitchell 1993a, 176–97.

12. See Whittaker 1990; Lane Fox 1987, 39–46; Edwards 1992c.

13. See Rich and Wallace-Hadrill 1991; Owens 1991; Price 79; Mitchell 1993a, 80–96, 198–216.

14. See Magie 1950, 572–76; Garnsey and Saller 1982; Bengtson 1979; Jones 1984.

15. See Smallwood 1981 for discussion of the three wars against the Jews. On these and other rebellions, see Goodman 1991b; Magie 1950, 582. Continued concern for internal threats is apparent from such things as the curtailing of clubs, viewed sometimes as the source of political turmoil. See Wilken 1984, 12–13, 33–35.

16. MacMullen 1988, 2–4.

17. Millar 1981, 196–97; Jones 1992, 171–73.

18. On the "new men," see Alföldy 1985, 118; Jones 1992, 2–3.

19. See Degrassi 1947. Augustus had the list of Roman triumphs that began with Romulus, founder of Rome, and ended with Augustus's triumph over the Parthians prominently displayed, probably on his arch celebrating his triumph over the Parthians.

20. On the iconography, see Edwards, 1992b.

21. Wallace-Hadrill 1981, 319.

22. K. Scott 1936, 2; Blake 1959; Syme 1936.

23. Gruen 1990.

24. Wallace-Hadrill 1990, 158.

25. Vinson 1989, 432.

26. French 1980, 707–11.

27. Millar 1964, 174.

28. Millar 1977, 380–85; Reynolds, Beard, and Roueché 1986, 133–34.

29. When the Flavians come to power, ethnic regions in Galatia, for example, were increasingly categorized. This type of classification ended by the early part of Hadrian's reign. See Mitchell 1993b, 4.

30. Rogers 1991, 13–16.

31. Millar 1981, 3.

32. Brown 1978, 36.

33. Ibid., 34. The use of religious symbols by local elites is amply illustrated by Lane Fox 1986.

34. Gordon 1979.

35. See, e.g., Kearsley 1988.

36. See Sherk 1980, 1002–3; Turner 1954, 61–64; Burr 1955. Ti. Iulius Alexander Iulianus is mentioned in the Arval Acts of 118 c.e. and is probably the same as Ioulios Alexandros (Dio 68.20.2); the praetorian legate of Trajan who captured Seleucia may well have been Alexander's son or grandson. Turner notes: "Such a graduation of promotion, by which an energetic knight at length obtained entry to the Senate by means of *adlectio* and thereby bequeathed senatorial rank to his son, was part of the spirit of the age" (1954, 63). This is certainly true, whatever the merits of the historical connections made between the two figures. A famous decree of Tiberius Iulius Alex-

ander as prefect exhibits the power he wielded. See the one prominently placed on the outer gate of a grand entryway to a prominent temple in Hibis in Winlock 1941, 36–38, pls. 1–2, 30; White and Oliver 1938, pls. 1, 8.

37. See Yavetz 1987, 139–41; Macro 1980, 683.

38. Dodge 1988; Ward-Perkins 1992; Fant 1988.

39. See Segal 1995, 1987.

40. Strange 1992, 342–43. "Striking" and "fundamental" changes occurred in architectural style during the last half of the first century and early decades of the second according to MacDonald (1982, ix).

41. MacMullen, 1990, 6; Alföldy 1985, 103, 104. In certain cities of the Greek East the prestige associated with one of their members becoming a senator is aptly illustrated by an inscription touting the appointment of an unidentified man to the Roman Senate: "in all time he was fifth from the whole of Asia to enter the Senate, and from Miletus and the rest of Ionia the first and only" (Charlesworth 1936, 44; see also Woodward 1926–27, 120).

42. Alföldy 1985, 94. See also Charlesworth 1936, 43–45.

43. Galsterer 1988, 86–87.

44. Millar 1990, 8–10.

45. See Alföldy 1985, 113; Charlesworth 1936, 44.

46. Plutarch, *Praecepta gerendae reipublicae* [Precepts of statecraft] c.17.813–14. Quoted in Bowie 1974, 183 n. 49.

47. See, e.g., Herod Agrippa II's speech depicting the power of Rome over mighty nations and proud peoples, notably the Greeks (*BJ* 2.358–87) and Josephus's observation about the Romans' forethought "in making their servant class useful to them not only for the ministrations of ordinary life but also for war" (*BJ* 3.70).

48. Some recent and important works include R. Smith 1993, 1990b, 1987, 1988, 1990a; Smith and Erim 1991; Roueché and Erim 1990; Erim and Roueché 1982; Reynolds 1982, 1981, 1986; *MAMA* 8; Roueché 1989; de la Genière and Erim 1987; Erim 1986 (contains a lengthy bibliography on material published before 1985); MacDonald 1992, 1976.

49. See Reynolds 1987, 83.

50. Vinson 1989, 432–33; Ramage 1983.

51. Reynolds 1987, 83.

52. Reynolds 1982, 167–68.

53. Ibid., 183–84.

54. Ibid., 113–15.

55. Reynolds 1987, 83.

56. For the statue of Domitian, see Erim 1973, Erim 1990b, 152–53. For the head of the Flavian priest, see Inan and Rosenbaum 1966, 171–72, no. 228. For the bust of Trajan, see Inan and Alföldi-Rosenbaum 1979, 207–8; no. 181, pl. 134.

57. D'Ambra 1993, 107–8.

58. Chariton, *The Loves of Chaereas and Callirhoe* (London, 1764), cited by Heiserman 1977, 221–22 n. 3.

59. Reardon 1982b, 25.

60. Zanker 1988, 3.

61. I agree with Brigitte Egger that women could have been the principal readers. But women could relate as strongly to the association of Callirhoe with a powerful deity as they could to Callirhoe's "erotic omnipotence" (Egger 1994). But see the cautionary remarks by Stephens 1994; see also Konstan 1994.

62. Plepelits 1976, 28–29. For *Chaereas and Callirhoe* I use the critical edition by

Warren Blake (1938), although as B. P. Reardon has recently noted, it contains a number of inadequacies (1982a).

63. E. Rohde dated Chariton's work in the fifth or sixth centuries as the last of the Sophistic romances (1960, 485–93). Papyrus fragments of *Chaereas and Callirhoe* found at Faiyum and Oxyrhynchus indicate a first or second century C.E. date. For a more detailed discussion of the fragments and the date of Chariton's work see Perry 1967, 343 ff.; Grenfell, Hunt, and Hogarth 1900, 41, 46, 74–82; Perry 1930; Hägg 1983, 5–6. Because Chariton identifies himself as a secretary to a rhetor named Athenagoras, Consuelo Ruiz-Montero (1980) believes that the mention of a rhetor Athenagoras by Ammianus (A.P. 11, 150) suggests that Chariton's romance was written at the end of the first or the beginning of the second century. See also Ruiz-Montero 1994a, 1989.

64. But see the cautionary remarks by Stephens 1994. For a listing of the fragments and their location, see Pack 1965, 33, Reardon 1982a. Numerous fragments of a number of different ancient romances further indicate the widespread popularity of this genre. See Stephens and Winkler 1995; Pack 1965, 136–37; Zimmermann 1936; Lavagnini 1922.

65. Grenfell Hunt, and Hogarth 1900, 41. See Lucke 1985.

66. Wesseling 1988, 72.

67. Public dedications to Aphrodite by secretaries or clerks elsewhere in the empire indicate their use of the same media as the elite classes to express their affiliation with cosmic powers. See *IG* 4.209, 211, for dedications by clerks to Aphrodite.

68. For a sample of the inscriptions see *MAMA* 8, no. 552 (Chariton), nos. 437–38, 462, 475 (Athenagorus). E. Rohde's conclusion that Aphrodisias in Caria is the site based on these inscriptions has carried the day (1960, 520 ff.). See also Plepelits 1976, 1–3; Schmeling 1974, 17–18; Hägg 1983, 5. For other places with the name, see s.v. "Aphrodisias" in *RE*.

69. Cities and urban life operate on many levels in the ancient romances. See Said 1994.

70. Nock makes this observation in a review of K. Kerenyi's *Die griechischeorientalische Romanliteratur in religionsgeschlichtlichen Beleuchtung:* "Kerenyi is . . . probably in the right in emphasizing against Rohde the importance of the explicit religious element in the plot of Chariton" (1972a, 173). Nock, however, does not agree with Kerenyi's thesis that the religious component comes from the sacred myth of Isis and Osiris.

71. Parsons 1982, 190. Parsons makes this point about a fragment called *Phoenicica* by Lollianos that presents heroes, brigands, and human sacrifice.

72. Perry 1967, 45. Perry does suggest spiritual edification as a possible function but generally ignores it in his analysis of Chariton's text.

73. Wesseling 1988, 77.

74. Anderson 1982, 21.

75. Merkelbach 1962, 159, 339–40.

76. For the former view, see Reardon 1976; 1971, 309–412; 1969, 291–309. For the latter, see Schmeling 1974, 129.

77. Winkler 1980, 156.

78. Ibid., 165–66.

79. Valerius Maximus, *Memorable Deeds* 1.33.

80. See Claudius's edict of 41 C.E.; *CPJ*, vol. 2, no. 153 (pp. 36–55).

81. See Goodman 1994, 38–48.

82. Smallwood 1981, 293–427; *CPJ*, vol. 2, nos. 225–60. The revolt under Trajan

had powerful symbolic overtones for Egyptians, and the Jewish defeat was celebrated into the third century (*CPJ,* vol. 2, no. 450).

83. Payment of the Jewish tax is dramatically displayed in a series of ostraca from Egypt (*CPJ,* vol. 2, nos. 160–229). Most of the ostraca are dated according to the year of the reigning emperor, beginning with Vespasian in the year 71/72. The last ostracon dates to Trajan's rule in 116, a stark reminder of the decimation of the Jewish population that took place by 117 C.E. The taxpayers include slaves (e.g., 201, 206, 212, 218, 229), freedmen (171, 179–80, 199), and women (168–69, 171, 223). The listing of women suggests their participation in the economic life of society and a degree of independence. We see evidence of this from other quarters (discussed more fully in chap. 6). Notably, a dedication to the goddess Isis dated to the early second century mentions that Isis made women free. Luke depicts a number of women who provide for the movement out of their own means.

84. Schürer 1986, 150–53; Feldman 1993; Stern 1980, 1974.

85. See the discussion in *CPJ,* vol. 2, no. 418 (pp. 188–97).

86. Smallwood 1981, 485–86.

87. See now the excellent studies of Goodman 1994; Schürer 1986, 150–76; Feldman 1993, 288–382; Wilson 1992. Scholars have frequently argued that proselytization was a significant aspect of Judaism in the first centuries of this era and that many of these proselytes converted to Christianity. Certainly the assertion that the movement had spread to the ends of the earth fit the rhetoric of many cults of this period, whether or not in practice they actually had much influence. The debate over the so-called god-fearers has settled generally into two camps: those who argue that proselytization was an effective activity of Judaism and, later, of Christianity (see Feldman 1993; Georgi 1986, 83–150) and those who view the mention of proselytization by authors a literary device and largely exaggerated (see, e.g., Kraabel 1992a,b, 1994). For a discussion of the issues, see also Cohen 1992b; McKnight 1991. Certainly, some Jewish writers emphasized that Judaism surmounted the normal social boundaries separating Jews and Gentiles and had extended throughout the *oikoumene.* Like local elites at Ephesus, writers like Josephus interpreted the spread of Jews throughout the *oikoumene* and the attraction of the cult as evidence of the power and prestige of the Jewish god and, by implication, of the Jews. See chapter 5.

88. Cohen 1989.

89. For bibliography, see Vermeule 1981; Edwards 1992b.

90. Smith 1988; Edwards 1992b, 299–300.

91. Edwards 1992b, 301–6; Goodman 1994, 42–44.

92. On *The Jewish War,* see Attridge 1984, 192–93; Bilde 1988, 79; Rajak 1984a. On *Antiquities of the Jews,* see Attridge 1984, 210–11; Bilde 1988, 104; Rajak 1984a, 237–38. On *Vita,* see Bilde 1988, 104–6. On *Against Apion,* see Bilde 1988, 113.

93. See Cohen 1979.

94. See Rajak 1984a, 79.

95. Wilken 1984, xiv.

96. Suetonius, *Claudius* 25; Wilken, 1984, 50; Smallwood, *The Jews Under Roman Rule,* p. 24.

97. Smallwood, 1981, 210–16.

98. For a judicious discussion of the sources see ibid., 217–19. See also Benko 1984, 1980.

99. Thompson 1990, 16, 164; contra Sordi 1986.

100. For a summary with bibliography, see Pervo 1994.

101. Snyder 1985, 2. The appearance of distinct Christian symbols may have

resulted as well from increased toleration in certain local areas. In Phrygia, around the Upper Tembris valley, a number of Christian gravestones have been found dating from the middle of the second to the late third centuries. The earliest symbols probably included a cross and the Eucharist. See Gibson 1978; *MAMA* 10:xxxvi–xli; Mitchell 1993b, 38. By the mid–second century, a Christian community existed at Cadi, a small town in Phrygia, willing to identify their religion openly on gravestones. Two are securely dated to 157/58 and 179/80 c.e. A third, dedicated to a father and mother, ends with the word "Christians" (*chrisianoi*) and is dated somewhat earlier (to the mid–second century) by the editors of *MAMA* 10 (xxxvi). The editors of *MAMA* 10 rightly note that the number of early Christian inscriptions from southern Phrygia, all from rural areas, suggests a substantial Christian population before the end of the second century, which challenges the common notion that post-Pauline Christianity was almost totally urban in character (*MAMA* 10:xxxix). This does not indicate, however, that such rural areas were outside the influence of the network of cities that held the empire together.

102. See Finney 1994, 105–15. Finney notes that "Christians looked like their neighbors and behaved like them." Culturally they "spoke the same languages, ate the same foods, used the same money, patronized the same markets, wore the same clothes, exploited the same natural resources, labored in the same workplaces, lived in the same neighborhoods, buried their dead in the same plots, and acknowledged the same political authorities. The result: their high degree of adaptation to the prevailing Greco-Roman environment provided the new religionists with a social mechanism that guaranteed a low profile, in material culture, a profile best described as invisible" (109).

103. Smallwood 1981, 210–19.

104. Perhaps the Elkesaites, followers of a prophet Elkesai, who stressed ritual purity (through immersion and dietary practices) should be viewed as Jewish Christians. See Klijn and Reinink, 1974; Ferguson 1993, 577.

105. Sordi 1986, 43–44. But see Smallwood 1981, 318–82.

106. Meeks 1983, 1–2.

107. For succinct statements of the opposing sides of the issue, see Kraabel (1981), who argues that "god-fearers" is a rhetorical device used by Luke, and Feldman (1993, 342–68), who argues that epigraphic evidence indicates otherwise.

108. Cadbury 1968, 353. "Luke" serves as a convenient title for the author of the Gospel of Luke and Acts of the Apostles; its selection is not meant to suggest any identification with a known historical personage; see Maddox 1982, 3–6.

109. See the discussion by Alexander (1993).

110. Conzelmann 1987, xxxiii; Fitzmyer 1985, 53–57; Esler 1987, 27–29. Colin Hemer's (1989a) effort to date Luke–Acts earlier than 70 c.e. is not persuasive.

111. On the prologue, see Alexander, 1993; L. Alexander, "Luke's Preface," *NT* 28 (1986), pp. 48–74; Richard J. Dillon, "Previewing Luke's Project," *CBQ* 43 (1981), pp. 205–227. For an excellent overview see D. Aune, *The New Testament in Its Literary Environment*, pp. 116–157.

112. See Halvor Moxnes, "Patron-Client Relations and the New Community in Luke-Acts," pp. 241–270.

113. D. Aune, *The New Testament in Its Literary Environment*, pp. 138–140; R. Pervo, *Profit with Delight*, pp. 1–10.

114. See D. Gill, "Acts and the Urban Élites," in Gill/Gempf, 1994:109–110, 113–118.

115. Much debate has centered on the character of Luke's presentation. Was it

intended as an apologetic for the Roman leadership? Was it an antagonistic, though subtle, broadside against Roman rule and power? Or was it an attempt to make the Roman world palatable for Christian converts? As my study will suggest, none of these positions quite works. Rather, Luke redefines the power relations before him—imperial rule, regional and local authorities, other religious groups—by portraying the Christian god and the movement associated with it (i.e., the people Luke displays in the narrative) as the real power. He advocates tolerance of other power networks (except certain Jewish groups), but such groups are subject to the real authority as Luke sees it, the Christian god.

Chapter 3

1. For a discussion of the role of tradition, see Handler and Linnekin 1984.

2. See MacMullen 1981, 2–4.

3. Hobsbawn calls the result "invented tradition," understood to mean "a set of practices, normally governed by overtly or tacitly accepted rules and of a ritual or a symbolic nature, which seek to inculcate certain values and norms of behaviour by repetition, which automatically implies continuity with the past" (Hobsbawm and Ranger 1983, 1). See also Hobsbawm 1972; Bloch 1977.

4. Lane Fox 1986, 68; Millar 1993a, 236–37, 250–51.

5. Cartledge and Spawforth 1989.

6. Rogers 1991, 111–15; Oster 1987; Edwards 1991, 199–200.

7. Heracles remained the primary figure on Greek imperial coins of Tyre for a long period and appears often in literary traditions; see Millar 1993c, 264–66. Chariton of Aphrodisias reflects the popular association of Tyre with Heracles in his novel: "the Tyrians . . . are by nature a most warlike race who seek to maintain a reputation for bravery so as to avoid the appearance of disgracing the god Heracles, who is their most prominent divinity, and to whom they have dedicated their city almost exclusively" (7.2.7). A temple built to Heracles at Tyre is also mentioned by Josephus (*CA* 1.118).

8. Horsley 3:30–31 (includes bibliography).

9. The evidence for Jerusalem's importance is early. Cicero defends Flaccus, who was accused of stealing a large sum of money intended for the Jerusalem Temple (*Pro Flacco* 28). Luke has Jews from Parthia, Medes, Elam, Mesopotamia, Cappadocia, Pontus, Asia, Phrygia, Pamphylia, Egypt, Cyrene, Rome, Crete, and Arabia gather in Jerusalem for the Passover (Acts 2:9–10). Members of the country of Adiabene were active in the revolt against Rome. For the Parthian connection, see Neusner 1969a,b. Of course, direct involvement with the Temple discontinued after its destruction in 70 C.E., although the importance of Jerusalem as a symbol continued. For additional discussion of the key role that antiquity played for Jews, see Goodman 1994, 42–45; Feldman 1993, 177–95.

10. The leaders of the first revolt used silver, a direct affront to the Romans; see Crawford 1985, 270.

11. Such concerns, of course, continued throughout this period and afterward, as work on the Second Sophistic has shown. See Bowersock 1969. For a discussion of the period prior to and including the Antonine period, see Andrei 1984.

12. Cartledge and Spawforth 1989, 107.

13. Bowie 1974, 194.

14. Ibid., 199. See also Ramsay 1897, vol. 1, pt. 2, p. 606 n. 495.

15. Parke 1985, 72.

16. A similar motivation may explain the appearance of bronze statues of deities

from Greek mythology placed in newly built early-second-century C.E. baths in Apamea on the Orontes. See Millar 1990, 14.

17. See Millar 1993a.

18. See Bowie 1974, 206; Charlesworth 1936, 14–15.

19. See Magie 1950, 566–82; Alcock 1989a, 103–5.

20. See Millar 1993a, 246.

21. Millar 375–85; Galsterer 1988, 88.

22. Bowersock 1969, 43–58.

23. Jones 1970.

24. Ibid., 229–34, 248.

25. Bowie 1974, 208.

26. See also Millar 1993a, 250.

27. Much of what follows depends on an important study by Diana E. E. Kleiner (1983).

28. Ibid., 14–15.

29. Garnsey and Saller 1987.

30. Ibid., 10–11.

31. Ibid., 85.

32. Ibid., 87–88, 93.

33. Ibid., 90–91; see also 55.

34. See Josephus, *BJ* 7.219–43.

35. Kleiner 1983, 13, 91.

36. Ibid., 92.

37. Ibid., 98. See also Kleiner 1986.

38. Millar 1981, 202.

39. See Mitchell 1974. Compare C. Quadratus from Pergamum, who was consul in 93 C.E., and proconsul of Asia in 108–9, and T. Julius Celsus Polemasanus, who was consul in 92 C.E. and proconsul in 106–7 as well as governor of Bithynia. The latter's son built the magnificent library at Ephesus to commemorate his rule. See Harris 1980, 881.

40. *New Docs.* 1:31. See also Edson 1948, 181–82; Sokolowski 1974, 441–45.

41. *New Docs.* 1:18–20; Roussel 1929, 137–68.

42. *New Docs.* 1:21–23. See also Düll 1977, 4–5, who discusses a dedication by a Dionysiac cult to Titus, a chief *místos* at first-century Stobi in Yugoslavia.

43. See Reynolds, Beard, and Roueché 1986, 146, who note that such archaizing is also evident in an inscription from Spain dedicated in the early imperial period.

44. Mitchell 1993a, 206–11.

45. Zanker 1988; Wallace-Hadrill 1986, 1981.

46. The Ephesians, for example, claimed that Artemis of Ephesus festivals went back to the nineteenth century B.C.E. See Robert 1978, 473–76.

47. They even rehabilitated the tarnished image of Claudius. See Levick 1990, 190–93.

48. Millar 1977.

49. Reynolds 1982.

50. Millar 1977, 450–51.

51. MacMullen 1981, 96.

52. See Hunter 1994.

53. A fragment of the *Metiochus and Parthenope* romance indicates the importance of historiography for the early romances; see Maehler 1976, 1–20. See also Reardon 1991, 141–48; Hägg 1983, 16–17; and Perry, who remarks: "What Thucydides did for

the Peloponnesian War, that Chariton has done for the daughter of Hermocrates!" (1967, 137). Perry also notes the mixed nature of Chariton's composition and that his style and structure compare favorably to the contemporary biography and the historical monograph (143–48).

54. The Athenians are not viewed in a positive manner in Chariton's text. Perhaps his "anger" at them goes back to the time when Athens sent Carian slaves to their deaths against Sicily in the Peloponnesian War (Aelius Aristides 1.242). The loss of status of Athens in the Flavio-Trajanic period combined with the increased prestige of Asia Minor cities like Aphrodisias may also have some bearing.

55. Callirhoe belongs in the upper strata of Syracusan society. Little is known about the real daughter of Hermocrates from the two sources that mention her (Plutarch, *Dionysus* 3; Diodorus Siculus 3.112). See discussion by Perry 1967, 353, n. 25; and Plepelits 1976.

56. Steiner 1969.

57. Erim 1967; Squarciapino 1959, 1960, 1966; Inan and Rosenbaum 1966, 30–31.

58. At Aphrodisias, Kenan Erim has found a head of Alcibiades, portrayed as "a beardless, long-haired young man," apparently sculpted during the Roman period 1983, 233.

59. For Hellenistic and Roman epics, see review by Philip Hardie (1992) of D. C. Feeney's *The Gods in Epic: Poets and Critics of the Classical Tradition.* Hardie remarks, "As power surges round the circuit, gods, heroes, and epic poet all tend to become versions of one another" (253).

60. For example, the emperors from Augustus through Nero are portrayed in heroic guise and associated with numerous mythic images of the Greek past in panels forming two sides of the Julio-Claudian Sebasteion at Aphrodisias. See R. Smith 1990b, 1987.

61. See Müller 1976; Perry 1967, 77 ff., 169–70. Cf. *Odyssey* 6.232; *Iliad* 10.26; Apollonius Rhodius, *Argonautica* 1.774–80.

62. See also Reardon 1991, 74–75 (esp. n. 50).

63. Erim 1986, 26–27; cf. 25. See also Robert 1987, 349–54, who discusses the Iranian presence at Aphrodisias; cf. Robert 1965.

64. Erim 1986, 100–101.

65. Smith 1994.

66. For the argument that this child draws on the powerful myth of the child that Aphrodite gave to the world, Aeneas, see Edwards 1991, 195–96; see also LaPlace 1980, 124–25.

67. This topic is developed further in chapters 4 and 6.

68. See chapter 6.

69. Millar 1993a, 237.

70. Nock 1972, 2:625.

71. Rajak 1985; Kant 1987; Rutgers 1992.

72. *IGRR* 1.1024.

73. Smith 1993; Robert 1966; Reynolds 1982, 156–64.

74. Kant 1987, 690–92.

75. Schürer, 3.1 (1986), pp. 107–25.

76. *CPJ,* vol. 2, no. 153.

77. Rajak 1984b.

78. Smallwood 1981, 371–77.

79. Edwards 1992b; Thompson 1982.

80. Goodman 1989.

81. Feldman 1993, 177–200.
82. Goldberg 1990.
83. Brooke 1991.
84. Horbury and Noy 1992, 214–16.
85. Ibid., 95–102.
86. Ibid., 1. The inscription is dated between the second century B.C.E. and the early part of the second century C.E. Many inscriptions from Leontopolis are called Jewish because of their association with Jewish inscriptions that come from the same cemetery. The prevailing assumption is that because of that association they also may be Jewish, a distinct possibility but not entirely assured. The potential difficulties in identifying Jews using this method have been usefully discussed by Kraemer (1991).
87. Cf. Horbury and Noy 1992, 74–77, 90–94. As Horbury and Noy also note (1992, 63), the mention of Hades might also evoke certain biblical passages such as the Septuagint's version of Isaiah 5:14 or Wisdom of Solomon 1:14.
88. Collins 1984.
89. Lamentations Rabbah, dated in its latest form to the sixth century C.E., also depicts God destroying the Temple so it would not fall into the hands of the wicked. See Kirschner 1985.
90. Applebaum in Safrai and Stern 1974, 136; Lüderitz 1983.
91. This assumes that Joyce Reynolds is correct that the inscription refers to a public amphitheater and not a private Jewish building (1977, 246–47).
92. Horbury and Noy 1992, 213.
93. Feldman 1993, 233–87; Gager 1972; Cohen (1989) names seven ways in which non-Jews associated with Judaism.
94. "God will strike this person with poverty, with fever and cold shivers, irritation, blight, derangement, blindness, and distraction of mind" (*New Docs.* 3:123–24).
95. See Schürer, 2:59, 97; Geiger 1990, 142.
96. Attridge and Oden 1981, 1–9; Geiger 1990, 149–50; Barr 1974–75.
97. Millar 1983b; Grabbe 1992, 1:161; Hill 1911.
98. Bickerman 1980, 348.
99. Hengel 1980, 53.
100. Mildenberg 1990, 70.
101. Ibid., 73.
102. Porton 1976.
103. Yarden 1991.
104. See Hachlili 1988, 251, 255. See also *CIJ*, vol. 1, no. 200 (p. 139). The exception appears to be funerary monuments. In Cos, for example, on a first- or second-century funerary monument is the image of a menorah; inscribed above it is the name "Eutyclus." See Sherwin-White 1976, 186–87. Cf. *CIJ*, vol. 1, no. 283 (pp. 198–99), where Greek inscriptions have below them a menorah, shofar (horn), and lulab (palm). *Shalom* is written in Hebrew script to the left of the symbols, and the inscription is flanked by theater masks. Unfortunately, the sarcophagus is not dated.
105. See the early-second-century tomb in Rome that depicts the famous scene in Daniel where his three friends walk through the furnace (Wilpert 1903, pl. 13, 1:357–58). The power of symbols that draw on the past continues into the present, as aptly illustrated in the State of Israel's choice of the menorah (also found on the arch of Titus) as the symbol of the new nation. See Handelman and Shamger-Handelman 1990.
106. See letter by Claudius to Greeks and Jews in Alexandria in *CPJ*, vol. 2,

no. 153 (10 Nov. 41 C.E.). Claudius relies on the precedent established by Augustus to allow Jews to continue practicing their particular customs without interference.

107. Gager 1972, 25–79.

108. Goodman 1987.

109. Bowie 1974, 209.

110. Murphy 1985a,b.

111. Lane Fox 1986, 27.

112. Rajak 1991.

113. Cohen 1982.

114. See also Feldman 1989.

115. Edwards 1994b.

116. Millar 1993b.

117. Bickerman 1980, 355.

118. Elliott 1993, 369; MacDonald 1986, 1983.

119. *First Apology* 20–22, 30–60.

120. Grant 1988.

121. Pagels 1985, 313.

122. See Droge 1989.

123. Walker (1990, 31) calls this period "one of the obscurest portions of Church history."

124. Corbo 1993.

125. For bibliography and rebuttal see Taylor 1993, 1989–90; Strange 1977.

126. The protoevangelism of James 18 suggests that a "cave of the Nativity" existed in the early second century C.E. See Lane Fox 1986, 476; Hunt 1982. Some have suggested that the so-called house of Peter in Capernaum became a Christian shrine by the second century. See the judicious discussion in Taylor 1993. Such beginnings set the stage for full-blown pilgrimages in the third and especially the fourth centuries under Constantine. Other possible Christian realia include Christian graves dating as early as the mid–second century in Phrygia, the tomb in Rome with the three friends of Daniel burning in the flame, and *P. Oxy.*, vol. 17, no. 3057, which is dated to the late first or early second century C.E. on palaeographic grounds and which P. Parsons, the translator, suggests is Christian (Parsons 1980). The evidence is tenuous at best. The text is discussed fully, with bibliography, in *New Docs* 6:169–77.

127. Pliny, *Correspondence with Trajan* 96.

128. Elliott 1981, 84–87.

129. Lane Fox 1986, 321–22.

130. Finn 1982.

131. Hagner 1973; Hall 1968.

132. Jeffers 1991; Barnard 1967; Barnes 1984; Danielou 1964; Frend 1985, 1984.

133. *Ignatius to the Ephesians* 1.2, in Lake 1959, 173–75.

134. Wilpert 1903, vol. 1, pls. 13, 78.1, 172.2, pp. 357–58.

135. The evidence and discussion can be found in Price 1984b, 199–200; cf. Lane Fox 1986, 476.

136. 1 Clement 4.1–5.7.

137. On these genres, see Bowersock 1995.

138. The discussion of this connection is voluminous. See Evans and Sanders 1993; Esler 1987, 201–19.

139. David Moessner argues persuasively that Luke uses Moses' rejection by the people and his journey through the wilderness to the Promised Land as the paradigm for Jesus, Peter, and Stephen (1989, 296–307).

140. Esler 1987, 216.

141. Goodman 1991b, 227–38.

142. Pliny, *Correspondence with Trajan* 96.

Chapter 4

1. *CIL,* vol. 2, no. 1963.

2. See F. T. Van Straten 1974, 159–89; Pleket 1981.

3. *IGUR* 1245, lines 3–6, in *New Docs.* 4:43; for additional examples, see pp. 42–46. See also Van der Horst 1991, 121.

4. See Lane Fox 1986. See also the discussion of the long tradition of tirades against the atheist from Plato to Plutarch by Meijer (1981).

5. Roussel 1931, 116.

6. Roussel 1931; Bowersock 1987.

7. Hatzfeld 1927, 64. Quoted in MacMullen 1981, 167 n. 18.

8. MacMullen 1981, 46–47; much of the following discussion regarding this cult is indebted to the work of R. MacMullen.

9. Ibid., 47.

10. Roussel 1927, 124; MacMullen 1981, 167 n. 18.

11. MacMullen 1981, 47.

12. See Kotansky 1991, 111. On the mysteries at Ephesus, see *New Docs.* 6:201–2.

13. For such requests, see Winkler 1991.

14. See, e.g., the Isis aretalogy from Maroneia in Macedonia in the latter part of the second or early part of the first century B.C.E. Isis, the inscription states, instituted justice, laws, and provided tranquility to cities. Parents are honored by their children because of her intervention. See Grandjean 1975; Solmsen 1979; *New Docs.* 1:10–12.

15. See the fine study of this phenomenon in Asia Minor by Simon Price (1984b).

16. Garnsey and Saller 1987, 166–67.

17. *ILS* 8794 = *Syll.* 3.814; translation from Price 1984a, 83.

18. On power networks within Greek cities, see Millar 1993a, 241.

19. On patronage, see Saller 1982; Wallace-Hadrill 1989.

20. S. Price details the association of imperial and local cults at some length (1984b, 146–56).

21. Price 1984a, 83 n. 37.

22. Ibid., 89.

23. Aristides, *Orationes* 26 (K) 32. Quoted in Price 1984a, 93.

24. "What is a god? The exercise of power." Quoted in Price 1984a, 95; *Philologus* 80 (1924–25), p. 339.

25. Individuals would also associate themselves and their professions with cosmic power. See the example of a purple-seller, Euschemon, who dedicated a statue and shrine to Agathe Tyche at Miletopolis in Mysia (Hasluck 1907, 61–62, no. 2).

26. *TAM.* 5:167a.

27. Lane Fox 1986, 128–29.

28. See *New Docs.* 2:90.

29. For evidence of the cult, see Lane 1971–78, vols. 1–4.

30. *New Docs.* 2:90.

31. Ibid., 3:27.

32. Petzl and Malay 1987; *New Docs.* 5:143.

33. Summarized in *New Docs.* 3:27–28.

34. Ibid., 3.28.

35. Ibid., 73–74.
36. Wild 1984.
37. Walker 1979, 246.
38. Ibid., 247. A statue of Aphrodite was also dedicated to Isis at this time. For a discussion of the important role played by women as benefactors, see *New Docs.* 4:242–44; Van Bremen 1985.
39. See Boyce and Grenet 1991.
40. Gordon 1994.
41. Boyce and Grenet 1991, 261; Gordon 1972; Ulansey 1989, 95–103; Beck 1988.
42. Patrich 1990.
43. Bowersock 1990, chap. 3. See also Millar 1987.
44. See *Anatolian Studies* 3 (1983), 234; Galinsky 1969, 5–6; Reynolds 1980, 70.
45. Reynolds 1991, 15–19; 1982, document 55.1.1, p. 184; 1986, 111–12.
46. Robert 1989, 39–41.
47. Smith 1990b, 89.
48. Reynolds 1990, 40; 1986, 111.
49. Reynolds 1991.
50. Reynolds 1986, 111. See also the inscription on the bath complex, which ends with the dedication to Aphrodite Epiphane, the *prometor* of the emperors (Robert 1989, 41 n. 1.).
51. See Price 1984b; Lane Fox 1986.
52. Smith 1990b, 100.
53. *LIMC* 2.1, p. 1, and 2.2, no. 2.
54. Citations are from Reynolds 1982 (see also ibid., p. 80).
55. Stern 1980, 508.
56. Williams 1987, 32–33.
57. Inan and Rosenbaum 1966, 171, pl. 126, nos. 1–2.
58. Inan and Alföldi-Rosenbaum 1979, 39, no. 186, pls. 138.1, 274.1–5, 139.1–4.
59. Erim 1990a, 15, 18, 17 (fig. 9); see also Smith 1990a, 128.
60. Reynolds 1982, document 18, p. 127.
61. Lane Fox (1986, 102–67) examines visitations of the gods.
62. *CIG* 2811.
63. Cormack 1954.
64. Versnel 1990.
65. Roscher 1884–1937, s.v. "Homonoia." Artemis of Ephesus is the most obvious parallel to Aphrodite's political and social role at Aphrodisias. See Fleischer pls. 41a–b; 79a; Oster 1990; LiDonnici 1992.
66. Howgego 1985, 40–41.
67. *BMC Caria*, no. 161, p. 53, pl. 44; no. 162, p. 53; *BMC Phrygia*, no. 166, p. 257; MacDonald 1976, 31; Oster 1990, 1700–1701.
68. *BMC Phrygia*, no. 25; Vermeule 1968, 160–61.
69. Price 1984b, 126–27.
70. Ibid., p. 127. L. Robert (1974, 198) notes that a late inscription found in the Sarapeion at Thessalonica was dedicated to Aphrodite Homonoia (ca. 182–83 C.E.), situating Aphrodite squarely within family and civic life (see *IG* 10.2.1). Some of the rights of local magistrates in the Flavian period are detailed in a set of inscribed laws found in Spain. See Gonzalez 1986; MacDonald 1976, 127.
71. See Johnston 1989, 323–24; Klose 1987, 53 ff.
72. Dio of Prusa, *Oracles* 38.22; Harris 1980.
73. See Reynolds 1982, 6–11.

74. Fleischer 1973, 146 ff.

75. Galinsky 1969, 217; Laumonier 1958, 497–98; Fleischer, in *LIMC* 2.1, pp. 153–54.

76. See *Anatolian Studies* 14 (1964), 26, gives Erim's description of this statue. For photographs of some of the many statues of Aphrodite of Aphrodisias, see *LIMC* 2.2, pp. 154–56.

77. See Laumonier 1958, 500.

78. Galinsky 1969, esp. 217; see also Laumonier 1958, 497–98; R. Fleischer also observes that this statue of Aphrodite at Aphrodisias is similar to one of Artemis at Ephesus and that the decoration and zones depict the power of the goddess over nature, the heavens, earth, and water, a conception, he argues, that dates to the late Hellenistic and early Roman periods (see *LIMC* 2.1, pp. 153–54).

79. Other sites include Ephesus, Athens, Salone, Leptis Magna, and Baalbek (where a bronze statuette was found). See Noelke 1983.

80. Babelon 1908, no. 2207; *LIMC* 2.2, no. 3a.

81. See Price 1984b, 101–32; MacMullen 1981, esp. 18–42.

82. The imperial Greek coins from Aphrodisias indicate its close association with the Roman emperors; see MacMullen 1981, 30.

83. Reynolds 1991, 15; 1987, 83; *MAMA* 8.435–36, 448.

84. Translation from Reynolds 1982, 167.

85. See ibid., 172–73; Robert 1971, 81–82; Campbell 1936.

86. Reynolds 1982, 113–15.

87. Laumonier 1958, 499; see Cameron 1991, 78–79.

88. Reynolds 1987, 83.

89. Smith 1993.

90. Reynolds 1981, 320.

91. Ibid., 322–23.

92. *BMC Caria,* no. 66; cf. no. 68 (Harpocrates); Witt 1971, 11, 44, 89–93, 107–10; Garnsay and Saller 1987, 170–73.

93. Versnel 1990.

94. Aphrodite's power is acknowledged, e.g., by crowds on Dionysius's estate (2.2.5); by Dionysius, a local elite in Miletus (2.3.6); and by Stateira, the queen of Persia (5.9.1). Also, Chariton has Callirhoe go to the temple of Aphrodite (2.2.7, 2.3.5).

95. This allusion to Helen is one of several in the narrative (2.6.1, 5.2.8, 5.5.9). Callirhoe, however, unites nations rather than causing them to go to war. And although Helen's beauty attracts nations, crowds do not consistently worship her (*proskunein*), nor does she unite warring factions. Even her beauty, according to Dionysius, pales against Callirhoe's. "I imagined that my life would be happier than that of Menelaus, the husband of Helen of Sparta, for really I do not believe that Helen was as beautiful as she is. But besides this she also has the power of convincing speech [*peitho*]" (2.6.1). *Peitho* was closely associated with Greek magistrates. See the excellent discussion by Sokolowski (1964, 3–4). *Peitho* (persuasion) was an important attribute associated with Aphrodite, sometimes as another form of her. See Robinson 1933, 602–4. *Peitho* also symbolized "civic obedience to the state and its authorities" (Sokolowski 1964, 6).

96. G. Galinsky has observed this relationship in the Aphrodite and Eros on the Boston Throne, which functioned as part of an altar or monument sacred to Aphrodite. He quotes approvingly G. Richter's observation that Aphrodite was the goddess of love, who could bestow or withhold all things pertaining to love and marriage (Galinsky 1969, 252). Indeed, as Galinsky notes, the close association between Eros and Aphrodite caused their symbols to be interchangeable (253).

97. See the important discussion by Beye (1982, 127–28). See *Chaereas and Callirhoe* 6.4.5.

98. A similar attitude was evinced toward the Fates (*moira*) in a funerary epitaph for a midwife, Julia Prinigenia, who died in the early imperial period (*IGUR* 1240; *New Docs.* 4:23). See also a later inscription from Nikaia in Asia Minor (second or third century C.E.) that says about a young man who has died: "For this is what the Fates' [*moiron*] thread spins for us, to come once more to Hades" (*New Docs.* 4:25). The motif is common from the third century B.C.E. on. See *New Docs.* 4:29.

99. See discussion by Reardon (1969, 293 ff., 297 nn. 16–17). G. Anderson correctly observes that it is a common feature in the ancient romances to show divine intervention prevailing over Fate (1984, 2). See also Hägg 1983, 13; Helms 1966, 120.

100. Gerald Sandy discusses the role of Fate in the novels, including this passage (1994, 1557–62), but inexplicably discounts this passage as depicting Aphrodite's power over Fate (1558).

101. A close parallel occurs in Apuleius, who has the high priest of Isis describe the power of Isis over Fortune. "You [Lucius] have endured many toils and been driven by Fortune's great tempests and mighty storm winds; . . . the blindness of Fortune, while torturing you with the worst of perils, has brought you in its random wickedness to this holy state of happiness. . . . Behold! Lucius, set free from his tribulations of old and rejoicing in the providence of great Isis, triumphs over his Fortune" (Apuleius, *Meta.* 11.15).

102. Aphrodite's role in maintaining group cohesiveness and goodwill occurs elsewhere in the Greek East. Diodorus notes that the Charites were closely associated with Aphrodite and encouraged sacrifices on behalf of the corporate group to obtain the goodwill of the people and the authorities (5.7.3; see also Sokolowski 1964, 5).

103. For a discussion of Josephus's works as apologetic historiography, see Sterling 1992.

104. Goodman 1994, 51–59. However, if the epitaphs from Leontopolis are Jewish, they suggest that some Jews did not emphasize an afterlife or an all-powerful Jewish god. See Horbury and Noy 1992, 51–182, for excellent bibliography and discussion; also Feldman 1993, 65–69. Of particular interest also are the dedications found near the temple of Pan at El-Kanais. One possibly dating between the second or first century B.C.E. or even into the Roman period reads: "Bless God. Theodotos son of Dorian, the Jew, returned safely from overseas [or saved from the sea]" (Horbury and Noy 1992, 207, no. 121). The inscription was one of sixteen texts located immediately west of the temple of Pan. (Bernand 1972). Horbury and Noy appear to suggest (following Bernand) that the dedication is to the Jewish god since this inscription (1) is not in the temple proper, (2) appears to have been set apart from other inscriptions by a frame drawn around it, and (3) has no explicit dedication to the god Pan (as is the case with the other clearly Jewish text: Horbury and Noy 1992, no. 122; Bernand 1972, no. 34). Several problems exist with this interpretation. Most of the other inscriptions in the area are explicitly dedicated to Pan, and there seems little doubt that this area was associated with the temple. Indeed, the inscription that is directly above this inscription reads "To Pan, Savior, from Didymarchus son of Eumelos, of Perge. I have come" (Bernand 1972, 101, no. 39). There seems no reason to doubt that the area is part of the sacred space associated with the temple. Thus the writer of the inscription must have known the nature of the area. In addition, other inscriptions in the area have similar boxes drawn around them (Bernand 1972, nos. 48–50, pl. 41.3, 4, 5; no. 72, pl. 47.1, 2; no. 80, pl. 50.1), including the inscription to Pan noted earlier. The writers of the two Jewish inscriptions, therefore, purposely placed in the temple area dedications listing their

Jewish identities (whatever that meant). What can we conclude from this? Ross Kraemer suggests that this may represent evidence for Jews honoring other gods in certain instances (1992b, 322). Conceivably the dedicator presents or acknowledges his deity at the cult site of the resident deity. It was common in the pagan world to offer dedications to one deity at the site of another. Finally, it might be a subtle way to acknowledge the power of one's deity without drawing attention to the fact. Although I lean toward Kraemer's interpretation, the other two remain strong possibilities.

105. Smallwood 1981, 220–25. The fear in Egypt was extreme among some non-Jews during the Jewish revolt of 115–17 C.E., as vividly evidenced by a series of letters to a combatant from his family. Another letter expresses fear about traveling through the land because of the danger. The most virulent examples come from the Acts of the Pagan Martyrs. Feldman may be right to caution us about universal hostility against Jews (certainly for the post-Trajanic period), but our evidence for the Flavio-Trajanic period suggests a good deal of prejudice, animosity, and fear in key areas of the empire, a point Feldman also fully demonstrates (1993, 107–76).

106. *CPJ* 1:48–92.

107. *CIJ*, vol. 1, no. 690a (pp. 67–68); cf. a manuscript text from 86 C.E. in *P. Oxy.*, vol. 1, no. 48.

108. *CIJ*, vol. 1, no. 68; see also Calderini 1965, 418–20.

109. The phrases "friend of Rome" and "friend of caesar" are common terms that reflect the connection between Rome and local elites, often client kings. See Braund 1984 and *New Docs.* 3:87–89 for discussion and numerous examples. Both Agrippa I and Agrippa II of Judaea bear the title of king (*OGIS* 419–20, 424), as does Agrippa I's nephew, Herod Eusebes (*OGIS* 427). The importance of such formulas can be seen in legal documents from Dura Europus. A deed of a gift dated to 87 C.E. begins: "In the reign of the king of kings Arsaces, benefactor, just, manifest god, and friend of Greeks" (Welles, Fink, and Gilliam 1959, no. 18, pp. 98–104). The formal similarity to the Gorgippia transaction should be obvious. A Parthian king following Seleucid tradition frames the social act by asserting his divine associations and Hellenic affiliation but with no hint of incorporating or acknowledging Roman power. The pattern of address continues for some time (cf. Welles, Fink, and Gilliam 1959, no. 19 (88/89 C.E.), no. 20 (121 C.E.), no. 21 (100–150 C.E.), no. 23 (134 C.E.), no. 24 (159/60 C.E.). A land deal between two brothers in 180 C.E. reflects a completely altered situation.

> In the consulship of Bruttius Praesens for the second time and of Julius Verus for the second time, in the twentieth year of the principate of Imperator Caesar Marcus Aurelius Antoninus and the fourth of his son Imperator Caesar Lucius Aurelius Commodus, Augusti, and 491 of the former reckoning, on the fourth of the month Peritius, in Europos toward Arabia. In the year when Lysanias, son of Zenodotus and grandson of Heliodorus, was priest of Zeus; Theodorus, son of Athenodotus and grandson of Artemidorus, was priest of Apollo; Heliodorus, son of Diocles and grandson of Heliodorus, was priest of the Ancestors; and Danymus, son of Seleucus and grandson of Danymus, was priest of King Seleucus. (Welles, Fink and Gilliam 1959, no. 25)

Both Roman and Seleucid dating systems frame the event, as does the lengthy list of religious affiliations. A new day had come in which Rome with its affiliated local elites, not Parthia, now controlled this region (Rome took over in 165 C.E.). The contract changes clearly reflect the integration of Roman and Seleucid/Parthian powers within which social and legal actions had to take place; see Cotton, Cockle, and Millar 1995.

110. *CIJ* 1.690 (translated by M. Reinhold, p. 93); *CIJ* 1.683 (p. 495); Kant 1987, 683–84.

111. See Lewis 1989; Cotton 1993.

112. Lewis suggests initially that Babatha may have fled her village to escape the wrath of the Romans. Later he says that her choice of that particular cave was "no doubt dictated by the fact that nearby En-gedi was a Bar Kokhba stronghold, plus the fact that her stepdaughter owned property there" (Lewis 1989, 5). Her reasons may never be known. But the proximity to Bar Kochba's stronghold seems unlikely to be accidental (ibid., 4).

113. Cf. the similar archive of Salome Komaise, daughter of Levi (Cotton 1995); for additional discussion of this connection see chapter 7.

114. Two administrators who lease land date their legal document, written in Aramaic, "on the first day of Iyyar, in the first year of the redemption of Israel [by ?Simeon] bar Kosiba [Kochba], Prince of Israel" (Apr. 132 C.E.). Millar 1993c, app. B. no. 1. Cf. other examples using similar formulas in Millar 1993c, nos. 2–13.

115. Goodman 1991a, 172–73; Lewis 1989, 67 (P. Yadin 16). Individuals apparently used various legal systems to compose legal documents, indicating that complete submission to the Roman legal system did not occur.

116. P. Yadin 16, line 34 (in Lewis 1989); cf. Cotton 1995, no. 2, line 2, which reads: "son of Levi, I swear by the tyche of the Lord Caesar that I have in good faith registered as written above, concealing nothing" (p. 176). See also a document from Hermoupolis Magna in Egypt, dated to 90 C.E., that reads: "And I swear by the tyche of Imperator Caesar Domitianus Augustus Germanicus that there is no house or other landed property belonging to me, and that I have no other sons or anyone else undeclared apart from those mentioned above" (*CPJ* 3:485, pp. 62–64; cf. Goodman 1991a, 174).

117. Goodman suggests something similar and draws possible implications for the revolt in 66–73. Rather than postulating ancient hostility as the cause of the first revolt, increased social and political polarization in Judaea may have brought a number of Jewish communities into the conflict that had had perfectly amiable relations with their Gentile neighbors (1987; 1991a, 175).

118. Schürer, 3.1:36–38.

119. Stern 1974b: 1560.

120. Goodman 1987, 152–53; Millar 1981, 200.

121. Quoted from Ewing 1895, 49, no. 19 (Waddington 2413b).

122. Kokkinos 1992 argues that Agrippa was not viewed as Jewish.

123. Stern 1987, 76–77.

124. Ibid., 77.

125. Feldman and Hata 1987, 25.

126. Cf. Rajak 1984a, 100, who notes that Roman generals often express the role of God in history (e.g., *BJ* 3.144, 484, 494; 4.366, 370, 626). God acts through natural disasters (*BJ* 1.369–73). Herod sees an earthquake as a snare that God set to trap invading Arabs (*BJ* 1.373).

127. Rajak 1984a, 78–79.

128. Ibid., 92–98.

129. In Josephus's account of Herod the Great, Herod acknowledges the key role God and the Romans (especially Augustus) play in establishing *homonoia* with his household. As noted earlier, disruption and lack of concord within the family struck at the very fabric of society. The integration of divine power and Roman power to maintain stability in Herod's realm depicts how Josephus saw the relationship. This attempt

at *homonoia* contrasted sharply with the strife (*stasis*) that was to rip the family apart (*BJ* 1.431; cf. *CA* 16.146–59).

130. R. Grant 1966; *Ignatius of Antioch, Letter to the Romans* 5:3.

131. Perkins 1985.

132. See Squires 1993.

133. Tiede 1980, 32–33. Talbert (1984, 96–98) also draws important parallels to the role of necessity in the ancient world and the important role it had in many ancient genres.

134. Most appropriate are the following examples: Acts 3:20, 22:15, 26:16 (*procheiridzein*); Acts 10:41 (*procheirpotonein*); Acts 4:28 (*prooridzein*).

135. Luke 2:49; 4:23; 9:22; 12:12; 13:14, 16, 33; 15:32; 17:25; 18:1; 19:5; 21:9; 22:7, 37; 24:7, 26, 44. Acts 1:16, 21; 3:21; 4:12; 5:29; 9:6, 16; 14:22; 15:5; 16:30; 19:21, 36; 20:35; 23:11; 24:19; 25:10; 27:24. F. Danker (1981, 46–47) has rightly observed that *dei* operates in the same manner as *pronoia*. See also Squires 1993, 5–7.

136. See Tiede (1980, 27) for discussion of and evidence for this position.

137. Compare Kee 1983a, 211–12; Squires 1993, 166–77.

138. See Kee 1983a, 181, 219–20.

139. In the second century Justin Martyr develops this theme at great length in his apologetics and his debate with Trypho.

140. Edwards 1992b.

141. *CPJ*, vol. 2, nos. 160–229. The ostraca stop abruptly in the year 116 C.E. except for one lone example from the mid–second century (no. 460).

142. Tcherikover in *CPJ*, vol. 1, pp. 81–83.

143. Goodman 1994; 1989, 41–43.

144. Some issues still remain for Goodman's thesis. The Edfu ostraca, for example, show no real break in their style from Vespasian through Trajan. Intriguing is the fact that none occur from Nerva in the Edfu collection. This may simply be an accident of course. But it lends support to Goodman's point. Yet the impact may have been shorter than Goodman proposes or the tax was simply not strictly enforced. Or most likely, the Egyptian community sought to maintain its strong Jewish identity.

145. *AJ* 20.100; Tcherikover suggested that Josephus toned down his views toward this apostate Jew so as not to offend Titus (*CPJ*, vol. 1, p. 79). Goodman (1989, 41) rightly argues that Josephus still saw him as part of the Covenant, even if a wayward member.

Chapter 5

1. For works on this topic, see Foucault 1986; Lincoln 1982; Harley and Woodward 1987, 502–9.

2. Nicolet 1991, 189; see also Sack 1986.

3. Quoted from Nicolet 1991, 194.

4. See J. Z. Smith 1987.

5. On "mental maps," see Gould and White 1986.

6. On territoriality, see Sack 1986; Wells 1992.

7. See Edwards 1992b, 304.

8. See Nicolet 1991, 189.

9. MacDonald 1982, ix; cf. the excellent and more comprehensive discussion in MaCready and F. Thompson 1987. For a careful analysis of the issues involved, see Yegül 1991.

10. Much of the following discussion is indebted to R. Smith's excellent work on the complex (1990b, 1988, 1987).

11. The complex was founded during the reign of Tiberius; significant additions were made during the reign of Claudius and perhaps Nero (R. Smith 1987, 90; Reynolds 1981, 319–22). R. Smith, project director at Aphrodisias, informs me that it continued to stand well into the fifth century.

12. R. Smith 1987, 137–38; see also Nicolet 1991.

13. Smith 1988, 51–53, pl. 7.3, 4.

14. Augustus stands with Nike and a trophy above a bound captive (R. Smith 1987, pl. 4); Germanicus is shown with a captive (pl. 10); Claudius is shown defeating Britannia (pl. 14); and Nero is shown conquering Armenia (pl. 16).

15. Smith 1988, 51–59.

16. Ibid., 59.

17. Smith persuasively demonstrates the appropriation of Roman models (ibid., 70–77).

18. R. Smith 1988, 1987.

19. R. Smith 1987, 94.

20. On the spread of worship of this triad, see Garnsey and Saller 1987, 167.

21. E.g., the cities of Keretapa (1 *Ephesos* 2.234) and Hyrkanis (1 *Ephesos* 5.1498); see also (1 *Ephesos* 2.235–41) dedications date toward the end of the first century and early part of the second (Price 1984b; Friesen 1993, 29–49).

22. Ramsey MacMullen (1981) disputes this. Yet deities in the second century had become important. In addition, to arguments in the text, see *IG 14* (Suppl.), 2461, where an inscription from Massilia in the imperial period refers to several gods in association with a young man who has recently died.

23. On the worship of Mithras, see Beck 1984; Martin 1987, 113–18; Campbell 1968. On the cult of Isis, see Leclant 1986. Also see the inscription by Demetrios from Magnesia on the Maenander, who copied a stele in Memphis, a sacred city associated with Isis (*New Docs.* 1:18–28); Magie 1953. On the cult of Artemis of Ephesus, see Oster 1976; Rogers 1991; Trebilco 1994. On the cult of Zeus originating in Doliche, see Horig and Schwertheim 1987; *New Docs.* 4:118–26; Millar 1993c, 248–49 (who notes that the cult drew on ancient Hittite iconography); Momigliano 1987, 189–90; Kan 1943. On the cult of Jupiter Optimus Maximus Heliopolitanus, see Millar 1990, 23; Hajjar 1977, 188–220, 261–416. MacMullen (1981, 117–18) notes that some of these cults flowered only in the late second and third centuries. They had roots in the first century, however.

24. Numerous examples exist that indicate the close ties people had to their home-lands. A young man from Rome who died and was buried at Antioch in Mygdonia in the early part of the second century C.E. had his ashes taken back by his relatives for reburial in Rome (*IGUR* 1151; for other parallels see *New Docs.* 4:36–38). In the first century, Jews from the city of Scythopolis sought burial at Jerusalem, the holy city (Edwards 1992c, 70). The loss of homeland, of course, is sorely felt by Callirhoe throughout the ancient romance *Chaereas and Callirhoe,* a theme that figures in the other romances as well.

25. Price 1984b, 131.

26. Robert 1967; Oster 1990, 1703 n. 333.

27. Translated in Price 1984b, 130–31; see *Syll.* 3.867; 1 *Ephesos* 1a.24.

28. Fleischer 1973, map 2; *New Docs.* 4:74–82.

29. Noelke 1983.

30. Ibid., 128.

31. Fleischer 1981, 308; Squarciapino 1962, 69–70.

32. Noelke 1983, 129–30.

33. Ibid., 130. See, e.g., *MAMA* 8.413d.

34. On the spread of the cult of Artemis of Ephesus, see Oster 1990, 1703–6; Noelke 1983, 128. On the spread of the cult of Mithras, see Gordon 1976; Ulansey 1989. On Isis, see Witt 1971; Garnsey and Saller 1987, 171–72. On Men, see *New Docs.* 3:30–31 for discussion. Greg Horsley notes that the Men cult seems to be more public in central Asia Minor (e.g., in Antioch of Pisidia); in Greece and western Asia Minor, however, the finds are generally associated with individuals or local sanctuaries. This suggests a spread from east to west, although the evidence for this remains inconclusive. On Dionysus, see C. Gasparri, "Bacchus," in *LIMC* 3.1, pp. 540–66, and *LIMC* 3.2, pp. 428–56; C. Augé, "Dionysos (In Peripheria Orientali)," in *LIMC* 3.1, pp. 514–31, and *LIMC* 3.2, pp. 406–19; S. Boucher, "Bacchus (In Peripheria Occidental)," in *LIMC* 4.1, pp. 908–23, and *LIMC* 4.2, pp. 612–31. For a fine discussion of recent research on the god Dionysus, see Hutchinson 1991.

35. See chapter 4.

36. Nicolet 1991; Scott 1994, 485.

37. Parke 1985, 200.

38. MacMullen 1981, 98–99.

39. Ibid., 99.

40. Suetonius's description of the persecution of Christians under Nero may say more about his period than Nero's. To be sure, sporadic persecution took place, as evidenced by Paul's letters. But widespread recognition as a group separate from one of the many Jewish groups in the empire does not seem to happen until the late first (Acts) and early second centuries (Pliny).

41. MacMullen 1981, 100.

42. Ibid., 101.

43. Friesen 1993, 144–45.

44. On this point, see Goodman 1994, 20–37.

44. Nicolet 1991, 29–56, 171–87; R. Smith 1990b, 1987; Scott 1994, 490–91.

46. For an analysis of the role of the barbarian in Greek thought up through Xenophon's *Cyropaedia,* see Georges 1994.

47. See the famous Isis hymn from Oxyrhynchus (*P. Oxy.,* vol. 11, no. 1380).

48. On the connection of the Mithras cult to the military, see Vermaseren 1963.

49. E.g., Hägg 1983, 25–26, 36, 89; Reardon 1976.

50. See Hägg's excellent analysis (1971).

51. In a paper kindly shared with me, Loveday Alexander discusses Chariton's employment of the Ionian view of the *oikoumene* (Alexander n.d.).

52. It matters little whether such a temple existed or whether such a festival actually occurred at Syracuse. The readers would understand the implications of the festival. See Schmeling 1974, 83.

53. Chariton also shows the reader how Greek, and thus superior, his characters are as opposed to the barbarians they encounter, something his city, Aphrodisias, emphasizes as well. The theme of the superiority of the Greek over the barbarian was a long-standing one. See Georges 1994, 244–46.

54. See MacMullen 1981, 2–4. This criterion had its variants. Tacitus remarks that Ephesus received approval to continue as a site for asylum based on ancient myths, whereas Aphrodisias and Stratonicea used a decree from Julius Caesar and a rescript from the deified Augustus, who praised their fidelity (another type of tradition) (*Annals* 3.62–63).

55. The temple cult established by Onias in Leontopolis and destroyed during the Jewish revolt of 66 C.E. was never a serious rival to the Temple in Jerusalem (Philo, *The Special Laws* 1.67; Josephus, *AJ* 13.67–77, *BJ* 7.420–41).

56. Smallwood 1981, 375–76.

57. Alexander, 1992, 981–82; Alexander 1982; Scott 1994; Schmidt 1990.

58. Scott (1994, 512) argues that Josephus downplays the centrality of Israel and that *omphalos* here refers to Jerusalem as geographical center of Judaea, not the world (contra Jubilees). Yet Jerusalem and its temple hold for Josephus powerful associations with the fabric of the cosmos itself, as I show elsewhere. Cf. Jubilees 8:19.

59. Alexander 1992, 984. The former, for example, apparently influences the author of 1 Enoch (17–36).

60. This information was conveyed to me by Robert Whiting, managing editor of the Neo-Assyrian Text Corpus Project, University of Helsinki, Finland. Discussion of the map can be found in Gomilev and Quznetzov 1969. See also Benjamin Mazar's brief discussion (1975, 24).

61. Philo has the universe itself as the Temple, with the stars as votive offerings and the angels as priests (*The Special Laws* 1.66).

62. See discussion in Edwards 1992b, 294–95.

63. *OTP* 2:548.

64. Edwards 1992a, 1994b.

65. Cf. the attitude of the Qumran community. See Goranson 1992.

66. On symbolic discourse in Judaism, see Neusner 1992, 90–91.

67. Kraabel 1979, 502; Kraabel 1992b, 26–27; see also Lightstone 1984, 117; Goldman 1966.

68. Lightstone 1984, 118.

69. Gafni 1981; Weiss 1992; Lightstone 1984, 71–78.

70. Lightstone 1984, 57–87.

71. Kraabel 1992b, 27.

72. Neusner 1973, 67–80; Segal 1986, 132–33.

73. This information was conveyed to me by Esther Eschel.

74. Grant 1992.

75. See Attridge 1989.

76. White 1990.

77. Cf. Taylor 1993, 1989–90; Markus 1994.

78. Gnostics took a different course, but Jesus still remained central.

79. Here again the question of god-fearers (i.e., Gentiles) comes to the forefront. Whether such a group existed or not, certain Christian writers portray their movement as widespread and, in some cases, attractive to outsiders.

80. For a useful discussion of "territoriality" as used by Luke, see Robbins 1991, 212–21.

81. See Elliott 1991, 213–24.

82. Contra Neyrey 1991, 286.

83. See discussion in Alexander n.d. Richard Bauckham has made this observation in a recent lecture, according to a report given to me by Loveday Alexander; see also Scott 1994, 524–43.

84. Metzger 1970; Weinstock 1948, 43–46; contra Conzelman 1987, 14–15.

85. See Talbert 1984, 91–103; Peterson 1993.

86. Robbins 1991, 211–15.

87. Ibid., 219.

88. Conzelmann 1961, 18–94.

89. See Ladouceur 1980; Miles and Trompf 1976. See also Trompf 1984, 236 n. 8, who cites C. H. Talbert and draws attention to the similarities in *Chaereas and Callirhoe* (3.3.10, 3.3.18, 3.4.9–10).

Chapter 6

1. Tacitus, *Histories* 4.81 (Loeb).

2. Under Roman rule the laws of heredity and requirements at Eleusis appear to have changed, however. See Alderink 1989, 1458–59.

3. See Van Straten 1981.

4. See also Van Bremen 1985; Pleket 1981.

5. The Greek writer Hermippus from Berytus, writing in the early second century, included among his works a treatise entitled "On Slaves Who Distinguished Themselves in Paideia" (in Adler II, 414; see also Millar 1990, 17).

6. On this topic, see McClelland 1989; Barry 1993; Brantlinger 1983.

7. On patronage, see Saller 1982; Garnsey and Saller 1987, 148–59; Wallace-Hadrill 1989.

8. Engelmann 1976, no. 13; *New Docs.* 1:111–12.

9. Merkelbach 1976, no. 16; *New Docs.* 1:72.

10. See Kraemer 1992a, 80–92.

11. Van Bremen 1985.

12. Kraemer 1992a, 89–91.

13. Ibid., 90–92.

14. *New Docs.* 1:57.

15. *New Docs.* 1:5. See also Smith and Taussig 1990; D. E. Smith 1980.

16. On the importance of communal meals in Greek and Roman cults, see also Will 1976; Stambrough 1978.

17. On burial societies, see Fraser 1977, 58–70; *New Docs.* 2:49–50.

18. *New Docs.* 1:31.

19. On the popularity of Sarapis, see Engelmann 1975.

20. See *New Docs.* 2:90.

21. Sokolowski 1964; see also Croissant and Salviat 1966.

22. Sokolowski 1964, 2.

23. Ibid., 6.

24. Cameron 1991, 79.

25. Ibid.

26. 1 *Ephesos* 2.234.

27. Discussed in *New Docs.* 4:49–50. E.g., Aristio also served as *neokoros* of the temple (1 *Ephesos* 2.237, 241); *grammateus* of the demos (1 *Ephesos* 4.1128, 1129, 1129a); *prytany* (1 *Ephesos* 2.427); and *gymnasiarch* (1 *Ephesos* 3.638). See also the lives of his contemporaries T. Flavius Pythio (Asiarch in 104/105), his son T. Flavius Aristoboulos (1 *Ephesos* 5.1500) and P. Vedius Antoninus. See discussion by G. Horsley in *New Docs.* 4:51.

28. 1 *Ephesos* 2.213; *New Docs.* 4:94.

29. Reynolds 1982.

30. *New Docs.* 4:94.

31. See Apuleius's portrayal of an Isis ceremony, where an official of the cult first pronounced prayers "for the prosperity of the great Emperor, the Senate, the Knights, and the entire Roman people, for the sailors and ships under the rule of our world-wide

empire. Then he proclaimed, in the Greek language and with Greek ritual, the opening of the navigation season" (Apuleius, *Meta.* 11.17).

32. For discussion and translation of the inscription, see *New Docs.* 4:10–17.

33. *New Docs.* 4:13. See also a similar honorific inscription for Laevia Paula in 1 *Ephesos* 3.614B.

34. Cf. the posthumous honorific inscriptions for Apollonis of Ayazviran in Lydia (*New Docs.* 3:9, 96/97 C.E.) and Iulia Gordos (*New Docs.* 2:18, 75/76 C.E.).

35. A dedication to Aphrodite in Sicily lists a number of officials, including a Pausanius Sosius, who was a clerk, *hupographeus,* like Chariton. The inscription offers evidence that clerks sometimes acknowledged the power of Aphrodite (*IG* 14.209). (See also *IG* 14.211, where Purrichos Aristogeitos, also a clerk, dedicates to Aphrodite.) See Robert and Robert 1959 for the complete list of names. The fact that *IG* 14.209 comes from Sicily, the narrative starting point of Chariton's novel, is interesting though probably accidental. Sicily had a famous cult of Aphrodite, which Chariton may have known about.

36. See 1.1.1–2 and 8.8.15–16. Both E. Haight (1943, 32) and T. Hägg (1971, 216) note the connection between Callirhoe and Aphrodite.

37. References to Aphrodite as goddess of love were readily available in literary sources such as Homer, which Chariton clearly uses in his work; see Blake's "Index Analyticus," 1938, 134 ff., for Chariton's citations of Homer.

38. Inscriptions on several tombs at Aphrodisias warn those who might be tempted to disturb the tombs of the penalties that must be paid to Aphrodite (*MAMA* 8:547, 555, 565, 573, 576). See also Laumonier 1958, 500. L. Farnell presents evidence that at various sites in Greece and Asia Minor Aphrodite was associated with death (1897, 2:652–53, 754–55).

39. At Aphrodisias, a third-century C.E. *aedicula* of Aphrodite features Aphrodite drying her hair on a half shell held by two tritons; see *Anatolian Studies* 32 (1982), 13. Iris Love (1978) has shown that nearby Cnidos had an active cult of Aphrodite Euploia. L. Farnell (1897, 2:636–38) provides additional references to this aspect of Aphrodite.

40. See J. Helms's (1966, 45–66) discussion of Callirhoe's personality.

41. *"Thaoumastos ti chrema parthenou."*

42. Kenneth Scott (1938, 384) translates *agalma* as "cult image," perhaps too extreme but more plausible than Warren Blake's (1939) "admiration," Georges Molinié's (1979) *"trésor,"* or Karl Plepelits's (1976) *"Entzücken."* Scholars generally consider *agalma* to be an object placed in the temple for worship; for references see A. Nock 1972a, 204 n. 5. Simon Price (1984b, 178), however, notes that translating *agalma* as cult statue assumes a cult association that does not always occur. Some private citizens did not receive the honors of a public cult during the imperial period even though they had images (*agalmata*) placed in sacred locations, even at Aphrodisias (*MAMA* 8:412). *Agalma* can also refer to a bronze vase (Van Straten 1981, 75). This does not diminish the fact that the divine *kallos* of Callirhoe shines through the narrative. See also the discussion of the term by W. Burkert 1985, 65, 91, 94, 187.

43. "Parthenos" is an unusual epithet for Aphrodite (although see Reinach 1908, 500, regarding a late-second-century C.E. example). M. LaPlace (1980, 124–25) plausibly suggests an allusion to Athena Parthenos. For discussion on the role of cult statues in antiquity, see Nock 1972a, 202–51; Price 1984b, 170–206.

44. *Hellenica* 11/12 (Paris, 1960), p. 124 n. 2. An important parallel, noted earlier, is the honorific inscription for Apollonis, who has a number of statues (*agalmata*) set up in her honor in various civic and religious contexts.

45. *IGUR* 1268.

46. *New Docs.* 4:41.

47. Cf. Petri 1963, 11–12; Helms 1966, 42–45. They note the close relationship between Callirhoe and the goddess Aphrodite but downplay its importance for the narrative. Peter Walsh (1970, 55 n. 2, 200) cites the similar role played by Psyche in Apuleius's *Metamorphoses.*

48. E.g., Xenophon of Ephesus, *Ephesiaca* 1.2.6–8, 1.12.1, 2.2.4; Heliodorus, *Aethiopica* 1.2, 1.7, 2.23, 2.39, 3.4, 10.9. The pattern goes all the way back to Homer, who refers to individuals as "godlike" and "like unto Zeus in counsel."

49. See Nock 1972a, 233–34. Such identification, Nock argues, often depicts the ruler as another form of the deity, although, inexplicably, he calls such comparisons "trite" (233).

50. Magie 1950, 512.

51. Vermeule 1968, 457. See also Nock, 1972a, 226–27; Aymard 1934.

52. *MAMA* 8:514 (p. 548).

53. Nock 1972a, 233–35.

54. Price 1984b, 30.

55. See van Unnik's (1947) discussion of the important role of hair. Further evidence for the importance of hair as a manifestation of the divine is indirectly provided by Athenaios, who snidely remarks that Apelles' inspiration to paint his Aphrodite rising from the sea came from an incident involving a certain Phryne. "At the great assembly of the Eleusinia and at the festival of Poseidon in full sight of the whole Greek world . . . [Phryne] removed her cloak and let down her hair before stepping into the water" (13.590). Cf. Apuleius's description of Isis's appearance as she rose from the water: "First of all her hair, thick, long, and lightly curled, flowed softly down, loosely spread over her divine neck and shoulders" (*Meta.* 11.3).

56. *MAMA* 8:413; see also Lane Fox 1986, 102–67.

57. Chariton compares Callirhoe to Artemis in order to highlight Callirhoe's divine appearance (see 1.1.16, 3.8.6, 4.7.5, 6.4.6). A close association existed between the cult statues of Artemis of Ephesus and Aphrodite of Aphrodisias. See Fleischer 1981. In *Chaereas and Callirhoe,* however, the emphasis falls on Callirhoe's relationship to Aphrodite. Indeed, Callirhoe's appearance before crowds at Syracuse, which is compared to Artemis's appearance before hunters (1.1.16), offers a contrast; Artemis appears to hunters in the country, whereas Aphrodite's representative appears to crowds in the city.

58. *Skene* is used several times in Chariton's narrative to describe a tent or awning from which someone suddenly emerges, causing surprise, amazement, and worship on the part of onlookers. Instances include the following: Callirhoe's appearance before astonished crowds, who prostrate themselves (*proskunein*) before her on her entrance into Babylon (5.3.9); Stateira's stepping off the ship that returned her to the king (8.5.5); and Callirhoe and Chaereas's appearance in regal trappings on their return to Syracuse (8.6.7–8). For a different use of the term, see 1.4.8.

59. For a discussion of the Eleusinian mysteries, with a description of their effect on people, see Mylonas 1961; D'Alviella 1981. Chariton's allusions to the mysteries (1.1.15, 4.1.9, 8.1.10) do not prove the existence of a mystery cult of Aphrodite at Aphrodisias. The discussion between Goodenough and Nock regarding the possible references to a Jewish mystery cult in Philo indicates the difficulty of identifying actual mystery practices on the basis of the literary evidence alone. See Goodenough 1969; Nock 1972a, 459–68. No evidence yet appears for mystery practices in connection with the cult of Aphrodite of Aphrodisias.

60. A. Scobie has suggested that the act of proskynesis by the Babylonians reflects a practice "generally detested by the Greeks;" in *More Essays on the Ancient Romance and Its Heritage,* p. 24. Scott agrees in part:

> The attitude on proskynesis, freely paid the Great King or his wife by Persian subjects but refused by Greeks, is characteristic of the proud days when the Greek states were independent, and it is an attitude glorified in literary tradition. In the romances the gesture of adoration is often induced by gratitude, which, we know, was a common motive for the deification of a benefactor. Heroes and heroines are endowed with superhuman beauty which often wins them divine honors and causes people to regard them as epiphanies. (1938, 388–89)

In *Chaereas and Callirhoe,* proskynesis is performed before several different individuals by various groups and individuals: (a) before Callirhoe, as if she were a deity, by Greek citizens at Syracuse (1.1.16); by crowds on Dionysius's estate; by the people of Miletus; by barbarians (Stateira, 5.9.1; and the crowds, 5.3.9); (b) before the cult statue of Aphrodite by Callirhoe and Chariton (once); (c) before the king of Babylon by Dionysius, Mithridates, and subjects; and (d) before the queen by servants and the crowd when she returns from her captivity.

61. Cf. Kenneth Scott's (1938, 386) assessment. He argues against Graham Anderson's view that mystery language appears only as incidental allusions. Anderson's statement that "even the nights at Eleusis or the Olympic Games fail to produce as much enthusiasm as Callirhoe's trial" (1982, 18) does not recognize that it is Aphrodite's power on display here. How better to express the excitement and awe that her power engenders than to allude to such experiences?

62. For a brief discussion of the use of popular Stoic thought in the ancient romances, see Berger 1984, 1264–68, 1278–81. See also Helms 1966. Chaereas appears in a bad light when he betrays these qualities of proper conduct. The best example occurs when his lack of self-control and unfounded jealousy cause the apparent death of Callirhoe (1.4.12–13).

63. The stress on the free status of the Greek in relation to barbarians during this period is discussed by E. Gruen (1984, 1:132–57). The popularity of this motif in the Greek world is exhibited in the Sebasteion reliefs at Aphrodisias (R. Smith 1987). Barbarians are often portrayed as sensual, irrational, effeminate, cruel, weak, and servile (Georges 1994, xv, 244–46).

64. R. Smith 1987, 98.

65. The passage 5.1.1 indicates that Aphrodite arranged (*politeuein*) the marriage.

66. Love as a malady is a popular topos that cuts across genres. See Miralles 1977, 20.

67. Control of the passions (especially anger) is an important component of Chariton's text, and the lack of such control is generally accompanied by subsequent problems (Chaereas kicks his wife, causing her apparent death and their separation; Dionysius, Mithridates, and the Persian king lose their ability to govern effectively and fairly). Xenophon of Athens details the potent force of Eros for political figures in his *Cyropaedia* (5.1.8ff). In *Chaereas and Callirhoe,* Dionysius typifies the attributes outlined in Xenophon's text. He becomes completely incapable of fulfilling any of his political and social obligations. The following illustrates the pattern. Having just met Callirhoe in the temple of Aphrodite, Dionysius returns home:

[H]is whole soul [*psyche*] was in the shrine of Aphrodite, and he recalled every detail; her face, her hair, how she turned to him, how she had looked at him, her dress, her words; even her tears excited him. Then you could observe a struggle between reason and passion, for although sunk deep in the waves of desire, yet like a man of noble nature he tried to bear up. . . . But Eros eagerly came to attack his best intentions and considered his self-restraint [*sophrosyne*] outrageous [*hybris*], and for that reason inflamed all the more a loving soul [*psyche*] which sought to play the philosopher. (2.4.3–4, 6)

68. Bompaire 1977.

69. Persuasively argued by M. LaPlace (1980, 124–25).

70. If Chariton writes from Aphrodisias, why the emphasis on Syracuse, where the journey starts and begins? Several possibilities exist. The historical framework—the Peloponnesian War—of course necessitates Syracuse and Sicily as the home base of the narrative. Further, the use of mythic images associated with other geographic regions was not a problem, as is well illustrated in the Sebasteion at Aphrodisias. The images further support the power and prestige of Aphrodite and, by association, her city. In addition, a number of cult centers of Aphrodite are emphasized throughout the narrative, allowing Chariton to use the symbolic power contained with each. Finally, even Chariton is not willing to situate Aphrodite anachronistically at Aphrodisias when the city apparently did not claim to associate with the goddess until much later. When Chariton mentions Aphrodisias at the very beginning of the narrative, however, he effectively associates his account within that civic framework.

71. B. Perry (1930, 129 n. 43) notes that the comparison of Callirhoe's death to the sacking of a city is meant seriously by Chariton.

72. M. Seve (1979) dates the inscription to the second half of the first century.

73. Van Bremen 1985; Gordon 1990a, 230.

74. On the status of women under Greek and Roman law, see Cantarella 1989, 142.

75. Ibid., 152.

76. Callirhoe complains to Tyche that she has now become the talk of all Asia and Europe (5.5.3).

77. This recalls Aphrodite's role as the goddess of the sea (Aphrodite Euploia); see also 8.1.12.

78. Cf. Plutarch's statement that the "honor and charm, and mutual love and trust, that grow up daily [in a happy marriage] prove the wisdom of the Delphians in calling Aphrodite the goddess who joins together" (*Amat.* 23). Kenneth Scott draws attention to Empress Domitia's association with Concordia/Harmonia, which he believes symbolizes the "harmonious relations within the imperial household" or "harmony in wedlock" (1936, 85–86).

79. See Plutarch, who explicitly associates marriage and the political sphere: "A man, therefore, ought to have his household well harmonized who is going to harmonize State, Forum, and Friends" (*Moral* 144C, "Advice to Bride and Groom"). See Shapiro 1990, 479; Thraede 1992, 179–91; Sheppard 1984–86, 229–52.

80. *IG* 4.1098.

81. *SEOR* 3.819.

82. Many of the protagonists in the ancient Greek romances are of the elite classes. See Ninos fragment; Xenophon's *Ephesiaca*.

83. See the emphasis on the Son of Man and Messiah in 1 Enoch 46–48 and Dan. 7:12.

84. On 2 Baruch, see Murphy 1985b. On 4 Ezra, see Levine 1992b, 129–31. On Pseudo-Philo, see Murphy 1993. Also see Holladay 1977; Tiede 1972.

85. On the Sibylline Oracles, see Collins 1983b.

86. See Tiede 1972, 101–206.

87. Neusner 1992, 1988a, 1979.

88. See Rajak 1984a, 96–97.

89. The development of rabbinic Judaism is, of course, more complicated than this single issue. See Neusner 1979.

90. Goodman 1987, 231–51; idem, 1992a; Cohen 1992a, 172–73.

91. For a general discussion, see Bowsker 1983, 30–32.

92. Green 1979. Cohen 1992a, 164 n. 21. But see also Goodman, 1983, 108–9; cf. Lightstone 1984, 17–56.

93. T. Hullin 2:13; Cohen 1992a, 158.

94. Cohen 1989.

95. Smallwood 1981, 371–76; Goodman 1989; Goodman 1992a, 136–38.

96. Applebaum, *Jews and Greeks in Ancient Cyrene,* p. 178.

97. *CIJ,* vol. 2, no. 757.

98. Ibid., no. 738.

99. Quoted from Kraemer 1992a, 119.

100. *MAMA* 6:264 (translated by M. Reinhold, p. 95). It is possible, though not as likely, that Julia Severa did not build the synagogue especially for Jews but rather that her name, as a famous local personality, was associated with it.

101. *MAMA* 6:265, p. 98.

102. *MAMA* 6:263–65. See discussion in Kraabel 1983.

103. Kraemer 1992a, 119–23.

104. Rajak and Noy 1993, 86–87; Brooten and Safrai 1993; Brooten 1982; Kraemer 1992a, 106–27. For a discussion of literary evidence, see Brown 1992.

105. Abodah Zarah 3:4 (Neusner 1988b, 665).

106. *New Docs.* 3:123–25, no. 96.

107. See Preisendanz 1973.

108. See now Gager 1992; Bonner 1950, 26–32; cf. *CIJ,* vol. 1, p. 24.

109. Gager 1992, 24; see also MacMullen 1966, 95–127.

110. See Gray 1993, 35–79.

111. For a detailed discussion of the evidence, see ibid.

112. Feldman 1993, 201–32; Holladay 1977, 47–102.

113. Gray 1993.

114. Ibid., 80–111.

115. See Judas, an Essene who predicts the death of Antigonus (*BJ* 1.78–79).

116. Horsley and Hanson 1985.

117. Gray 1993, 118–19.

118. See Edwards 1994b, 156–58.

119. Goodman 1987.

120. Schoedel 1985, 22. See Ephesians 4:1–2, 13:1; Magnesians 6:1, 15; Trallians 12:2.

121. Horton 1976; Hurst 1990; Attridge 1989.

122. Bogaert 1968; *New Docs.* 5:139.

123. Cameron 1991, 48.

124. Ibid., 49.

125. Epistles 2.10, translated by Walsh and quoted in Cameron 1991, 50.

126. Shepherd of Hermas, *Visions* 8.7–9; Cameron 1991, 51.

127. Cameron 1991, 79–80.

128. Kee 1983a, 190–200. I use "myth" to refer to sacred stories that give meaning and direction to individuals. See the discussion in Mol 1977.

129. General consensus has it that Luke used the Septuagint as his major source; no attempt is made here to discern the sources that may stand behind the text. The major focus of my study is the final product of the author.

130. Jesus is viewed by his followers as "a prophet powerful in speech and action" (Luke 24:19).

131. Cf. Luke 9:1ff. and 10:1ff.

132. Walaskay 1983, 38–49.

133. Moxnes 1991, 258–60. Cf. Danker 1982.

134. A close parallel in *Chaereas and Callirhoe* occurs when Callirhoe acknowledges that her wanderings are part of Aphrodite's divine plan (8.8.8). There is, however, no explicit statement in the narrative that she serves as a witness, even though the effect of the story makes clear to the reader that she represents the power and presence of Aphrodite.

135. Acts 13:4–12, however, only states that the proconsul of Cyprus becomes a believer. Nothing is said about his receiving baptism or the Holy Spirit. This of course would represent a considerable coup on the part of the Christian movement. By rights, the proconsul's primary allegiance (besides Rome) should be directed toward the local cult, in this case the famous cult of Aphrodite.

136. David Moessner (1989, 1982) primarily stresses the necessity of the death of Moses in leading his people to a new land as a paradigm for the death of Jesus. Cf. E. Richard's discussion of this section (1978).

137. Acts 2:19, 22, 43; 4:30; 5:12; 6:8; 7:36; 14:3; 15:12.

138. See Jervell 1984. Jervell's agenda is different from mine; he seeks to compare Paul's actual message with that of the Lucan Paul. I seek to understand the portrayal of these figures solely in the context of Luke's agenda.

139. E.g., Deut. 13:2–3, 28:46, 34:11. Cf. Neh. 9:10; Wisd. of Sol. 8:8, 10:16; Isa. 20:3; Jer. 39:20–21; Dan. 6:28.

140. It is possible that this offers a better explanation for Luke 10:1–10 (the appointment of the seventy) than the one normally proposed, that is, as symbolic of the universal mission of the church. It is ironic that the mission of the seventy seems to have gone no further than the area around the Sea of Galilee (note the few mentions of geographical place-names). Another possibility may be an important reference in Num. 11:16–30, in which Moses appoints seventy elders to aid in the daily operation of the camp. Of course, both may have made sense to the audience of Luke. See Pervo 1987.

141. Cf. Acts 4:1–4, 29–31; 8:1–3, 14; 9:31; 11:19; 12:18–24; 13:4–12, 45–51; 14:4–7; 17:5–13; 20:19–20. Those who join the movement, Luke implies, must expect persecution. For example, Stephen claims to a Jewish audience that their fathers had killed those who foretold the coming of the Righteous One (Acts 7:52). Stephen's prophetic statement foreshadows his own demise.

142. Cadbury 1968, 311–13.

143. See discussion in Talbert 1984, 91–103. The thrice-repeated version of Saul's (Paul's) conversion also serves to establish a mythic pattern for the readership of Luke–Acts.

144. I thank Loveday Alexander (n.d.) for this observation.

145. Peter's meeting with Cornelius also stresses this aspect. When Cornelius prostrates (*proskunein*) himself before Peter, Peter responds, "Stand up; I too am a man" (Acts 10:26).

146. Josephus presents a similar rendering in *CA,* showing clearly that power came from the Jewish god, not Greek deities.

147. *New Docs.* 3:30.

148. Pliny, *Correspondence with Trajan* 96.

149. Cameron 1991, 47–88.

150. Smith 1993.

151. As, e.g., Ti. Claudius Diogenes. See Reynolds 1981, 319–22; R. Smith 1987, 90.

152. Alderink 1989, 1459.

153. Neusner 1979, 1971.

154. Bauckham 1993.

Chapter 7

1. W. Burkert 1987, 12.

2. Pfanner 1983.

3. On celebrating his triumphs in Germany, see Charlesworth 1936, 24–25; Edwards 1992b, 304–5.

4. For a discussion and a bibliography, see Kleiner 1989.

5. Quoted from Charlesworth 1936, 45; found in *IGRR* 4.661.

6. Goodman 1982; 1987, 154.

7. Lewis 1989, 1985–88; Cotton 1993.

8. Lewis 1989, 67.

9. Cf. similar contracts in the archive of Salome Komaise, daughter of Levi, in Cotton 1995, 171–203.

10. Reynolds 1982, 183–84: "To the first mother Aphrodite and the Demos. Imperator Caesar Nerva Traianus Augustus, Germanicus, Dacicus, restored (this) with the legacy from Adrastus Grypus son of Pereitas, through Callicrates Grypus son of Pereitas, priest, superintendent of the work."

11. Price 1984b, 161.

12. *IG* 5.1.1208; quoted from Hopkins 1983, 249–50.

13. This topic is discussed at length in Hopkins 1983, 250–52.

14. Lane Fox 1986, 168–261; Mitchell 1993b, 11–19.

15. Robin Lane Fox (1986) provides an excellent discussion of oracles, especially for the second and subsequent centuries.

16. Burkert 1987, 13.

17. See North 1986, 253.

18. Lane Fox 1986, 171–83; Mitchell 1993b, 11–13.

19. Levin 1989, 1606–15.

20. Parke 1985, 76–79.

21. Collins 1974, 1987.

22. Lane Fox 1986, 117–19; Miller 1994, 8–9.

23. *New Docs.* 2:40–43.

24. Drawing on a cliché of the times, Chariton depicts the pirate Theron holding his tongue about his guilt because one is eternally the optimist (3.3.16).

25. Lane Fox 1986, 166–67.

26. *New Docs.* 4:135.

27. Versnel 1981, 63.

28. Robin Lane Fox (1986, 154–64) has a useful discussion of the role of dreams, especially as depicted in the books of Artemidorus of Daldis.

29. Brown 1978, 65.

30. Price 1986, 13.

31. Quoted from Miller 1994, 135.

32. Von Straten 1981.

33. Burkert 1987, 13.

34. Ibid., 14.

35. Shipwrecks were so feared that they became a symbol of premature death on sarcophagi. See Nock 1972b, 638 n. 96.

36. Canetti 1973, 305.

37. Pearson 1993.

38. On the inscription, translation, and discussion, see *New Docs.* 2:58–60.

39. Millar, 1977.

40. The inscription is translated in *New Docs.* 4:136.

41. Cf. the case of a woman in Athens in the period of Hadrian who is given the title "dream interpreter" after building a monumental shrine to Isis near the Acropolis (Walker 1979; *New Docs.* 4:244).

42. *New Docs.* 2:100.

43. Cf. a similar stele, dated to 96/97 C.E., for a certain Apollonios from Ayazviran in Lydia donated by his extended family and a religious association (*New Docs.* 3:37–38). See also the late-first-century stele from the necropolis at Nikaia in Bithynia dedicated to Italos, a slave, by his master, who in return for the slave's industrious and faithful service "fulfilled these sacred rites for him as a favour (*charis*)" (*New Docs.* 3:39).

44. A tomb inscription from Ephesus for a silversmith and his wife dating to the time of Claudius or later states that anyone who defaces the inscription or inappropriately puts a corpse in the tomb must pay 1,000 denarii to the silversmiths' guild (*New Docs.* 4:7–10). See also the inscription of Apollonis in *New Docs.* 4:10–17; Gager 1992, 177–78; Lattimore 1962.

45. Doerner 1978, 319, 376–77; *New Docs.* 3:121–22.

46. θρησκεια, "religion." See Robert 1938, no. 938, pp. 227–35, esp. 227.

47. Quoted from deZulueta 1932.

48. The role of curses, which are primarily found in Asia Minor, is discussed in a fine study by J. Strubbe (1991). See also Kraemer 1992a, 122–24; van der Horst 1991, 54–60. Typical is a first-century tomb inscription from Crete that reads: "You who pass by, do not injure my sacred grave, lest you incur the sharp anger of Agesilaos and Persephone, maiden daughter of Demeter. But as you go by, say to Aratius: may you have light earth upon you" (translated in van der Horst 1991, 55).

49. Jones 1983.

50. Hopkins 1983, 224.

51. See Hopkins 1983, 201–3.

52. Morris 1992, 166.

53. Shaw 1991, 67.

54. This inscription is discussed thoroughly in Rogers 1991.

55. Ibid., 186–88.

56. Ibid., 157.

57. Ibid., 173.

58. See MacMullen 1990, 198–203; Lincoln 1985; Momigliano 1987, 120–41.

59. Lincoln 1989, 174.

60. Gailey 1992, 44.

61. Morris 1992, 51.

62. Wrede 1987.

63. Alcock 1993, 214, 259.

64. For a discussion of the problems involved in defining the term "magic," see Remus 1982.

65. Barton 1994a, 9–31; Aveni 1992; O'Neil 1986, 18–51; Sachs and Hunger 1988; Sachs and Hunger 1989.

66. Barton 1994a, 41–63; 1994b, 40–62.

67. According to Apuleius, Isis wears the symbol for the moon on her forehead and has "over the surface of her cloak glittering stars," and at the center of her cloak, "the full moon exhaled fiery flames" (*Meta.* 11.3–4). Cf. Mithras's cloak with bright stars, in the photo of the fresco from the Mithraeum at Marino, Italy, by L. Martin on the cover of Ulansey 1989.

68. Cumont 1960, 51; Beck 1977; Gordon 1976; Ulansey 1989.

69. Barton 1994a, 53–63; 1994b, 47–62. Cf. the domed ceiling of the temple of Bel at Palmyra, dated to the first century C.E., which, according to Lucille Roussin (forthcoming), had "seven planetary deities in hexagonal relief compartments framed by the circle of the zodiac." Cf. Lehman 1945, esp. 3.

70. See Jones 1992, 119–23, for the reign of Domitian and earlier; see Barton 1994a, 53–56, for attacks on astrology.

71. See, e.g., Phillips 1991; Brashear 1995, 3391 n. 4, 3446–47; Gager 1992, 24–25; MacMullen 1966, 102–4, 120–26; Kee 1986.

72. J. Gager 1992, 24–25.

73. *New Docs.* 5:140.

74. Lane Fox 1986, 36; Gager 1992, 24–25.

75. *Thessalus* 1968.

76. Lane Fox 1986, 37.

77. Jordan 1985, 151.

78. Ibid., 152.

79. Ibid., no. 158, p. 190.

80. Elderkin 1937, 391–92.

81. *SEG* 30.326.

82. Elderkin 1937, 391–92.

83. Cf. a similar curse found in a well at Delos, dating between the first century B.C.E. and the first century C.E., which because of the theft of a necklace invokes the gods to curse the thief's brain, soul, muscles, hands, and everything from his head down to his toenails (Jordan 1985, no. 58, p. 168).

84. Jordan 1985, no. 59, pp. 168–69. Cf. similar first- and second-century *defixiones* from Sicily (ibid., no. 109, p. 177; no. 112, p. 178), Asia Minor (no. 168, p. 194), and Panticapeum in the north Black Sea area (no. 170, p. 195).

85. Thessalus, e.g., organized a world fraught with uncertainty by associating with highly powerful and visible arenas: the ancient power of Asclepius, imperial power (in his dedication), and magical rites. He had countless counterparts who sought love, victory in competitive events, help in business ventures, almost any human endeavor.

86. Martin 1987, 84.

87. Hägg 1971.

88. Quoted from *New Docs.* 4:31; see Schwertheim 1980, 493, pl. 34; Sibyl. 3:480–81 ("Alas for all the virgins whom Hades will wed and unburied youths whom the deep will attend").

89. See Edwards 1991, 195–96.

90. P. Alexander 1986.

91. Barton 1994a, 68–71; *OTP* 1:935–59.

92. Juvenal describes a Jewish woman who tells fortunes and interprets dreams (6.542–47).

93. See Rajak and Noy 1993, esp. 84–85.

94. Schürer, vol. 1, pp. 308–10; Hachlili 1988, 9–64.

95. Exceptions existed, of course, as noted in earlier chapters.

96. Kant 1987, 702–3; Hachlili 1988, 254–56.

97. See the menorah found in an undated grave near the city of Aphrodisias in Smith and Ratté 1995, esp. 38–39.

98. Hachlili 1988, 236–56.

99. See 4 Ezra 9:26–37; 2 Bar. 38:1–2, 46:4, 77:16, 84:1–9.

100. Hachlili 1988, 166–87.

101. Kraabel 1992b, 26.

102. See van der Horst 1991, 56–57.

103. Quoted from van der Horst, 59.

104. See van der Horst, 57–59, for examples and discussion.

105. Quoted from van der Horst 1991, 149.

106. See van der Horst 1991, 149.

107. Quoted from van der Horst, 150.

108. Quoted from van der Horst, 155.

109. Quoted from van der Horst, 156–57.

110. Sibyl. 5:238–40.

111. See discussion in Gray 1993; Aune 1983, 103–52.

112. Neusner 1988a.

113. On the Essenes, see Schürer, vol. 2. pp. 555–97. On the Sibylline Oracles, see Collins 1987. Cf. The Similitudes of Enoch (dated to the latter part of the first century C.E.), which details how the high officials, governors, kings, and landlords will be judged for their misdeeds (62:1–63:12); and Sibyl. 3:350–80.

114. Thompson 1990, 13–14.

115. Davies 1991; Brooke 1991.

116. Brooke, 1991, 159.

117. The Pseudepigrapha and Apocrypha include a large number of these texts.

118. Anderson 1991.

119. Kant 1987, 692–94.

120. Quoted from van der Horst 1991, 124.

121. Sibyl. 5.207–12. Cf. Sibyl. 5.512–31; Rev. 12:7; Nonnus, Dionysiaca 38.347–409. The first-century B.C.E. Treatise of Shem sets out a series of predictions based on what zodiac sign begins the year (OTP 1:481–86).

122. OTP 1:944–45.

123. Josephus seems to imply this in his discussion of the Essenes, who he says "make investigations into medicinal roots and the properties of stones" (BJ 2.136) and foretell the future (BJ 2.159). Cf. AJ 15.373–75 and AJ 13.311.

124. P. Alexander 1985, 375–79; Duling 1975. For Moses, see the discussion in Feldman 1993, 285–87, though most of the evidence is late.

125. Such as "wickedness, immorality, natural disaster, deformity, disease, and death" (OTP 1:953).

126. See the excellent discussion in OTP 1:935–58; see also Barton 1994a, 68–70.

127. In 1 Enoch (dated between the second century B.C.E. and the first century C.E.) angels consort with human women and teach them medicine, incantations and their interpretation, astrology, and how to understand the courses of the moon and stars (1 En. 7:1, 8:3–4). The visions granted to Enoch show the reader that the sun and moon

follow their courses "in accordance with the commandment of the Lord of the Spirits" (1 En. 41:6; cf. 69:20–21). In the Similitudes of Enoch (dated to the first century C.E.; *OTP* 1:6–7), those who acquired the power from the angels to practice sorcery or have knowledge of the occult powers will be doomed in the future by the court of the Lord (1 En. 65:6). In the Book of Heavenly Luminaries of 1 Enoch, the angel Uriel describes in great detail the workings of the cosmos. Uriel was appointed by "the Lord, god of eternal glory" so that "all created objects which circulate in all the chariots of heaven—should rule in the face of the sky and be seen on the earth to be guides for the day and the night" (1 En. 75:3). Some of those in charge of specific courses of the stars will err, and those stars will "change their courses and functions and not appear during the seasons which have been prescribed for them." In a direct slap at astrologers, the author states that some will then err and mistake the stars as gods (1 En. 80:6–7).

128. See, e.g., Milik 1961; Yadin 1969.

129. Kotansky 1991.

130. Herod the Great has a dream warning of his brother's death (*BJ* 1.328); Archelaus has a dream that an Essene named Simon interprets as revealing the length of his rule (*BJ* 2.112–13); Archelaus's wife, formerly married to his murdered brother Alexander, has a vision of Alexander, who says he will reclaim her. Two days later she dies (*BJ* 2.114–16).

131. Building programs continued under Herod Antipas and Philip (*BJ* 2.168).

132. Martin 1987, 106–7.

133. Ulansey 1991.

134. Hachlili 1988, 301–9; see also Barton 1994a, 68–70.

135. This becomes clear when Josephus says that in revenge for Herod's prosperity and beneficence to others Tyche "visited Herod with troubles at home" (*BJ* 1.431). Tyche's ability to switch sides is especially clear in *BJ* 4.40.

136. Material evidence for early Christianity is sparse, as already noted. Some suggest that the *"apenrho"* (a p struck through an x) found in a second-century C.E. tomb in Jerusalem represents a Christian convert. But the sign has also been found in non-Christian contexts, including one associated with a mummy that dates to 29 B.C.E. (*New Docs.* 5:141).

137. See the numerous narrative references to this lifestyle in *Chaereas and Callirhoe*.

138. Laws 1980, 195–218.

139. Cf. the apparently negative attitude toward the Temple in Acts 7:48–49. See also Hebrews 7–9, which portrays the earthly temple as a copy and shadow of the heavenly temple (8:5).

140. Miller, 1994, 132.

141. The Shepherd of Hermas 1.2.4.2. Adapted from F. Crombie 1985, 12.

142. Miller 1994, 134.

143. Thompson 1990, 14. See the discussion of Justin Martyr's criticism of imperial rule in Pagels 1985.

144. In his encounter with the Lystrans, who mistake him and Barnabas for Hermes and Zeus (Acts 14:12–13), Paul makes clear that God has ultimate control. "We also are men, of like nature with you, and bring you good news, that you should turn from these vain things to a living God who made the heaven and the earth and the sea and all that is in them" (Acts 14:15). See Martin 1995.

145. Cf. the similar coalition in Iconium (Acts 14:5).

146. Cf. Acts 17:4, 12.

147. See Didache 3:4. Admonitions against the use of magical means to influence

future events found their parallels in Jewish literature. See Pseudo-Phocylides 149; 2 En. 10:4 (document J); *Sibyl.* 3:220–30; Kee 1986; Arnold 1989.

148. Garrett 1989.

149. Conzelman 1961.

150. See the discussion in Esler 1987, 209–10.

151. They need not be part of the administrative or military establishment (contra ibid., 210). Merchants like Lydia, the purple-dye maker in Acts, also benefited from the imperial system and would be reluctant to reject it out of hand.

Bibliography

Adler, A., ed. 1928–38. *Suidae Lexicon*. 5 vols. Leipzig: B. G. Teubner.

Alcock, Susan E. 1989a. "Archeology and Imperialism: Roman Expansion and the Greek City." *JMA* 2.1:87–135.

———. 1989b. "Greek Society and the Transition to Roman Rule." Ph.D. diss., Cambridge University.

———. 1993. *Graecia Capta: The Landscapes of Roman Greece*. Cambridge: Cambridge University Press.

Alcock, Susan E., and Robin Osborne, eds. 1994. *Placing the Gods: Sanctuaries and Sacred Space in Ancient Greece*. Oxford: Clarendon Press; New York: Oxford University Press.

Alderink, Larry J. 1989. "The Eleusinian Mysteries in Roman Imperial Times." In *ANRW* 2.18.2:1457–98.

Alexander, Loveday. 1986. "Luke's Preface in the Context of Greek Preface-Writing." *Novum Testamentum* 28:48–74.

———. 1993. *The Preface to Luke's Gospel: Literary Convention and Social Context in Luke 1.1–4 and Acts 1.1*. SNTSMS 78. New York: Cambridge University Press.

———. n.d. "'In Journeyings Often': Voyaging in the Acts of the Apostles and in the Greek Romance." Typescript.

———, ed. 1991. *Images of Empire*. Sheffield: Sheffield Academic Press.

Alexander, P. 1982. "Notes on the "Imago Mundi" of the Book of Jubilees." *JJS* 33:197–213.

———. 1986. "Incantations and Books of Magic." In Schürer 1986, 342–79.

———. 1992. "Geography in the Bible (Early Jewish)." In *ABD* 2:977–88.

Alföldy, G. 1985. *The Social History of Rome*. Trans. David Braund and Frank Pollock. London and Sydney: Croom Helm.

Anderson, B. 1991. *Imagined Communities: Reflections on the Origin and Spread of Nationalism*. New York: Verso.

Anderson, Graham. 1982. *Eros Sophistes: Ancient Novelists at Play*. Chico, CA: Scholars Press.

———. 1984. *Ancient Fiction: The Novel in the Graeco-Roman World*. Totowa, NJ: Barnes & Noble Books.

———. 1994. *Sage, Saint, and Sophist: Holy Men and Their Associates in the Early Roman Empire*. New York and London: Routledge.

Andrei, O. 1984. *A. Claudius Charax di Pergamo: Interessi antiquarie e antichità cittadine nell'età degli Antonini*. Bologna: Pàtron.

Appelbaum, Shimon. 1979. *Jews and Greeks in Ancient Cyrene*. Leiden: E. J. Brill.

Arnold, C. E. 1989. *Ephesians: Power and Magic, the Concept of Power in Ephesians in Light of Its Historical Setting*. SNTSMS 63. Cambridge: Cambridge University Press.

Arvidsson, C., and L. E. Blomquist, eds. 1987. *Symbols of Power: The Aesthetics of Political Legitimation in the Soviet Union and Eastern Europe*. Stockholm: Almqvist & Wiskell International.

Asad, Talal. 1983. "Anthropological Conceptions of Religion: Reflections on Geertz." *Man* 18:237–59.

Attridge, Harold W. 1984. "Josephus and His Works." In *Jewish Writings of the Second Temple Period*, ed. M. Stone, 185–232. Compendia Rerum Iudaicarum ad Novum Testamentum, sec. 2, Assen: Van Gorcum; Philadelphia: Fortress Press.

———. 1989. *The Epistle to the Hebrews: A Commentary on the Epistle to the Hebrews*. Philadelphia: Fortress Press.

Attridge, Harold W., and Robert A. Oden, Jr. 1981. *Philo of Byblos: The Phoenician History*. CBQ Monograph Series 9. Washington, DC: Catholic Biblical Association of America.

Aune, D. 1983. *Prophecy in Early Christianity and the Ancient Mediterranean World*. Grand Rapids, MI: Eerdmans.

———. 1987a. "The Apocalypse of John and Graeco-Roman Revelatory Magic." *NTS* 33.4:481–501.

———. 1987b. *The New Testament in Its Literary Environment*. Ed. Wayne A. Meeks. Library of Early Christianity. Philadelphia: Westminster Press.

Aveni, A. 1992. *Conversing with the Planets: How Science and Myth Invented the Cosmos*. New York: Times Books.

Aymard, J. 1934. "Vénus et les impératrices sous les derniers Antonins." *Mélanges d'Archéologie et d'Histoire* 51:178–96.

Babelon, E. 1908. *Inventaire sommaire de la Collection Waddinton de la Bibliothèque Nationale*. Paris: C. Rollin et Feuardent.

Bagatti, B. 1971. *The Church from the Circumcision, History, and Archaeology of the Judaeo Christians*. Jerusalem: Franciscan Printing Press.

Bakker, Jan Theo. 1994. *Living and Working with the Gods: Studies of Evidence for Private Religion and Its Material Environment in the City of Ostia (100–500 A.D.)*. Amsterdam: J. C. Gieben.

Barnard, L. W. 1967. *Studies in the Apostolic Fathers and Their Background*. New York: Schocken Books.

Barnes, T. D. 1984. *Early Christianity and the Roman Empire*. London: Variorum.

Barr, J. 1974–75. "Philo of Byblos and His 'Phoenician History.'" *BRL* 57:17–68.

Barrett, John C., Richard Bradley, and Martin Green. 1991. *Landscape Monuments and Society*. Cambridge: Cambridge University Press.

Barry, William D. 1993. "Aristocrats, Orators, and the 'Mob': Dio Chrysostom and the World of the Alexandrians." *Historia* 42.1:82–103.

Barton, Tamsyn S. 1994a. *Ancient Astrology*. London and New York: Routledge.

———. 1994b. *Power and Knowledge: Astrology, Physiognomics, and Medicine Under the Roman Empire*. Ann Arbor: University of Michigan Press.

Bauckham, Richard. 1993. *The Climax of Prophecy: Studies on the Book of Revelation*. Edinburgh: T. & T. Clark.

Beard, Mary. 1985. "Writing and Ritual: A Study of Diversity and Expansion in the Arval Acta." *PBSR* 53:114–62.

Beard, Mary, and J. North, eds. 1990. *Pagan Priests: Religion and Power in the Ancient World*. Ithaca: Cornell University Press.

Beck, R. 1977. "Cautes and Cautopates: Some Astronomical Considerations." *JMS* 2.1:1–17.

———. 1984. "Mithraism Since Franz Cumont." In *ANRW* 2.17.4:2002–115.

———. 1988. *Planets and Planetary Orders in the Mysteries of Mithras*. Leiden: E. J. Brill.

Bengtson, Herman. 1979. *Die Flavier: Vespasian, Titus, Domitian*. Munich: Beck.

Benko, Stephen. 1980. "Pagan Criticism of Christianity During the First Two Centuries A.D." In *ANRW* 2.23.2:1054–118.

———. 1984. *Pagan Rome and the Early Christians*. Bloomington: Indiana University Press.

Berger, Klaus. 1984. "Hellenistische Gattungen in Neuen Testament." In *ANRW* 2.25.2.

Berger, Peter. 1967. *The Sacred Canopy: Elements of a Sociological Theory of Religion*. Garden City, NY: Doubleday.

Bernand, André. 1972. *Le paneion d'El-Kanaïs: les inscriptions grecques*. Leiden: E. J. Brill.

Betz, H. D. 1986. *The Greek Magical Papyri in Translation Including the Demotic Spells*. Vol. 1, *Texts*. Chicago: University of Chicago Press.

Beye, Charles R. 1982. *Epic and Romance in the Argonautica of Apollonius*. Carbondale and Edwardsville: Southern Illinois University Press.

Bickerman, Elias. 1980. *Studies in Jewish and Christian History*. Arbeiten zur Geschichte des antiken Judentums und des Urchristentums. Vol. 9, pt. 2, Leiden: E. J. Brill.

———. 1986. "Pliny, Trajan, Hadrian, and the Christians." In *Studies in Jewish and Christian History*. Arbeiten zur Geschichte des antiken Judentums und des Urchristentums. Vol. 9, pt. 3, 152–71. Leiden: E. J. Brill.

Bilde, P. 1988. *Flavius Josephus Between Jerusalem and Rome: His Life, His Works, and Their Importance*. Sheffield: JSOT Press.

Billault, A. 1989. "De l'histoire au roman: Hermocrate de Syracuse." *REG* 102:540–48.

Blake, Marion E. 1959. *Roman Construction in Italy from Tiberius Through the Flavians*. Washington, DC: Carnegie Institute of Washington.

Blake, Warren. 1938. *Charitonis Aphrodisiensis: De Chaerea et Callirhoe amatoriarum narrationum libri octo*. Oxford: E Typographeo Clarendoniano.

———. 1939. *Chariton's "Chaereas and Callirhoe."* Ann Arbor: University of Michigan Press.

Bloch, Maurice. 1977. "The Past and the Present in the Present." *Man* 18:278–92.

Bogaert, R. 1968. *Banques et banquiers dans les cités grecques*. Leiden: E. J. Brill.

Bompaire, Jacques. 1977. "Le décor sicilien dans le roman grec et dans la littérature contemporaine." *REG* 90:55–68.

Bonner, Campbell. 1950. *Studies in Magical Amulets*. Ann Arbor: University of Michigan Press.

Boon, James A. 1982. *Other Tribes, Other Scribes: Symbolic Anthropology in the Comparative Study of Cultures, Histories, Religions, and Texts*. Cambridge: Cambridge University Press.

Borman, Lukas, Kelly Del Tredici, and Angela Standhartinger, eds. 1994. *Religious Propaganda and Missionary Competition in the New Testament World: Essays Honoring Dieter Georgi*. Leiden: E. J. Brill.

Boulding, Kenneth E. 1990. *Three Faces of Power*. Newbury Park, CA: Sage Publications.

Bowersock, G. W. 1965. *Augustus and the Greek World*. Oxford: Clarendon Press.

———. 1969. *Greek Sophists in the Roman Empire*. Oxford: Clarendon Press.

————. 1983. *Roman Arabia*. Cambridge: Harvard University Press.

————. 1987. "The Mechanics of Subversion in the Roman Provinces." In *Opposition et résistances à l'empire d'Auguste à Trajan,* ed. K. Raaflaub and A. Giovannini, 33:291–317. Hardt: Geneva.

————. 1990. *Hellenism in Late Antiquity*. Cambridge: Cambridge University Press.

————. 1991. "The Babatha Papyri, Masada, and Rome." *JRA* 4:336–44.

————. 1995. *Martyrdom and Rome*. Wiles Lectures. Cambridge: Cambridge University Press.

Bowie, E. L. 1974. "Greeks and Their Past in the Second Sophistic." In *Studies in Ancient Society,* ed. M. I. Finley, 166–209. Past and Present Series. Boston: Routledge & Kegan Paul.

————. 1977. "The Novels and the Real World." In *Erotica Antiqua: Acta of the International Conference on the Ancient Novel,* 91–96. Bangor, Wales.

————. 1985. "The Greek Novel." In *The Cambridge History of Classical Literature*. Vol. 1, *Greek Literature,* ed. P. E. Easterling and B. M. W. Knox, 683–99. Cambridge: Cambridge University Press.

Bowie, E. L., and S. J. Harrison. 1993. "The Romance of the Novel." *JRS* 83:159–78.

Bowsker, B. M. 1983. "Recent Developments in the Study of Judaism, 70–200 C.E." *Second Century* 3.1:1–68.

Boyce, M., and F. Grenet, with a contribution by R. Beck. 1991. *A History of Zoroastrianism*. Vol. 3, *Zoroastrianism Under Macedonia and Roman Rule*. Leiden: E. J. Brill.

Brantlinger, Patrick. 1983. *Bread and Circuses: Theories of Mass Culture as Social Decay*. Ithaca: Cornell University Press.

Brashear, William M. 1995. "The Greek Magical Papyri: An Introduction and Survey; Annotated Bibliography (1928–1994)." In *ANRW* 2.18.5:3380–684.

Braund, David. 1984. *Rome and the Friendly King: The Character of the Client Kingship*. London and Canberra: Croom Helm; New York: St. Martin's Press.

Brooke, George J. 1991. "The Kittim in the Qumran Pesharim." In Alexander 1991, 135–59.

Brooten, B. 1982. *Women Leaders in the Ancient Synagogue*. Brown Judaic Series 36. Chico, CA: Scholars Press.

Brooten, B., and Channa Safrai. 1993. *Women and Temple: The Status and Role of Women in the Second Temple of Jerusalem*. Berlin and New York: Walter de Gruyter.

Brown, Cheryl A. 1992. *No Longer Be Silent: First-Century Jewish Portraits of Biblical Women*. Louisville, KY: Westminster / John Knox Press.

Brown, Peter. 1978. *The Making of Late Antiquity*. Cambridge: Harvard University Press.

————. 1992. *Power and Persuasion in Late Antiquity: Towards a Christian Empire*. Madison: University of Wisconsin Press.

Burchard, C. 1987. "The Importance of Joseph and Aseneth for the Study of the New Testament: A General Survey and a Fresh Look at the Lord's Supper." *NTS* 33:102–34.

Burkert, Walter. 1983. *Greek Religion*. Trans. by John Raffan. Cambridge: Harvard University Press.

————. 1987. *Ancient Mystery Cults*. Cambridge: Harvard University Press.

Burnett, A., M. Amandry, and P. P. Ripollès. 1992. *The Roman Provincial Coinage I*. Vol. 1, *From the Death of Caesar to the Death of Vitellius (44 BC–AD 69)*. London: British Museum Press.

Burr, Victor. 1955. *Tiberius Iulius Alexander*. Bonn: Rudolf Hubelt.

Cadbury, H. J. 1968. *The Making of Luke–Acts*. 1927. Reprint, London: S.P.C.K.

Calder, William M. 1935. "Silius Italicus in Asia." *CR* 49:216–17.

Calder, William M., and J. M. R. Cormack, eds. 1962. *Monumenta Asiae Minoris Antiqua*. Vol. 8. Manchester: Manchester University Press.

Calderini, A. 1965. *La manomissione e la condizione dei liberti in Grecia*. Rome: L'erma di Bretschneider.

Cameron, Averil. 1991. *Christianity and the Rhetoric of Empire: The Development of Christian Discourse*. Sather Classical Lectures 55. Berkeley and Los Angeles: University of California Press.

Campbell, D. J. 1936. "The Birthplace of Silius Italicus." *CR* 50:56–58.

Campbell, L. A. 1968. *Mithraic Iconography and Ideology*. Leiden: E. J. Brill.

Canetti, Elias. 1973. *Crowds and Power*. Harmondsworth: Penguin.

Cannadine, David, and Simon Price, eds. 1987. *Rituals of Royalty: Power and Ceremonial in Traditional Societies*. Cambridge: Cambridge University Press.

Cantarella, Eva. 1989. *Pandora's Daughters: The Role and Status of Women in Greek and Roman Antiquity*. Trans. Maureen B. Fant. Baltimore: Johns Hopkins University Press.

Carr, E. L. 1962. *What Is History?* New York: Knopf.

Cartledge, Paul, and Anthony Spawforth. 1989. *Hellenistic and Roman Sparta: A Tale of Two Cities*. London and New York: Routledge.

Castriota, D., ed. 1986. *Artistic Strategy and the Rhetoric of Power: Political Uses of Art from Antiquity to the Present*. Carbondale: Southern Illinois University Press.

Charlesworth, M. P. 1936. "The Flavian Dynasty." *CAH* 11:1–45.

Cherry, J. F. 1987. "Power in Space: Archaeological and Geographical Studies of the State." In *Landscape and Culture: Geographical and Archaeological Perspectives,* ed. J. M Wagstaff, 146–72. Oxford: Basil Blackwell.

Chesnutt, Randall D. 1988. "The Social Setting and Purpose of Joseph and Aseneth." *Journal for the Study of the Pseudepigrapha* 2:21–48.

Chilton, Bruce. 1992. "Jews in the New Testament." In *ABD* 3:845–48.

Chuvin, Pierre. 1990. *A Chronicle of the Last Pagans*. Cambridge: Harvard University Press.

Clinton, K. 1989. "The Eleusinian Mysteries: Roman Initiates and Benefactors, Second Century B.C. to A.D. 267." In *ANRW* 2.18.2:1400–1539.

Cohen, A. P. 1989. *The Symbolic Construction of Community*. London: Ellis Horwood & Tavistock Publications, 1985. Reprint, London: Routledge.

Cohen, S. J. D. 1979. *Josephus in Galilee and Rome: His Vita and Development as a Historian*. Leiden: E. J. Brill.

———. 1982. "Josephus, Jeremiah, and Polybius." *History and Theory* 21:366–81.

———. 1989. "Crossing the Boundary and Becoming a Jew." *HTR* 82.1:13–33.

———. 1992a. "The Place of the Rabbi in Jewish Society." In Levine 1992a, 157–73.

———. 1992b. "Was Judaism in Antiquity a Missionary Religion?" In *Jewish Assimilation, Acculturation, and Accommodation: Past Traditions, Current Issues, and Future Prospects,* ed. M. Mor, 14–23. New York: University Press of America.

Coles, S. G. 1989. "The Mysteries of Samothrake During the Roman Period." In *ANRW* 2.18.2:1564–98.

Collins, John J. 1974. *The Sibylline Oracles of Egyptian Judaism*. Missoula, MT: Scholars Press.

———. 1983a. *Between Athens and Jerusalem: Jewish Identity in the Hellenistic Diaspora*. New York: Crossroad.

———. 1983b. "Sibylline Oracles: A New Translation and Introduction." In *OTP* 1:317–472.

———. 1984. *The Apocalyptic Imagination: An Introduction to the Jewish Matrix of Christianity.* New York: Crossroad.

———. 1987. "The Development of the Sibylline Tradition." *ANRW* 2.20.1:421–59.

Congresso internazionale di studi Flaviani. 1983. 2 vols. Rieti: Centro di Studi Varroniani.

Conzelmann, Hans. 1961. *The Theology of St. Luke.* Trans. Geoffrey Buswell. New York: Harper.

———. 1987. *Acts of the Apostles: A Commentary on the Acts of the Apostles.* Trans. James Limburg, A. Thomas Kraabel, and Donald H. Juel; ed. Eldon Epp with Christopher Matthews. Philadelphia: Fortress Press.

———. 1992. *Gentiles, Jews, Christians: Polemics and Apologetics in the Greco-Roman Era.* Trans. M. Eugene Boring. Minneapolis: Fortress Press.

Corbo, Virgilio. 1969. *The House of St. Peter at Capharnaum.* Jerusalem: Franciscan Printing Press.

———. 1975. *Cafarnao I: Gli edifici della citta.* Jerusalem.

———. 1993. "The Church of the House of St. Peter at Capernaum." In Tsafrir 1993, 71–76.

Cormack, J. M. R. 1954. "Epigraphic Evidence for the Water-Supply of Aphrodisias." *ABSA* 49:9–10.

———. 1964. "Inscriptions from Aphrodisias." *ABSA* 59:16–29.

Cotton, Hannah. 1993. "The Guardianship of Jesus Son of Babatha: Roman and Local Law in the Province of Arabia." *JRS* 83:94–108.

———. 1995. "The Archive of Salome Komaise Daughter of Levi: Another Archive from the 'Cave of Letters.'" *ZPE* 105:171–208.

Cotton, Hannah, W. E. H. Cockle, and F. G. B. Millar. 1995. "The Papyrology of the Roman Near East: A Survey." *JRS* 85, 214–35.

Crawford, M. 1980. "Money and Exchange in the Roman World." *JRS* 70:40–48.

———. 1985. *Coinage and Money Under the Roman Republic: Italy and the Mediterranean Economy.* London: Methuen.

Croissant, F., and F. Salviat. 1966. "Aphrodite gardienne des magistrats." *BCH* 90:460–71.

Crombie, F., trans. 1985. "The Pastor of Hermas." In *The Ante-Nicene Fathers.* Vol. 2, *Fathers of the Second Century,* ed. A. Roberts and J. Donaldson, 3–58. Buffalo: Christian Literature Publishing Co.

Cumont, Franz. 1960. *Astrology and Religion Among the Greeks and Romans.* New York: Dover.

D'Alviella, G. 1981. *The Mysteries of Eleusis: The Secret Rites and Rituals of the Classical Greek Mystery Tradition.* Wellingborough, U.K.: Aquarian Press.

D'Ambra, Eve. 1993. "The Cult of Virtues and the Funerary Relief of Ulpia Epigone." In *Roman Art in Context: An Anthology,* ed. Eve D'Ambra, 104–14. Englewood Cliffs, NJ: Prentice-Hall.

Danielou, Jean. 1964. *The Theology of Jewish Christianity.* Trans. John A. Baker. London: Darton, Longman & Todd; Chicago: Henry Regnery Co.

Danker, F. 1981. "The Endangered Benefactor in Luke–Acts." In *SBLSP,* ed. Kent H. Richards, 20:39–48. Atlanta: Scholars Press.

———. 1982. *Benefactor: Epigraphic Study of a Graeco-Roman and New Testament Semantic Field.* St. Louis: Clayton Publishing House.

Davies, P. G. 1991. "Daniel in the Lion's Den." In Alexander 1991, 160–78.

———. "Divine Agents, Mediators, and New Testament Christology." *JTS* 45.2:479–503.

Degrassi, A. 1947. "Fasti consulares et triumphales." *Inscriptiones Italica* 13.1:1–142.

de la Genière, J., and K. T. Erim, eds. 1987. *Aphrodisias de Carie: Colloque de l'Université de Lille III*. Paris: Editions Recherche sur les Civilisations.

De Ste Croix, G. E. M. 1974. "Why Were the Early Christians Persecuted?" In *Studies in Ancient Society*, ed. M. I. Finley, 210–49. Past and Present Series. Boston: Routledge & Kegan Paul.

deZulueta, F. 1932. "Violation of Sepulture in Palestine at the Beginning of the Christian Era." *JRS* 22:184–97.

Dilke, O. A. W. 1985. *Greek and Roman Maps*. London: Thames & Hudson.

Dillon, Richard J. 1981. "Previewing Luke's Project from His Prologue (Luke 1:1–4)." *CBQ* 43:205–27.

Dodge, Hazel. 1988. "Palmyra and the Roman Marble Trade: Evidence from the Baths of Diocletian." *Levant* 23:215–30.

Doerner, F. K., ed. 1978. *Tituli Asiae Minoris*. Vol. 4, *Tituli Bithyniae*, pt. 1. Vienna: Academiam Scientiarum Austriacum.

Droge, Arthur J. 1989. *Homer or Moses? Early Christian Interpretations of the History of Culture*. Hermeneutische Untersuchungen zur Theologie 26. Tübingen: J. C. B. Mohr, Paul Siebeck.

Duling, Dennis. 1975. "Solomon, Exorcism, and the Son of David." *HTR* 68:235–52.

———. 1985. "The Eleazor Miracle and Solomon's Magical Wisdom in Flavius Josephus's *Antiquitates Judaicae* 8.42–49." *HTR* 78.1–2:1–25.

Düll, Siegrid. 1977. *Die Götter Kulte nordmakedoniens in römischer Zeit*. Münchener Archäologische Studien 7. Munich: Fink.

Edson, C. 1948. "Cults of Thessalonica." *HTR* 41.3:153–204.

Edwards, D. 1987. "Acts of the Apostles and Chariton's *Chaereas and Callirhoe*: A Literary and Sociohistorical Study." Ph.D. diss., Boston University.

———. 1991. "Surviving the Web of Roman Power: Religion and Politics in the Acts of the Apostles, Josephus, and Chariton's *Chaereas and Callirhoe*." In Alexander 1991, 179–201.

———. 1992a. "Dress and Ornamentation." In *ABD* 2:232–38.

———. 1992b. "Religion, Power, and Politics: Jewish Defeats by the Romans in Iconography and Josephus." In Overman and MacLennen 1992, 293–310.

———. 1992c. "The Socio-economic and Cultural Ethos of the Lower Galilee in the First Century: Implications for the Nascent Jesus Movements." In Levine 1992a, 53–73.

———. 1994a. "Defining the Web of Power in Asia Minor: The Novelist Chariton and His City Aphrodisias." *JAAR* 62.3:699–718.

———. 1994b. "The Social, Religious, and Political Aspects of Costume in Josephus." In *The World of Roman Costume*, ed. Judith Lynn Sebesta and Larissa Bonfante, 153–59. Madison: University of Wisconsin Press.

Edwards, D., and T. McCollough, eds. Forthcoming. *Archaeology and the Galilee*. University of South Florida Studies in the History of Judaism. Atlanta: Scholars Press.

Egger, Brigitte. 1994. "Looking at Chariton's Callirhoe." In Morgan and Stoneman 1994, 31–48.

Eisenstadt, S. 1979. "Observations and Queries About Sociological Aspects of Imperialism in the Ancient World." In *Power and Propaganda: A Symposium on Ancient Empires*, ed. Mogens Trolle Larson, 21–33. Mesopotamian Copenhagen Studies in Assyriology 7. Copenhagen: Akademisk Forlag.

Elderkin, G. W. 1937. "Two Curse Inscriptions." *Hesperia* 6:382–95.

Elliott, John H. 1981. *A Home for the Homeless: A Sociological Exegesis of I Peter, Its Situation, and Strategy*. Philadelphia: Fortress Press.

———. 1991. "Temple Versus Household in Luke–Acts: A Contract in Social Institutions." In *the Social World of Luke–Acts: Models for Interpretation*, ed. J. Neyrey, 211–46. Peabody: Hendrickson.

Elliott, J. K., ed. 1993. *Apocryphal New Testament*. New York: Oxford University Press.

Engelmann, H. 1975. *The Delian Aretalogy of Sarapis*. Leiden: E. J. Brill.

———, ed. 1976. *Inschriften griechischer Städte aus Kleinasien* Vol. 5, *Die Inschriften von Kyme*. Bonn: Habelt.

Epictetus. 1959–61. *Epictetus: The Discourses as Reported by Arrian, the Manual, and Fragments*. 2 vols. Trans. W. A. Oldfather. Loeb Classical Library. Cambridge: Harvard University Press; London: William Heinemann.

Erim, Kenan T. 1967. "The School of Aphrodisias." *Archaeology* 20.1:18–27.

———. 1973. "A Portrait Statue of Domitian from Aphrodisias." *Opuscula Romana* 9:135–42.

———. 1983. "Aphrodisias." *Anatolian Studies* 33:231–35.

———. 1986. *Aphrodisias: City of Venus–Aphrodite*. New York and London: Facts on File.

———. 1990a. "Recent Work at Aphrodisias, 1986–88." In Roueché and Erim 1990, 9–35.

———. 1990b. "Portrait Sculpture of Aphrodisias." In Roueché and Erim 1990, 152–60.

Erim, Kenan T. and Charlotte M. Roueché. 1982. "Sculptors from Aphrodisias." *PBSR* 50:102–15.

Esler, Philip F. 1987. *Community and Gospel in Luke–Acts. The Social and Political Motivations of Lucan Theology*. SNTSMS 57. Cambridge: Cambridge University Press.

Evans, Craig A., and James A. Sanders. 1993. *Luke and Scripture: The Function of Sacred Tradition in Luke–Acts*. Minneapolis: Fortress Press.

Ewing, W. 1895. "Greek and Other Inscriptions Collected in the Hauran." *Palestine Exploration Fund Quarterly Statement*.

Fant, J. Clayton. 1988. "The Roman Emperors in the Marble Business: Capitalists, Middlemen, or Philanthropists?" In *Classical Marble: Geochemistry, Technology, Trade*, ed. N. Herz and M. Waelkens, 147–58. Boston: Kluwer Academic.

Faraone, Christopher A., and Dirk Obbink, eds. 1991. *Magika Hiera: Ancient Greek Magic and Religion*. Oxford: Oxford University Press.

Farnell, Lewis. 1897. *The Cults of the Greek States*. 5 vols. Oxford: Clarendon Press.

Fears, J. R. 1981. "The Cult of Jupiter and Roman Imperial Ideology." In *ANRW* 2.17.1:3–141.

Feeney, D. C. 1991. *The Gods in Epic: Poets and Critics of the Classical Tradition*. Oxford: Oxford University Press.

Feldman, L. H. 1989. "Josephus's Portrait of Joshua." *HTR* 82.4:351–76.

———. 1993. *Jew and Gentile in the Ancient World: Attitudes and Interactions from Alexander to Justinian*. Princeton: Princeton University Press.

Feldman, L. H., and G. Hata, eds. 1987. *Josephus, Judaism, and Christianity*. Detroit: Wayne State University Press.

Ferguson, Everett. 1993. *Backgrounds of Early Christianity*. 2d ed. Grand Rapids, MI: W. B. Eerdmans.

Finn, T. M. 1982. "Social Mobility, Imperial Civil Service, and the Spread of Early Christianity." *Studia Patristica* 17:31–37.

Finney, Paul Corby. 1994. *The Invisible God: The Earliest Christians on Art*. Oxford: Oxford University Press.

Fitzmyer, J. 1981. *The Gospel According to Luke I–IX*. Garden City, NY: Doubleday.

———. 1985. *The Gospel According to Luke X–XXIV*. Vol. 2. Garden City, NY: Doubleday.

Fleischer, R. 1973. *Artemis von Ephesos und verwandte Kult statuen aus Anatolien und Syrien*. EPRO 35. Leiden: E. J. Brill.

———. 1981. "Artemis Ephesia und Aphrodite von Aphrodisias." In *Die orientalischen Religionem im Römerreich*, ed. M. J. Vermaseren, 298–311. Leiden: E. J. Brill.

———. 1984. "Aphrodisias." In *LIMC* 2.1:2–154.

Foucault, M. 1972. *The Archaeology of Knowledge*. Trans. A. Sheridan Smith. London: Tavistock.

———. 1980. *Power and Knowledge: Selected Interviews and Other Writings, 1972–77*. Ed. C. Gordon. New York: Pantheon Books.

———. 1986. "Space, Knowledge, and Power." In Hoy 1986, 239–56.

Fowden, G. 1988. "Between Pagans and Christians." *JRS* 78:173–82.

Fraser, P. M. 1977. *Rhodian Funerary Monuments*. Oxford and New York: Clarendon Press.

Freedberg, D. 1991. *The Power of Images: Studies in the History and Theory of Response*. Chicago: University of Chicago Press.

French, D. H. 1980. "The Roman Road System of Asia Minor." In *ANRW* 2.7.2:688–729.

Frend, W. H. C. 1984. *The Rise of Christianity*. Philadelphia: Fortress Press.

———. 1985. *Saints and Sinners in the Early Church*. Wilmington, DE: Michael Glazier.

———. 1988. *Archaeology and History in the Study of Early Christianity*. London: Variorum Reprints.

Frey, J. B. 1933. "Les Juifs à Pompeii." *RB* 42:365–84.

Friesen, Steven J. 1993. *Twice Neokoros: Ephesus, Asia, and the Cult of the Flavian Imperial Family*. Leiden: E. J. Brill.

Fulford, M. 1987. "Economic Interdependence Among Urban Communities of the Roman Mediterranean." *World Archaeology* 19.1:58–75.

Gafni, I. 1981. "Reinterment in the Land of Israel: Notes on the Origin and Development of the Custom." In *The Jerusalem Cathedra*, ed. L. Levine, 1:96–104. Detroit: Wayne State University Press.

Gager, John G. 1972. *Moses in Greco-Roman Paganism*. SBLMS 16. Nashville and New York: Abingdon Press.

———. 1975. *Kingdom and Community: The Social World of Early Christianity*. Englewood Cliffs, NJ: Prentice-Hall.

———. 1985. *The Origins of Anti-Semitism: Attitudes Towards Judaism in Pagan and Christian Antiquity*. Oxford: Oxford University Press.

———, ed. 1992. *Curse Tablets and Binding Spells from the Ancient World*. Oxford: Oxford University Press.

Gailey, C. 1992. "Culture Wars: Resistance to State Formation." In *Power Relations and State Formation*. Ed. T. Patterson and C. Gailey, 35–56. Salem, WI: Sheffield Publishing Co.

Galinsky, G. K. 1969. *Aeneas, Sicily, and Rome*. Princeton: Princeton University Press.

Galsterer, Hartmut. 1988. "Municipium Flavium Irnitanum: A Latin Town in Spain." *JRS* 78:78–90.

Garnsey, P., and Richard P. Saller. 1982. *The Early Principate, Augustus to Trajan*. Oxford: published for the Classical Association at the Clarendon Press.

————. 1987. *The Roman Empire: Economy, Society, and Culture.* Berkeley and Los Angeles: University of California Press.

Garrett, Susan R. 1989. *Demise of the Devil: Magic and the Demonic in Luke's Writings.* Minneapolis: Augsburg Fortress.

Geertz, C. 1966. "Religion as a Cultural System." In *Anthropological Approaches to the Study of Religion,* ed. Michael Banton, 1–46. London: Tavistock Publications.

————. 1975. "Thick Description: Toward an Interpretive Theory of Culture." In *The Interpretation of Culture,* ed. C. Geertz, 3–30. London: Hutchinson.

————. 1977. "Centers, Kings, and Charisma: Reflections on the Symbolics of Power." In *Culture and Its Creators: Essays in Honor of E. Ehils,* ed. J. Ben-David and T. N. Clark, 150–71. Chicago: University of Chicago Press.

Geiger, Joseph. 1990. "Local Patriotism in the Hellenistic Cities of Palestine." In *Greece and Rome in Eretz-Israel: Collected Essays,* ed. A. Kasher, U. Rappaport, and G. Fuks, 141–50. Jerusalem: Israel Exploration Society.

Georges, Pericles. 1994. *Barbarian Asia and the Greek Experience: From the Archaic Period to the Age of Xenophon.* Baltimore: Johns Hopkins University Press.

Georgi, Dieter. 1986. *The Opponents of Paul in Second Corinthians: A Study of Religious Propaganda in Late Antiquity.* Philadelphia: Fortress Press.

Gibson, Elsa. 1978. *The "Christians for Christians" Inscriptions of Phrygia.* Harvard Theological Studies 32. Missoula, MT: Scholars Press, 1978.

Gill, David W. J., and Conrad Gempf, eds. 1994. *The Book of Acts in Its First Century Setting.* Vol. 2, *The Book of Acts in Its Greco-Roman Setting.* Grand Rapids, MI: Eerdmans.

Goldberg, A. 1990. "The Rabbinic View of Scriptures." In *A Tribute to Geza Vermes: Essays on Jewish and Christian Literature and History,* ed. P. Davies and R. White, 153–66. Sheffield: JSOT Press.

Goldman, Bernard. 1966. *The Sacred Portal: A Primary Symbol in Ancient Judaic Art.* Detroit: Wayne State University Press.

Gomilev, L. N., and E. A. Quznetzov. 1969. "Two Traditions of Ancient Tibetan Cartography." In *Geology and Cartography Papers.* bull. 24. Leningrad University.

Gonzalez, J. 1986. "The Lex Irnitana: A New Copy of the Flavian Municipal Law." *JRS* 76:147–243.

Goodenough, E. R. 1969. *By Light, Light: The Mystic Gospel of Hellenistic Judaism.* Amsterdam: Philo Press.

Goodman, M. 1982. "The First Jewish Revolt: Social Conflict and the Problem of Debt." *JJS* 33:417–27.

————. 1983. *State and Society in Roman Galilee, A.D. 132–212.* Totowa, NJ: Rowman & Allanheld.

————. 1987. *The Ruling Class of Judaea: The Origins of the Jewish Revolt Against Rome, A.D. 66–70.* New York: Cambridge University Press.

————. 1989. "Nerva, the *Fiscus Judaicus,* and Jewish Identity." *JRS* 79:40–44.

————. 1990. "Identity and Authority in Ancient Judaism." *Judaism* 39:192–201.

————. 1991a. "Babatha's Story." *JRS* 81:169–75.

————. 1991b. "Opponents of Rome: Jews and Others." In Alexander 1991, 222–38.

————. 1992a. "The Roman State and the Jewish Patriarch in the Third Century." In Levine 1992a, 127–39.

————. 1992b. "Diaspora Reactions to the Destruction of the Temple." In *Jews and Christians,* ed. J. D. G. Dunn, 27–38. Tübingen: J. C. B. Mohr.

————. 1994. *Mission and Conversion: Proselytizing in the Religious History of the Roman Empire.* Oxford: Clarendon Press.

Goranson, S. 1992. "Sectarianism, Geography, and the Copper Scroll." *JJS* 43:282–87.

Gordon, R. L. 1972. "Mithraism and Roman Society: Social Factors in the Explanation of Religious Change in the Roman Empire." *Religion* 2.2:92–121.

———. 1976. "The Sacred Geography of a *Mithraeum:* The Example of Sette Sfere." 1.2:119–65.

———. 1979. "The Real and the Imaginary: Production and Religion in the Graeco-Roman World." *Art History* 2:5–34.

———. 1980. "Reality, Evocation, and Boundaries in the Mysteries of Mithras." *JMS* 3:19–99.

———. 1990a. "The Veil of Power: Emperors, Sacrificers, and Benefactors." In Beard and North 1990, 199–234.

———. 1990b. "Religion in the Roman Empire: The Civic Compromise and Its Limits." In Beard and North 1990, 235–55.

———. 1994. "Who Worshipped Mithras?" *JRA* 7:459–74.

Gould, P., and R. White. 1986. *Mental Maps.* 2d ed. Boston and London: Allen & Unwin.

Gould, Stephen Jay. 1989. *Wonderful Life: The Burgess Shale and the Nature of History.* New York: W. W. Norton.

Grabbe, Lester L. 1992. *Judaism from Cyrus to Hadrian.* 2 vols. Minneapolis: Fortress Press.

Grandjean, Y. 1975. *Une nouvelle arétalogie d'Isis à Maronée.* Leiden: E. J. Brill.

Grant, Robert. 1966. *The Apostolic Fathers.* Vol. 4. Camden, N.J.: Thomas Nelson & Sons.

———. 1977. *Early Christianity and Society.* New York: Harper & Row.

———. 1988. *Greek Apologists of the Second Century.* Philadelphia: Westminster Press.

———. 1992. "Early Christian Geography." *Vigiliae Christianae* 46:105–11.

Gray, Rebecca. 1993. *Prophetic Figures in Late Second Temple Jewish Palestine: The Evidence from Josephus.* Oxford: Oxford University Press.

Green, W. 1979. "Palestinian Holy Men: Charismatic Leadership and Rabbinic Tradition." In *ANRW* 2.19.2:619–47.

Gregory, Andrew P. 1994. "'Powerful Images': Responses to Portraits and the Political Uses of Images in Rome." *JRA* 7:80–99.

Grenfell, B. P., A. S. Hunt, and D. G. Hogarth. 1900. *Fayûm Towns and Their Papyri.* London: Egypt Exploration Fund.

Griffiths, J. G. 1978. "Xenophon of Ephesus on Isis and Alexandreia." In *Hommages à Maarten. J. Vermaseren,* Vol. 1, ed. M. de Boer and T. Edridge, 409–37. EPRO 68. Leiden: E. J. Brill.

Gruen, E. S. 1984. *The Hellenistic World and the Coming of Rome.* 2 vols. Berkeley and Los Angeles: University of California Press.

———. 1990. *Studies in Greek Culture and Roman Policy.* Leiden: E. J. Brill.

Hachlili, R. 1988. *Ancient Jewish Art and Archaeology in the Land of Israel.* Leiden: E. J. Brill.

Hadidi, A., ed. 1982. *Studies in the History and Archaeology of Jordan.* Vol. 1. Amman, Hashemite Kingdom of Jordan: Department of Antiquities.

Hägg, T. 1971. *Narrative Technique in Ancient Greek Romances: Studies of Chariton, Xenophon Ephesius, and Achilles Tatius.* Göteborg: Paul Astrom.

———. 1983. *The Novel in Antiquity.* Berkeley and Los Angeles: University of California Press.

———. 1987. "Callirhoe and Parthenope: The Beginning of the Historical Novel." *Classical Antiquity* 6.2:184–204.

Hagner, Donald A. 1973. *The Use of the Old and New Testaments in Clement of Rome.* Supplements to Novum Testamentum 34. Leiden: E. J. Brill.

Haight, E. H. 1943. *Essays on the Greek Romances.* Port Washington, NY: Kennikat Press.

Hajjar, Y. 1977. *La triade d'Heliopolis-Baalbek.* Vol. 1. Leiden: E. J. Brill.

Hall, A. 1968. "1 Clement as a Document of Transition." *La Ciudad de Dios* 181:682–92.

Handelman, Don, and Lea Shamger-Handelman. 1990. "Shaping Time: The Choice of the National Emblem of Israel." In *Culture Through Time: Anthropological Approaches,* ed. Emiko Ohnuki-Tierney, 193–226. Stanford: Stanford University Press.

Handler, Richard, and Jocelyn Linnekin. 1984. "Tradition, Genuine or Spurious?" *Journal of American Folklore* 97:273–89.

Hannestad, Niels. 1986. *Roman Art and Imperial Policy.* Århus: Århus University Press.

Hardie, Philip. 1992. Review of D. C. Feeney 1991. *JRS* 82:252–56.

Harley, J. B., and David Woodward. 1987. *The History of Cartography.* Vol. 1, *Cartography in Prehistoric, Ancient, and Medieval Europe and the Mediterranean.* Chicago: University of Chicago Press.

Harris, B. F. 1980. "Bithynia: Roman Sovereignty and the Survival of Hellenism." In *ANRW* 2.7.2:881–90.

———. 1991. "Dio of Prusa: A Survey of Recent Work." In *ANRW* 2.33.5:3852–81.

Hasluck, F. S. 1907. *JHS* 27.2:61–67.

Hatzfeld, J. 1927. "Inscriptions de Panamara." *BCH* 51:57–122.

Heiserman, A. 1977. *The Novel Before the Novel.* Chicago: University of Chicago Press.

Helms, Johannes. 1966. *Character Portrayal in the Romance of Chariton.* The Hague and Paris: Mouton.

Hemer, Colin J. 1989a. *The Book of Acts in the Setting of Hellenistic History.* Ed. Conrad H. Gempf. Tübingen: J. C. B. Mohr.

———. 1989b. *The Letters to the Seven Churches of Asia in Their Local Setting.* JSNT Supplement Series 11. Sheffield: JSOT Press.

Hengel, M. 1979. *Acts and the History of Earliest Christianity.* London: SCM Press.

———. 1980. *Jews, Greeks, and Barbarians: Aspects of the Hellenization of Judaism in the Pre-Christian Period.* Trans. John Bowden. London: SCM Press.

Hill, G. F. 1911. "Some Graeco-Phoenician Shrines." *JHS* 31:56–64.

Hobsbawm, E. J. 1972. "The Social Function of the Past: Some Questions." *Past and Present* 55:3–17.

Hobsbawm, E. J., and Terence Ranger, eds. 1983. *The Invention of Tradition.* Cambridge: Cambridge University Press.

Holladay, Carl H. 1977. *Theios Aner in Hellenistic Judaism: A Critique of the Use of This Category in New Testament Christology.* SBLDS 40. Missoula, MT: Scholars Press.

Hopkins, Keith, ed. 1983. *Death and Renewal: Sociological Studies in Roman History.* Cambridge: Cambridge University Press.

Horbury, William, and David Noy. 1992. *Jewish Inscriptions of Graeco-Roman Egypt.* Cambridge: Cambridge University Press.

Horig, Monika. 1984. "Iupiter Dolichenus." In *ANRW* 2.17.4:2136–79.

Horig, Monika, and Elmar Schwertheim. 1987. *Corpus Cultes Iovis Dolichen.* EPRO 106. Leiden: E. J. Brill.

Horsley, Richard A., and John S. Hanson. 1985. *Bandits, Prophets, and Messiahs: Popular Movements at the Time of Jesus.* Minneapolis: Winston Press.

Horton, F. 1976. *The Melchizedek Tradition: A Critical Examination of the Sources to the Fifth Century and in the Epistle of Hebrews.* Cambridge: Cambridge University Press.

Howgego, C. J. 1985. *Greek Imperial Countermarks*. London: Royal Numismatic Society.

———. 1992. "The Supply and Use of Money in the Roman World, 200 B.C. to A.D. 300." *JRS* 82:1–31.

———. 1994. "Coin Circulation and the Integration of the Roman Economy." *JRA* 7:5–22.

Hoy, David, ed. 1986. *Foucault: A Critical Reader*. Oxford and New York: Basil Blackwell.

Hunt, E. D. 1982. *Holy Land Pilgrimage*. Oxford: Clarendon Press; New York: Oxford University Press.

Hunter, R. L. 1994. "History and Historicity in the Romance of Chariton." In *ANRW* 2.34.2:1055–86.

Huot, Jean-Louis. 1991. "Grand oublie du conflit du Golfe: Le patrimoine culturel de l'Irak." *Archeologia* 62.2:12–39.

Hurst, L. 1990. *The Epistle to the Hebrews: Its Background of Thought*. Cambridge: Cambridge University Press.

Hurtado, Larry. 1988. *One God, One Lord: Early Christian Devotion and Ancient Jewish Monotheism*. Philadelphia: Fortress Press.

Hutchinson, Valerie J. 1991. "The Cult of Dionysos / Bacchus in the Graeco-Roman World: New Light from Archaeological Studies." *JRA* 4:222–30.

Inan, Jale, and Elisabeth Alföldi-Rosenbaum. 1979. *Römische und frühbyzantische Porträtplastik aus der Türkei*. Vol 1. Mainz: Philipp von Zabern.

Inan, Jale, and Elisabeth Rosenbaum. 1966. *Roman and Early Byzantine Portrait Sculpture in Asia Minor*. London: Oxford University Press.

Jaczynowska, M. 1981. "Le culte de l'Hercule romain au temps du Haut-Empire." In *ANRW* 2.17.2:631–61.

Jeffers, James S. 1991. *Conflict at Rome: Social Order and Hierarchy in Early Christianity*. Minneapolis: Fortress Press.

Jervell, J. 1984. "The Signs of an Apostle: Paul's Miracles." In *The Unknown Paul: Essays on Luke–Acts and Early Christian History*. Trans. Roy A. Harrisville, 77–95. Minneapolis: Augsburg.

Johnston, Ann. 1989. "The Coinage of Smyrna." *JRA* 2:319–25.

Jones, A. 1949. *The Greek City: From Alexander to Justinian*. Oxford: Clarendon Press.

Jones, Brian W. 1984. *The Emperor Titus*. London: Croom Helm; New York: St. Martin's Press.

———. 1992. *The Emperor Domitian*. London: Routledge.

Jones, C. P. 1970. "A Leading Family of Roman Thespiae." *HSCP* 74:223–55.

———. 1978. *The Roman World of Dio Chrysostom*. Cambridge: Harvard University Press.

———. 1983. "A Deed of Foundation from the Territory of Ephesos." *JRS* 73:116–25.

Jordan, D. R. 1985. "A Survey of Greek Defixiones Not Included in the Special Corpora." *GRBS* 26:151–97.

Kan, A. H. 1943. *Juppiter Dolichenus: Sammlung der Inschriften und Bildwerke*. Leiden: E. J. Brill.

Kant, Laurence H. 1987. "Jewish Inscriptions in Greek and Latin." In *ANRW* 2.20.2:671–713.

Katz, Steven T. 1984. "Issues in the Separation of Judaism and Christianity After 70 C.E.: A Reconsideration." *JBL* 103.1:43–76.

Kearsley, R. 1988. "A Leading Family of Cibyra and Some Asiarchs of the First Century." *Anatolian Studies* 38:43–45.

Kee, H. 1983a. *Miracle in the Early Christian World.* New Haven: Yale University Press.

———. 1983b. "The Socio-cultural Setting of Joseph and Aseneth." *NTS* 29:394–413.

———. 1986. *Medicine, Miracle, and Magic in the New Testament Times.* SNTSMS 55. Cambridge: Cambridge University Press.

———. 1990. "The Transformation of the Synagogue After 70 C.E.: Its Import for Early Christianity." *NTS* 36:1–24.

Kirschner, Robert. 1985. "Apocalyptic and Rabbinic Responses to the Destruction of 70." *HTR* 78.1–2:27–46.

Kleiner, Diana E. E. 1983. *The Monument of Philopappos in Athens.* Archaeologica 30. Rome: Giorgio Bretschneider.

———. 1986. "Athens Under the Romans: The Patronage of Emperors and Kings." In *Rome and the Provinces: Studies in the Transformation of Art and Architecture in the Mediterranean World,* ed. Charles B. McClendon, 8–20. New Haven: New Haven Society of the Archaeological Institute of America.

Kleiner, F. S. 1989. "The Study of Roman Triumphal and Honorary Arches 50 Years After Kähler." *JRA* 2:195–206.

Klijn, A. F. J., and G. J. Reinink. 1974. "Elchasai and Mani." *Vigiliae Christianae* 28:277–89.

Klose, D. 1987. *Die Munzprägung von Smyrna in der römischen Kaiserzeit.* Berlin: W. de Grüyter.

Koenen, L. 1967. "Eine Einladung zur Kline des Sarapis." *ZPE* 1:121–30.

Kokkinos, Nikos. 1992. "The Herodian Dynasty: Origins, Role in Society and Eclipse." Ph.D. diss., Oxford University.

Konstan, David. 1994. *Sexual Symmetry: Love in the Ancient Novel and Related Genres.* Princeton: Princeton University Press.

Kotansky, Roy. 1991. "Incantations and Prayers for Salvation on Inscribed Greek Amulets." In Faraone and Obbink 1991, 107–37.

Kraabel, A. T. 1979. "The Diaspora Synagogue: Archaeological and Epigraphic Evidence." In *ANRW* 2.19.1:477–510.

———. 1981. "The Disappearance of the God-Fearers." *Numen* 28:113–26.

———. 1983. "Impact of the Discovery of the Sardis Synagogue." In *Sardis from Prehistoric to Roman Times,* ed. George M. A. Hanfmann, 178–90. Cambridge: Harvard University Press.

———. 1992a. "The Roman Diaspora: Six Questionable Assumptions." In Overman and MacLennan 1992, 1–20.

———. 1992b. "Unity and Diversity Among Diaspora Synagogues." In Overman and MacLennan 1992, 21–34.

———. 1994. "Immigrants, Exiles, Expatriates, and Missionaries." In Borman, Del Tredici, Standhartinger 1994, 71–88.

Kraemer, Ross Shephard. 1991. "Jewish Tuna and Christian Fish: Identifying Religious Affiliation in Epigraphic Sources." *HTR* 84.2:141–62.

———. 1992a. *Her Share of the Blessings: Women's Religions Among Pagans, Jews, and Christians in the Greco-Roman World.* New York: Oxford University Press.

———. 1992b. "On the Meaning of the Term 'Jew' in Graeco-Roman Inscriptions." In Overman and MacLennan, 1992, 311–30.

Ladouceur, D. 1980. "Hellenistic Preconceptions of Shipwreck and Pollution as a Context for Acts 27–28." *HTR* 73:435–49.

Lake, Kirsopp, trans. 1959. *Apostolic Fathers.* Loeb Classical Library. Cambridge: Harvard University Press.

Lane, E. N. 1991. "Men: A Neglected Cult of Roman Asia Minor." In *ANRW* 2.18.3:2161–74.

———. 1971–78. *Corpus Monumentorum Religionis Dei Menis.* 4 vols. EPRO 19. Leiden: E. J. Brill.

Lane Fox, Robin. 1986. *Pagans and Christians in the Mediterranean World from the Second Century A.D. to the Conversion of Constantine.* New York: Knopf.

LaPlace, Marcel. 1980. "Les légendes troyennes dans le "roman" de Chariton, Chairéas et Callirhoé." *REG* 93:83–125.

Lattimore, R. 1962. *Themes in Greek and Latin Epitaphs.* Urbana: University of Illinois Press.

Laumonier, Alfred. 1958. *Les cultes indigènes en Carie.* Paris: E. de Boccard.

Lavagnini, B., ed. 1922. *Eroticorum Graecorum Fragmenta Papyracea.* Leipzig: B. G. Teubner.

Laws, Sophie. 1980. *The Epistle of James.* Harper's New Testament Commentaries. San Francisco: Harper & Row.

Leclant, Jean. 1986. "Isis, déesse universelle et divinité locale dans le monde greco-roman." *BCH* 14:341–53.

Lehmann, K. 1945. "The Dome of Heaven." *AB* 27:1–27.

Levick, Barbara. 1990. *Claudius.* New Haven: Yale University Press.

Levin, S. 1989. "The Greek Oracles in Decline." In *ANRW* 2.18.2:1599–1649.

Levine, Lee, ed. 1992a. *The Galilee in Late Antiquity.* New York and Jerusalem: Jewish Theological Seminary of America; Cambridge: Harvard University Press.

———. 1992b. "Judaism from the Destruction of Jerusalem to the End of the Second Jewish Revolt: 70–135 C.E." In *Christianity and Rabbinic Judaism,* ed. Hershel Shanks, 125–49. Washington, DC: Biblical Archaeology Society.

Lewis, N. 1985–88. "A Jewish Landowner in Provincia Arabia." *Scripta Classica Israelica* 8 / 9:132–37.

———. 1989. *The Documents from the Bar Kokhba Period in the Cave of Letters Greek Papyri.* Jerusalem: Israel Exploration Society, Hebrew University of Jerusalem, and Shrine of the Book.

LiDonnici, Lynn R. 1992. "The Images of Artemis Ephesia and Greco-Roman Worship: A Reconsideration." *HTR* 85.4:389–415.

Lieu, Judith, John North, and Tessa Rajak, eds. 1992. *The Jews Among Pagans and Christians in the Roman Empire.* London and New York: Routledge.

Lightstone, Jack N. 1984. *The Commerce of the Sacred: Mediation of the Divine Among Jews in the Graeco-Roman Diaspora.* Brown Judaic Studies 59. Chico, CA: Scholars Press.

———. 1988. *Society, the Sacred, and Scripture in Ancient Judaism: A Sociology of Knowledge.* Studies in Christianity and Judaism 3. Waterloo, ON: Wilfrid Laurier University Press.

Lincoln, Bruce. 1982. "Places Outside Space, Moments Outside Time." In *Homage to George Dumézil,* ed. Edgar Polomé, 69–84. Washington, DC: Journal of Indo-European Studies Monograph Series, Institute for the Study of Man.

———. 1989. *Discourse and the Construction of Society: Comparative Studies of Myth, Ritual, and Classification.* Oxford: Oxford University Press.

———, ed. 1985. *Religion, Rebellion, Revolution: An Interdisciplinary and Crosscultural Collection of Essays.* London: Macmillan.

Love, Iris. 1978. "Knidos." *American Journal of Archaeology* 82:324–25.

Luck, Georg. 1985. *Arcana Mundi: Magic and the Occult in the Greek and Roman Worlds.* Baltimore: Johns Hopkins University Press.

Lucke, C. 1985. "Zum Chariton Text auf Papyrus." *ZPE* 58:21–33.

Lüderitz, Gert. 1983. *Corpus jüdischer Zeugnisse aus der Cyrenaika*. Wiesbaden: Dr. Ludwig Reichaut.

Lukés, S. 1977. *Essays in Social Theory*. London: Macmillan.

MacDonald, D. 1976. *Greek and Roman Coins from Aphrodisias*. British Archaeological Reports Supplementary Series 9. Oxford: British Archaeological Reports.

———. 1992. *The Coinage of Aphrodisias*. London: Royal Numismatic Society.

MacDonald, Dennis. 1983. *The Legend and the Apostle: The Battle for Paul in Story and Canon*. Philadelphia: Fortress Press.

———. 1986. *The Apocryphal Acts of the Apostles*. Decatur, GA: Scholars Press.

MacDonald, William L. 1982. *The Architecture of the Roman Empire*. Vol. 1. New Haven: Yale University Press.

MacMullen, Ramsay. 1966. *Enemies of the Roman Order: Treason, Unrest, and Alienation in the Empire*. Cambridge: Harvard University Press.

———. 1971. "Social History in Astrology." *Ancient Society* 2:105–16.

———. 1981. *Paganism in the Roman Empire*. New Haven: Yale University Press.

———. 1982. "The Epigraphic Habit in the Roman Empire." *AJP* 103:233–46.

———. 1984. *Christianizing the Roman Empire (A.D. 100–400)*. New Haven: Yale University Press.

———. 1988. *Corruption and the Decline of Rome*. New Haven: Yale University Press.

———. 1990. *Changes in the Roman Empire: Essays in the Ordinary*. Princeton: Princeton University Press.

MaCready, S., and F. Thompson, eds. 1987. *Roman Architecture in the Greek World*. Society of Antiquaries of London Occasional Papers 10. London: Thames & Hudson.

Macro, Anthony D. 1980. "The Cities of Asia Minor Under the Roman Imperium." In *ANRW* 2.7.2:658–97.

Maddox, R. 1982. *The Purpose of Luke–Acts*. Edinburgh: T. & T. Clark.

Maehler, Herwig. 1976. "Der Metiochus–Parthenope–Roman." *ZPE* 23:1–20.

Magie, D. 1950. *Roman Rule in Asia Minor*. 2 vols. Princeton: Princeton University Press.

———. 1953. "Egyptian Deities in Asia Minor." *AJA* 57.3:163–87.

Mann, Michael. 1986. *The Sources of Social Power*. Vol. 1. Cambridge: Cambridge University Press.

Marcus, J. 1974. "The Iconography of Power Among the Classic Maya." *World Archaeology* 6:83–94.

Markus, R. 1994. "How on Earth Could Places Become Holy? Origins of the Christian Idea of the Holy Places." *Journal of Early Christian Studies* 2.33:257–71.

Martin, L. H. 1987. *Hellenistic Religions: An Introduction*. Oxford University Press.

———. 1995. "Gods or Ambassadors of God? Barnabas and Paul in Lystra." *NTS* 41.1:152–56.

Mazar, Benjamin. 1975. *The Mountain of the Lord*. Garden City, NY: Doubleday.

McCarthy, T. 1992. "The Critique of Impure Reason: Foucault and the Frankfurt School." In Wartenberg 1992, 121–48.

McClelland, S. 1989. *The Crowd and the Mob: From Plato to Canetti*. London and Boston: Unwin Hyman.

McKnight, Scot. 1991. *A Light Among the Gentiles: Jewish Missionary Activity in the Second Temple Period*. Minneapolis: Fortress Press.

Meeks, W. 1983. *The First Urban Christians: The Social World of the Apostle Paul*. New Haven: Yale University Press.

Meijer, P. A. 1981. "Philosophers, Intellectuals, and Religion in Hellas." In *Faith, Hope, and Worship: Aspects of Religious Mentality in the Ancient World,* ed. H. S. Versnel, 216–63. Studies in Greek and Roman Religion 2. Leiden: E. J. Brill.

Merkelbach, Reinhold. 1962. *Roman und Mysterium in der Antike.* Munich: Beck.

———. 1976. *Die Inschriften von Assos.* Bonn: Habelt.

Metzger, B. 1970. "Ancient Astrological Geography and Acts 2:9–11." In *Apostolic History and the Gospel,* ed. W. Gasque, 123–33. Exeter, Eng.: Paternoster Press.

Mildenberg, Leo. 1990. "Rebel Coinage in the Roman Empire." In *Greece and Rome in Eretz Israel,* ed. G. Fuks, U. Rappaport, and A. Kasher, 62–74. Jerusalem: Israel Exploration Society.

Miles, Gary B., and Garry Trompf. 1976. "Luke and Antiphon: The Theology of Acts 27–28 in the Light of Pagan Beliefs About Divine Retribution, Pollution, and Shipwreck." *HTR* 69:259–67.

Milik, J. T. 1961. "Textes hébreux et arameens." In *Discoveries in the Judaean Desert.* Vol. 2, *Les Grottes de Murabba'at,* ed. P. Benoit, J. Milik, and R. DeVaux, 67–205. Oxford: Oxford University Press.

Millar, F. 1964. *A Study of Cassius Dio.* Oxford: Clarendon Press.

———. 1977. *The Emperor in the Roman World (31 B.C.–A.D. 337).* Ithaca: Cornell University Press.

———. 1981. *The Roman Empire and Its Neighbours.* 2d ed. London: Duckworth Press.

———. 1983a. "Epigraphy." In *Sources for Ancient History,* ed. M. Crawford, 80–136. Cambridge: Cambridge University Press.

———. 1983b. "The Phoenician Cities: A Case-Study of Hellenization." *PCPS* 209: 55–71.

———. 1984. "State and Society: The Impact of Monarchy." In *Caesar Augustus: Seven Aspects,* ed. F. Millar and E. Segal, 37–60. Oxford and New York: Clarendon Press.

———. 1987. "Empire, Community, and Culture in the Roman Near East: Greeks, Syrians, Jews, and Arabs." *JJS* 38:143–64.

———. 1990. "The Roman *Coloniae* of the Near East: A Study of Cultural Relations." In *Roman Eastern Policy and Other Studies in Roman History,* ed. Heikki Solin and Mika Kajava, 7–58. Societus Scientiarum Fennica Commentationes Humanarum Litterarum 91. Helsinki: Societas Scientiarum Fennica.

———. 1993a. "The Greek City in the Roman Period." In *The Ancient Greek City-State,* ed. Mogens Herman Hansen, 232–60. Historisk-filosofiske Meddelelser 67. Copenhagen: Royal Danish Academy of Sciences and Letters.

———. 1993b. "Hagar, Ishmael, Josephus, and the Origins of Islam." *JJS* 44.1:23–45.

———. 1993c. *The Roman Near East (31 B.C.–A.D. 337).* Cambridge: Harvard University Press.

Miller, Patricia Cox. 1994. *Dreams in Late Antiquity: Studies in the Imagination of a Culture.* Princeton: Princeton University Press.

Miralles, Carlos. 1977. "Eros as Nosos in the Greek Novel." In Reardon 1977, 20–21.

Mitchell, Stephen. 1974. "The Plancii in Asia Minor." *JRS* 64:27–39.

———. 1993a. *Anatolia: Land, Men, and Gods in Asia Minor.* Vol. 1, *The Celts in Anatolia and the Impact of Roman Rule.* Oxford: Clarendon Press; New York: Oxford University Press.

———. 1993b. *Anatolia: Land, Men, and Gods in Asia Minor.* Vol. 2, *The Rise of the Church.* Oxford: Clarendon Press; New York: Oxford University Press.

Moessner, David P. 1982. "Jesus and the 'Wilderness Generation': The Death of the Prophet Like Moses According to Luke." In *SBLSP* 21:319–40, ed. Kent H. Richards. Chico, CA: Scholars Press.

———. 1983. "Paul and the Pattern of the Prophet Like Moses in Acts." In *SBLSP*, 22:203–12, ed. Kent H. Richards. Chico, CA: Scholars Press.

———. 1989. *Lord of the Banquet: The Literary and Theological Significance of the Lukan Travel Narrative*. Philadelphia: Fortress Press.

Mol, Hans. 1977. *Identity and the Sacred*. New York: Free Press.

Molinié, Georges. 1979. *Chariton: Le roman de Chairéas et Callirhoé*. Paris: Budé.

Momigliano, A. 1987. *On Pagans, Jews, and Christians*. Middletown: Wesleyan University Press.

Morgan, J. R., and R. Stoneman, eds. 1994. *Greek Fiction: The Greek Novel in Context*. London: Routledge.

Morris, Ian. 1992. *Death-Ritual and Social Structure in Classical Antiquity*. Cambridge: Cambridge University Press.

Moxnes, Halvor. 1991. "Patron–Client Relations and the New Community in Luke–Acts." In *The Social World of Luke–Acts: Models for Interpretation*, ed. J. Neyrey, 241–70. Peabody, MA: Hendrickson.

Müller, Carl Werner. 1976. "Chariton von Aphrodisias und die Theorie des Romans in der Antike." *Antike und Abendland* 22.2:115–36.

Murphy, Frederick J. 1985a. "2 Baruch and the Romans." *JBL* 104.4:663–69.

———. 1985b. *The Structure and Meaning of Second Baruch* SBLDS 78. Atlanta: Scholars Press.

———. 1993. *Pseudo-Philo: Rewriting the Bible*. Oxford: Oxford University Press.

Musurillo, Herbert A. 1954. *The Acts of the Pagan Martyrs*. Oxford: Clarendon Press.

Mylonas, George E. 1961. *Eleusis and the Eleusinian Mysteries*. Princeton: Princeton University Press.

Neusner, Jacob. 1969a. *History of the Jews of Babylonia*. Vol. 1, *The Parthinian Period*. Leiden: E. J. Brill.

———. 1969b. *History of the Jews of Babylonia*. Vol. 2, *The Early Sasanian Period*. Leiden: E. J. Brill.

———. 1971. *The Rabbinic Traditions About the Pharisees Before 70*. 3 Vols. Leiden: E. J. Brill.

———. 1973. *From Politics to Piety: The Emergence of Pharisaic Judaism*. Englewood Cliffs, NJ: Prentice-Hall.

———. 1978. "The Jews East of the Euphrates and the Roman Empire I. 1st–3rd Centuries A.D." In *ANRW* 2.9.1:46–69.

———. 1979. "The Formation of Rabbinic Judaism: Yavneh (Jamnia) from A.D. 70–100." In *ANRW* 19.2:21–42.

———. 1988a. "Beyond Myth, After Apocalypse: The Mishnaic Conception of History." In *The Social World of Formative Christianity and Judaism: Essays in Honor of Howard Kee*, ed. J. Neusner, P. Borgen, E. Frerichs, and R. Horsley, 91–106. Philadelphia: Fortress Press.

———. 1988b. *The Mishnah: A New Translation*. New Haven: Yale University Press.

———. 1992. "The Two Vocabularies of Symbolic Discourse in Ancient Judaism." In Overman and MacLennan 1992, 79–104.

Neusner, Jacob, Peder Borgen, Ernest Frerichs, and Richard Horsley, eds. 1988. *The Social World of Formative Christianity and Judaism*. Philadelphia: Fortress Press.

Neusner, Jacob, and E. S. Frerichs, eds. 1985. *"To See Ourselves as Others See Us": Christians, Jews, "Others" in Late Antiquity*. Chico, CA: Scholars Press.

Neusner, Jacob, W. S. Green, and E. S. Frerichs, eds. 1987. *Judaisms and Their Messiahs*. Cambridge: Cambridge University Press.

Neyrey, J. 1991. "The Symbolic Universe of Luke–Acts: 'They Turn the World Upside

Down.'" In *The Social World of Luke-Acts: Models for Interpretation*, ed. J. Neyrey, 271–304. Peabody, MA: Hendrickson.

Nicolet, Claude. 1991. *Space, Geography, and Politics in the Early Roman Empire*. Jerome Lectures 19. Ann Arbor: University of Michigan Press.

Nock, A. D. 1972a. *Essays on Religion and the Ancient World*. Vol. 1, ed. Zeph Stewart. Cambridge: Harvard University Press.

———. 1972b. *Essays on Religion and the Ancient World*. Vol. 2, ed. Zeph Stewart. Cambridge: Harvard University Press.

Noelke, Peter. 1983. "Zwei unbekannte Repliken der Aphrodite von Aphrodisias in Köln." *AA* 1:107–31.

North, J. 1986. "Religion and Politics, from Republic to Principate." *JRS* 76:251–58.

———. 1994. "The Development of Religious Pluralism." In Lieu, North, and Rajak 1992, 174–93.

Noy, David. 1993. *Jewish Inscriptions of Western Europe*. Vol. 1, Italy (*Excluding the City of Rome*), Spain and Gaul. Cambridge: Cambridge University Press.

———. 1995. *Jewish Inscriptions of Western Europe*. Vol. 2, *The City of Rome*. Cambridge: Cambridge University Press.

O'Neil, William M. 1986. *Early Astronomy: From Babylonia to Copernicus*. Sydney: Sydney University Press.

Oster, Richard E. 1976. "The Ephesian Artemis as an Opponent of Early Christianity." *JbAC* 19:27–44.

———. 1987. *A Bibliography of Ancient Ephesus*. American Theological Library Association Bibliography Seires 19. London: Scarecrow Press.

———. 1990. "Ephesus as a Religious Center Under the Principate I: Paganism Before Constantine." In *ANRW* 2.18.3:1661–728.

Overman, J. A. 1988. "The God-Fearers: Some Neglected Features." *JSNT* 32:17–26.

Overman, J. A., and W. S. Green. 1992. "Judaism (Greco-Roman Period)." In *ABD* 3:1037–54.

Overman, J. A., and R. S. MacLennan, eds. 1992. *Diaspora Jews and Judaism: Essays in Honor of, and in Dialogue with, A. Thomas Kraabel*. University of South Florida Series in Ancient Judaism. Atlanta: Scholars Press.

Owens, E. J. 1991. *The City in the Greek and Roman World*. London and New York: Routledge.

Pack, Robert A. 1965. *The Greek and Latin Literary Texts from Greco-Roman Egypt*. 2d ed. Ann Arbor: University of Michigan Press.

Pagels, E. 1985. "Christian Apologists and the 'Fall of the Angels': An Attack on Roman Imperial Power?" *HTR* 78:301–25.

Parke, H. W. 1985. *The Oracles of Apollo in Asia Minor*. London and Dover, NH: Croom Helm.

Parsons, P. J. 1980. "The Earliest Christian Letter." In *Miscellanea Papyrologica*, 289. Florence: Gonnelli.

———. 1982. "Facts from Fragments." *Greece and Rome* 29.2:184–95.

Patrich, J. 1990. *The Formation of Nabatean Art: Prohibition of a Graven Image Among the Nabateans*. Jerusalem: Magness Press; Leiden: E. J. Brill.

Pearson, Mike Parker. 1993. "The Powerful Dead: Archaeological Relationships Between the Living and the Dead." *CAJ* 3.2:203.

Perkins, Judith. 1985. "The Apocryphal Acts of the Apostles and Early Christian Martyrdom." *Arethusa* 18.2:211–35.

Perry, B. E. 1930. "Chariton and His Romance from a Literary-Historical Point of View." *AJPh* 51:93–134.

————. 1967. *The Ancient Romances: A Literary-Historical Account of Their Origins.* Berkeley and Los Angeles: University of California Press.

Pervo, Richard I. 1987. *Profit with Delight: The Literary Genre of the Acts of the Apostles.* Philadelphia: Fortress Press.

————. 1994. "Early Christian Fiction." In *Greek Fiction: The Greek Novel in Context,* ed. J. Morgan and Richard Stoneman, 239–55. London and New York: Routledge.

Peterson, David. 1993. "The Motif of Fulfillment and the Purpose of Luke–Acts." In *The Book of Acts in Its First-Century Setting.* Vol. 1, *Ancient Literary Setting,* ed. Bruce W. Winter and Andrew D. Clarke, 83–104. Grand Rapids, MI: W. B. Eerdmans.

Petri, Remy. 1963. *Ueber den Roman des Chariton.* Beitrage zur Klassischen Philologie 11. Meisenheim am Glan: Anton Hain.

Petzl, G., and H. Malay. 1987. "A New Confession—Inscription from the Katakekaumene." *GRBS* 28:459–72.

Pfanner, M. 1983. *Der Titusbogen: Beiträge zur Erschliessung hellenistischer und Kaiserzeitlicher Skulptur und Architektur,* Vol. 2. Mainz: Philipp von Zabern.

Phillips, C. R., III. 1991. *"Nullen Crimen sine Lege:* Socioreligious Sanctions on Magic." In Faraone and Obbink 1991, 260–76.

Pleket, H. W. 1981. "Religious History as the History of Mentality: The 'Believer' as Servant of the Deity in the Greek World." In *Faith, Hope, and Worship: Aspects of Religious Mentality in the Ancient World,* ed. H. S. Versnel, 152–92. Leiden: E. J. Brill.

Plepelits, Karl. 1976. *Chariton von Aphrodisias: Kallirhoe.* Stuttgart: Anton Heisermann.

Pliny. 1952. *Correspondence with Trajan.* Trans. W. Hutchinson. Loeb Classical Library. Cambridge: Harvard University Press.

Porton, Gary. 1976. "The Grape-Cluster in Jewish Literature and Art of Late Antiquity." *JJS* 27:159–76.

Potter, David. 1994. *Prophets and Emperors: Human and Divine Authority from Augustus to Theodosius.* Cambridge: Harvard University Press.

Preisendanz, Karl. 1973. *Papyri Graecae Magicae: Die griechischen Zauberpapyri.* 2 vols. Stuttgart: B. G. Teubner.

Price, Jonathan J. 1994. "The Jewish Diaspora of the Graeco-Roman Period." *Scripta Classica Israelica* 13:169–86.

Price, S. 1980. "Between Man and God: Sacrifice in the Roman Imperial Cult." *JRS* 70:28–43.

————. 1984a. "Gods and Emperors: The Greek Language of the Roman Imperial Cult." *JHS* 104:79–95.

————. 1984b. *Rituals and Power: The Roman Imperial Cult in Asia Minor.* Cambridge: Cambridge University Press.

————. 1986. "The Future of Dreams from Freud to Artemidorus." *Past and Present* 113:3–37.

Raden, G. T. B. 1963. "Comments on the History of the Jews in Pannonia." *Acta Archaeologica* 25:267–78.

Rajak, T. 1984a. *Josephus: The Historian and His Society.* Philadelphia: Fortress Press.

————. 1984b. "Was There a Jewish Charter?" *JRS* 74:107–23.

————. 1985. "Jews and Christians as Groups in a Pagan World." In Neusner and Frerichs 1985, 247–61.

————. 1991. "Friends, Romans, Subjects: Agrippa II's Speech in Josephus's *Jewish War.*" In Alexander 1991, 122–34.

———. 1992. "The Jewish Community and Its Boundaries." In Lieu, North, and Rajak 1992.

Rajak, T., and David Noy. 1993. *"Archisynagogoi:* Office, Title and Social Status in the Greco-Jewish Synagogue." *JRS* 83:75–93.

Ramage, E. S. 1983. "Denigration of Predecessor Under Claudius, Galba, Vespasian." *Historia* 32:201–14.

Ramsay, W. 1897. *Cities and Bishoprics of Phrygia.* Vol. 1, pts. 1 and 2. Oxford: Clarendon Press.

Reardon, B. 1969. "The Greek Novel." *Phoenix* 23:291–309.

———. 1971. *Courants littéraires grecs des IIe et IIIe siècles après J.-C.* Annales littéraires de l'Université de Nantes 3. Paris: Les Belles Lettres.

———. 1976. "Aspects of the Greek Novel." *Greece and Rome* 23:118–31.

———. 1977. *Erotica Antiqua: Acta of the International Conference on the Ancient Novel.* Bangor, Wales.

———. 1982a. "Une nouvelle edition de Chariton." *REG* 95:157–73.

———. 1982b. "Theme, Structure, and Narrative in Chariton." In *Later Greek Literature,* ed. John J. Winkler and Gordon Williams, 1–27. YCS 27. Cambridge: Cambridge University Press.

———, ed. 1989. *Collected Ancient Greek Novels.* Berkeley and Los Angeles: University of California Press.

———. 1991. *The Form of Greek Romance.* Princeton: Princeton University Press.

Reinach, Theòdore. 1906. "Inscriptions d'Aphrodisias." *REG* 19:205–98.

———. 1908. "Parthenon (Greek)." *BCH* 32:499–513.

Remus, H. 1982. "'Magic or Miracle'? Some Second-Century Instances." *Second Century* 2.3:127–56.

Reynolds, Joyce. 1977. *Excavations at Sidi Khrebis Benghuzi (Bernice).* Vol. 1. Libya: Department of Antiquities.

———. 1980. "The Origins and Beginning of Imperial Cult at Aphrodisias." *PCPS* 206:70–84.

———. 1981. "New Evidence for the Imperial Cult in Julio-Claudian Aphrodisias." *ZPE* 43:317–27.

———. 1982. *Aphrodisias and Rome.* JRS Monograph 1. London: Society for the Promotion of Roman Studies.

———. 1986. "Further Information on Imperial Cult at Aphrodisias." *StClas* 24:109–17.

———. 1987. "The Inscriptions." In de la Genière and Erim 1987, 81–85.

———. 1990. "Inscriptions and the Building of the Temple of Aphrodite." In Roueché and Erim, 1990, 37–40.

———. 1991. "Epigraphic Evidence for the Construction of the Theatre: 1st B.C. to mid-3rd A.D." In Smith and Erim 1991, 15–28.

Reynolds, Joyce, Mary Beard, and Charlotte Roueché. 1986. "Roman Inscriptions, 1981–85." *JRS* 76:124–46.

Reynolds, Joyce, and R. Tannenbaum. 1987. *Jews and God-Fearers at Aphrodisias.* Vol. 12. Cambridge: Cambridge Philological Society.

Rich, John, and Andrew Wallace-Hadrill, eds. 1991. *City and Country in the Ancient World.* London and New York: Routledge.

Richard, E. 1978. *Acts 6:1–8:4: The Author's Method of Composition.* Missoula, MT: Scholars Press.

Robbins, V. K. 1991. "Luke–Acts: A Mixed Population Seeks a Home in the Roman Empire." In Alexander 1991, 202–21.

Robert, Louis. 1938. *Etudes épigraphiques et philologiques*. Paris: Libraire Ancienne.

———. 1946. "Un corpus des inscriptions juives." *Hellenica* 3:90–108.

———. 1960. *Hellenica* 11/12.

———. 1965. "Aphrodisias." *Hellenica* 13:109–238.

———. 1966. "Inscriptions d'Aphrodisias." *L'Antiquité Classique* 36:408–10.

———. 1967. "Sur des inscriptions d'Ephese." *RPh* 41:7–84.

———. 1971. "Les colombes d'Anastase et autres volaties. 1. Les colombes d'Anastase aux Thermes de Cyrène. 2. Les colombes d'Aphrodisias et d'Ascalon.
3. Une épitaphe à Kibyra." *JS*, 81–105.

———. 1974. "Les inscriptions de Thessalonice." *RPh* 48:180–246.

———. 1978. "Documents d'Asie Mineure." *BCH* 102:395–543.

———. 1987. *Documents d'Asie Mineure*. Paris: De Boccard.

———. 1989. "Inscriptions d'Aphrodisias." In *Opera Minora Selecta*, 6:1–56. Amsterdam: Adolf M. Hakkert.

Robert, L., and J. Robert. 1959. "Bulletin épigraphique." *REG* 72:229–39.

Robiano, Patrick. 1984. "Tychè chez Chariton et Hélidore." *REG* 97:543–49.

Robinson, David M. 1933. "A New Inscription from Macedonia." *American Journal of
Archaeology* 37:602–4.

Rogers, Guy M. 1991. *The Sacred Identity of Ephesos: Foundation Myths of a Roman City*.
London and New York: Routledge.

———. 1993. "The Gift and Society in Roman Asia: Orthodoxies and Heresies." *Scripta
Classica Israelica* 12:188–99.

Rohde, E. 1960. *Der griechische Roman und seine Vorläufer*. With appendix by Wilhelm
Schmid. Hildesheim: Georg Olms Verlagsbuchlandlung.

Rokeah, D. 1982. *Jews, Pagans, and Christians in Conflict*. Jerusalem: Magness Press;
Leiden: E. J. Brill.

Roscher, W. H. 1884–1937. *Ausführliches Lexikon der griechischen und römischen Mytho-
logie*. 6 vols. in 9. Leipzig: B. G. Teubner.

Roueché, Charlotte. 1989. *Aphrodisias in Late Antiquity*. JRS Monograph 5. London:
Society for the Promotion of Roman Studies.

Roueché, Charlotte, and Kenan T. Erim, eds. 1990. *Aphrodisias Papers*. Vol. 1, *Recent
Work on Architecture and Sculpture*. JRA Supplementary Series 1. Ann Arbor: Editorial Committee for the JRA.

Roussel, P. 1927. "Les mystères de Panamara." *BCH* 51:123–27.

———. 1929. "Un nouvel hymne à Isis." *REG* 42:137–68.

———. 1931. "Le miracle de Zeus Panamaros." *BCH* 55:70–116.

Roussin, Lucille. Forthcoming. "The Zodiac in Synagogue Decoration." In *Archaeology
and the Galilee*, eds. Edwards and McCollough. Atlanta: Scholars Press.

Ruiz-Montero, Consuelo. 1980. "Una observación para la cronología de Caritón de
Afrodisias." *Estudios Clásicos* 25:63–69.

———. 1989. "Caritón de Afrodisias y el mundo real." In *Piccalo mondo antico, le donne,
gli amori: Costumi, il mondo reale nel romanzo antico*, ed. P. Liviabella and A.
Scarcella, 106–49. Universita di Perugia: Edizioni Scientifiche Italiane.

———. 1994a. "Chariton von Aphrodisias: Ein Ueberblick." In *ANRW* 2.32.2:1006–
54.

———. 1994b. "Xenophon von Ephesos: Ein Ueberblick." In *ANRW* 2.34.2:1088–
138.

Rutgers, L. 1992. "Archaeological Evidence for the Interaction of Jews and Non-Jews in
Late Antiquity." *AJA* 96:101–18.

———. 1994. "Roman Policy Towards the Jews: Expulsions from the City of Rome During the First Century C.E." *Classical Antiquity* 13.1:56–74.

Sachs, A., and H. Hunger. 1988. *Astronomical Diaries and Related Texts from Babylonia: Diaries from 652 B.C. to 262 B.C.* Vol. 1. Vienna: Oesterreichischen Akademie der Wissenschaften.

———. 1989. *Astronomical Diaries and Related Texts from Babylonia: Diaries from 261 B.C. to 165 B.C.* Vol. 2. Vienna: Oesterreichischen Akademie der Wissenschaften.

Sack, Robert D. 1986. *Human Territoriality: Its Theory and History.* Cambridge Studies in Historical Geography 7. Cambridge: Cambridge University Press.

Safrai, S., and M. Stern, eds. 1974. *The Jewish People in the First Century: Historical Geography, Political History, Social, Cultural, and Religious Life and Institutions.* Vol. 1. Compendia Rerum Iudaicarum ad Novum Testamentum, sec. 1. Assen: Van Gorcum; Philadelphia: Fortress Press.

Said, S. 1994. "The City in the Greek Novel." In Tatum, 1994, 216–36.

Saller, R. P. 1982. *Personal Patronage Under the Early Empire.* Cambridge: Cambridge University Press.

Sanders, E. P. 1990. *Jewish Law from Jesus to the Mishnah: Five Studies.* London: SCM Press, Philadelphia: Trinity University Press.

———. 1992. *Judaism: Practice and Belief, 63 B.C.E.–66 C.E.* Philadelphia: Trinity Press International.

Sandy, Gerald N. 1994. "Apuleius' 'Metamorphoses' and the Ancient Novel." In *ANRW* 2.34.2:1511–74.

Schmeling, Gareth. 1974. *Chariton.* Twayne's World Authors Series 295. New York: Twayne Publishers.

Schmidt, F. 1990. "Jewish Representations of the Inhabited Earth During the Hellenistic and Roman Periods." In *Greece and Rome in Eretz Israel,* ed. A. Kasler et al., 119–34. Jerusalem: Yad Izhak Ben-Zvi and Israel Exploration Society.

Schoedel, William R. 1985. *Ignatius of Antioch: A Commentary on the Letters of Ignatius* Philadelphia: Fortress Press.

Schubert, W. 1984. *Jupiter in den epen der Flavierzeit.* Studien zur Klassischen Philologie 8. Frankfurt: Peter Lang.

Schürer, Emil. 1973–87. *The History of the Jewish People in the Age of Jesus Christ (175 B.C.–A.D. 135).* Vols. 5 1–3, pt. 1, 2. Revised and edited by Geza Vermes, Fergus Millar, and Martin Goodman (vol. 3 only). Edinburgh: T & T Clark.

Schwertheim, E. 1980. *Die Inschriften von Kyzikos und Umgebung.* Vol. 1. Bonn: Habelt.

———. 1983. *Die Inschriften von Kyzikos und Umgebung.* Vol. 2. Bonn: Habelt.

Scobie, A. 1973. *More Essays on the Ancient Romance and Its Heritage.* Beiträge zur klassischen Philologie 46. Meisenheim am Glan: Anton Hain.

Scott, J. 1994. "Luke's Geographical Horizon." In Gill and Gempf 1994, 483–544.

Scott, Kenneth. 1936. *The Imperial Cult Under the Flavians.* Stuttgart and Berlin: W. Kohlhammer.

———. 1938. "Ruler Cult and Related Problems in the Greek Romances." *CP* 33:380–89.

Segal, A. 1995. *Theatres in Roman Palestine and Provincia Arabia.* Leiden: E. J. Brill.

———. 1987. "Theatres in Eretz-Israel in the Roman–Byzantine Period." In *Eretz-Israel* 19:106–24 (in Hebrew); 75–76 (English summary).

Segal, Alan. 1986. *Rebecca's Children: Judaism and Christianity in the Roman World.* Cambridge: Harvard University Press.

Sève, M. 1979. "Un décret de consolation à Cyzique." *BCH* 103:327–59.

———. 1981. "Inscriptions de Thasos." *BCH* 105:183–98.

Shapiro, H. Alan. 1990. "Homonoia." *LIMC* 5.1:476–79.

Shaw, B. D. 1991. "The Cultural Meaning of Death: Age and Gender in the Roman Family." In *The Family in Italy from Antiquity to the Present,* ed. D. I. Kertzer and R. P. Saller, 66–90. New Haven: Yale University Press.

Sheppard, A. R. R. 1984–86. "Homonoia in the Greek Cities in the Roman Empire." *Ancient Society* 15–17:229–52.

Sherk, Robert K. 1980. "Roman Galatia: The Governors from 25 B.C. to A.D. 114." In *ANRW* 2.7.2:954–1052.

Sherwin-White, S. M. 1976. "A Note on Three Coin Inscriptions." *ZPE* 21:183–88.

Sichtermann, H., and G. Koch. 1975. *Griechische Mythen auf römischen Sarkophagen.* Tübingen: Ernst Wasmuth.

Smallwood, E. 1981. *The Jews Under Roman Rule: From Pompey to Diocletian: A Study in Political Relations.* Leiden: E. J. Brill.

Smith, D. E. 1980. "Social Obligation in the Context of Communal Meals: A Study of the Christian Meal in 1 Corinthians in Comparison with Graeco-Roman Communal Meals." Ph.D. diss., Harvard University.

Smith, D. E., and Hal Taussig. 1990. *Many Tables: The Eucharist in the New Testament and Liturgy Today.* Philadelphia: Trinity Press.

Smith, Jonathan Z. 1980. "Fences and Neighbors: Some Contours of Early Judaism." In *Approaches to Ancient Judaism,* Vol. 2, ed. W. S. Green, 1–25. Chico, CA: Scholars Press.

———. 1987. *To Take Place: Toward Theory in Ritual.* Chicago: University of Chicago Press.

Smith, R. R. R. 1987. "The Imperial Reliefs from the Sebasteion at Aphrodisias." *JRS* 77:88–138.

———. 1988. "Simulacra Gentium: The Ethne from the Sebasteion at Aphrodisias." *JRS* 78:50–77.

———. 1990a. "Late Roman Philosopher Portraits from Aphrodisias." *JRS* 80:127–55.

———. 1990b. "Myth and Allegory in the Sebasteion." In Roueché and Erim 1990, 89–100.

———. 1993. *The Monument of C. Julius Zoilos.* Mainz am Rhein: P. von Zabern.

———. 1994. "Spear-Won Land at Boscoreale: On the Roman Paintings of a Roman Villa." *JRA* 7:100–127.

Smith, R. R. R., and K. T. Erim, eds. 1991. *Aphrodisias Papers.* Vol. 2, *The Theatre, a Sculptor's Workshop, Philosophers, and Coin-Types.* JRA Supplementary Series 2. Ann Arbor: Editorial Committee for the JRA.

Smith, R. R. R., and C. Ratté. 1995. "Archaeological Research at Aphrodisias in Caria." *American Journal of Archaeology* 99:33–58.

Snyder, G. 1985. *Ante Pacem: Archaeological Evidence of Church Life Before Constantine.* Macon, GA: Mercer University Press.

Sokolowski, F. 1964. "Aphrodite as Guardian of Greek Magistrates." *HTR* 57.1:1–8.

———. 1974. "Propagation of the Cult of Sarapis and Isis in Greece." *GRBS* 15:441–48.

Solmsen, F. 1979. *Isis Among the Greeks and Romans.* Cambridge: published for Oberlin College by Harvard University Press.

Sordi, Marti. 1986. *The Christians and the Roman Empire.* Trans. Annabel Bedini. London and Sydney: Croom Helm.

Squarciapino, M. Floriani. 1943. *La scuola di Afrodisias.* Rome: Cuggiani.

———. 1959. "Afrodite d'Afrodisias." *Bollettino d'Arte,* pp. 97–106.

———. 1960. "Afrodite di Afrodisia." *Archeologia Classica* 12:208–11.

———. 1962. *I culti orientali ad Ostia*. Leiden: E. J. Brill.

———. 1966. "Afrodite di Afrodisia." *Rendiconti della Pontificia Accademia Romana di Archeologia* 38:143–56.

———. 1987. "Afrodite d'Aphrodisias." In de la Genière and Erim 1987, 65–79.

Squires, John T. 1993. *The Plan of God in Luke–Acts*. Cambridge: Cambridge University Press.

Stambrough, J. 1978. "The Functions of Roman Temples." In *ANRW* 16.1:554–608.

Steiner, Grundy. 1969. "The Graphic Analogue from Myth in Greek Romance." In *Classical Studies Presented to Ben Edwin Perry*, 123–37. Illinois Studies in Language and Literature 58. Urbana: University of Illinois Press.

Stephens, S. A. 1994. "Who Read Ancient Novels?" In Tatum 1994, 405–18.

Stephens, S. A., and J. J. Winkler, eds. 1995. *Ancient Greek Novels: The Fragments*. Princeton: Princeton University Press.

Sterling, Gregory E. 1992. *Historiography and Self-definition: Josephus, Luke–Acts, and Apologetic Historiography*. Leiden: E. J. Brill.

Stern, Menahem. 1974a. *Greek and Latin Authors on Jews and Judaism*. Vol. 1, *From Herodotus to Plutarch*. Jerusalem: Israel Academy of Sciences and Humanities.

———. 1974b. "The Jewish Diaspora." In Safrai and Stern 1974, 117–83.

———. 1980. *Greek and Latin Authors on Jews and Judaism*. Vol. 2, *From Tacitus to Simplicius*. Jerusalem: Israel Academy of Sciences and Humanities.

———. 1987. "Josephus and the Roman Empire as Reflected in the Jewish War." In Feldman and Hata 1987, 71–80.

Strange, J. F. 1977. "The Capernaum and Herodium Publications (Part 1)." *Bulletin of the American Schools of Oriental Research* 226:65–73.

———. 1992. "Six Campaigns of Sepphoris: The University of South Florida Excavations, 1983–1989." In Levine 1992a, 339–55.

Strauss, Mark L. 1995. *The Davidic Messiah in Luke–Acts: The Promise and Its Fulfillment in Lukan Christology*. Sheffield: Sheffield Academic Press.

Stravinsky, Igor. 1947. *Poetics of Music in the Form of Six Lessons*. Trans. Arthur Knodel and Ingolf Dahl. Cambridge: Harvard University Press.

Strubbe, J. H. M. 1989. "Joden en Grieken: On verzoen lijke vijanden? De integratie van Joden in Kleinaziatische steden in de Keizertijd." *Lampas* 22:188–204.

———. 1991. "Cursed Be He That Moves My Bones." In Faraone and Obbink 1991, 33–59.

Sullivan, Richard D. 1984. "Royal Coins and Rome." In *Ancient Coins of the Graeco-Roman World,* ed. W. Heckel and R. Sullivan, 143–58. Waterloo, ON: Wilfred University Press.

Syme, R. 1936. "Flavian Wars and Frontiers." In *CAH* 11:131–87.

Talbert, Charles H., ed. 1984. *Luke–Acts: New Perspectives from the Society of Biblical Literature Seminar*. New York: Crossroad.

Tatum, James, ed. 1994. *The Search for the Ancient Novel*. Baltimore: Johns Hopkins University Press.

Taylor, Joan E. 1989–90. "Capernaum and Its 'Jewish-Christians': A Re-examination of the Franciscan Excavations." *Bulletin of the Anglo-Israel Archaeological Society* 9:7–28.

———. 1993. *Christians and the Holy Places: The Myth of Jewish–Christian Origins*. Oxford: Clarendon Press.

Thane, Pat, G. Crossick, and R. Floud, eds. 1984. *The Power of the Past: Essays for Eric Hobsbawm*. Cambridge: Cambridge University Press.

Thessalus. 1968. *Thessalos von Tralles*. Trans. Hans-Veit Friedrich. Meisenheim am Glan: Anton Hain.

Thompson, L. A. 1982. "Domitian and the Jewish Tax." *Historia* 31:329–42.

Thompson, L. L. 1990. *The Book of Revelation: Apocalypse and Empire*. Oxford: Oxford University Press.

Thraede, Klaus. 1992. "Homonoia." *RAC* 122/123:176–290.

Tiede, David L. 1972. *The Charismatic Figure as Miracle Worker*. SBLDS 1. Missoula, MT: Scholars Press.

———. 1980. *Prophecy and History in Luke–Acts*. Philadelphia: Fortress Press.

Trebilco, P. R. 1991. *Jewish Communities in Asia Minor*. Cambridge: Cambridge University Press.

———. 1994. "Asia." In Gill and Gempf 1994, 291–362.

Trompf, Garry W. 1984. "On Why Luke Declined to Recount the Death of Paul: Acts 27–28 and Beyond." In Talbert 1984, 225–39.

Tsafrir, Yoram. 1993. *Ancient Churches Revealed*. Jerusalem: Israel Exploration Society.

Turner, E. G. 1954. "Tiberius Iulius Alexander." *JRS* 44:54–64.

Ulansey, David. 1989. *The Origins of the Mithraic Mysteries: Cosmology and Salvation in the Ancient World*. New York: Oxford University Press.

———. 1991. "The Heavenly Veil Torn: Mark's Cosmic Inclusio." *JBL* 110.1:123–25.

Van Bremen, Riet. 1985. "Women and Wealth." In *Images of Women in Antiquity*, ed. Averil Cameron and Amalie Kuhrt, 223–42. Detroit: Wayne State University Press.

Van der Horst, P. W. 1983. "Chariton and the New Testament: A Contribution to the Corpus Hellenisticum." *Novum Testamentum* 25:348–55.

———. 1989a. "The Altar of the 'Unknown God' in Athens (Acts 17:23) and the Cult of 'Unknown Gods' in the Hellenistic and Roman Periods." In *ANRW* 2.18.2:1426–56.

———. 1989b. "Jews and Christians in Aphrodisias in the Light of Their Relations in Other Cities of Asia Minor." *Nederlands Theologisch Tijdschvift* 43:106–21.

———. 1991. *Ancient Jewish Epitaphs*. Kamper: Kok Pharos.

Van Henten, J. W., and P. W. van der Horst, eds. 1994. *Studies in Early Jewish Epitaphs*. Leiden: E. J. Brill.

Van Straten, F. T. 1981. "Gifts for the Gods." In *Faith, Hope, and Worship: Aspects of Religious Mentality in the Ancient World*, ed. H. S. Versnel, 65–151. Studies in Greek and Roman Religion 2. Leiden: E. J. Brill.

———. 1974. "Did the Greeks Kneel Before Their God?" In *Bulletin Antieke Beschaving* 49:159–89.

van Unnik, E. C. 1947. "Les cheveux défaits des femmes baptisées." *Vigiliae Christianne* 1:77–100.

Veeser, H., ed. 1989. *The New Historicism*. New York: Routledge.

Vermaseren, M. J. 1963. *Mithras, the Secret God*. London: Chatto & Windus.

Vermeule, C. 1968. *Roman Imperial Art in Greece and Asia Minor*. Cambridge: Belknap Press of Harvard University Press.

———. 1978. *Roman Art: Early Republic to Late Empire*. Boston: Department of Classical Art, Museum of Fine Arts.

———. 1981. *Jewish Relations with the Art of Ancient Greece and Rome: "Judaea Capta Sed No Devicta*. Art of Antiquity 5.4.2. Boston: Museum of Fine Arts.

Versnel, H. S. 1981. "Religious Mentality in Ancient Prayer." In *Faith, Hope, and Worship: Aspects of Religious Mentality in the Ancient World*, ed. H. S. Versnel, 1–64. Studies in Greek and Roman Religion 2. Leiden: E. J. Brill.

————. 1990. *Inconsistencies in Greek and Roman Religion* Vol. 1, *Ter Unus: Isis, Dionysus, Hermes. Three Studies in Henotheism.* Leiden: E. J. Brill.

Veyne, Paul. 1990. *Bread and Circuses: Historical Sociology and Political Pluralism.* Trans. B. Pearce. London: Penguin Press.

Viereck, Paul, and Friedrich Zucker. 1926. *Papyri Ostraka und Wachstafeln aus Philadelphia im Fayum.* Berlin: Weidmannsche.

Vinson, M. P. 1989. "Domitia Longina, Julia Titi, and the Literary Tradition." *Historia* 38.4:431–50.

Walaskay, Paul W. 1983. *"And So We Came to Rome": The Political Perspective of St. Luke.* SNTSMS 49. Cambridge: Cambridge University Press.

Walker, S. 1979. "A Sanctuary of Isis on the South Slope of the Athenian Acropolis." *ABSA* 74:243–57.

Walker, Williston. 1990. *A History of the Christian Church.* 3d ed. New York: Charles Scribner's Sons.

Wallace-Hadrill, A. 1981. "The Emperor and His Virtues." *Historia* 30:298–323.

————. 1986. "Image and Authority in the Coinage of Augustus." *JRS* 76:66–87.

————. 1990. "Roman Arches and Greek Honours: The Language of Power at Rome." *PCPS*, n.s., 36:143–81.

————, ed. 1989. *Patronage in Ancient Society.* London and New York: Routledge.

Walsh, Peter. 1970. *Apuleius' "Metamorphoses" in the Romen Novel.* Cambridge: Cambridge University Press.

Ward-Perkins, J. B. 1992. *Marble in Antiquity: Collected Papers of J. B. Ward-Perkins.* Ed. H. Dodge and B. Ward-Perkins. London: British School at Rome.

Wartenberg, Thomas E., ed. 1992. *Rethinking Power.* Albany: State University of New York Press.

Weber, M. 1949. *Methodology of the Social Sciences.* Trans. and ed. E. A. Shils and H. A. Finch. Glencoe, IL: Free Press.

Weinstock, W. 1948. "The Geographical Catalogue in Acts II, 9–11." *JRS* 38:43–46.

Weiss, Zeev. 1992. "Social Aspects of Burial in Beth She'arim: Archaeological Finds and Talmudic Sources." In Levine 1992a, 357–71.

Welles, C. Bradford, R. O. Fink, and J. Frank Gilliam. 1959. *The Excavations at Dura-Europos: Final Report.* Vol. 1, *The Parchments and Papyri.* New Haven: Yale University Press.

Wells, Peter. 1992. "Tradition, Identity, and Change Beyond the Roman Frontier." In *Resources, Power, and Interregional Interaction,* ed. E. Schortman and P. Urban, 175–92. New York: Plenum Publishing Co.

Wesseling, Berber. 1988. "The Audience of the Ancient Novels." In *Gröningen Colloquia on the Novel,* ed. H. Hofman, 1:67–79. Gröningen: Egbert Forsten.

White, H. G. E., and J. H. Oliver 1938. *The Temple of Hibis in El Khargeh Oasis.* Pt. 2, *The Greek Inscriptions.* New York: Metropolitan Museum of Art Egyptian Expedition.

White, L. M. 1990. *Building God's House in the Roman World: Architectural Adaptation Among Pagans, Jews, and Christians.* Baltimore: published for the *Bulletin of the American Schools of Oriental Research* by Johns Hopkins University Press.

Whittaker, C. R. 1990. "The Consumer City Revisited: The Vicus and the City." *JRA* 3:110–18.

————. 1994. *Frontiers of the Roman Empire: A Social and Economic Study.* Baltimore: Johns Hopkins University Press.

Wild, Robert A. 1984. "The Known Isis-Sarapis Sanctuaries of the Roman Period." in *ANRW* 2.17.4:1739–1851.

Wilken, R. 1984. *The Christians as the Romans Saw Them*. New Haven: Yale University Press.

Will, E. 1976. "Banquets et salles de banquet dans les cultes de la Grèce et de l'Empire romain." In *Mélanges d'histoire et d'archéologie offerts à Paul Collart,* 353–62. Lausanne: Bibliothèque historique vaudoise.

Williams, C. K., II. 1987. "The Refounding of Corinth: Some Roman Religious Attitudes." In *Roman Architecture in the Greek World,* ed. Sarah Macready and F. H. Thompson, 26–37. London: Society of Antiquaries.

Wills, Garry. 1990. *Under God: Religion and American Politics*. New York: Simon & Schuster.

Wilpert, J. 1903. *Die Malereien der Katakomben Roms*. 2 vols. Freiberg im Breisgau: Herdersche Verlagshandlung.

Wilson, Stephen G. 1992. "Gentile Judaizers." *NTS* 38.4:605–16.

Winkler, John J. 1980. "Lollianos and the Desperadoes." *JHS* 100:155–81.

———. 1985. *Auctor and Actor: A Narratological Reading of Apuleius's "The Golden Ass."* Berkeley and Los Angeles: University of California Press.

———. 1991. "The Constraints of Eros." In Faraone and Obbink 1991, 214–43.

Winlock, H. E. 1941. *The Temple of Hibis in El Khargeh Oasis*. Pt. 1, *The Excavations*. New York: Metropolitan Museum of Art Egyptian Expedition.

Witt, R. 1971. *Isis in the Graeco-Roman World*. Ithaca: Cornell University Press.

Woodward, A. M. 1926–27. "Note-Book of Sir William Gell." *ABSA* 28:107–27.

Woolf, G. 1992. "Imperialism, Empire, and the Integration of the Roman Economy." *World Archaeology* 23.3:283–93.

Wrede, H. 1987. "Monumente der antikaiserlich philosophischen Opposition." *JDAI* 102:279–390.

Yadin, Yigael. 1969. "Tefillin (Phylacteries) from Qumran" (in Hebrew). *Eretz-Israel* 9:60–83.

Yadin, Yigael, Jonas C. Greenfield, and Ada Yardeni. 1994. "Babatha's Ketubba." *IEJ* 44.1–2:75–101.

Yarden, L. 1991. *The Spoils of Jerusalem on the Arch of Titus*. Åström: Söleborg.

Yavetz, Z. 1987. "The Urban Plebs: Flavians, Nerva, Trajan." In *Opposition et résistance à l'empire d'Auguste à Trajan,* ed. Kurt A. Raaflaub and A. Giovannini, 135–81. Geneva: Fondation Hardt.

Yegül, Fifret K. 1991. "'Roman' Architecture in the Greek World." *JRA* 4:345–55.

Zanker, P. 1988. *The Power of Images in the Age of Augustus*. Trans. A. Shapiro. Ann Arbor: University of Michigan Press.

Zeev, M. P. Ben. 1995. "Caesar and Jewish Law." *RB* 102.1:28–37.

Zimmermann, F., ed. 1936. *Griechische Roman-Papyri, und verwandte Texte*. Heidelberg: F. Bilabel.

Author Index

Index

Citations